The Kalish Book

(Kalisz, Poland)

Published by the Israel-American Book Committee; Tel Aviv 1968

Published by JewishGen

An Affiliate of the Museum of Jewish Heritage—A Living Memorial to the Holocaust
New York

The Kalish Book (Kalisz, Poland)

Published by the Israel-American Book Committee in Tel Aviv 1968

Project Coordinator: Judy Wolkovitch
Layout and Name Indexing: Jonatan Wind
Cover Design: Rachel Kolokoff-Hopper

Published by JewishGen, Inc.
An Affiliate of the Museum of Jewish Heritage
A Living Memorial to the Holocaust
36 Battery Place, New York, NY 10280

Printed in the United States of America by Lightning Source, Inc.

Library of Congress Control Number (LCCN): 2021934555

ISBN: 978-1-954176-09-6 (hard cover: 444 pages, alk. paper)

Cover Credits:

Cover Graphic Design: Rachel Kolokoff Hopper

Front and Back Cover: Color and texture by Rachel Kolokoff Hopper

Front Cover: Illustration from the Kalish Book, page 74

Back Cover: Illustration from The Kalish Book, page 12
                             Photo from The Kalish Book, *Great Synagogue Choir*,
                             page 382

Background map from The Kalish Book, page 243 (218)

Illustration on spine from The Kalish Book, page 111 (92)

JewishGen and the Yizkor Books in Print Project

This book has been published by the **Yizkor Books in Print Project**, as part of the **Yizkor Book Project** of JewishGen, Inc.

JewishGen, Inc. is a non-profit organization founded in 1987 as a resource for Jewish genealogy. Its website [www.jewishgen.org] serves as an international clearinghouse and resource center to assist individuals who are researching the history of their Jewish families and the places where they lived. JewishGen provides databases, facilitates discussion groups, and coordinates projects relating to Jewish genealogy and the history of the Jewish people. In 2003, JewishGen became an affiliate of the **Museum of Jewish Heritage—A Living Memorial to the Holocaust** in New York.

The **JewishGen Yizkor Book Project** was organized to make more widely known the existence of Yizkor (Memorial) Books written by survivors and former residents of various Jewish communities throughout the world. Later, volunteers connected to the different destroyed communities began cooperating to have these books translated from the original language—usually Hebrew or Yiddish—into English, thus enabling a wider audience to have access to the valuable information contained within them. As each chapter of these books was translated, it was posted on the JewishGen website and made available to the general public.

The **Yizkor Books in Print Project** began in 2011 as an initiative to print and publish Yizkor Books that had been fully translated, so that hard copies would be available for purchase by the descendants of these communities and also by scholars, universities, synagogues, libraries, and museums.

These Yizkor books have been produced almost entirely through the volunteer effort of researchers from around the world, assisted by donations from private individuals. The books are printed and sold at near cost, so as to make them as affordable as possible. Our goal is to make this important genre of Jewish literature and history available in English in book form, so that people can have the personal histories of their ancestral towns on their bookshelves for themselves and for their children and grandchildren.

A list of all published translated Yizkor Books in the project with prices and ordering information can be found at:
http://www.jewishgen.org/Yizkor/ybip.html

Lance Ackerfeld, Yizkor Book Project Manager
Joel Alpert, Yizkor-Book-in-Print Project Coordinator
Susan Rosin, Yizkor-Book-in-Print Project Associate Coordinator

JewishGen
Yizkor Book Project

This book is presented by the
Yizkor-Books-In-Print Project
Project Coordinator: Joel Alpert

Part of the Yizkor Books Project of JewishGen. Inc.
Project Manager: Lance Ackerfeld

These books have been produced solely through efforts of volunteers
from around the world. The books are printed using the Print-on-Demand technology and sold at
near cost, to make them as affordable as possible.

Our goal is to make this intimate history of the destroyed Jewish shtetls
of Eastern Europe available in book form in English, so that people can
experience the near-personal histories of their ancestral town on their
bookshelves and those of their children and grandchildren.

All donations to the Yizkor Books Project, which translated the books,
are sincerely appreciated.

Please send donations to:

Yizkor Book Project
JewishGen, Inc.
36 Battery Place
New York, NY, 10280

JewishGen, Inc. is an affiliate of the
Museum of Jewish Heritage
A Living Memorial to the Holocaust

Notes to the Reader:

We apologize ahead of time for the poor quality of images in the book. Often these images had been scanned from the original Yizkor books which were of poor quality to begin with, being copies of old photographs. Each transfer results in loss of quality. We have done the best we could, given the original material and the resources and technology at hand. Even though images often appear of higher quality on computer screens, that does not transfer to high quality images in print. A reader can view the original scans on the web sites listed below.

Within the text the reader will note "{34}" standing ahead of a paragraph. This indicates that the material translated below was on page 34 of the original book. However, when a paragraph was split between two pages in the original book, the marker is placed in this book after the end of the paragraph for ease of reading.

Also please note that all references within the text of the book to page numbers, refer to the page numbers of the original Yizkor Book.

The original book can be seen online at the New York Public Library site:

https://digitalcollections.nypl.org/items/8c692020-7a70-0133-a895-00505686a51c

or at the Yiddish Book Center web site:

https://www.yiddishbookcenter.org/collections/yizkor-books/yzk-nybc301552/lask-i-m-the-kalish-book

In order to obtain a list of all Shoah victims from Kalish, the reader should access the Yad Vashem web site listed below; one can also search for specific family names using family name option. These lists are continually updated by Yad Vashem, so it is worthwhile to periodically search these lists.

There is much valuable information available on this web site, including the Pages of Testimony, etc.
http://yvng.yadvashem.org

A list of this book and all books available in the Yizkor-Book-In-Print Project along with prices is available at:
http://www.jewishgen.org/Yizkor/ybip.html

Geopolitical Information:

Kalisz, Poland is located at 51°45' N, 18°05' E and 59 miles W of Łódż, 66 miles SE of Poznań (Posen)

	Town	District	Province	Country
Before WWI (c. 1900):	Kalisz	Kalisz	Kalisz	Russian Empire
Between the wars (c. 1930):	Kalisz	Kalisz	Łódż	Poland
After WWII (c. 1950):	Kalisz			Poland
Today (c. 2000):	Kalisz			Poland

Alternate names for the town:
Kalisz [Pol], Kalish [Rus, Yid], Kalisch [Ger], Calisia [Lat], Kolish

Nearby Jewish Communities:

Koźminek 11 miles ENE
Stawiszyn 12 miles N
Ostrów Wielkopolski 13 miles WSW
Raszków 15 miles W
Mikstat 16 miles SSW
Pleszew 16 miles NW
Grabów nad Prosną 16 miles S
Błaszki 17 miles ESE
Odolanów 21 miles SW
Rychwał 22 miles N
Kowale Pańskie 24 miles ENE
Ostrzeszów 24 miles SSW

Warta 24 miles E
Tuliszków 25 miles NNE
Dobra 26 miles ENE
Turek 26 miles NE
Krotoszyn 27 miles W
Koźmin 27 miles W
Kobyla Góra 28 miles SSW
Jarocin 28 miles WNW
Russocice 30 miles NE
Zagórów 30 miles NNW
Sieradz 30 miles ESE
Lututów 30 miles SSE

Jewish Population: 7,580 (in 1897), 15,300 (in 1931)

BALTIC SEA   LITHUANIA

RUSSIA   Vilnius ●

POLAND   BELARUS

GERMANY

● Poznan   Warsaw ●

Kalish *   ● Lodz

● Prague

CZECH REPUBLIC   ● Krakow   UKRAINE

SLOVAKIA

0 ├─────────────┤ 250 miles

0   250 Km   500 Km

POLAND - Current Borders

Map of Poland with **Kalish**

TABLE OF CONTENTS

The English version, prepared by I. M. Lask, was completed and printed on the Eve of Passover 5678 (1968).

The Kalish Book
(Kalisz, Poland)

Published by the Israel-American Book Committee

Tel Aviv 1968

**Our sincere appreciation to Genia Hollander
for typing the English text to facilitate its addition to this project.**

———

This is "The Kalish book",
Published by the Israel-American Book Committee; Tel Aviv 1968 (E 329 pages)

Note: The original book can be seen online at the NY Public Library site: <u>Kalisz (1968)</u>

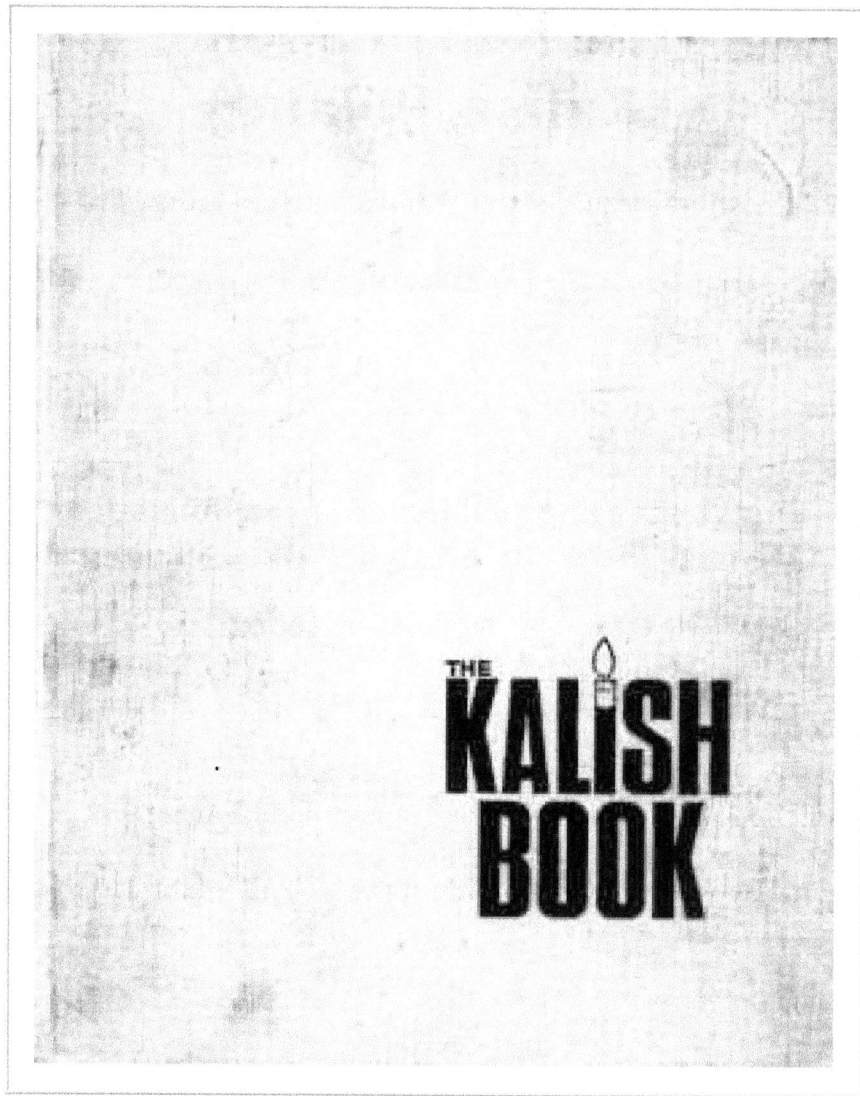

[Page 6]

Members of the Publication Committees

Publication Committee in Israel	Publication Committee in the U.S.A.
Zvi Arad	Joseph Arnold, President
Eliezer Birnbaum, Treasurer	Sam Berke, Vice-President
Joseph Holtz	Abraham Bandel, Chairman
Gershon Wroclawski	Samuel Okladek, Financial Secretary
Dr. Saul Zalud	Israel Diamant, Treasurer
Abraham Zohar, Secretary	Peretz Walter, Secretary
Baruch Tall, Chairman	Hersh Arkush
Mendel Sieradzki	Max Smolen
Menahem Szklanowski	Nahum Median
	Jacob Levi
	Samuel Roth
	Kalman Aronovitch former secretaries
	Hava Shurek

Jerusalem members: Moshe Carmeli, Joseph Rosenbaum

Haifa members: Arieh Eifodi, Shimshon Green, Eliahu Winter, Fishel Katz, Moshe Fuyara, Israel Friede

Graphic Design and Layout: Samuel Brand

The Hebrew and Yiddish text of the first volume were composed in the year 1964, seven centuries after the promulgation of the Kalish statutes (1264).

The Hebrew and Yiddish text of the second volume were brought to the press during the six-day war of Israel, 5-10 June, 1967 (28 IYYAR, 2 SIVAN 5727).

The Kalish Book is issued by the societies of former residents of Kalish and the vicinity in Israel and the U.S.A.

Composed and printed at Eylon Press, 11 Hasharon St., Tel-Aviv.
Photographs printed at the M. Anabi Offset Press, Tel-Aviv.

THE KALISH BOOK

The Kalish Statute Designed and Illuminated by Arthur Szyk

Foreword

The decades after the Nazis exiled the Jews of Kalish from their homes to the ghettoes and the death camps;

Fifteen years after the end of World War II and the appearance of the survivors who brought the dread tidings of the destruction of the Kalish Community and the extermination of the Jews who had been its members;

The vestiges of the Community in the State of Israel, in the United States of America and in other countries of the dispersion, resolved to set up their Memorial to thirty thousand fathers, mothers, brothers, sisters, sons and daughters who had fallen facing the foe and who had been slain to Hallow the Holy Name.

The Committees of the "Kalish Book" in Israel and America gleaned the material page by page, testimony by testimony, article by article, and item by item. With efforts that continued for years, they collected the material for this Kalish Book.

Here is the history of a very ancient community which existed for almost a thousand years. On numberless occasions throughout the generations, the community fell only to rise again and continue its life and way of living until at last it was eradicated so that not even a sign of it is left.

May this Book be an everlasting witness to an outstanding Jewish Community which reeled and fell. May its history serve as a memory for coming generations and a source of pride to those who came forth from our City so that they may preserve and continue the tradition of the Community and Holy Congregation of Kalish.

The Editorial Committee

[Page 8]

Yizkor

Jewry, remember the City and Mother in Israel cut down with her children. The city remains as it had been, untouched.

The houses raise high, the gardens blossom, the River Prosna twines as of old with banks that are now paved with tombstones out of the Jewish graveyard.

Yet the thirty thousand Jews of Kalish have been cut down one and all never brought to a Jewish grave. Their ashes are part of the ashes of millions burnt; their bones flung afar in alien fields – all they had was left behind in the city where aliens batten upon it.

Seven hundred years ago and more, they arrived in the city and at once became the yeast in the dough; they minted coins for the kind; they toiled and they traded. Swiftly, they spread beyond the narrow bounds of the Jewish callings of those times and engaged in crafts and commerce. Skilfully, wisely, they laboured until they made their city into a leader in all embroidery and lace-making work.

This was a city of Jews, a Jewish city, a city of merchants and craftsmen, the city of the learned "Magen Abraham" and "Nefesh Haya"; the city of Revolutionaries in 1905 and of ghetto fighters who came from Youth Movements, went to their brethren all over the country and with their blood wrote pages of valour in the record of Polish Jewry; city of pioneer Halutzim who went ahead to show the way to the Homeland; city of all-year-round Jews who filled synagogues and stieblech with the chanting of prayer and the study of Torah; city of youngsters in many a party contending together, their hearts full of the Love of Israel, flaming with zeal for the

Honour of Israel; city of Erect Jewish
Workers with skilful hands who were
honoured at home among their own people
and in the eyes of their Gentile comrades.

[Page 9]

But the murderers came like robbers at noon,
encompassing them with deceit and trickery
and brought them to the flames before they
could utter their prayer, before they could lift
up their hands.

See them go to the Market Building, to the
railway wagons with little bundles and huge
eyes, sad Jewish eyes. For seven hundred
years they had contended here with hostile,
envious neighbours who drove them away
and oppressed them; sevenfold they fell and
sevenfold they rose; their right to eat and pray
to God which they purchased with anguish,
yearning, intercession and money. Here or
there, the hand of a Jew was raised to repay
murderers their deserts. So it went on day
after day, century on century. Read the tale of
their chronicles in the city and you will know
what brought the sad sheen to their eyes.

Women pass clutching the babes to their
breast, running naked to gas chambers, some
stumbling and perishing. Children pass and
their wise eyes know the whole of the naked
truth. The old folk pass with their hands
clutching their prayer books. Men pass along
and their backs are bowed with the burden of
seven hundred years. Lads leap from the
wagons and smash against the stone
permanent way. The hopes of the people pass
and iron-shod jackboots trample them
underfoot in the sun.

Remember and Never Forget!

Let the people remember their offspring and write their names large and hallow their memory. You who were born in this city or whose fathers and mothers were born there repeat and repeat to your children: Your fathers before you were pure in their lives and were martyrs in death. And their souls are bound up forever in the bundle of life.

[Page 10]

Memorial Stones

...The deeds of humankind will swiftly pass away and vanish from memory unless they are preserved by verbal witness or written documents.

(From the Kalish Statute, 10ᵗʰ September 1264).

Kalish is one of the middle-sized cities of Poland. In the year 1938, it had a population of 68,000. Its size determined the style of life there and saved the inhabitants from the monotony of the hamlets and small towns and that absence of a centre which marks the residents of a metropolis. Like the Prosna flowing slowly through the city, so the inhabitants wove the pattern of their daily lives. Most of them earned their living by light industry and retail trade. Special mention should be made of the Lace Industry which reached considerable dimensions and opened commercial horizons to the city through exports – first to the expanses of Russia before World War I and afterwards to Poland and the West.

Kalish, which lay on the former frontier between Russia and Germany, absorbed a Western atmosphere over the years. This atmosphere combined with the cultural life and enlightenment activities which were part of the local tradition. There were three governmental Secondary Schools; a Public Library bearing the name of Adam Mickiewicz and a Society for Popular Music whose handsome Concert Hall welcomed the leading musicians of the world. The Municipal Theatre, where renowned companies staged their performances, lies on the riverbank at the entrance to the magnificent park.

After the destruction that followed the outbreak of World War I, Kalish was rebuilt with modern streets and new houses. It had an extensive circle of intellectuals who included most of the members of the free professions. From their midst came the Polish writers Adam Asnik, Maria Konopnicka and Maria Dombrowska.

There were 25,000 Jews in Kalish whose life, in general, resembled that of their brethren in other Polish cities.

For the greater part, they engaged in retail trade, handicrafts, as agents and in the free professions. They played a considerable part in establishing the Lace Industry and expanding it. Among them, a minority enjoyed very considerable economic success. The majority made a bare living, suffering from the manifestations of anti-Semitism and the animosity of the dominant majority.

Their social life was lived in and around the Jewish Community in which all parties and economic bodies were represented.

Elections to the Community Council were important occasions. More than once, there were "explosive" election campaigns which were participated in by all the parties in the Jewish Street: The Bund, Agudat Israel, General Zionists, Labour Eretz Israel, Left Poalei

Zion, the Hassidic "Stieblech", the Hassidim of the Rebbes of Gur and Alexander, Craftsmen, Retail Merchants, Trade Unions, etc. Kalish was a citadel and stronghold of various Hassidic groups and each of these maintained its own "Stiebel". As a whole, the Jews of the city prided themselves on the renowned authorities who had served there as Rabbis.

Secular life was equally lively. The political parties had their clubs where lectures and entertainments were held. Intellectuals and youngsters found reading matter in the libraries of these clubs. Two Yiddish weeklies: "Kalisher Leben" and "Kalisher Woch" were published and reflected the daily life of the Jewish Community.

Thanks to local initiative, a Jewish Gymnasium or Secondary School was established and educated the younger generation for years, providing them not only with their general training but also with the foundations of a national Hebrew education.

Sabbaths and festivals were clearly to be recognized in the Jewish Quarter which ran from the Old Market to the Maikow Fields, criss-crossed with streets that were always full of life. Kalish Jewry was blessed with an ever-fresh and effervescent younger generation. The Hebrew Gymnasium, the Government Gymnasium, the Trade School and the many Yeshivot, educated hundreds of young men and women whose influence could be felt. Zionist and Halutz youth, trade union youth, school children and members of Sports Organizations had their own regular meeting places in the Old and New parks. Many of their best came to Eretz Israel over the years and joined those who were building up the Homeland.

The Kalish Book describes the daily life of the Jewish Community, its struggle for economic, cultural and social existence from the early days until the end. In these pages, the survivors of the Community have done their best to set up a Memorial to their brethren. May it serve as a landmark for the coming generations of our offspring.

Baruch Tall

The History of the Jews in Kalish

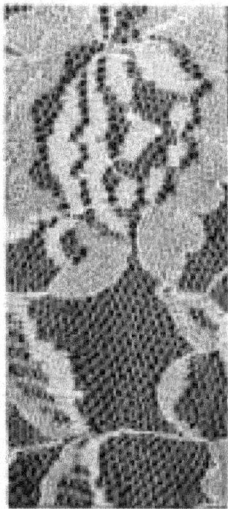

[Page 15]

History of the Jews in Kalish

By Dr. N.M. Gelber

The Beginnings

Kalish, on the River Prosna, has been a city with considerable municipal rights of autonomy ever since the 13th century, by which time the population already consisted of Poles, Jews and Germans from Silesia. It belonged to the Hanseatic League and was made a Free City in the year 1360. Under King Kasimir the Great, in the mid-14th century, it became the second capital of Poland. At the period of the Reformation, it became a Protestant refuge. Early in the 17th century, the first astronomical observatory in Europe was constructed there. Throughout the Middle Ages and after the city, which was strongly fortified and had four gates, suffered the usual vicissitudes of siege, revolt, warfare, pillage, fires, etc.

Jews were to be found in Silesia by the middle of the 12th century and had entered Great Poland by the first decades of the 13th century. Several places called Zydowo (Jew-town) are referred to at that time, one being close to Kalish. According to Thadinski, the historian of the city, Jews were already resident in Kalish as early as 1139. By the end of the 12th century there were Jewish minting specialists in the city as proved by one-sided coins known as "Brakmats" bearing the imprint: "Joseph Kalish" in Hebrew characters. It appears that at this period, Jews were masters of various mints in Germany and in Austria and also supplied the metal for the coins. Jewish minters seem to have been among the first to reach Western Poland and they operated a mint in Kalish for seven years.

The Kalish Privileges

On 10th September 1264, the Jews of Kalish were granted the "Kalish Privileges", consisting of 37 articles. Thirteen of these deals with matters of Jewish credit and two with Jewish trade. Under these privileges, the Jews had the status of "servi camerae" (servants of the Treasury or of the local Government authority). For this, they had to pay the local duke certain amounts in return for which he gave them his protection. They were subject to his jurisdiction or that of a special judge appointed by him and known as "Judge of the Jews". However, they were not under the jurisdiction of the city in which they dwelt. Criminal cases were judged by the duke in person.

Internal Jewish disputes were dealt with in Jewish courts but the Judge of the Jews might intervene at the request of either of the contending parties. The Jewish court was held in the synagogue. Jews might not be brought for trial during their Festivals but otherwise, they had to appear in Court as soon as summoned. Any person who did not appear when summoned for the first or second time had to pay a fine.

[Page 16]

No Jew might be required to take oath on their Torah Scrolls save in major trials for sums exceeding the value of 50 marks of fine silver, or when he was summoned before the duke. In minor trials, he had to take oath in front of the synagogue and at its doors.

If a Christian brought action against a Jew, whether on a criminal or civil charge, he had to bring a Jewish witness as well as a Christian.

Any person injuring a Jew, who was the property of the duke, had to pay a fine to the duke's treasury and damages to the Jew. Any person murdering a Jew was sentenced to death and his property was to be confiscated by the ducal treasury. Similar punishments were provided for wounding a Jewess, destroying a Jewish cemetery or taking a pledge from a Jew by force. Any person throwing stones at a synagogue had to pay the authorities a fine of 2 "stones" of pepper. A person kidnapping a Jewish child by force was judged as a thief.

In accordance with the Bull of Pope Innocent IV, which was published after a blood libel charge at Fulda in Germany in 1253, it was severely prohibited to bring any such charge against any Jews whatsoever within the Duchy, namely that of using human blood, "since all Jews refrain by reason of their faith from consuming blood in any fashion whatsoever."

If a Jew should be charged with the murder of a Christian child, the matter had to be proved by three Christians and an equal number of Jews. If it should be proved, the Jew would be punished but not by the customary punishment for this crime. If he should prove himself innocent by the said witnesses, then the Christian would not unjustly be sentenced to the punishment which the Jew would otherwise have had to bear because of his malice.

A Christian suspected of murdering a Jew might prove his innocence through trial by combat and the court would appoint the person with whom he would have to do battle.

If the Jews transfer the bodies of the dead after their fashion from one city to another or from one district to another or from one country to another, the tax collectors are not authorized to levy any payment upon them; and if they do so, they will be punished as robbers.

If a Jew is compelled to raise an outcry at night on account of any great urgency and the Christian neighbours do not give him the necessary aid and do not gather at the sound of the outcry, then each Christian neighbour shall pay thirty soldi to the judge or to the local authority.

Thirteen articles deal in detail with interest charged by Jews. If a Christian claimed that he pawned an article with a Jew for an amount less than the latter demanded, the latter had to take oath that he was telling the truth. Christian religious apparel and wet or blood-stained garments might not be accepted as pledges. Jews might accept horses as pledges only openly and by daylight. If a Christian found a stolen horse held by a Jew, the Jew would be deemed innocent if he took oath that the horse had been pledged with him openly and in the daytime; that he had lent money to its owner and had no reason to believe that the horse was stolen.

If a Jew advanced money against land or deeds of outstanding individuals and could prove this by the documents and the seals, the Jew would be allocated the land as with any other pledges and he would be protected by the authorities against all duress and compulsion.

[Page 17]

Jews transporting wares were not to pay any higher customs duty or octroi than the citizens of the city in which the Jew might be staying at that time. Jews might buy and sell anything, might touch bread like Christians and any person restraining them from so doing would be fined. A further clause reads: "Likewise, we desire that no man shall be billeted in the house of a Jew." This exemption from the duty of billeting was otherwise granted only to the clergy and the nobility and would seem to indicate the special status of the Jews in the eyes of the law.

The Kalish Privileges were afterwards extended to all the Jews in the Duchy of Great Poland. Subsequently, they were confirmed and expanded in the years 1334 and 1364-65 by Kasimir the Great and extended to the whole of Poland. At that time, the document was entrusted to a Kalish Jew named Falk.

Similar privileges it should be noted had already been granted to Jews from the mid-13th century in Austria, Hungary and Bohemia. However, the Polish privileges included certain clauses that were not to be found in the others.

The original text was printed in a collection of laws prepared by Jan Laski, approved by the Polish Seim (Parliament) in Radom and published in 1506. Certain changes for the worse were made and the inclusion of the law was justified by the declaration of the then reigning King Alexander: "We, King Alexander, command that the Privileges be included in the Code of Laws not in order to confirm them afresh but as a precautionary measure to protect the Jews".

Polish scholars sometimes describe these Privileges as the Magna Charta of Polish Jewry. While considerable attention is paid to Jews as moneylenders (i.e., the bankers of the Middle Ages), they also seem to have played a very significant part as merchants who maintained the flow of goods throughout the country and from one territory to another. The recognition of the Jewish, i.e., Rabbinical Court as the legal authority in internal Jewish affairs and disputes helped to secure the growth of the subsequent internal autonomy of Polish Jewry which has been a decisive factor in shaping the lives of East European Jewry and their descendants.

Lieutant-Colonel Berek Joselewicz of the Fifth Mounted Regiment, died for Poland at the Battle of Kotsk, 5 May 1809.

Jewish Physicians sent by Don Joseph Nassi, Duke of Naxos and the Cyclades, Grand Vizier of Sultan Suleman the Magnificent, in Order to Treat Barbara Radziwil, Wife of his Sovereign Friend Sigismund Augustus King of Poland.

A Jew With a Petition Writer

Jewish Seamen Export Produce through the Port of Danzig

A Funeral Procession Starts Out

Robbery in the Jew's Quarter

A Jew is Attacked

A Jew Takes Oath

A Christian Gives Evidence in a Case Concerning a Jew

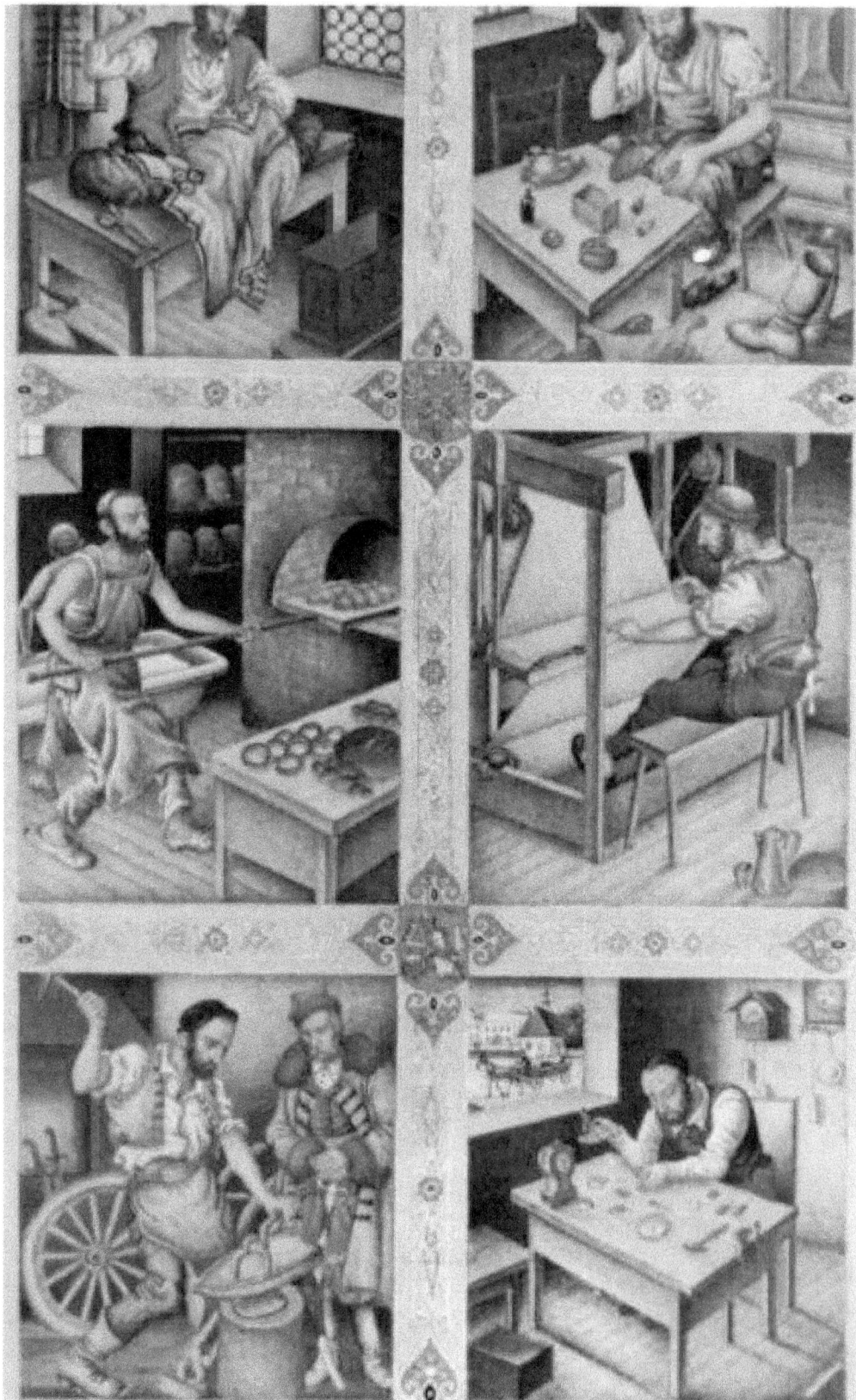

Jewish Craftsmen at Work

A Din Torah

Boleslaw the Great Signs the Statute in Kalish 1264

The Kalish Statute, Yiddish Version

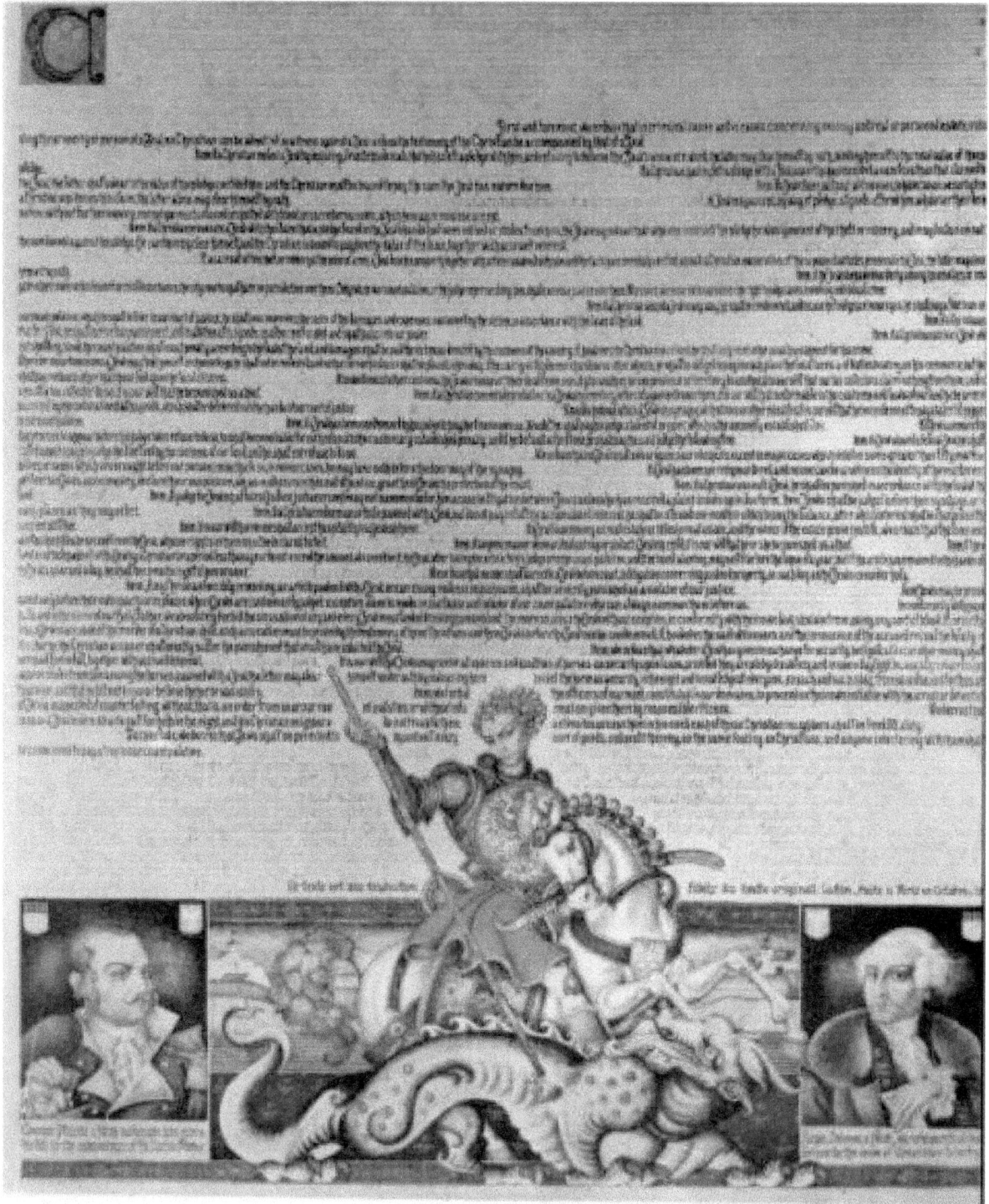

The Kalish Statute, English Version

The Kalish Statute, Hebrew Version

Jewish Minters Strike the First Polish Coins in the Reign of Mieszek III

Jewish Representatives before Kasimir the Great

Early Days

As frequently happens in Jewish history, the presence of Jews is known through some calamity. In this case, it is known that in Kalish they suffered from hunger in 1282 on account of pestilence. The first step taken by the community as such was to establish a cemetery which goes back to the year 1287 and was paid for at the rate of six talents of pepper and two talents of saffron as an annual leasehold rental.

The early Jewish community was set up not in the commercial centre but nearby, apparently on the left bank of the River Prosna. To begin with, Jews were engaged in crafts such as tailoring, butchering, gold and silver working; and there were also those who engaged in agriculture. Following the prohibition of lending money on interest by the Church, an increasing number of Jews began to engage in finance so that by the time of Kasimir the Great, Kalish and Posen lying further north were important Jewish banking and credit centres.

[Page 18]

However, the Black Death, which spelt calamity throughout Central Europe, had its effect in Poland as well. The coming of the Flagellants spelled the end of the Jewish community. A lament for the massacres that took place records the slaying of Jews in Kalish, Cracow and Glogau. However, the German massacres led in turn to a Jewish migration into Poland. Many settled in Kalish and the Jewish community began to expand once more. There was a period of relative prosperity interrupted by the campaigns of the Hungarian king Ludwig in 1383, while about forty years later, a convocation of the Catholic Church led to the imposition of anti-Jewish regulations including the wearing of the Jewish badge.

From the middle of the 14th century, Jews began to appear more frequently by name, being referred to in various legal records as claiming the payment of debts, most of which are by no means considerable.

Names found in these lists include: Michael, Abraham, Yehudya, David, Daniel, Shabdai (Sabbethai), Aaron, Shlomo and Jonah Michael. Women mentioned include: Zelda, Zemela and Dina. Other names are Jurdan, Kavian and Benish.

By the early 15th century, Kalish Jews were engaging in partnerships in respect of various financial transactions. At this time, Jews are referred to in the courts by the names of Iko (Isaac) and Kossol.

Growth of the Community

A Jewish street existed from the middle of the 14th century. As remained customary for many centuries, this was rather more of a square or quarter built around the synagogue which was burnt in the late 16th century. The Jewish Quarter ran from the centre of the city to the walls. Before the fire of 1537, Jews were permitted to hold six houses of their own; other houses being presumably rented. When the city was rebuilt, the number of Jewish houses was increased to eleven. By an agreement reached in 1540, eleven Jewish families were permitted to deal in certain kinds of goods within the Christian quarter and Jews were permitted to maintain four taverns for spirits.

Some years later, the municipality supplied the Jews with piped water against an annual payment of four florins. By 1553, the community already had nineteen houses apart from communal buildings consisting of the community building and offices, dwellings of the rabbi, *shamash* (beadle) and communal staff, and the *hekdesh* (communal lazar-house and hostel), the bath-house and *mikveh* (ritual bath). As time went on, Christian citizens including aldermen sold their houses to the Jews, particularly if they happened to lie within the Jewish Quarter.

In respect of Polish law, the main purpose of the organized Jewish community was to facilitate the collection of taxes and other charges owing to the Government. Internally speaking, the community or *kehilla* engaged in the conduct and regulation of religious, economic, social and educational affairs and represented its members vis-à-vis Government and municipal authorities. Until well on in the 16th century, each Jewish community was an independent body and there was no territorial organization linking them. From time-to-time, they would associate for some ad hoc purpose which was usually temporary.

[Page 19]

In the early days the community was headed by an unspecified number of *parnassim* (wardens), five, four or three in number. When Kasimir the Great confirmed the Kalish Privileges, the leaders of the Kalish community represented the Jews of Great Poland. Thirty years later, the revised Charter which had been extended to all Polish Jewry was, as already mentioned, entrusted to the Jew Falk of Kalish who, presumably, headed the community at that time. Other known leaders of the community were Daniel who was chosen as arbitrator in disputes and David Ogbut of Cracow who built houses in the early part of the fourteen-hundreds.

Under King Wladislaw Jagiello the Jewish community of Kalish, was subjected to increasing economic pressure. In 1430 the King gave instructions that Palta Joseph and Canaan, Jews of Kalish, should appear before the Royal Court because they had not paid taxes to the Treasury from their profits in financial transactions. They did not appear in Court and a fine of fifteen hundred grzebni was imposed upon them. Instances of this kind alarmed the community and led them to resolve to leave the city. The authorities opposed this and demanded that the wealthy Jews of the community should personally guarantee, on pain of a financial fine of sixty grzebni, that those who departed would not take their property with them until they had settled their debts for taxes. Kavian, apparently as community head, and other wealthy Jews gave security for this as we learn from an existing document. About a generation earlier, a false florin had been found in the possession of the Kalish Jew Mark who was flung into prison.

Kavian, together with Jehuda, Smalko and Jurdan, bailed him out on a guarantee of 100 grzebni. Mark proved that he had never gone abroad and had purchased the bad florin from the Kalish citizen, Kurczak, in the belief that it was good money. Kurczak witnessed that Mark's claim was correct and he was acquitted. A similar incident occurred in 1441 to two Jewesses who were also set free.

The number of Jews in Kalish increased following the expulsion from Prague in 1542 though most of those expelled settled in Lublin and Cracow. Jews from Hungary also settled in the city.

The major expansion of Polish Jewry took place in the 15th and 16th centuries when Kalish residents began to move to new communities which offered better economic opportunities. As already noted, the authorities did their best to prevent any mass withdrawal. In this connection, various wealthy Jews were charged with breaches of the law, particularly in 1448 and escaped imprisonment only by paying large sums as security. At this time, the community as such paid an annual tax of one hundred grzebni to the king's secretary, Canon Martin Swenka who was himself heavily burdened with debt. The tax was paid by the Canon promised the community that he would obtain a royal privilege exempting it from all further taxation for two years together with the assistance of Government officials in collecting debts owed by Christians to the Jews. A special agreement in this connection was signed in 1445. However, it is not known whether the Canon succeeded in carrying out his part. In 1453, a joint delegation from seven communities including Kalish endeavoured to obtain a confirmation of their privileges at the royal chancellery. After six years of intercession and considerable financial outlay, a memorandum summarizing all privileges was prepared and was signed by the reigning monarch in respect of the Jews of Great Poland and Small Poland. However, under ecclesiastical pressure, the privileges were withdrawn soon after.

[Page 20]

The first named rabbi of the Jews was Michael who is referred to in a document of 1427. Somewhat later, reference is made to the Jewish judge Abraham Kapust of Pesari and the Jewish assessors Michael and Palty. At about the same time, there were three shamashim or beadles of the court and the community, Abraham, Shmuel and Israel by name, whose quarrels brought them before the civil court and are a matter of record.

In 1458, there was a fire in the course of which the Jewish houses were all burnt and their property pillaged. During the same year, they had to pay the rector of the general school, apparently for preventing his older pupils from engaging in anti-Jewish riots of the kind known as "schueler geleif". Riots broke out in the year 1542 and were participated in not only by the rabble but also by various notables of the city. The rioters burst into the synagogue and profaned the Torah Scrolls. The heads of the Jewish community blamed the Municipal Council. The latter in return prohibited the Jews from appearing in public or even leaving their dwellings from Good Friday to Easter Monday inclusive. At that time, the Government authorities warned the Municipality that they would have to pay a fine of two thousand grzebni if disturbances broke out again. However, there were more riots in 1565 when three Jews were killed. The municipal authorities did not appear in court and the accused were not punished.

Some years earlier, the Jews of Kalish had been accused of stealing the Host from the church and a number were sentenced to death. In 1571, legal steps were taken by the brothers Shmuel and Moshe Mordechovitch and the rabbi against the citizens of Kalish on account of the murder of their brother Elia by a student. The matter was settled in due course by payment of compensation. A few years later, the following brief entry is found in the Pinkas (Record Book) of the Cracow community: "In the Holy Congregation of Kalish, the students destroyed the synagogue and took the Torah Scroll and ripped it apart in the year 5351 (1591).

Sixty years earlier, King Zygmunt had set out to protect the Jews against the charges of using Christian blood for religious purposes and had published a declaration confirming all the long-established privileges of the Jews in the cities of Great Poland including Kalish. Once again, the citizens were prohibited from judging the Jews in their courts.

It should be noted that the beginnings of the 15th century were marked by a struggle on the part of the Polish cities to restrict the long-established Jewish freedom for trade. Indeed, in 1521 a delegation of burghers persuaded the king to cancel all privileges. Sometime later, the merchants of Posen broke the Jewish warehouses open in their town and destroyed the content, being followed by similar measures in various other towns including Kalish. In spite of this, Jewish trade re-established itself and between 1550 and 1570 Jews conducted the greater part of all commercial transactions with the seaport of Danzig as well as in all parts of Poland.

[Page 21]

Thus, in 1580-81, the Jews of Kalish transported close to 4,500 fells and skins of all kinds through the Kalish Customs Station; also 972 stones of wool (more than 80% of the total handled): 30 stones of tallow; 295 stones of wax and 5 stones of pepper.

In 1579 the Jews of the city paid less than one fifth of all local taxes – 130 zloty. Forty Jews paid nothing on account of their poverty meaning that 30% of the Jewish community were poverty-stricken. At that period, the Jews were required to pay: The Jewish poll-tax; extraordinary taxes and Charges and imposts in money, kind and work.

By the middle of the 17th century, Kalish Jews were regular visitors at the Leipzig and Breslau Fairs. On many occasions two or three were sent as representatives of them all but on other occasions, more than thirty Jews went from Kalish. Towards the end of the century, the participation of over six hundred Jews from Poland is recorded. Of these, more than a hundred came from Kalish. The goods they brought to these fairs included fells, furs, etc. Their purchases included textiles, silks, general merchandize and peddler's goods, metals, ironware and jewellery. Asher Abraham and his sons Amshel and Moshe visited the Leipzig Fair regularly from 1686 until 1736. Others were Hanoch, Jacob, Marcus and Moshe belonging to the Hertz, Marcus, Shmerelovitch and Wolf families. There were others who regularly visited the Breslau Fair. Names mentioned include: Asher, Isaac, Jacob Leibel, Michael, Moshe and Shmuel Abraham in the final decades of the 17th century. Marcus Isaac and his son Isaac Marcus Derar, Jacob Barbar, Koppel Goldschmidt (who belonged to the merchant family of Yuchan Alexander), Jacob Ahs, Jacob Lippman, Aaron, Jacob Lazarus, Samuel Yochan and Abraham and Marcus

Kaplan. By the turn of the century, a number of Polish Jews including several from Kalish had settled in Breslau.

Jews engaged in the following crafts: Tailors, bakers, weavers, furriers, cord-makers, gold and silversmiths. In the early 16th century, there was a Jewish painter named Beinish (Byenas). An interesting Order issued by King Zygmunt in 1513 provides that Jewish butchers might sell meat which was not kosher only in their own homes, i.e. to non-Jews.

In the middle of the 17th century, Jews were also harness-makers, saddle-makers, blacksmiths, oven-makers, carpenters, bag-makers, rope-makers, engravers and glaziers. There were severe restrictions on craftsmen who were not members of the local guilds, who might, however, sell their wares at fairs and markets. Any journeyman joining a guild paid one zloty and eighteen groszy. The only guild from which Jews were then excluded was that of the Barber-surgeons but presumably this exclusion did not apply within the Jewish community as such. During all this time, the Christian merchants of Kalish were endeavouring to combat their Jewish fellow-townsmen and competitors in every way possible, including measures that can be classed as anti-Semitic and economic boycott.

Regional Government bodies repeatedly demanded that Jews should not be allowed to farm any excise or customs duties and that they should be required to pay the same war tax as others when there was danger of a Tartar invasion into the Ukraine, Wolhynia and Podolia. Christian tax farmers who employed Jewish officials and collectors were liable to fines together with the said Jews. Extortion by false charges was also part of the normal scene. In 1620, the Posen community paid various bribes, etc. in this connection on behalf of the Jews of Kalish who were then undergoing a period of economic distress.

[Page 22]

During an epidemic in the year 1623, Kalish Jewry suffered from the incitement of a Polish physician named Sebastian Szleszkowski who declared in a work on the pestilence that it was due to "Divine retribution for the protection and defence which the nobility and the municipalities grant to the Jews." He claimed that the Jewish physicians were systematically poisoning their Christian patients. In several brochures, he continued his violent attacks on Jewish physicians and on those who consulted them in spite of the prohibitions by the Holy Church. From his writings and that of a predecessor who wrote the first Polish anti-Semitic documents, it would appear that there must have been quite a number of Jewish physicians in Poland at the time; and there must have been a certain amount of social intercourse between the Jewish and Polish communities including eating and drinking together. Szleszkowski's solution for the Jewish problem of his time was to isolate the Jews in special villages where they would be treated in the same way as the serfs of the nobility.

Following a false charge by a converted Jew in 1641, Christians broke into the Kalish Synagogue and ripped two Torah Scrolls apart. However, all such events were minor details compared with their fate during the invasion of Poland by the Swedish forces between 1655 and 1660, in addition to the general sufferings of the population. In the course of hostilities, close to 1800 synagogues were destroyed; Torah Scrolls were ripped to pieces and hundreds of Jews were killed. Forty communities were exterminated in Great Poland alone. In Kalish itself, close to 600 Jewish families were slain according to a Hebrew record of the period entitled: "Tit Hayeven" (The Nether Hell) which enumerates those slain in Polish Jewish communities from the Cossack Massacres of 1648 until the end of the Swedish wars in 1660 and arrives at the figure of 600,000 – a stupendous number for those days. However, survivors and new settlers re-established the community with the financial aid of the Posen community and thanks to loans received from Posen, Lissa and Krotoszin as well as certain clergy, totalling 28,000 zloty.

In 1670, the Jews of Kalish and Posen were required to pay 3,000 zloty on account of the poll-tax for the year 1669. During the same year, a number of Jewish refugees from Vienna settled in the town. Five years later, Kalish was visited by one of those fires which were endemic in Polish cities and their Jewish quarters. At about this time, the burghers took steps to ensure that the Jews should be confined within the area specified in 1540. In 1676, King Jan Sobieski confirmed the old Kalish Privileges.

Autonomous Jewish Life

The Jews, who were under royal protection, were regarded as the King's servants. This meant that in terms of the feudal system, they owed direct allegiance to the king alone. The internal source of Jewish life was Jewish Talmudic law as it had evolved throughout the ages under the guidance of the Rabbinical authorities known as the *Poskim*. The constitutional base of Jewish life was the Kalish Privileges of 1264 which prescribed conditions relating to trade, loans at interest, the functions of Jewish and general courts, oaths and general regulations governing the life of the community. Various details in these Privileges might vary from one community to another. For ordinary purposes, the Jewish community existed on the basis of contract; either with the local Municipal Authorities in the case of Free Cities or else with the local Regional or Central Government Authorities.

[Page 23]

The *Kahal* was equivalent to the Municipality. In Kalish, its affairs were conducted by five *Parnassim* or wardens who were responsible for income and expenditure. They were elected by the community which also laid down the general lines of administration and exercised administrative, financial, judicial and educational functions besides the conduct of worship and religious affairs. The communal representatives represented the Jews vis-à-vis the authorities and the *Kahal* was the first and in certain cases the highest legal instance. It was organized in: a) The heads or *Parnassim*, numbering three to five; b) The Worthies and c) The Congregation or representatives of the community.

After the *Parnassim* or heads were elected, they took an oath of allegiance to the king and state. Their election required official confirmation. It was the practice for them to hold responsibility each for a month in turn, so that the person responsible in the community at any given time was known as the *Parnass Hahodesh*. The Worthies, three to five in number, could replace the *Parnassim* or might sit in judgment with a Jewish judge on behalf of the authorities. The number of members in the *Kahal* seems to have varied from time to time.

There were also the following committees: 1) Major charity wardens, 3-7 in number; 2) Holders of the accounts; 3) Market wardens to supervise weights and measures, ensure that the streets were kept clean, supervise night watchmen and the kashrut of butter, cheese and wine. (It should be remembered that the latter three food items have to be ritually kosher for observant Jewry to this day). Sub-committees supervised animal slaughter and the sale of meat, the hiring of men-servants and maid-servants, etc. 4) School Wardens; 5) Synagogue Wardens; 6) Wardens collecting donations and contributions to support the inhabitants of the Holy Land; 7) Wardens for *Pdyon Shevuyim*, the redemption of captives particularly during hostilities, revolts, etc., in the 17th century; 8) Communal Fund Wardens; 9) Assessors for the allocation of communal taxes; 10) Heads of the Artisan Societies, i.e. the Jewish Guilds.

Other committees were set up ad hoc to ensure the observation of sumptuary laws (against excessive display and extravagance in clothing, etc.,) to supervise morals, etc. Lawsuits between Jews were brought before the *Dayanim* or subordinate Rabbinical judges. There were two or three *Batei Din* or Rabbinical Courts, each composed of 3-5 *Dayanim*.

Persons were elected to office for a period of one year. Elections were held in all communities including Kalish on the 3rd day of Passover, i.e. on the first of the intermediate days. Former office holders might be re-elected.

The method of election known in Posen and apparently also used in Kalish was as follows: The heads of the community placed 21 names of leading householders in the ballot box and withdrew seven by lot. These were the referees who appointed the new *Kahal* and also gave them general instructions.

[Page 24]

Both religious and civil functionaries were required by the community. The Rabbi headed the communal hierarchy and was not only the leading official but likewise the spiritual authority and supervisor of the religious and general cultural life of his congregation. In the 16th century, the Rabbis were usually members of well-to-do families who were not concerned with salary and were therefore completely independent of the heads and wardens of the congregation. This helped to secure the traditional status of the rabbi in Eastern Europe until the time of the Catastrophe, even though the status in question began to decline in the 17th and 18th centuries. Though the names of the early Kalish rabbis are not known, they are referred to in various sources in terms of very high respect. It is interesting to note that the community never appointed one of its own members to serve as its rabbi.

From the early 17th century on, the known rabbis of the city included quite a number of outstanding figures who played a prominent part both in rabbinical and public affairs and also in the literature of their period. A leading rabbi, born in Kalish, was Jacob ben Joseph Striemer. He was a follower of Sabbethai Zvi until the latter's apostasy when he became violently anti-Sabbatian. Subsequently, he conducted a Talmud Torah (Jewish day school) in Adrianople, Turkey and is recorded as one of the Ashkenazi sages in Jerusalem in the year 1700.

Under Polish law, the rabbi was authorized to issue decisions on all matters brought before him in accordance with the laws of Israel. The only authority to whom he was responsible was the king himself. He signed all the resolutions of the Kahal, conducted the elections and ensured that they were properly carried out. However, he was selected and appointed by the *Parnassim* and was, therefore, dependent upon them unless he was himself well-to-do.

When elected, the rabbi received a certificate of appointment specifying his rights and duties, the fees he might charge for weddings, wills, issuing legal judgements and also the businesses in which members of his family were allowed to engage. In the 17th and 18th centuries, his salary in communities as large as Kalish varied from 3-10 zloty per week. He was also paid for the two sermons which he traditionally delivered on the Sabbath before Passover and the Sabbath between the New Year and the Day of Atonement.

Mention should also be made of the Head of the Yeshiva or Talmudical Academy who might sometimes compete with the local rabbi in respect of the precedence and authority deriving from his learning. In many cases, the two offices were combined.

Other officials included: the communal scribe or secretary who needed to be able to speak Polish at least. For public affairs, a special Christian official who was sometimes a nobleman assisted him in the Civil Courts and Regional Government offices. There were Shamashim (Beadles or attendants of various kinds) for the synagogue, the cemetery, the tax assessors, the Jewish and general court. The Court *Shamash* developed in due course into the *Shtadlan* or intermediary with the non-Jewish authorities. The first known in Kalish was Reb Leib Shtadlan who exercised this function for many years at the end of the 17th century, and from 1700-1709 was also *Shtadlan* in Posen where he received five gulden a week for his services.

[Page 25]

The community also maintained a physician, apothecary, barber-surgeons, a midwife, watchmen, collectors, messengers and postmen. Charitable activities were extensive including charity for the local poor and wayfarers, support for indigent householders, supervision of young Jewish students and orphans, dowries for brides, medical aid and hospitalisation. Physicians with medical degrees are referred to only in the 18th century but the physician, Moshe ben Benjamin Wolf of Mezeritch, who was in Kalish in the second half of the 18thcentury, wrote medical works including one containing extensive passages in German.

The expenses of the community included the taxes paid to the Government treasury. The regular taxes required of Jews were:

1. The "Stacyjne" levied in money or goods for the upkeep of the Royal Court and Kitchen. This was afterwards transformed into a fixed payment which each community paid either to the King himself or to his assigns.
2. The Szos of the Jews: a special municipal tax levied only on property held by Jews.
3. The Poll-tax which commenced in 1549 and amounted to 1 zloty per person. This was supposed to exempt Jews from other taxes which, however, were not abolished as it was clear whether the Poll-tax was levied on the family or the individual. At first, each community paid for itself. Subsequently, the Jewries of each part of Poland paid through the chief community. To facilitate the collection of this tax, the body known as the *Vaad Arba Aratzot* (Council of the Four Lands) was established and a total amount was fixed by agreement with the Chancellor of the Exchequer. This amount was then distributed by the Jews themselves among the various lands and communities. The powers vested in the Council in order to facilitate collection of this tax enabled it to achieve a virtual national autonomy and brought about the spirit of group unity which has characterized East European Jewry and their offspring ever since.
4. A Billeting Tax which was paid by the Jews in lieu of billeting troops with them. Sometimes the community paid the rent for barracks and officers' quarters away from the Jewish quarter or else, they paid directly to regimental funds.

Extraordinary taxes included:

1. Coronation fees levied when a new king was crowned.
2. Special levies to pay off national debts upon royal edict.
3. For the requirements of war. Charges of this kind were levied quite frequently during the 17th century.
4. Contributions to gifts sent to the Turkish Sultan and Tartar Khans (as tokens of goodwill and to persuade them to refrain from incursions into Polish territory).

All kinds of gifts, presents, payments, etc., to nobles, officials, town councils, churches, clergymen, schools (as insurance against the student riots called *Schuelergeleif*). Certain sums are clearly recorded as bribes and fines and amercements were paid to occupying forces.

[Page 26]

General taxes levied on all town folk (citizens) alike were:

1. Municipal Szos which was a property tax dating from the 17th Century.
2. Foodstuffs tax including an excise duty on liquor paid by the community and collected from the individual Jews.
3. Octroi, toll fees on bridges and roads, municipal weight fees, frontier customs duties.

It was the function of the community to raise all these amounts, each member being assessed as to his share. Notice of three days was given for payment. If a man did not pay, he was declared "contumacious" and if this was repeated, he was excommunicated and not permitted to enter the Synagogue. If he refused to leave the Synagogue, he would be imprisoned until he paid or made suitable arrangements for payment.

Other sources of income included: *Hazaka* (occupation rights or permits). These included the right of residence, of possessing a house, plot or dwelling or engaging in trade, handicrafts or selling. One of the purposes of the *Hazaka* fee was to prevent harmful and unfair competition or price-raising.

Then came payments on weddings, burials, dowries and the grant of certain honorific titles. A property tax was also levied on occasion. If direct taxes were insufficient, taxes were levied on meat, milk, wine, honey and other staple foodstuffs. The community farmed the taxes out and on occasion, an income tax was also levied.

After the vicissitudes of the mid-17th century, however, all these sources proved inadequate and the Kalish community had to borrow loans repeatedly in the early part of the 18thcentury. Many of these loans were raised from Christians in Breslau.

A Kalish Jew named Gad Uziel is named as one of the first assessors when the forerunner of the Council of the Four Lands was set up for the communities of Great Poland in 1519.

Special courts dealing with disputes in Fairs and Markets were established, and by the early 16th century had led to the establishment of a Jewish High Court for the whole of Poland. This too helped to lead to the establishment of the *Vaad Arba Aratzot* which comprised Great Poland, Little Poland, Reissen (White Russia) and Lithuania. Kalish played a leading part at this council and on the Council of Great Poland itself. It was the practice of the community to send persons who exercised no other communal functions whatsoever to these Councils. By the middle of the 17th century, Kalish held the hegemony over the Council of Great Poland which met once and sometimes twice a year.

The internal economic functions of the latter can be judged by the fact that in 1684 it passed a *Takana* (Regulation) against monopolization of Jewish trade and imposed a tax on wool purchases to ensure that there would be no unfair competition between purchasers of wool from the big estate owners and nobles. This Regulation reads as follows:

"No visitor is permitted to purchase any goods in communities other than his own save specifically from Jews; and he is not permitted to stay in them more than three days and no longer. Likewise, those who live outside the State have no permission to purchase any goods in the vicinity of any community in accordance with the ancient regulation and Jewish villagers are prohibited from taking them on the wagon and carrying them to make the rounds in the small towns in order to purchase any goods whatsoever; and even if they have already purchased goods from Jews who dwell in the villages, then whenever the members of the community come there, it will be first come first served in respect of those goods." Similar regulations are repeated in more stringent terms from time-to-time.

[Page 27]

The Wardens of the Council of Great Poland from Kalish included: Rabbi Samuel ben Yaakov in the 1670's who was also the *Parnass* of the Council of the Four Lands. He also took steps to redeem a certain Rabbi Yekutiel Kaufman Katz from captivity. Others were: Reb Yitshak Isaac ben Azriel Zelig, son-in-law of Reb Mendel of Kalish, also known as Reb Isaac Reb Mendel; Shlomo ben Hayyim and Reb Yehuda ben Yosef; Yosef ben Arieh, Yehuda Leib Halevi; Shmuel ben Yonah Katz; Shmuel Feivish ben Yehuda Leib Preger, referred to as a scholar; Joseph Halevi of Kalish; Hirsch ben Asher; Meyer ben Yaakov; Michael Pak, a merchant of Kalish who represented Jewry at the Council of the Four Lands in 1602 and was followed in due course by Rabbi Israel ben Nathan Shapiro; Shmuel ben Yaakov; Yehuda Leib Obornik; Meir ben Dov Joseph; Joseph ben Eliahu Venczinek; Mordechai Joseph; Jacob ben Zelig who was imprisoned together with other delegates on account of claims from Breslau against them and Polish Jewry in general; Leibel Feivish; Yitshak known as Isaac ben Azriel and Joseph ben Arieh Yehuda.

In 1685, the Council of Great Poland borrowed loans from the Order of Jesuits in Posen and also owed considerable sums to the Jesuits in Kalish. They paid an annual interest of 7-10% and in 1964 the Council became bankrupt. Creditors, whose numbers were by no means few, attacked Jews on the roads, seized their goods in the fairs and markets, imprisoned them in fortresses and citadels. King Jan Sobleski appointed special commissioners to investigate the debts and spread the period of their repayment over several years. The total debt was then assessed at 400,000 zloty, to be paid off during the following three years. However, the communities were not in a position to meet these commitments.

The matter was dealt with by the Council of the Four Lands in 1699 but dragged on for years and commitments could not be met in 1713 when Isaac Zelig of Kalish, Warden of the Council, tried to obtain a consolidating loan but was unsuccessful. The creditors then began to demand that the Kalish community should pay the debt but the community declared that it was not in a position to do so. In 1714 the Lissa community took over part of the Kalish debts, including interest of more than 12,000 zloty per year and then became the head community of Great Poland.

The Eighteenth Century

In the course of the war between Sweden and Poland in 1706, Kalish was captured and the greater part of the city burnt down. A contemporary report by the Municipality reads as follows: "In the city of Kalish, all our Jewish houses were completely burnt to ashes together with the Synagogue, except for two houses by the wall; all the buildings and the ware. On Sunday evening before the Festival of the Birth of the Holy Virgin, this tremendous fire burst out in the square of Kalish. It spread so far and wide that only the plots were left instead of the houses. In this conflagration, forty-five were burnt as it was impossible to escape from the terrible flames."

[Page 28]

Two years later, an epidemic broke out during Passover on such a scale that the Lissa community prohibited all visits to kalish. The inhabitants fled to the fields and forests. The neighbouring communities came to their aid. It is reported that 450 persons died. The community of Posen was asked to aid and gave 1,000 zloty. In the year 1727, the communities of Posen, Lissa and Krotoszyn made a grant of 28,000 zloty to the impoverished community of Kalish.

The fire of 1706 was followed by fresh conflagrations in 1710, 1712 and 1713, while epidemics spread in 1708 and 1712. At this time, there were about 100 Jews in a total population of 700, the lowest known population in the history of the city.

In 1754, the townsfolk charged the Jews with endangering their lives and existence. Large fines were paid and the Jews escaped from the danger but not details are known.

The first authentic figures on the population date from 1765 when there were 809 Jews and 52 babies aged less than a year. There were 408 men and 401 women. Of these, 197 were married; 175 of the being independent and 22 being sons and sons-in-laws living with parents; 188 unmarried sons; 23 servants, apprentices and orphans. There were 175 married women, 22 married daughters and brides, 18 widows, 15 independent, 3 divorced, 174 unmarried girls, 12 servants and orphans. There were 215 families in all – 190 being independent and 25 living with the parents.

Since Jews used to evade censuses for religious and other reasons, it has been estimated that the total number in Kalish at the time may have been over 1,000.

More than another thousand lived in 8 hamlets and 8 villages in the vicinity, while the total number of Jews in the Kalish Government District was 6,465 in 29 cities which constituted 23 communities. (Certain small congregations came under the authority of the larger neighbouring communities).

Ten years later, there were 670 Jews, not including infants, liable to the poll-tax. It may be assumed that the Jewish population was still at around 900. For the year 1789, we have reliable figures showing that there were at the time 880 Jews, 334 being men, 318 women, 126 boys of whom 75 were more than a year old and 102 girls of whom 53 were more than a year old. It would appear that the entry of poor and sick Jews to the city was prohibited.

When the Prussian authorities conducted a census in 1793, there were 1,706 Jews. Some doubt is cast on the latter figure by a Palish historian who calculates that there must have been a total of 1,300 Jews in 1789. In 1792, another fire burst out and not a single house was left standing in the Jewish Quarter which was a separate part of the city. Special municipal regulations of 1755 required the Jews to keep the Quarter clean and clear gutters and drainpipes on pain of fine and imprisonment.

Throughout the century, the Jewish merchants faced the fierce competition of the townsfolk and citizens. The Christian Guilds did their best to reduce the opportunities and possibilities of the Jewish traders in every way possible. Countless municipal regulations attest to this.

[Page 29]

Jewish liquor merchants met with serious competition from a group of Greek merchants who settled in Kalish in the middle of the 18th century coming from Macedonia where they had been persecuted by the Turks. In general, Jewish liquor traders had to struggle very severely against the repressive measures of the families of hereditary brewers in the city.

In the course of time Jews also dealt in cattle, horses, oxen, grain and agricultural produce. There was a constant coming and going of agents who visited large estates and villages to purchase these wares and the Christian wholesalers combatted this trade continuously. In the year 1778, for instance, the community spent 6,000 zloty exclusively on trials with the municipal authorities in this connection. Shopkeepers and storekeepers who rented places in the Market Square were subjected to all kinds of restrictions and prohibitions by the municipal authorities and Christian associations in respect of kinds of goods to be sold, weight, prices and hours of sale. They faced constant threats of confiscation and expulsion.

In spite of this, the census of 1765 gives the following figures about the employment of heads of families: Trade, 18, 13 of whom were merchants, 2 shopkeepers, 2 hawkers and 1 agent; Crafts 79, of which 30 in free professions; and 63 heads of families without any profession.

Of 443 families recorded in 1786, 141 were householders and permanent residents; 99 were not permanent. Forty-two engaged in trade; 50 were agents and 5 had inns. As against 21% of the Jewish population engaged in trade, only 9% of the Poles were so engaged.

In 1789 the figures were as follows: Householders 69, or 153 with wives and children; merchants 70, or 174 with wives and children; craftsmen 100, or 234 with wives and children; innkeepers 4 or 17 with wives and children; shopkeepers 40, or 122 with wives and children; agents 30, or 107 with wives and children; apprentices and assistants 21, or 33 with wives and children. At this time, 43% of Jewish families made their living by trade, liquor and as agents. The corresponding percentage for Christian families was 10%.

The Jews traded in horses, cattle, grain and agricultural produce. In that century, the Jews also engaged in wholesale textile trade having wool woven for them by individual weavers or Polish workshops. They exported to Moravia, Bohemia, Silesia and Saxony. There were some Jews who leased flocks of sheep. Jews opened soap factories.

When the Polish Treasury took over the manufacture of tobacco, a workshop was opened in Kalish and Jews engaged in the sale of the product. Monetary and credit activities were also carried on. Loans were granted to Christian and Greek merchants and others at an annual interest of 7% or more, often against pledges of silver, gold and jewellery. At the same time, Jewish merchants borrowed from wealthy citizens, nobles, etc., including clergymen who charged a high rate of interest. There were constant relations with Silesia, particularly with Breslau where the Jewish merchants of Kalish established a synagogue of their own in 1698, maintaining a trustee and *shtadlan* to safeguard their interest. By the beginning of the 18th century, there were 6 such representatives in Breslau from Poland. In 1722 there were 8 and at one time there were even 12. The Breslau authorities authorized only 3 in 1738.

[Page 30]

A report dated 1779 on the Customs offices in the Kalish District and Kalish itself gives an account of the local and other Jewish merchants who returned from Frankfurt. A representative of the Kalish Jews was required to take oath that cattle imported were healthy. Agents made the rounds of the city and environs purchasing clothes, gold, silver and jewels, also agricultural produce, horses, cattle, liquor, etc. The Municipality took special steps to ensure that Jewish shopkeepers would not sell goods on the roads and in the streets. All trade had to be conducted in the market-place.

Jewish craftsmen listed in the 1765 census were: 27 tailors, 2 hat-makers, 16 furriers, 4 embroiderers, 10 cord makers, 2 glaziers, 1 bookbinder, 8 craftsmen of various kinds and 9 butchers. These Jewish craftsmen suffered from the persecution of the various Christian craft guilds which insisted that according to the privileges awarded to them, the Jews were not permitted to engage in various trades, particularly tailoring. In 1713, an agreement was reached between the Tailors' Guild and the Jewish tailors whereby Jewish residents of Kalish might engage in tailoring in return for an annual payment of 14 zloty to the Guild. In 1774, another agreement was reached whereby Shlomo, the Women's Tailor, was the only Jew authorized to engage in this calling against an annual payment of 3 zloty to the Guild. In the earlier part of the 17th century, indeed, the Jewish butchers had been authorized to maintain 12 butcher shops against an annual payment of 300 zloty while the Jewish furriers paid 16 zloty annually to the Furriers Guild.

By the second half of the 18th century, there were also Jewish shoemakers, saddle-makers and button-makers. In 1786 there were 101 Jewish craftsmen in Kalish as against 106 Christians. In 1789 there were 100 Jewish craftsmen with 98 wives, 16 boys and 20 girls or 234 persons in all, constituting 26.6% of the Jewish population. They were organized in societies which had a guild character and charged the same rates as the Christian guilds.

Although there was no Hebrew printing press in Kalish itself, men from Kalish are referred to throughout this period as printers, typesetters, proof-readers and publishers. Thus, in 1589, Abraham ben Yitshak Kera Ashkenazi of Kalish printed books in Salonica and afterwards in Venice and Mantua. In 1690, there was a type-setter in Amsterdam named Leib ben Naphtali Hirsch Fass of Kalish. Others at that time in Berlin were Shneur Zalman ben Yehonatan Katz and Hehoshua ben Avigdor, both from Kalish. The 18th century records Benjamin Sabbethai Bass, a printer; Zvi Hirsch ben Kalonymos in Duehrenfuerth; Kalonymos Baltzabon; Yitshak ben Eliahu in Frankfurt-on-Main; Benjamin ben Yehiel; Ezekiel ben Yaakov; Kalonymos ben Yehuda Leib, typesetter in Salonica and Zvi ben Reb Kalonymos Katz in Frankfurt-on-Main.

Mention should also be made of religious and communal functionaries including: Rabbis and Dayanim, cantors, sextons, slaughterers, beadles, *shtadlanim*, Torah scribes, barber-surgeons and barbers.

In 1778, a municipal committee for good order was set up. Among other duties, its task was to end the disputes and trials between Jews and townsfolk and restore peace between them. The committee achieved this purpose and an agreement was reached and signed between the Jewish community and the municipal authorities. The Jewish committee undertook to pay 1,100 zloty for the billeting of troops, for the water-pipe, the cemetery, synagogue, hospital and butcher shops at a monthly rate of 100 zloty. It was agreed that the billeting tax should cease if the troops left the town and payment would then be made pro rata to the number remaining. However, if so many soldiers arrived that the Christians could not billet them alone; the Jews would also have to do their share.

[Page 31]

Jewish merchants might trade in accordance with their ancient privileges but were not permitted to import liquor from Poland or abroad for blending and sale, with the exception of kosher wine for their own requirements. They might sell stockfish and honey. They had to take precautions not to harm Christian merchants. The community might maintain 4 drinking houses for beer and spirits but each might consist only of one room and be in the hands of one keeper. They had to buy their spirits and beer from Kalish citizens on pain of a fine to the municipality. However, in case of a shortage in Kalish, the municipality had to permit purchase elsewhere.

The Jews were guaranteed a fixed price of 6 zloty per barrel of liquor and any attempt by Kalish citizens to raise the price and/or lower the quality, would be punishable by a fine. Jews might not set up beer breweries or distilleries; they might not manufacture spirits in private houses or keep taverns or stables.

The tailoring and butchering agreements already established were confirmed though the annual fee for the butcher shops was raised afterwards to 400 zloty. An agreement of the Butcher's Guild required them to pay a levy of almost 1,100 zloty to the Furrier's Guild as before though there had never been any specific agreement. Two Jews only were permitted to sell salt in two houses of the Jewish Quarter to Jews and Christians alike, provided that weights were accurate and that the price was the same as among the Christian merchants. In return, the community had to pay the Salt-sellers' Guild 2 lbs of wax every three months. If a tannery were set up in Kalish, the Jews would not be permitted to purchase skins and export them from the city Jews were forbidden to import medicines and poisons.

Additional regulations prohibited Jews from abroad and residing temporarily in Kalish from engaging in any trade. No Jewish resident could serve as host to a Jew from abroad without the knowledge of the municipality. The gatekeepers were required to check suspect alien Jews at the gates of the city and bring them to the Mayor or Chief of Police. Jews had to share in the expenses of the water conduit leading to their own well and specially constructed for them. Jews were prohibited forever from purchasing, leasing and requisitioning houses, plots, shops in the centre of the city and all its streets and suburbs which had hitherto been inhabited by Christians, save for those buildings which they already held on some legal basis. A special resolution was adopted regarding Jewish beggars on the assumption that the latter spread contagious diseases and engaged in thievery. The committee recommended that they should not be admitted to the city but detained at the gates, given communal charity and sent away. The community could maintain only crippled poor who were resident in their hospital. They Police Chief had to ensure several times a year that the Jews were obeying this resolution, otherwise the communal heads would be fined. Those beggars caught would have to clean the streets for a month and would then be expelled, but not by vehicle.

[Page 32]

The Municipality and community were required to completely prohibit the Jews from admitting wayfarers into their homes without municipal permission and without the careful investigation by each one. The Jews were specially enjoined to keep their streets clean and in good repair. They had to maintain fire-extinguishing equipment at their own expense.

The implementation of this agreement was entrusted to the municipal authorities and was thenceforth used systematically in order to restrict the activities of the Jewish community and individuals for a full century to come until the sixties of the following century.

Towards the end of the 18th century, liberal and enlightened circles in Poland discussed the social, economic and political reorganization of their country and devoted much thought to the Jewish question. At the Great and Final Seim of Sovereign Poland (1788-1792) the cities, including Kalish, put forward a plan for setting up special Jewish craft and merchant societies subject to the supervision of the Christian associations. This ran counter to most of the plans which aimed to eliminate Jewish distinctiveness.

Throughout the century, the amount paid in poll-tax varied very considerably. Most of the figures are for the entire Posen-Kalish region and vary from almost 18,000 zloty in 1717 to over 35,000 zloty in 1734. In 1714, the city itself seems to have paid over 7,000 zloty; in 1756 the sum was 1,363; eight years later it was 39 zloty more and in 1790 it was 2,147 zloty. Whether this reflects difficulties in collection or changes in the Jewish population, is no longer clear. In addition, a number of special payments were made to the Municipality for the cemetery and the water conduit in lieu of billeting soldiers, etc. When there were no troops in Kalish, the Municipality used this amount to support the poor, orphans, widows and cripples. Jewish workshops made special payments to the guilds as already reported.

Between the years 1778 and 1792, the community paid a total of over 100,000 zloty for gifts and occasional outlay (presumably bribery and douçeurs) for various high officials and as the cost of legal proceedings. Total debts of the community to nobles, clergymen and the Committee of National Education, as recorded under a law of 1792, amounted to over 306,000 zloty on which an interest of more than 200,000 zloty was owed. Of this total, the Committee had paid almost 23,000 zloty principal and almost 54,000 zloty interest, leaving a debt of over 293,000 zloty in principal and close on 147,000 zloty in interest. Creditors among the clergy included the Jesuits, Franciscans, Bernardines, Lateran Canons, Hospital Canons and the Collegiate in Kalish.

It seems that there must have been repeated disputes between the community heads and the rabbis as can be judged by the fact that many rabbis stayed for only short periods. Between 1714 and 1763, at least five rabbis left the city on this account. When the Polish authorities set about liquidating the Jewish regional autonomous institutions in 1764, the representatives of Kalish were appointed liquidators.

[Page 33]

In the middle of the century, the Church controlled the country and Kalish together with many other communities and the Jews suffered from anti-Jewish incitement and Blood Libel cases. In 1763, seven Jews, five men and two women, were charged with murdering a Christian girl for ritual purposes. Details of the trial are unknown, but two Jews were sentenced to having their hands and heads cut off! (After conversion, they were merely beheaded). A third Jew was flung into a lime-pit and afterwards beheaded. One Jewess was sentenced to decapitation but after converting, only her hand was cut off. A fourth Jew refused to convert and was strangled, the guards mutilated his corpse dragging it the entire length of the Jewish street to the crossroads where they flung it to the dogs! The sixth and seventh victims, a man and a woman, refused to convert and were sentenced to beheading and the cutting off of their hands. The steps taken by the community are unknown.

Towards the end of the 18th century, the Redlich Family began to emerge and to move towards the prominent part they played in developing local industry during the 19th century. The first special privilege was issued to Samuel Joseph Redlich in 1793, during the final days of independent Poland. King Stanislaw Augustus Poniatowski took him under his special protection and gave him permission to trade and store goods freely. He, his wife and heirs were exempt from all mistreatment and were entitled to display silks, textiles and wool of all kinds during fairs in Kalish and any other city in the region, in shops and any public places. They could sell and exchange goods, brew beer and distil spirits and enjoy all the legal rights and privileges of the citizens of Kalish.

Under Prussia, 1793-1806

When Poland was partitioned for the second time in 1793, Prussia received the entire Western part of the country including the district in which Kalish lies. The territory contained 1,200,000 inhabitants and was called South Prussia. A treasury official was promptly given the task of ascertaining the rights of all communities and their institutions as well as the incomes of the Jews. In his report, he stated that he found appreciable numbers of Jewish craftsmen such as book-binders, butchers, shopkeepers, gold and silversmiths, tinkers, cord makers, furriers, tailors and mechanics. There were 1159 Jewish merchants and 1739 non-Jewish merchants in the whole of South Prussia who were required to keep accounts.

The King of Prussia visited Kalish in October 1793 and was received at a league's distance from the town by two groups of young Jews, one in green and the other in red Turkish garb. The heads of the community, led by the Jewish physician, Dr. Mayer and his eight-year-old son, gathered at the Triumphal Arch erected to welcome the monarch. The Jews who rode out to greet him arranged themselves in a circle around the arch, and the physician's son presented a poem which was received with thanks by the king. In 1800, there were 16,230 Jews in the department of Kalish. In Kalish itself, the Jews were 41% of the population and were chiefly engaged in commerce, the entire textile trade being in their hands. The weavers complained that the Jews paid them badly and lent them money at high interest. Trade in wool was also in Jewish hands and the weavers complained at the high cost of the raw material. At the same time, the Jews were more than 50% of all craftsmen in the city. They included tailors, shoemakers, bookbinders, glaziers, gold and silversmiths, button makers, furriers, hat makers, cord makers, musicians and weavers. The authorities refer to the high quality of the work done by the Jewish craftsmen and their satisfactory earnings. Dr. Jonah Mayer was the head of the community.

[Page 34]

The communal heads at the time included: Yehuda Leib Baruch; Naphtali ben Moshe Shimon; Yehuda Leib Crystal; Jacob Traube, Shimon Levy and Zalman Rosenbloom.

The Prussian Government wished to take steps to bring the Jewish community in line, more or less, with the Western world. A special decree was issued prohibiting marriage without Government permission. The age of the bridegroom was fixed at 25 and he was required to prove that he possessed property worth 3,000 thaler in ready money or property or that he was a craftsman who could make a living for a family. Such wedding licenses were issued only to those who could prove that their parents and grandparents had been regular inhabitants of South Prussia. Bridegroom and bride were required to undertake not to settle in any village or set up a factory. The Jewish communities decided to take joint steps against this measure.

A debate ensued among the higher Prussian officials. A circular was sent to them asking their opinions about the transfer of Jews from villages to cities, even those having the ancient privilege of not permitting Jewish residents; what were the most desirable conditions of their employment; whether they might be allowed to engage in all their crafts or the latter should be restricted; and finally, what the education of the children was to be.

It was generally agreed that Jewish residence should be permitted everywhere in order to promote urban development. Some recommended the transfer of Jews to agriculture. Many wished Jewish craftsmen to be given the same rights as Christians and objected to restrictions on craft occupations and wholesale trade but wished to leave the monopoly in the hands of Christians and to restrict peddling. The official language of Jewish institutions was to be German which was also to become the language of instruction in their schools.

A Ministerial Memorandum of 1795 sent to the King of Prussia expressed opposition to the marriage restrictions proposed in 1793 and suggested that marriage be permitted without restriction against a registration of fee of 1-5 thalers. Jews should likewise be granted freedom of religion and charged the same tax as Christians, with the exception of a Recruits' Tax. The poll-tax should be replaced by a billeting tax.

These proposals were confirmed and became law in June 1795. The Prussian Government then planned to introduce a reform in Jewish affairs and demanded copies of all documents granting privileges as well as attested information on: Cities where Jews might not settle; the source of privileges and whether they had been abolished expressly or tacitly; the attitudes of the charters given to the guilds regarding Jews and the Jewish privileges regarding Christians and how far the latter were still valid.

[Page 35]

A general list of mutual privileges of Jews, Municipalities and Guilds was then drawn up. The Jewish communities including Kalish had already tried to obtain confirmation of their Polish charters but the Government had adopted the political attitude of "restricting the Jews in respect of the former legislation". They were permitted to renounce their autonomous organization in communities. The latter, it was true, had already begun to decline in the 18th century, with the resultant partial collapse of Jewish autonomy.

While the Jews wished to preserve the legal basis of the communities and hence the legislation from which they derived in order to retain a certain measure of autonomy, the Prussian authorities, in line with the general attitude of Western Europe at the time, wished to eliminate autonomy to adapt Jewish life to that of Jews in Prussia and Silesia and expedite the process of their adaptation and assimilation in German culture. It should be remembered that Prussia had annexed territories containing more than 150,000 Jews. While they were well aware of their economic importance, they wished to adapt them to their own style of life.

In 1797, the General Regulations for the Jews granted rights of domicile in the new areas only to those who had already lived there at the time of the occupation and to professional men. Others were required to leave the territory within a fixed time. The remainder were to be registered and would receive "letters of protection" (Schützbriefe). Taxation was increased. The Polish poll tax was raised from 3 to 10 zloty and the Jews were required to pay the following:

1. Tolerance tax of 2.5 thalers once a fortnight for any Jew who came to a place where he was not a permanent resident. A foreign Jew was charged 3.5 thalers.
2. An individually assessed Protection Tax for the right to live in the state and engage in a profession.
3. Marriage licences from 2 to 150 thaler by individual assessment.
4. Army tax to be paid by every Jew between 14 and 60 to the sum of 1 thaler and a number of groschen each year. Volunteers to the forces were exempt.
5. Stamp duty on Hebrew books, rabbinical documents, building synagogues, foundation of cemeteries, etc.

Communal and rabbinical authorities were restricted to religious affairs. Rabbis were required to write and speak either German or Polish and their judicial authority was abolished. All claims were to be heard in general courts. A special clause specified the number of communal officials. The communities could not select their officials. The authorities would lay down principles in this connection as in non-Jewish institutions and would appoint the rabbis and officials. German and Polish became the languages of instruction in Jewish schools. The communities were forbidden to use the *Herem* or ban, to impose sanctions or take any steps requiring the Jew to submit to their orders. Slaughterers were permitted to slaughter and sell meat, in this way depriving the community of what had hitherto been its right. Thus, the Prussians abolished the Jewish community or Kehilla which they regarded as the principal obstacle in carrying out their fiscal and economic policy.

[Page 36]

While the Jews were promised improvements as their cultural situation improved in the Polish provinces, prohibitions were there from the beginning. Jew could not engage in interest transactions and all loans had to be arranged in court. Spirits could not be sold to peasants on credit, nor could Jews sell them any goods except for agricultural requirements. All peddling was prohibited. The number of merchants was restricted. Crafts were permitted only in the towns and were prohibited in villages. It was hinted that the occupations in which the Jews engaged could not ensure them a living and they were, therefore, to be permitted to engage in agriculture and obtain uncultivated land sufficient for the upkeep of a village family. Anybody undertaking to purchase land on his own account could profit from all advantages, being exempt from taxes for a number of years and could employ Christians for the first three years. Jews were to be encouraged to engage in agriculture, lease estates and breweries and engage in industrial enterprises. The Government would maintain schools where the youngsters would study under Government supervision and in accordance with Government instructions.

These regulations were received with fear and mistrust by the Jews. In Kalish, they meant the destruction of Jewish trade. At the time, almost all the merchants were Jews and many were engaged in crafts as well. The entire retail trade in the surrounding villages was in Jewish hands.

The leaders of the communities and a number of outstanding rabbis held a meeting at the end of August 1797 to determine the attitude to be adopted towards these regulations. The conference was attended by 31 representatives of communities of whom Yehuda Leib Barash and Moshe Shimon represented Kalish. After careful deliberations, they resolved to request the King to conduct a thorough on -going investigation into the state of the Jews. They wrote as follows:

"Some months ago, there appeared in print a *Règlement* by our pious Lord and King and Glorious Majesty regarding the special position of Israel under the rule of his Government in the state of South Prussia and New East Prussia, and in each district and region of the said states. Indeed, true utterances cannot be denied for the eyes of the Hebrew have been opened to see therein, with the aid of His Blessed Name, the kind-heartedness of His Excellent Majesty and the ministers. However, in respect of the matter of the residence of the congregation of Israel in the said state since ancient times, and the ways of their livelihood, coming and going, and that, henceforth, matters of conduct are to be innovated in accordance with what is written at certain points in the said *Règlement*, there may, Heaven forbid, come about a destruction of faith and, Heaven forbid, a deficiency may be brought about in our livelihoods so that the hands may be enfeebled, Heaven forbid.

Therefore, the men of the said states have set their hearts to gather together several men from the communities in the districts of the said states to discuss, counsel and seek. His Name aiding, to find an opportunity whereby to appear before the King and entreat him to grant his grace and give instructions for matters to be investigated by his ministers and counsellors and to inquire thoroughly into the real state of Israel by greater enquiry and investigation as far as possible. We then hope that with His Name's aid, they will extend the wings of their loving kindness and indeed establish the pillars of faith on their firm pedestals...and the sources of livelihood and food will not be dammed up if the desirable approach is followed. To this purpose, we have gathered together and come hither to the Holy Congregation of Kleczow, men from the near and distant cities of the aforesaid states, with adequate power and authorization from the leaders and heads of the congregations, to take wise counsel together regarding the efforts to be made on behalf of Israel with the Name's aid."

[Page 37]

The communal representatives were required to select a delegation to proceed to Berlin and act as a Committee of Ways and Means about raising funds for the cost of the journey; to which each community was required to contribute. A levy consisting of a third of the Polish polltax was imposed on each individual and the money was to be sent to certain specified trustees. Discussions were suspended as the representatives had to return home without going into full details. The participants agreed to meet at the Fair to be held in Frankfurt-on-the-Oder some months later where they would devote one or two days to this matter and choose representatives. Those present in Frankfurt would constitute a quorum for the purpose but could co-opt another eleven suitable persons.

A delegation of three proceeded to Berlin in October 1797 and the following month received a reply from the Government. This was moderate and included a number of ameliorations in favour of the Jews. In the course of time, the higher officials had to come to realize that many of the clauses of their *Règlement* could not be implemented under the circumstances. They ceased to expel Jews from the villages, permitted them to settle in all towns and join guilds and facilitated the issue of peddling permits, not only for villagers but also for town-dwellers. In 1800, however, only villagers were permitted to be peddlers once again.

In the Department of Kalish there were six Jewish families who engaged in agriculture. Some were subject to the Polish "squires" while the others cultivated their land well and remained in agriculture. However, the small total number of Jewish farmers led to the abolition of all the special benefits on their behalf at the end of 1803. Various restrictions were then introduced into Jewish trade, peddling in villages and the purchase of agricultural produce.

In the cities, the authorities took steps to ensure that the number of Jews should not exceed the number of Christian merchants. They were also ejected from breweries and inns and were no longer permitted to manufacture liquor and spirits, being required to hand their inns over to the Government and Christian nobles. However, by dint of intercession, this order was deferred for five years until 1808. The new restrictions would have had a very severe effect on the existence of the Jews of Kalish.

By 1804 there were 2,111 Jews in Kalish out of a total population of 7,085. Some of the merchants were gradually acquiring real estate and the authorities tended to disregard the fact that they were spreading beyond the Jewish Quarter which, in any case, they wished to expand. However, the local citizens registered a complaint with the Prussian King, objecting to the increase of the Jews and their growing connection with the liquor trade. They demanded that the Jews should be restricted to a special quarter once again.

[Page 38]

A Counsellor for Taxation was given the task of investigating the situation. He decided that the privileges of 1540 were to be retained; that Jews could dwell outside the Jewish Quarter as sub-tenants and, in general, the authorities would continue their policy of trying to ensure that Jews lived under the same conditions as non-Jews. At the same time, dwellings in Christian houses could be rented to Jews only with the special permission of the authorities and the Counsellor assured the citizens that the latter would prevent any change for the worse on either side. All this time, the struggle of Kalish Jewry for the right of making a living and residing in Christian streets continued at the day-to-day level.

Meanwhile, there were political developments elsewhere. In the autumn of 1806, Prussia was defeated at the Battle of Jena and Napoleon began a triumphal Eastern march – the French entering Warsaw at the end of October 1806. The Jews joined the Poles in welcoming the French forces with food, drink and songs of praise in Kalish and elsewhere.

The Duchy of Poland, 1807-1815

In the summer of 1807, the Treaty of Tilsit, signed by Napoleon I and the Russian Tsar Alexander I, provided for the establishment of the Duchy of Warsaw within the areas occupied by Prussia after the Second and Third Partitions of Poland. The Duchy was divided into six Departments of which Kalish was one. In 1808, there were 2,535 Jews in the city, or 41% of the population. Of the family heads, 161 engaged in commerce; 16 in the sale of liquors and 3 sold salt. Others were wholesalers like Joseph Samuel Redlich already mentioned; Samuel Sachs; Isaiah Mamlok; Philip Sachs and Simeon Peretz. In 1814, Getz Isser Loewe of Hamburg, afterwards known as Gustav Adolph, settled in Kalish and became one of the first local Jewish industrialists. Redlich engaged in extensive transactions in liquor and textiles and also exported grain and cattle.

In 1813, there were changes in the Russian-German frontier. A Customs Station was opened near Kalish and the new Jewish occupation of Customs Agent began. There were 115 family heads who were tailors as well as many under very difficult conditions and the community as such was ore poverty-stricken than ever, although some of the richer Jews did well.

Under the constitution introduced by Napoleon, all citizens were granted equal rights. This included the Jews. However, the officials charged with implementing this constitution did their best to prevent any true equality of rights in practice. In addition, the Jews did not want complete equality. What they desired was religious freedom and the abolition of such disabilities as prohibition of residence in various cities and streets; the prohibition to engage in certain branches of livelihood and the abolition of the special Jewish taxes and levies. Full equality would have imposed the same duties upon them as on other citizens such as conscription to the army which would have involved the desecration of the Sabbath, the eating of *trefa* (ritually unfit) food, shaving of the beard and ear-locks, etc.

[Page 39]

The following year, the implementation of the Equal Rights Clause was deferred for a period of 10 years. It was pointed out that the differences which isolated the Jews from the rest of the population prevented them from benefitting from civil liberties and made them unsuitable for military service. At the same time, the authorities began to whittle their civil rights away. They were forbidden to acquire land, but merchants were permitted to dwell in the cities, purchase and sell houses and land and leave these to their heirs. Jews could build houses in vacant plots not desired by Christians, provided that the latter agreed to this.

The Polish Minister of Justice masked anti-Jewish principles in a dress of liberalism, claiming that constitutional equality did not of itself transform all residents into citizens with equal rights. The citizen was a man who was faithful to the king and regarded Poland as his homeland. Since the Jews regarded themselves as a separate nation and longed to return to the land of their fathers, they could not be regarded as sons of the homeland.

In the Duchy of Warsaw, the following taxes were levied on the Jews: food tax; kosher meat tax; tolerance tax of 2.5-10 thaler per family according to economic condition; a marriage tax; and all the general economic taxes and levies.

The heaviest burden was the kosher meat tax. It was estimated that the average Jewish family in the Duchy ate 8lbs of meat a week and the tax was 6 groszy per pound; 8 for ducks; 1 for chicken; 8 for goose; 1 zloty for turkey. On an average, every family paid 84 zloty of meat tax per year. When this tax was increased in 1809 from 2,650,000 zloty to almost 3,343,000 zloty, it meant that the 4,346 Jewish families in the department of Kalish (3,309 in the cities and 1,037 in villages) found that they had to pay almost 440,000 zloty per year.

The kosher meat tax was farmed out at public auction. The farmer was permitted to collect the tax which was fixed by the number of Jewish families. This tax was four times as high as in Austria and the amount fixed by the auction was not collected in any department. The law had provided that if the amount calculated according to the consumption of meat was not reached at the auction, the tax would be imposed on and collected directly from the Jewish population.

This transformed the indirect consumption tax into a direct one. Collection was imposed on the communities and responsibility on their heads. The communities were authorized to impose a ban on those who opposed the tax or refused to pay it. In this way, the Government increased the powers of the community for formal reasons and gave the *Parnassim* the possibility of misusing those powers. At the same time, this right vis-à-vis the central authorities helped to increase local self-government in some measure. Meetings between sub-prefects and communal representatives to arrange the distribution of the tax among families were transformed in the course of time into Committees which, when necessary, sent delegations to the Central Government in Warsaw or the Grand Duke (the King of Saxony, who resided in Dresden), in order to reduce the taxes or diminish the joint responsibility of the *Parnassim*. However, their efforts proved fruitless. It was then proposed to hold a meeting of *Parnassim* which would elect a delegation representing the entire Jewish population, as had been done in 1797.

[Page 40]

The initiative in this connection was taken by the community of Posen which proposed that the meeting should be deferred for a month as the political situation was unclear and the outcome of the war which was being fought at the time between Austria and the Duchy was not certain. In the end, no conference was held and the distress of the Jews grew worse and worse. The taxes were being collected mercilessly and the economic impoverishment of the masses compelled the *Parnassim* in Warsaw to take certain steps.

A meeting was finally held in July 1810 and presented a memorandum to the Minister of Finance. Memorandums were afterwards presented to the King, the Ducal Council and the Minister of Finance, declaring that the terrible poverty of the Jewish population made it impossible to pay the amount of meat tax demanded. (The best sign of the situation is the fact that in the years 1809-1810, the Government succeeded in collecting only 44.3% of the calculated amount and in 1810-1811 only 43.4%). The Minister of Finance accordingly had to take thought with regard the Jewish affairs.

After the failure of the internal attempts of the Jews to hold a conference, it became clear that the Minister of Finance would have to summon a gathering at which the Jewish representatives could offer their own proposals. This was done early in 1811. The Jews of Kalish elected their representatives within a fortnight. These were Simon Levy and Joseph Moshe, a *Shtadlan* or mediator from Dzialoszyn.

The Jewish representatives speaking on behalf of all the Jews in the Duchy expressed their opposition to the kosher meat tax and particularly to the imposition of group responsibility on the communal heads, which were both immoral and not the practice in respect of other taxes. They proposed that the Jewish tax be calculated on a consumption of 3 kilograms per family per week, i.e. 6 groszy tax per pound. They also worked to achieve Jewish exemption from military service. They pointed out that it was unfair to demand this of a community which was burdened by discriminatory taxation, had no equal rights and was persecuted. At the end of 1811, Jewish representatives submitted a memorandum to the State Council and proposed that a tax of 3 million zloty should be levied on the Jewish population; 80% as meat tax and the rest as a recruiting tax.

In a debate at the Polish Seim a few days later, one delegate rejected the special Jewish taxes as being against the Constitution. A few days later, the Minister submitted a law providing that the kosher meat tax should be a consumption tax and not a direct tax. The Seim approved of this. A week later, it was agreed that the distribution of this tax of 3 million zloty should be handled by the Jewish representatives themselves. It was not approved by the Minister. The amount seemed too small to him and allocation among the communities and the families appeared illegal in his eyes. He demanded 800,000 zloty a year for exemption from military service.

The Jewish representatives declared that the Jewish population was unable to pay more than they had offered and undertook to take charge of allocation by Departments. They were prepared to pay the amount of tax for five months, i.e., until the end of May 1812 but could not guarantee payment beyond that time. The Minister rejected these proposals and began to negotiate with three partners to whom he wished to farm out the kosher meat tax of the entire Duchy.

[Page 41]

The representatives then proposed their own nominee as tax-farmer in chief but were too late. The three partners undertook to pay 2,650,000 zloty a year. The representatives continued their negotiations about the exemption tax. The Minister demanded 800,000 zloty – they offered 600,000 and finally, they compromised on 700,000. Payment was to be made quarterly and the agreement was to run until the Jews were finally granted equal rights in the spirit of the Decree of 1808. Under the resultant law, the Jews of the Kalish Department were required to pay 55,088 zloty every year as exemption tax. Their representative had taken an active part in the entire negotiations.

By this agreement, the representatives of the Jews constituted a permanent Jewish representation in the Department. If one of the delegates died or was suspended, another was to be appointed by the Prefect. This Standing Committee met as a Government body representing the Jewish population in the Duchy of Warsaw vis-à-vis its government. It met once in 1809, twice in 1810, twice in 1811 and thereafter in spring of 1814.

All this while there had been no change in the relations between the Jews and the organized burghers. The latter demanded that the number of Jews in the city and their trade in spirituous liquors be reduced. At the same time, the Municipality made a practice of levying more than half of the municipal taxes on the Jewish community though they were at most barely a third.

With the preparations for Napoleon's Russian Campaign in 1812, a system of runners was established to expedite transmission of orders and post. The Kalish Municipality required the Jewish community to maintain runners with a cost of 6,000 zloty a year. In addition, they had to provide candles to a value of more than 1,000 zloty for all army officials and officers in the city. At that time, there were 2,276 Jews in a total population of 7,256 but the former were called on to pay twice as much as the remainder.

When an explanation was demanded, the local Prefect said that the charges were levied not per capita but according to income. Candles were supplied only to General Staff officers, it was claimed. It should be remembered, declared the Prefect, that the Christians were required to supply wood without payment while the Jews demanded payment for the lights. There was, therefore, no reason to exempt them from this supply. He claimed that trade as well as crafts of tailoring; furriery, cord-making, etc. were almost entirely in Jewish hands. Meanwhile, the Municipality explained that the Jews did not have to pay 10,000 zloty as demanded but rather less than two-thirds of that amount.

The Ministry of the Interior informed the Prefect, in reply, that it was not his duty to require the Jews to supply runners for the carriage of letters from Kalish to Czestochowa since the post was at his disposal. The system of runners was, therefore, to be abolished at once. Nor were there any orders permitting the Prefect to order the Jews to supply candles to army officers instead of billeting. The Jews were required to billet soldiers like other residents. It was necessary to insist that they should provide clean furnished rooms for the officers but, if any of the latter refused to accept a room in a Jewish home, the Prefect was entitled to fix a certain payment instead on a basis of negotiations. As far as individual taxes were concerned, the Municipality had to first consult the community for it had actually imposed far too high a sum on the Jews.

[Page 42]

The reply was received and the authorities in charge of the city went on behaving as they saw fit.

When Jews could not pay the individual tax, the local constables broke into their homes, seized the family heads, took craftsmen and hired men from their work and sent them out of town. After the community had paid several thousand zloty on account of contributions, more than 9,000 zloty extra were demanded from them. This could not be paid so the Prefect ordered that the Synagogue should be closed and prohibited the Jews from praying there. Troops were stationed in front of the Synagogue and the community was required to pay for their upkeep.

Leizer Koppel and Hyman Stern, then the heads of the community, had to first appeal to the Ministry of the Interior and then to the State Council in Warsaw. They requested that these persecutions should cease and the fine illegally imposed by the Municipality be cancelled. Furthermore, they requested that the Municipality, when allocating taxes and public payments, should consult the community which knew the situation of each and every one of its members; and that the allocation of taxes should be based on the number and financial capacities of the Jews and not in an arbitrary fashion. In any case, though they were faithful citizens with the same freedom as other residents, they had to contribute more than the Christians on account of all kinds of extraordinary taxes such as the one on kosher meat. All the income of the community had been requisitioned by the Courts to cover old debts which amounted to 400,000 zloty. A tax was paid to the Municipality on every funeral and wedding as well as for every civil permit and documentary fee and as a water rate.

Finally, they pointed out that all classes had been given equal rights by Napoleon and also by the legislation of the Duchy. They appended the demand of the Municipality for immediate payments with notice of fines in case of non-payment and the order of the Mayor, dated 7th May 1812 for the closing of the Synagogue, etc.

After sending their memorandum to Warsaw, the heads of the community informed the Prefect of what they had done in accordance with various clauses of the constitution which he had contravened. They also requested that any steps against merchants and *Parnassim* should be deferred until after the impending Feast of Weeks and until the arrival of the decision of the Ministry of the Interior.

In his reply, the Prefect reiterated that almost all trade and handicrafts were in the hands of the Jews; that there were only 6 Christian merchants out of 167 and only 17 Christian tailors out of 145. The Christians had 3 apothecaries, 8 dealers in wine and spirits, 98 sellers of beer and spirits and salt and were required to pay the same tax as the Jews; "With regard to the Synagogue", the Prefect explained: "that since the Jews refused to pay the sum demanded, the Mayor had insisted on permission to close the Synagogue which contained many valuables." Finally, he stated that the Municipality had withdrawn the notice to the congregation. In his opinion, the latter had no right to complain about the tax burden and persecution. The Jews were supplying all the consumption of the Royal kitchen to the Generals and the General Staff at high prices and had actually already received the amount of the impost returned.

[Page 43]

In the absence of any reply from the Minister, a deputation was sent to Warsaw and submitted a memorandum in which they appealed to "a sense of justice and pity" in order to draw his attention to the unhappy position of the Jewish inhabitants of Kalish. Factual evidence was given in this memorandum regarding the conditions under which the Jews lived. The Jewish merchants were poverty-stricken and most could not even make a living from their trade. The non-Jewish wine merchants had far more property than all the trade of Kalish Jews. There were 100 Christian distillery owners and only 4 Jews who were actually merely lease-holders and had to pay 1,000 thaler a year, a payment from which the Christian innkeepers were entirely exempt. The townsfolk had houses that brought an income as well as Municipal privileges which the Jews lacked.

Yet, in spite of all the fixed rates, the burden of billeting; the providing of 100 Jews for service as runner – 20 of them regularly each day, the Municipality had not hesitated to impose a payment of 400 thalers on the Jews and now demanded an additional 1,000 thalers.

A fortnight later, the Minister of the Interior replied to the Prefect stating that his behaviour towards the Jews was not in accordance with the law. He disapproved particularly of his forcible intervention in respect of religious ceremonies by such steps as closing the Synagogue.

The Minister informed the Kalish representatives that they could safely go home and tranquilly wait for justice to take its course. When they returned home, they were summoned to the Mayor for an inquiry and the latter wished to know whether they had a full authorization from the community. "The Jews Flamm and Warta had an authorization in the Yiddish language written by the Jew Shlomo Zelig Krumm and drafted and signed by us heads of the community."

In response to demands for receipts, a number were produced. The two community heads signed the minutes of this investigation which was promptly transferred to the Prefect. The latter, in his reply to the Ministry, drew attention to the impudence of the Jews in bothering him and trying to mislead him in one form or another. The promised reply from the Minister did not come and the community heads appealed once again stating that the Prefect had no intention of changing his behaviour. On the contrary, he had imposed a new levy of 240 thalers after the General Staff had left Kalish and the Municipality had taken it by force from Leizer Mamlock.

Nothing is known regarding the end of this dispute.

The failure of Napoleon's Russian campaign led to the collapse of the Duchy of Warsaw. In March 1813, the Russian army entered and Tsar Alexander I set up a new government. Meanwhile, the latter continued to collect the kosher meat tax and the recruits' exemption tax. In 1814 two leading Jews from each Department were invited to Warsaw in order to advise the Government on how to ensure the receipt of the taxes of the Jews. Wolf Traube and Zalman Rosenbloom attended for the Kalish Department, while Simon Levy came from the Kalish community itself.

[Page 44]

At the meeting, they declared that the Jewish population had never offered 2,400,000 zloty per year and proposed that the amount should be negotiated for each Department separately. The Minister of Finance agreed in principle and the Departmental representatives afterwards stated the amount that they could pay. The Kalish delegates proposed 52,000 zloty without Government supervision. This amount would be divided between the communities who would give satisfactory securities for payment. After protracted negotiations, the Higher Council of State rejected the proposals and decided to take charge of the tax itself. The special exemption tax of the days of Napoleon's war was now replaced by a special war tax of 700,000 zloty.

Following the end of hostilities, this was not abolished but twice the amount continued to be collected from the Jewish population. A Government decree of October 1812 prohibiting the manufacture and sale of spirits to Jews was deferred until April 1815 thanks to the efforts of the heads of the community and some judicious bribery. Meanwhile, a circular of the Minister of the Interior and Police issued under the Duchy of Warsaw in January 1812 remained in force. This required Jews residing in the houses of Christians to approach "a degree of civilization" and shave their beards. The Prefect of the Kalish Department tried to carry out this instruction and informed his superiors that he had given the Jews of the Department who resided in the houses of Christians in the city of Kalish until September to carry out the conditions required for them to approach a civilized way of living including the shaving of their beards in order not to be compelled to vacate their dwellings.

The heads of the community appealed to the Prefect not to compel them to shave because according to the passage from the Book of Leviticus, submitted and certified by the authorities, this practice was against their religion which was protected by the Government like all other faiths. Furthermore, the constitution had promised the Jews easier regulations than hitherto.

In the opinion of the Prefect, the Government decrees applied only to Warsaw and Plock. He, therefore, had the honour to ask the Ministry of the Interior whether, in spite of the above facts, the Jews must be compelled to shave their beards.

The Minister rebuked the Prefect of Kalish in his reply for making such a strange demand of the Jews and advised him to read Ministerial instructions more carefully in the future.

Congress Poland, 1815-1831

General Situation

After the fall of Napoleon, the Vienna Congress set up a Kingdom of Poland under Russian suzerainty with a Constitution including the following clause.

[Page 45]

"The Israelite People shall continue to enjoy those civil rights which are assured to them by the present laws and provisions. Special regulations shall outline the conditions that shall facilitate the obtaining by the Jews of greater satisfaction from social standing."

The entire Constitution was approved by Tsar Alexander I to whom several Memorials were presented by representatives of Polish Jewry during 1814-15 in Paris and Berlin. However, the above clause remained a dead letter and the state of the Jews was unchanged. The Jews were 10% in a population of 3,300,000 and their affairs were being dealt with by the Autonomous Polish Government in Warsaw.

In 1808, there were 6,712 inhabitants in Kalish of whom 2,535 were Jews. In 1827 the numbers were 12,107 and 3,463. This was a decline from 37.8% to 28.5%.

It was decided to defer all change in the status of the Jews on account of the absence of Jewish general education and the prejudices of the Polish population. General education was to be introduced and the *Kehilla* structure abolished. Meanwhile, the Russian Governor opposed emancipation because the Jews increased disproportionately and harmed the position of the Christian workers. The Polish political elite held that the Jews were not ripe for emancipation and imposed new restrictions. In 1820, enlightened Jews proposed: Abolition of the *Kehilla*; regulation of activities of rabbis, etc. prohibition of Hebrew printing presses and the import of Hebrew books from abroad as well as the establishment of a Rabbinical Seminary under University auspices.

In 1821, the *Kehillot* were replaced under Government decree by Synagogue Councils with limited authority and responsible to the Government Council for Interior Affairs, Religion and Education in Warsaw. The Synagogue Council had to prepare an Annual Synagogue Budget for approval by the District Authorities.

Following this decree, the *Kalish Kehilla* was abolished and was replaced by a Synagogue Council of three members. Election of the rabbi by all congregation members also required District approval. From 1825, the Rabbi acted as Communal Registrar of Births, Marriages and Deaths. The Hevra Kadisha (Burial Societies) was abolished in 1822. In 1827, the Communal Funds were administered by the Municipal Treasurer who received 5% of the Budgetary Income. From 1860, the Treasurer took two-thirds of this while the Auditor took one third. Throughout this period, the Jews were heavily taxed in general. Communal taxes fell into 4 groups – the highest being above 50 Gulden and the lowest between 3-8 Gulden. Until 1843, the Jews paid a Recruits' Tax. From 1843 on, they were conscripted for military service. These and many similar regulations remained in force until 1916 when the German Occupation Authorities issued a more suitable Order for the Organization of Jewish Religious Societies.

Until 1840, some 42 rural Jewish communities were under the control of the Kalish Community.

Reb Abraham Abele ben Yehiel Mechel Hacohen died in 1809 but a new rabbi was appointed only in 1821. This was Reb Moshe Ephraim Ashkenazi, a descendant of the renowned scholar, Hacham Zvi Ashkenazi. After various disputes on competence, a special committee formulated "Perpetual Regulations" in 1823.

[Page 46]

These regulations provided inter alia that new community members, whether from the city or elsewhere, might be admitted only by majority approval. New tailors might be admitted only with the approval of the Tailors' Guild. Engagement contracts, etc., might be prepared only for accredited residents and only by specified communal functionaries.

An attempt to open a Jewish school in 1822 was bitterly opposed by the rabbi on the grounds that it would injure or even destroy Jewish faith.

In 1822 and 1825 the Community was called upon to repay debts outstanding from the days of Independent Poland, together with interest.

The Struggle for Rights of Residence and Work

In the years 1815-1826, the Jews suffered from the introduction and expansion of Government monopolies which deprived thousands of their livelihoods in Kalish and elsewhere. This in turn caused many to engage in smuggling, etc. with a corresponding outcry in the press, political literature and the Seim. Some began to engage in home textile manufacture. Village Jews swarmed to Kalish. A Jewish proletariat began to appear and the character of Jewish commerce changed.

A handful of Kalish Jews had grown wealthy during the 1807-1815 wars. These were wholesalers or spirit vendors. The majority of Jewish shopkeepers, etc. however, were impoverished and suffered from countless municipal by-laws and the constant outcry of the non-Jewish shopkeepers.

Trade between Kalish and Russia began to increase. Jews played a part in the sheep fairs of the city and began to develop spinning and weaving mills, supplying raw materials and disposing of the finished product. In 1820 Joseph, son of Samuel Joseph Redlich, was a leading importer of woollen yarns, spirit manufacturer, general agent, wool buyer and wholesale merchant. He prospered after his daughter married Ludwig Mamroth who had settled in Kalish and opened a successful bank with M. Landau.

In 1825, Redlich and his son-in-law contracted to open storehouses for woollen yarns throughout the Kalish District under District Government guarantee which enabled them to allow three months credit to the weavers. By 1830, Redlich's property was assessed at 2 million guldens and 's at 130,000 gulden. Indeed, the sale of woollen yarns was their virtual monopoly and they themselves also began dealing in woollens. By 1832, they were dealing in land and investing in the new factories at Lodz. During the First Polish Revolt of 1831-31, they continued to supply weavers with raw materials whether they could pay or not. Indeed, Redlich undertook to keep them employed provided he was allowed to import 30 hundred-weight of yarn duty-free. The condition was approved because he was the only contractor in the Kalish District who was concerned for the livelihood of weavers and poor manufacturers. The exemption was later repeated in spite of opposition.

At this time Jews were still primarily merchants. Their entry into industry only came during the following decades.

[Page 47]

Jews in non-Jewish Residential Quarters

As of 1799, there were 30 Jews who traded or worked in Christian houses. They included: 19 merchants, 8 craftsmen and one tenant without occupation. The local Christian craftsmen in particular were opposed to this and in 1822 they petitioned the Warsaw Ministry of the Interior to take steps as the number of Jews in their quarters was increasing daily and the Jews were stealing their livelihoods. In their Historical Survey, they claimed that out of 11 families in 1540, the Jews were now more than 100 families with dozens of houses in the centre of the town. They demanded that the Jews be restricted to the 11 families of the 1540 Privileges, that they be excluded from commerce engaged in by Christians and that they live in their own special quarters.

The real issue, as before, seems to have been the monopoly of the manufacture of spirits and beer-brewing held by certain old-established Christian families of Kalish who fought tooth and nail, by fair means and foul, against Jewish competition. In Warsaw, they found little support but the Kalish municipal authorities supported them by various administrative measures. Prolonged negotiations with the Warsaw authorities resulted in recognition of the status quo but no new Jewish wine or spirit dealers were permitted.

A Special Jewish Quarter

A new Town Plan submitted to the Government Commission of the Interior and Police in June 1827 provided for a special Jewish Quarter in accordance with an Order issued six years earlier. The Jews could reside and keep shops in only 11 streets including those of their earlier Quarter. Their former wooden houses, which were a fire and health hazard, had to be demolished and replaced by properly built houses. All Jews living elsewhere had to remove themselves to the Jewish Quarter by October 1833 and had to sell their property outside the said Quarter by December 1832. All rental agreements, leaseholds, etc. would be invalid as of October 1833 except for Jewish physicians, artists, etc. who submitted recognized attestations, wore the same clothes as the Christian residents and sent their children to general schools as of the age of 7. To prevent congestion, apartments of 2-3 rooms could be let only to a single family and those of 4-5 rooms to 2 families. No more than 5 families could live in any one house. The composition of the family was specific: Husband, wife, unmarried children, servant and one parent over 60 if not gainfully employed.

The old prohibition of residence by Jews from other places was to be upheld. Jews could trade outside the Quarter only on market days and at fairs.

The Central Authorities pointed out that the proposals could mean the creation of a Jewish town which would draw all the trade away from the Christian town. The proposals were accordingly amended to provide for prolongation of several streets and no more.

However, the wealthier Jewish merchants, wine dealers, etc. began to bombard the District and Central Governments with petitions and applications to live outside the proposed Jewish Quarters. Most of these were approved. Christian merchants then drew attention to the risk of epidemics resulting from the congestion of the Jewish inhabitants, even in originally non-Jewish houses. Following inquiry, the Municipality described all this as unauthorized, exaggerated and rancorous and explained the ulterior motives of the signatories.

[Page 48]

Attempts on the part of the land-owning Polish nobility to attract Jews to agriculture were rendered nil by the attitude of the implementing officials.

The Polish Revolt 1830-31. And After

The Polish Revolt of 1830 was supported by certain Westernized Jews in Warsaw where Jews were recruited for the Civic Guard and a Jewish unit was set up. However, the new Polish National Government prevented Jews from joining in the Revolt but required them to pay a double Recruits' Tax instead. Many communal leaders told the new authorities that they objected. Elsewhere, it was proposed that Jews should be attracted to the forces by temporary economic privileges. Nothing came of this.

In Kalish, the Jewish Community contributed to the cost of the Revolt and was also called upon to serve in the Forces though they demanded to be exempted either from military service or the payment of the Recruits' Tax. A demand for contributions to the Jewish Unit, under Joseph Berkowitz (son of the Jewish warrior – Berek Yosselowitz) found little support. A Jewish Committee set up in Warsaw recommended that the special tax be abolished and that Jews be drafted to the Forces. This followed a petition to the same effect by a certain Joseph Golochowski of Kalish.

Though these and parallel viewpoints were adjudged corrected, the financial requirements of the Revolt were held to make it necessary to double the tax and refrain from recruiting the Jews for the time being, though this could change later. (At the time, early 1831, the Jewish population in Poland was assessed at 380,000.)

Accordingly, the Jews of Kalish were called upon to pay the double tax. In June 1831, the Polish Seim levied almost 250,000 zloty on them. As a result of this purely fiscal approach, the Jews of the city refrained from volunteering or joining the Civic Guard.

The only known Jewish participant was Alexander Morgenstern, son of the Kalish physician, Dr. Michael Morgenstern, a Polish nationalist who in due course became a physician himself.

The citizens, meanwhile, retained their animosity and demanded a return to the 1788 restrictions. Jews ought not to enjoy any civic liberties and had no civic rights. The central authorities received repeated memorandums from the Municipality to this effect but no steps were taken. Indeed, several Westernized Jews were granted licences on the basis of pre-Revolt permits and were allowed to live outside the Jewish Quarter. This trend was to continue throughout the 1830's.

However, a Permit for a Jewish school obtained by Ludwig Mamroth in 1822 could not be used because of the opposition of Rabbi M.E. Ashkenazi, as already mentioned, and the wealthy merchants sent their children to school in Breslau or Berlin.

[Page 49]

Following the Revolt, the status of the rich Jews gradually improved. The claim that though they were taxed and had no civic rights began to fall on attentive ears in Warsaw. At the same time, citizens with Jewish tenants demanded that the latter should not be expelled as that would lead to financial loss for their landlords.

Between 1832 and 1860, Jews established workshops which developed into factories. Almost all of them manufactured textiles of various kinds. They and their companions demanded domiciliary and similar rights in the non-Jewish quarters, appealing all the way to the King of Poland, i.e. the Russian Tsar.

An Eviction Order against some 20 Jewish families was issued by the Municipality in April 1834. The leaders of the Community appealed to the District Council and were sharply rebuffed. Thereupon, the Community appealed to the Governor, General Paskiewicz; and the right of domicile in previously non-Jewish streets was approved for those who had resided in them before 1833. However, correspondence between the municipal authorities and the central authorities in Warsaw continued for some time. Meanwhile, Jews holding mortgages on property began to foreclose and demand possession.

In addition, the Municipality complained in 1839 that Kalish Jews were marrying Jewesses from elsewhere and demanding their registration as permanent residents of the city though this was against local and national regulations. Warsaw drily replied that according to Article 181 of the Civil Code, the wife had to follow the husband and hence should be registered accordingly in the Municipal Registers.

In 1844, the Governorate of Kalish was abolished and transferred to Warsaw. Many dwellings previously occupied by officials were vacated and Jews rented them. Municipal and Ministerial correspondence continued as before. In general, the Jews were subject to a constant fear of eviction. There was a fairly clear line of demarcation between "cultured" and other Jews. The former were not precisely discouraged and the

District authorities permitted them to live and do business in the Christian areas. By 1854, there were 23 Jews with houses outside the Jewish Quarter.

A secret Report of 1854 records 4,012 Jews in Kalish the previous year as against 7,120 Christians. In 1852, some 70 houses had been burnt down in the Jewish Quarters and their owners could not afford to rebuild them. Hence, Jews had to be allowed to live elsewhere, said the report. A later fire in 1855 strengthened this consideration.

During the 1830's, a Russian Governmental fiscal decision led to a large-scale increase in the brewing and liquor industry and trade. The old-standing feud of the Kalish liquor manufacturers and dealers was renewed against their Jewish competitors.

There were cholera epidemics in 1831-1848 and 1852, respectively. The Jewish Quarter caught fire in July 1852 when 78 houses were burnt including the 16th century synagogue. The Torah Scrolls were then saved with the aid of Franciscans and other clergy.

[Page 50]

Rabbi Solomon Eger, who was rabbi from 1834, adopted a liberal policy and approach in many respects. He approved of knowledge of Polish and German; supervised Jewish education and did not object to Jewish children attending general schools. However, he was summoned to Posen following the death of his father, the renowned Rabbi Akiba Eger who was rabbi there. His departure was followed by internal disputes between the "Enlightened" and the Orthodox Jews.

While in Kalish, however, he helped to establish the principle whereby non-Jewish weavers could work for Jewish factory-owners on the Sabbath, a matter of much economic consequence. His successors, Rabbi Elijah Roselaar, served for a decade until his death in 1850. Rabbi Solomon Eger agreed to return to Kalish but died in 1852 before he could do so.

Rabbi Zvi Hirsch Chayyes, who was a graduate of the Lemberg University, then served as rabbi until his death in 1856. He in turn was followed by Rabbi Meir Auerbach until the latter's departure for Eretz Israel in 1860.

In 1841 a serious dispute broke out between the established community and a certain David. who refused to pay communal taxes on the grounds of being a tax-payer in a Christian quarter. Several others also refused to pay. The Commission for the Interior decided that as Jews they had to pay communal taxes. After appeals by both sides, this test-case was decided in favour of the Community.

In 1854 a total of 9 Jewish boys were taken for the Russian Army, the oldest aged 14, in place of older draftees who did not appear before the Recruiting Committees. (These measures were widespread at the time throughout the Jewish Pale of Settlement. The children were known as "Kantonists" and were compelled to serve 25 years in the Russian Army, without any Jewish contacts.)

In 1843, there were almost 52,000 Jews in the Kalish Governorate of whom close to 46,000 lived in towns. Non-Jews were almost 663,000 of whom over 95,000 were town-dwellers. Economically productive, Jews were 10,614 in all of whom 1,575 had no regular occupation.

In 1832, the Jewish population of Poland numbered over 380,000 with more than 3,500,000 non-Jews. In 1843 there were almost 525,000 Jews and almost 4,200,000 non-Jews. Leaders of the community decided to encourage Jewish settlement on the land. When Jews became liable to military conscription, the authorities announced that land workers would be exempt as in Russia. At the time, there were 19 Jewish settlements including Boleslawow in the Kalish district, which had been established in 1814 and consisted of 6 families with 18 males.

Three representatives of communities near Kalish were elected to proceed to Warsaw in order to participate in the activities of a Committee set up to encourage the settlement of poor Jews on the land. Some 7,500 roubles were to be collected annually for the purpose during 3 years from wealthy local Jews. The Jews of the Kalish District were followed by Jews from other Governorates, in spite of high-level disapproval of their unauthorized steps. In 1859 there were almost 28,000 Jewish land-workers in Poland.

The Kalish District had 15 Jewish farmers with 79 dependants in 1854. In 1855, there were 15 with 98 dependants. In 1856 they numbered 35 with322 dependants. The numbers remained almost identical in 1857 and 1859. In 1860 there were 16 farmers with 133 dependants and in 1861, there were 15 with 126 dependants. Most of them also engaged in trade and handicrafts. Their numbers remained virtually unchanged until 1865.

[Page 51]

When the Polish peasants were liberated, the Jewish farmers were also granted land in perpetuity.

The Hospital. 1835-1914

An old-style "Hekdesh" (alms-house) to which the sick and poor were sent existed until the end of the 18th century and the sick were attended by a Jewish physician. In 1788 it was laid down that only Kalish-born Jews could be admitted and if any beggars from elsewhere were found there, the Community would be fined.

Under the pressure of Dr. Michael Morgenstern, the "Hospital" was expanded from 1 small room without proper equipment to a hall in the synagogue containing 5 beds. With the help of Ludwig Mamroth, government intervention and interest was secured in 1830. The Revolt of 1830, however, led to the cessation of activities which were renewed by Mamroth in 1833.

In 1835, Dr. Morgenstern wrote a disturbing report on medical and epidemiological conditions in the congested Jewish quarter. From 1829 Mamroth had been collecting for a new hospital and had well over 30,000 zloty in the spring of 1835. In May 1835, it was decided to set up a District Hospital as proposed by the Government. Temporary premises were obtained on 1-1-1836 and patients were also treated at home. The Hospital proper was opened in February 1837 with 20 beds.

A clergyman claimed the Hospital Funds on the grounds of a loan obtained by the Community in 1701 from the Lateran Order of Priests. However, the Courts decided that the Hospital did not owe any of this money. The Hospital was also exempted from taxes and imposts.

In 1870, the Hospital Committee was abolished, and the Hospital was placed under Government supervision.

The founder and first physician, Dr. M. Morgenstern, died during the cholera epidemic of 1848. Dr. B. Redlich succeeded him until his death in 1860. The Polish Dr. Stopczynski officiated devotedly until his death in 1873 and was replaced by Dr. Rymarkiewicz who died in 1898. Dr. Eduard Beatus, who had been his assistant from 1887, remained in charge until 1914.

Though the poorer Jews, and particularly those who were observant, viewed the Hospital with suspicion at first, gradually came to use it freely. The number of patients rose from 25 in 1837 to 382 in 1854, 578 in 1872 and 1552 in 1914.

A new building was added at the end of the century and the old building with 43 beds was practically transformed into an Old Age Home. Other changes followed World War I.

The 1863 Revolt

In 1859 the Estate-Owners Association set up agencies in Kalish and elsewhere for the purpose of eliminating Jewish merchants, etc. from trade in agricultural produce and implements. By 1861, however, tension declined under the influence of the Polish National Movement which called for Polish-Jewish fraternity. Participants in a Warsaw demonstration were killed in February 1861 and were mourned in Kalish by all sections of the population including the Jews who attended church commemorations whiles Poles attended synagogue services. Jews were admitted to the Merchants' Club and in October 1861, a Memorial Service for Archbishop , was held in the synagogue.

[Page 52]

Jews were granted equal rights in 1862 and were entitled to elect and be elected to Municipal and Regional Councils. Three Jews and one Jewish proxy were elected to the Kalish Regional Council. In Kalish proper, one Jew was elected among 12 councillors and 5 Jewish proxies out of 12. There were then 4,423 Jews in Kalish, who were more than one-third of the population.

Simultaneously, Jewish intellectuals began to play a more active part in communal life, trying to improve the traditional education methods, the state of the poor and the forms of relief. But they changed nothing. Apart from the conflict with the Orthodox, there was a split between the Germanophils and the Polonophils who demanded virtual assimilation.

They objected in particular to the (subsequently) Hovev-Zion Rabbi Hayyim Eliezer who refused to follow in the footsteps of his enlightened predecessors. Rabbi Wachs saw no reason for establishing a school which he held to be the task of the government. However, a school with 3 classes was opened in July 1862, thanks to Ludwig Mamroth who died the following year.

Meanwhile, various members of his Polonophil group had been the objects of police observation and questioning on suspicion of complicity in the Polish preparations. All Jewish groups were contributing considerable sums to the Polish National Movement by this time.

The Revolt broke out in January 1863. The Russians attributed considerable strategic importance to Kalish and stationed artillery in the New Market. They arrested both Jews and non-Jews, who were later exiled to Siberia. Kalish Jews fought in the Polish ranks and a special Jewish Women's Committee supplied the rebels with uniforms, food and medicines, and helped to recruit Jews. Some 40 Jews of Kalish and district are on record as joining the Revolutionary Units. A few of them were still alive when Poland became independent in 1918 and subsequently received military honours.

1864-1914

The suppression of the 1863 Revolt was followed by a period of repression of the Jews in Kalish and elsewhere. There was an economic crisis. However, it became the Governmental city again in 1866 and the resultant economic improvement was enhanced in 1871 when the railway was laid. The general economic expansion of the 60's and the transition to capitalist development that marked the 70's helped to change the economic structure of Jewish life from market-town and village self-sufficiency to modern industry. At the same time, the Jews were steadily eliminated from various crafts and economic activities which had formerly been their own preserve so that a process of pauperization set in. The Jewish authorities did not engage in any economic policy but the people themselves largely succeeded in surmounting the difficulties and finding or creating new economic positions. Thus, they transformed Kalish into a textile centre.

[Page 53]

When Polish Jews were given rights of urban domicile, the number in Kalish rose from 4,423 in 1862 to 6,706 in 1875.

In 1867 Jews of the Kalish District owned 37 factories of which 29 were textile plants. Some 760 Jews worked in textile factories. Jews also had knitting factories, cart and carriage works, china works, liquor breweries and oil presses. They owned tobacco workshops, paper mills, glass and woodworks and windmills. In 1875, Kalish itself had 19 Jewish-owned industrial plants employing 285 Jewish workers. A Polish journalist reports that the city was losing its German aspect and becoming Polish thanks to the Poles and Jewish intellectuals.

In 1884 a Commission to investigate the conditions of Polish Jewry, set up by Jan Bloch, made it clear that in the Kalish Governorate as elsewhere, the Jews were a productive and effective economic force. Their functions expanded in the 80's and 90's. Kalish textiles were in great demand both in Poland and abroad. By 1908, there were 14,318 Jews in the city.

During this half-century, German began to be replaced by Polish among the wealthier Jews who, at the same time, combatted the traditionalist attitude of the majority. However, by the early 20th century Kalish had virtually become a Hassidic city. A separate synagogue for the "enlightened" group, which had been planned in 1871, was opened only in 1911.

The Hassidic Movement had been growing stronger in and around the city from the end of the 18th century and indeed, several Hassidic rabbis settled in Kalish after 1918.

The Jewish school established in 1862 had Russian as its language of instruction. In 1875, there were 150 pupils and 4 teachers. The Orthodox school system had 7 Hadarim with 317 pupils. By 1903, there were 50 boys and 80 girls at the school. A women's trade school and a kindergarten were opened early in the century.

The "enlightened" group were largely in charge of the community during the late 70's and 80's. Rabbi Wachs left the community on their account in 1881 and proceeded to Piotrkow. He was followed until 1902 by Rabbi Shimshon Arnstein. In 1906 Rabbi Ezekiel , was appointed rabbi and served until 1932.

Various loan funds and other institutions of a social and economic character were established from 1871 onwards.

As time went on, Kalish became a transit centre for Jewish emigrants and in 1909, a special committee was set up to provide, if necessary, food, shelter and further funds for the journey.

Anti-Jewish riots took place on 26th June 1876 following clerical incitement, the peasants of the surrounding districts taking advantage of the absence of the Russian garrison on manoeuvres. It was reported that 13 Jews were killed and many wounded and much damage was done to Jewish personal and communal property. The anniversary of the pogrom was observed as a fast for many years.

[Page 54]

In 1881 Jews who were not citizens of Russia or Poland were expelled from Kalish under a law prohibiting the residence of such Jews in frontier areas. Similar expulsions took place in 1887, 1900 and 1902. The city underwent severe economic crisis in 1904-1907 which began under severe climatic conditions but continued owing to the Russian revolutionary situation. As elsewhere in the Russian Empire, the year 1905 was marked by widespread strikes, disturbances and demonstrations.

1914-1939

Upon the outbreak of hostilities, the Russian troops left the city, but a battle began, and streets were demolished by artillery. Kalish was virtually emptied and all life there came to a standstill. In the early days of the fighting, 33 Jews were killed by German soldiers.

During 1916, life began to return to normal and the communal institutions began functioning once again. In 1917, the Mizrahi (Religious Zionist) Organization opened a seven-class school for Jewish and general subjects; and a kindergarten, commercial school and religious national school for girls were also opened. Polish nationalist groups did their best to extrude the Jews from economic life and the Anti-Semitic Endek (National Democratic) Party grew stronger.

In autumn 1918, with renewed independence, Poland began systematic anti-Jewish propaganda which led to conflict, onslaughts and pogroms.

Throughout the winter of 1918-19, the excesses gradually spread reaching Kalish on March 13th 1919. A labour demonstration was used as an occasion for plundering Jewish shops and beating Jewish passers-by. Jewish butchers defended themselves with cleavers, but one was killed while a merchant died of his injuries. Nine Jews were seriously injured. The pogrom lasted all day long and the authorities took no serious steps to end it.

A similar attempt on May 1, 1920 was prevented thanks to vigorous Jewish resistance.

The resurgence of independent Poland gave rise to Jewish hopes of equality and national autonomy as provided in the Versailles Peace Treaty. After the early disturbances died down, the situation seemed to improve gradually until 1930. After that, the Jews lost whatever they had gained. There was an economic recession, and the authorities began to close Jewish schools and impose taxes directed against the Jews. The aim was to force them out of their economic and social positions by any measures possible. Large-scale emigration to Eretz Israel and elsewhere began.

After the Nazis came to power in Germany, they set out to create an atmosphere suiting them in Poland by mass incitement against the Jews. Kalish, on the Polish-German frontier, provided them with a satisfactory base. In 1937, representatives at the Municipality protested vigorously and were savagely attacked in the Polish press.

During the 20's, to be sure, Kalish Jewry had recovered much of its lost ground. A joint Jewish list obtained 5 seats on the Municipality in 1927 while other Jewish lists obtained another 6-11 seats in all out of 34.

[Page 55]

A new, largely Orthodox, Community Council was elected in 1931. The following year there was a crisis after the discovery of defalcations in *Shehita* (slaughtering) funds and the communal opposition brought *Shohatim* (slaughterers) of their own to the city. This gravely affected communal income.

A move to close the Jewish hospital and amalgamate it with the Polish hospital roused vigorous opposition and was defeated.

Economically speaking, Kalish Jewry succeeded in holding its own. In 1921 there were 15,566 Jews while 547 industrial enterprises were in Jewish hands. Of these, 65 were weaving factories; 340 manufactured clothing while the others engaged in brick-making, metalwork, machinery, joinery, leather, paper, foodstuffs, chemicals, building materials, graphics and cleaning. More than half of these employed hired labour. Jewish workers numbered 775.

Kalish had become a centre for lace manufacture and by 1937, there were 24 factories with 500 machines. Workshops with hand-machines had vanished. New economic branches such as knitting, brush-making, soap manufacture, iron wire, batteries and electric bulk manufacture were added in the 20's and 30's. Twelve flour mills found an extensive market in Silesia and the Posen District. Other manufacturers included: dolls, velvet, linoleum and by-products, carriages and buses, bakeries, sweets and confectionery.

The number of members of the free professions also grew. Wholesale and retail trade continued to be largely dependent on the size of the crops. Market-men, who took goods to the markets and fairs all over Poland, helped to dispose of the goods manufactured. However, they began to be subjected to attack by the Polish Endeks in the early 30's under the growing influence of the Nazis.

Political parties

A Hovevei Zion Society was established in 1884 with 20 members and its numbers rose to 150. As the Hovevei Zion Movement was illegal in Russia until 1890, the members were liable to arrests from time to time. A new epoch began in 1897 with the founding of a Zionist Society which proved very active. After World War I, all Zionist parties had branches of their own and maintained training farms to prepare their younger members for Eretz Israel. There was a general Jewish Sports Society as well as a branch of the Maccabi, while the Revisionists had their own Nordia Sports Club.

After 1918, a number of Religious Societies were organized all centred on the Agudat Israel.

The Bund began activities in 1900 and was successful among lace-makers. It also organized tailors, carpenters, shoe-makers, pastry-makers, shop assistants and apprentices and tried to win over intellectual and high-school pupils. In 1905, it organized demonstrations and strikes. After World War I, the party took an active part in Municipal and Communal politics, setting up Yiddish schools but otherwise, it was concerned exclusively with its own interests.

[Page 56]

The Polish Socialist Party (1895), the Bund (1897) and the Poalei Zion (1905) all tried to establish Trade Unions. After the War, a joint union including all Jewish and non-Jewish groups and sections was established and functioned until 1930. In addition, there were about 500 Jewish workers in separate unions for clothing workers, leather workers, shop-assistants, cooks, porters and barbers. Craft groups in which there were only a few Jews belonged to Polish unions.

***

Kalish had a very widespread Hebrew education system from the traditional Heder and Talmud Torah to kindergartens, elementary and secondary schools. A Zionist weekly: "Die Kalisher Woch" appeared in 1919. A non-party "Kalisher Leben" weekly appeared in 1927 and was later called: "Dos Neie Leben" and appeared until 1938. The Agudat Israel published: "Die Kalisher Woch" between 1929 and 1937 and a daily called: "Kalisher Express" was also published for a short time. In 1934, "Unzer Zeitung" a religious by-weekly was also published for a while.

All this vital and intensive Jewish life was brought to an end by the Nazi occupation. After 1943, Kalish Jewry no longer existed. A history of almost seven hundred years had been brought to a cruel and savage end.

The Men of the City

[Page 58]

The City of Blessed Memory

by Dr. S. Zalud

In the Middle Ages most cities were built according to a regular design. The streets were laid out like a chessboard; a number of squares were placed at a few crossings and the whole city was surrounded by a defensive wall. It was not possible to build like this in every area. The river Prosna and its little tributaries on whose banks Kalish was built made it possible to build only part of the city in the chessboard style. The Jewish Street, which began at the Old Market Square, went straight for more than a kilometre and a half across the Jewish Bridge to the Maikow Field. If you stood at the upper end of the street on a bright day, you could see the other end as well.

In this street and the many side-streets to the right and left, lived the cream of the Jewish community as well as the rank and file. Coming back from the Maikow Field, I would reach Nowa Street with two-storey or three-storey houses on either side and vacant lots here and there. These were the dwelling-houses of families with many children, various factories surrounded by timber sheds belonging to well-known merchants, stores for all kinds of lumber, the Shtieblech (Hassidic prayer-rooms) of various groups of Hassidim and the Hadarim (Hebrew classes) of Hebrew teachers at various levels.

The first street cutting across Nowa Street is Chopin Street; part running down to the river and the other to the New Market. At the corner, either by chance or purpose, is a large building separated from the others. It has factory windows and a large chimney stack rising high above it. Here a factory hooter sounds four times a day and the whole neighbourhood set their clocks by it. This is one of the first and finest piano factories in Poland. Chopin and pianos go well together. Beyond are Shtieblech again, more dwelling houses and stores. As the street approaches the market, we come to shops: retail, very retail and most exceedingly retail! By the river there are factories and dwelling houses. The Russian cavalry ground is followed by the Polish one. At the end of the street is the velvet fabric factory which is one of the first and best in Poland.

We are back at the corner of Nowa and Chopin Street and continue along a small stretch of Nowa Street to the next corner, Ciasna (Narrow) Street. This section is brighter and gayer. The sky above seems loftier because the houses are low and there are no high trees or orchards. In the evening, the street lamps are brighter here. Here is the Bakery; the scent of whose fresh bread accompanies you in the morning on the way to Heder. Here is your shoemaker; here is a new perfumery shop. On the corner is an old, low house with a huge rusty key on the roof telling everybody that in the cellar you will find a locksmith in a room four metres by four. On the same corner is a shop that sells cheeses of all kinds. Their smell spreads far and wide.... Ciasna Street also runs in both directions. Towards the market there are every so many little shops, then once again, a Heder and a Shtiebel. On holiday nights and particularly on Simhat Torah, harmonious and fervent Hassidic melodies burst from here, sung by mingled young and old voices.

You can hear the echoing dances and hand-clapping even when the street is fast asleep. At No. 4 is the "Arbeiter Heim" of the left-wing Poalei Zion up on the third floor. It is reached by ancient wooden stairs that are hard to climb. In the entrance is a preserved fish shop whose scents mingle with the others that reach the top floors. Here, Zerubabel, with his black beard, used to speak when he came to town to put heart into his Party. Here the various election stratagems were carefully plotted. Here as well, fervent song resounded though of a different kind.

[Page 59]

Across the river you suddenly reach an orchard. Beyond the slaughterer's home is a tannery with a huge iron gateway and its own distinctive fragrance. The villa of the Doctor is on the corner facing the bridge. Across the street is a one-time factory which in due course became the "Stilowy" Cinema. The next house, No. 19 is very varied. Here you find a modern mechanical workshop, a private House of Prayer, then another mechanical workshop and a Hassidic Shtiebel in the courtyard, as well as the Shomer Hatzair Quarters. From the various storeys around the courtyard come music and melody which reach their peak on Friday and festival nights. We had to close the windows in the summer in order to escape the music. That did not always help either and the evenings usually finished with lively arguments between the interested parties on the stairs or in the courtyard. Here the dreams were woven; here the resolutions were framed. And from here, many started out on their own way in life.

Now we are back again at the corner of Nowa and Ciasna Streets. Here is a "general store" for odds-and-ends, fenced with boards, trading in the minutest coin of the realm. Next to it is a spacious lace factory. Nearby, in the heart of the Jewish street, is a tavern where things are very lively on Saturday night and Sunday.

Take another twenty paces. On the corner of Babina Street is the Jewish pharmacy which swiftly obtained many customers from all over town including Christians when it was established after the liberation of Poland. The owner also set up a medical laboratory and did well.

Opposite is a large and spacious corner house with an extensive internal courtyard. Here we find a weaving factory and the city bookbinder, the owner of a lace factory, a well- known surgeon, the District Judge and the hostel for secondary students. Here lived the Community's cantor and many others. In this house, I was born.

Beyond Babina Street, the first broad street running across is a spur of the Prosna. It is shallow here because of the numerous little weirs and dams. On either side of the street are acacia trees. You can smell their blossoms far away. We used to use them for learning our fate when we were in love. She loves me – she loves me not...

And now comes the Jewish bridge which seems to be very high because the water here runs shallow. It is built of seasoned oak. Don't be afraid, it won't collapse. So far, no heavy lorries cross it – only light carts or carriages harnessed to one horse, two or sometimes three (if the squire of Winiari or of Bezhazini is passing). Or maybe the cart of a carrier or a farmer passes here. It is kept up and looked after. A Russian cavalry unit camps in the neighbourhood and passes here together with a band on horseback when they make their way to the centre of the city.

[Page 60]

The opposite bank is called Nadwodna Street. It is the Jewish butchers' quarter. The doors are all of red iron. These butchers are all kosher and one day... but we shall come back to them. As for the bridge, there is not the slightest trace now left of all the generations who used to cross it.

I see Jews in groups and bands leaning against the parapets; and not only at the Tashlikh ceremony on New Year's Day but all year-round. Some discuss high policy while others argue which rabbi to elect and others again quarrel about party control in the community. And some are just passers-by. On clear winter nights, and particularly at the close of the Sabbath, you would find crowds from the various synagogues hallowing the new moon with the old formula: Peace be with you, peace by with you, with you be peace.

Amid a large group of Jews of all kinds, young and old, densely bearded or shaven, pious or secular, well-dressed or in rages – in the middle of them, all and towering head and shoulders above them, you were bound to find Enzel young and Enzel old. A Jewish cap with a peak is set a trifle slanted on his head, sometimes less slanted, sometimes more but never straight, not even on Sabbaths or festivals.

Enzel always feels hot: he sweats even in winter. The barber attends to his little beard once a week or once a fortnight without using a razor, of course and sometimes he cuts it a little too short. Then Enzel goes around without his little beard for quite a time joking about it, of course. Enzel jokes in the street like an ever-flowing fountain. He serves as the Badhan or jester at marriages and a fine chief jester he is, mingling his speech with wise words of Torah and fine phrases, with laughter and tears, accompanied by the Klezmerim, the local musicians who have learnt to suit their melody to his fine and accomplished style. Enzel is an accepted and successful match-maker. But his successes do not get him anywhere. His children are hungry but they have also learnt to smile and even laugh. His wife is the only one who has not learnt how to laugh except on the days when Enzel returns from a circumcision or a wedding in a wealthy home and brings all kinds of good things with him. He sells the Warsaw Yiddish dailies "Haint" and "Moment". He knows all that is written in them and mocks them and adds his own jokes. In the course of conversation, he starts on a deep and difficult Talmudic discussion, forgets all about making a living and comes home in the evening carrying his papers with him. And then his wife.... He also sells fringes and prayer shawls. If you meet Enzel late in the evening by himself and he does not notice you, you see the deep sorrow on his face. I have also seen Enzel the jester weeping.

Two houses face one another at the beginning of Zlota Street: the "Street of Gold". In former times, the gold dealers and goldsmiths were all to be found here. Now it is a neglected and filthy turning. There is a shop at each step, one just like the other, all tiny in the wooden buildings. They sell every kind of trifle: Jewish ritual requirements and tools and utensils of craftsmen, things needed by small tailors, cobblers, linen seamstresses and shroud-sewers and makers of ironware. There are grocery shops above all. In most of them, a piece of herring is sold for the smallest coin in circulation. Before your eyes they will cut a piece from the entire little fish. Some people will come and buy several heads for one farthing: Little cookhouses and beer houses. Well, and then come two big houses facing one another on the river bank; the Lustig House, the first, and the Shmerkovitz House, the second.

[Page 61]

In the corner facing the bridge are wooden stairs of middling width which over the years have developed the habit of creaking at every step. There are iron railings on both sides. These steps lead to the General Store for literature, newspapers, writing utensils and everything of that kind. Here you obtain everything that has arrived in town except for Yiddish dailies "Haint" and "Moment" and the Hebrew "Hazefira". Here you can order any periodical; say: "Hashahar" or "Hashahar Lanoar" (for youth) at your convenience and pleasure. When you enter the shop your eyes grow bright, even after sunset. All the heads here are reddish including those of the grandchildren and they all have a Jewish grace and charm. In 1913, during the Beilis Trial, my late father would wait impatiently for the paper to arrive from this shop.

At the entrance of a small shop opposite stand an elderly couple. What do they sell? They have no window but every cultured person in town knows that you find anything here: The "Tze-ena Ure-ena" or Women's Yiddish Pentateuch, from the oldest editions to the most recent. The whole of Jewish and Hebrew literature, scholarly, sacred and profane, rare editions and everyday publications can be found here. Ever since I can remember, the old couple are aged, bespectacled and with white hair. But their eyebrows are black and thick. Through the simple lenses and the silver frames, lively eyes gaze bright and grow weary towards evening. It is a strange shop: two metres by six. The colour of the ceiling is hard to judge, so old it is; but it is lofty and to my eyes towers almost to the skies. All the walls are set with cases crammed with books arranged in order or piled higgledy-piggledy; some bright with lettering and other worn with age.

The bookseller is not interested in modern technology. The shop is lighted with an oil-lamp although the city has long had gas and more recently electricity. If ever he has to fetch a book from the top shelves, he clambers up and down a ladder at tremendous speed – a lamp or candle in one hand and the book required in the other. More than once I used to think of the Ladder of Jacob in the Bible.

When the school year began, hundreds of pupils came to buy and sell schoolbooks. A table stood outside with heaps of books upon it and the bookseller used to buy and sell at astonishing speed. Whether he earned or lost didn't matter. Schoolchildren got a book. You could see that this gave him pleasure. The children used to line up as far as the bridge but this market only used to last a few days.

In the square opposite is the large synagogue which has been standing, it would seem, ever since the Creation. It has burnt down and been rebuilt several times, so history tells. The windows are longish and are of coloured glass. Lower down, with normal windows and mesh curtains, are the women's sections. High above the roof is a round tower whose colour changes according to the colour of the sky from blue to greenish to grey. Surrounding it is a round balcony with a parapet, but I never saw anybody on it although the tower has a small door. The old folk tell that ever so many years ago the communal Shamash (beadle) used to mount the tower and summon the congregation to rise and serve the Creator, shouting "In Shul arein." (Come to synagogue!). I myself can remember a Shamash who engaged in this holy task but in a different fashion. He used to walk along the Jewish Street and with a special wooden mallet dedicated to the purpose; he would knock at the doors of the houses shouting: "Come to the Synagogue!" That was why he was known as Simha Klapper or banger. Nobody knew his real family name. He also used to knock on the table of the Bema in the synagogue and shout: "Sha sha sha" before the rabbi's sermon and before prayers.

[Page 62]

The interior of the Great Synagogue was awe-inspiring even when it was empty with its spaciousness, its height and its magnificence. Here was a spiritual centre; a centre of joy and of sorrow in days of stress and calamity. Memorials were held here for the Kishinev Pogrom and the Lemberg Pogrom. With thousands of Jews within and thousands outside. And who will ever forget the prayers?

The synagogue had a custom of its own: Between afternoon and evening prayers on the Sabbath, the ample congregation waited for the stars to appear. The sun sank. It grew darker and darker and through the windows, one could see the swaying shadows of the trees as though they had already begun to pray without waiting. Then suddenly the assistant cantor would begin to sing, first in a whisper then with his voice growing louder and louder and all the congregation would respond. The echoes spread afar and the whole Jewish Street knew that this was the accompanying of the Sabbath on her departure; until the prayers began.

Before the first Penitential Prayers that began a month before the New Year and commenced with the evening prayer at the close of the Sabbath, a special prayer was said. This was the Psalm: "To the Chief Musician with Neginot, a psalm and song." The cantor, Reb Noah Lider, had prepared a special melody for the choir and the whole congregation sang with them in four voices. This was a great experience. The melody has passed to many congregations all over the world and is still widely sung today.

The synagogue had a garden of old ornamental trees which surrounded the building. But it was unprotected and neglected. So, the synagogue wardens decided to preserve it. But where was the money to come from? The Brokman and Mamrot families erected a fine iron fence with two main gates and lesser gateways hung on concrete pillars. It was all painted properly and in the gateway was a memorial tablet for the benefactors. Now they are all one: synagogue, fence, congregation and the Brokman and Mamrot families...

In Zlota Street opposite the synagogue, was a Jewish tavern. Its owner was a short, solid Jew whose cheeks were always red. He had the short dense beard of a young man and a pencil behind his white ear. The gentiles of the vicinity who came to the market on

Tuesdays and Fridays used to prefer his vodka and the salt and pickled herrings of his wife as well as the stuffed fish. The place was always full to overflowing after morning prayers when all those who had said the annual Kaddish (Memorial prayer for kinsfolk) used to come out of the synagogue and treat the congregation to a glass of something, in accordance with established practice. Since there was no lack of death anniversaries, things were always lively and cheerful here.

[Page 63]

A panting and dishevelled housewife suddenly comes dashing in. Guests have arrived unexpectedly. The wife of the innkeeper delivers her from her distress. A meal flavoured with plenty of onions is ready in a moment.

Next to the synagogue is the Talmud Torah. The House of Study always has people praying there from before dawn until late at night. You will find quorums for prayer, groups studying a daily page of Talmud or Ein Yaakov (the legendary and homiletic sections of the Talmud). Others are reciting Psalms. The voices resound with their singular melodies – fresh young voices. Many, many years ago I came to the House of Study in the middle of the day in order to recite Psalms for my older brother who was about to undergo an operation. I recited the whole book aloud – from Psalm 1 to Psalm 150 and hundreds of voices responded. To this day I can hear those wonderful voices echoing in my ears. Their faces I see as in a dream for that is what it has all become. Only legends remain.

From here to the Old Market Square, there are shops on either side, tiny and middling. Here as well herring is sold by the slice next to a shop which sells everything from drapery to ironware. And why is a crowd suddenly collecting at the street corner next to Nagurski House? Let us come over and see. The barber surgeon is standing there with a curious crowd all around him, listening to his stories about his real and imaginary sick patients as well as his jokes.

This fellow is a solid little Jew, fat and round as a barrel with a big head that is almost round as well and a face that has been cropped of its beard. Nobody has ever seen him really clean-shaven but his beard is like a fine brush. The hair never changes its length. His glasses hang on a silk thread hidden behind the collar of his smoking jacket. He used to put them on to inspect someone's throat or startle somebody or, particularly, when he was going to give a portion to someone who had insulted him. Before speaking he would put on his spectacles, angrily look the other fellow in the face, take them off again and only then commence. And then the party concerned would have done better to let the earth swallow him up, rather than hear all the pinpricks and stabs and stings as well as insults that the barber surgeon let him have before he went his way. He was always prepared to examine people in the street free of charge. All that was necessary for the man was to open his mouth wide, poke out his tongue and yell: "A a a a h" with all this strength. He had a fine practice and was a serious fellow but went his way with joy and laughter.

Here is the large square and in the centre of it is the large Town Hall built in Italian style on pillars, with the finest shops of the town behind them. This is a square three-storey building with a lofty tower on the roof which also has several floors in it. At the top is the ever-correct town clock with its four faces – one for each of the cardinal points. The clock stopped once and once only! That was when the Germans shelled the town before occupying it in 1914. When I was a child we used to play hide-and-seek around these pillars, particularly in the evenings after the shops were closed. But when the square was rebuilt with new and modern-style houses and shops, it was no longer worth much as a memory. All the romance departed from the Old Market Square (the Stary Rynek) and its name was also changed.

[Page 64]

From the square the streets run off in various directions. Two are main thoroughfares. One, four kilometres long, runs to the railway station and is named Wroclawska. Facing it, rather shorter and running towards a huge Russian Orthodox Church Square, is the Warsaw Street and beyond is the Sukienice Browarna. In Warsaw Street before the Church Square there used to be another little square with tremendous oak trees. Underneath them were many seats for the pleasure of those who lived there, namely higher officials and such like as well as passers-by. In the middle of the square was a monument in the form of a little obelisk on which various names and dates were inscribed: Friedrich Wilhelm; Maria Theresa; Czar Alexander; the three heroes or villains in the drama of the Partition of Poland; then the Emperor's Conference of 1814. Next to the monument is a big water-pump. Here is the deepest and tastiest water of the entire city. The municipal water pumpers used to deliver this pure water to the outlying inhabitants at high prices, all depending on the distance. Jews used to draw this water for baking matzos or "Matzah Wasser". In the course of time, however, a pump was fixed in the courtyard of every self-respecting house while an internal water supply was laid on in a few buildings. In spite of this, there were long queues lining up at the "Pomenik" pump until quite recently.

Beyond this point, Warsaw Street grows narrower and quieter, almost without shops. Here is the Asnik Municipal Gymnasium (secondary school) and beyond comes the gigantic Square of the Russian Orthodox Church which was dismantled in 1921 after the "Miracles on the Vistula", when the invading Russian communists were defeated and withdrew. On the other side of the square was the Evangelical Church. All the District offices are found in the House of the Jesuit Order and on the corner is the well-known Municipal Church with the big tower and giant clock which insisted on its existence every quarter of an hour. At midnight, the twelve strokes could be heard in each corner of the town and the vicinity. A trumpeter used to appear every morning on the balcony of the Tower, ever since the time of its foundation, so ran the tale, and played the well-known old song: *Kiedy Ranne Wstaja Zorze......*

And here is the bridge with a more handsome appearance: the Iron Bridge. The big house on the corner belongs to one of the local industrialists. Opposite is Niecala Street where the Doll Factory and the handsome dwelling of its owner. Then again, a wooden bridge crosses the Bernardinka next to the Church and a path leads to Stawiszyn. Here is the Jewish Old Age Home, a fine building by the standards of times gone by.

Here lived the Hebrew teacher Zwik who had a "reformed Heder". It was the largest Heder in the city and was supported by both the community and private funds. During recent years, the Heder had not been held in his home. He had gone up in the world. At one time the pupils studied in his dwelling, even on washing days. This teacher Zwik raised whole generations in town. All the outstanding folk, and they in particular, sent him their sons. My elder brother who was about twenty years older than me, was his pupil; and so was I and my sister's little boy. He went to join his children in America when he was about eighty years old.

[Page 65]

Teacher Zwik was an outstanding example of the enlightened Lithuanian intellectual. He had extensive familiarity with all the humanities and was a fervent advocate of Modern Hebrew. His bible lessons more than fifty years ago were of a very high standard. Even in his old age, he scarcely needed to glance at the bible text or commentaries for he knew them all by heart. His lessons in the Ethics of the Fathers and Psalms were of a remarkable character. He used to conduct them in his Heder, free of charge every Sabbath after the afternoon prayers, according to season. On these occasions, he gave us some idea of the world and the fullness thereof and told us about the latest research and discoveries in the world of nature. At his funeral in New York, large numbers of Kalish townsfolk attended and many of his pupils carried his coffin.

Leizer Moshe Cohen and his sons were the grocery wholesalers of the city and had a large spice shop with five opaque windows and excellent wares within coming from all parts of the world: You would find tea, sugar, coffee of the best and dried fruits. I can remember the fragrance that was wafted from there into the street. Business went on by itself. Leizer Moshe was entirely dedicated to communal affairs – gratis. He was a member of all the charitable and good deed societies.

Sometimes you would see Benjamin Hayyim Wolkowicz, a most worthy Jew, hurrying out of his home in Babina Street, his well-combed beard waving in the breeze, his coat unbuttoned, his stick in hand and a worried look on his face. Sometimes, he would emerge together with a roly-poly Jew with a big beard and gold-framed glasses who was always smiling and friendly. Where was he going? They would be going to an important discussion with their comrade Leizer Moshe Cohen. In the shop they would sit down to a glass of tea and after a brief discussion of current affairs, would get down to the point.

The conversation might last for hours until they set out for the Afternoon synagogue prayers together. Zlota Street has narrow pavements so the three of them walked in the middle of the road. In front of the synagogue or the House of Study, they would run into Tsalel Halter as though by appointment, and they rejoiced that God had brought them together since Tsalel Halter was a supreme giver of good counsel. A tall Jew with a friendly and shrewd face and eyes, his beard straight and well-tended, he was the lawman of Jewish Kalish, lawyer, judge, defending counsel and prosecutor. He always knew in advance and with absolute certainty all the paragraphs of the law and the judgments that would be handed down. Officially, he was a petition writer and in secret, a lawyer. Everybody honoured his ample knowledge. If judgment was given against his client and not as prophesized by him, then Fate was to blame... Tsalel Halter would hear out the problem as stated by friends, would express his views and then turn with slow and assured paces, his hands clasped behind his back, to say the Afternoon Prayers in his Hassidic Shtiebel.

After Evening prayers, Tsalel Halter could not go straight home. Deep in thought, he went down Zlota Street, entered the synagogue garden by the gate at the corner next to the House of Study, crossed the garden and came out by the main gate, crossed the street, dropped into the bookshop to riffle the pages of a book, went out, crossed the bridge, stood still a moment and returned. Beyond the Lustig House, he vanished into the narrow street turning left, looked in on the Jewish Hospital, crossed the street, glanced at the garden of the Jewish Girls' Orphanage and came out on Kanonicka Street. Now he turned left, passed the Jewish Community building next to the ritual bath on the river bank, crossed the bridge and gazed at the Fire Brigade Building as you enter the large square of the New Market.

[Page 66]

A man was lighting the gas lamps in the streets and around the square with a long stick. Lights came on in the houses. The Fire Brigade Band was meeting for a rehearsal. A gentle tune could be heard. Tsalel Halter leaned against the Bridge parapet, glanced for a moment at the shallow water of the Prosna and retraced his steps across the bridge to Kanonicka Street where he lived in a dwelling that occupied a whole floor. A light goes on in his study facing the Church of Holy Mikolai from which can be heard the tinkle of the little bells that summon to Vespers.

In Rzeznicza Street, at the corner of Sukienice Street, stands the house of one of the veteran heads of the community, an industrialist who is one of the first wardens of the synagogue. Few people have seen his laugh. He is a serious man of affairs, always active with hard lines to his face that shows unflinching resolution. His eyes are dark-grey and deep-set with dense eye-brows above them. He has a thick moustache and a little pointed beard. He walks with a valuable stick that has been artistically carved. On it he leans wherever he goes. He buys his hats when he goes abroad to the Baths each summer. Down below in his house is the barbershop of the Barber-surgeon who is an expert in setting leeches. The barber stands in the doorway enjoying a pleasant chat with passers-by. The shop is attended to by the young assistants who know nothing of "medicine". Only the better-class clients enjoy the personal attentions of the master himself....

***

Anybody who arrived in Kalish by train in the days before the buses or the diligence used to come to town by carriage. A row of carriages was lined up in the station square which lay several kilometres from the heart of the city. Not far from the station on the way to Skalmierzyce, the frontier post between Russia and Germany before 1914 stands the big building of the new flour mill.

Among the first houses to be seen at the entrance to the city were the large buildings of the Boraks brothers in Wroclawska (Gornoszlonska) Street. The Boraks family came from Stawiszyn towards the end of World War I and settled in Kalish. They were horse dealers on an international scale. The home of Leon Boraks swiftly became an open house, particularly for the young friends of his sons and daughters. He often placed his summer home at the disposal of the youth movements in summer for holidays and leisure. Adek, the youngest of the Boraks family was one of the heads of the Halutz underground in Poland and fell fighting in the Bialystok Ghetto.

The carriage passes the spot where the city gate once used to stand according to tradition. To the right is the Saint Trojca Hospital. To the left is the Nazarene Church and the Nazarene Girls School. Further on, near the handsome building of the Trade Bank and just opposite another bridge over the Prosna, we reach the Josephine Alley, the Venus Cinema, and the Europa Hotel on the right. On the left is the Electric Power Station operated by the river current with the aid of a dam. Beyond is an up-to-date bathhouse with public showers – modern times.

[Page 67]

There is a spacious building in the middle of a little square halfway along the Josephine Alley, facing the bridge beyond the dam. This building marks the end of Sukienice Street. It is the old District Court. Its large halls serve the lawmen and as offices for the public notaries. Under the sloping little roof is a painted pair of scales with a gilded text in Latin: "Suum Cuiquae". Nearby is a handsome residential building with a spacious courtyard. Within and on either side is a dwelling house with the "Oasis" cinema, the first in Kalish, at the far end. For the opening of the cinema the owner had a documentary film brought of recordings of Eretz Israel in 1912-14. All the fine folk of the city, the orthodox leaders, and heads of the synagogue, the wardens and the others were invited to this opening.

From the Oasis cinema begins the broad Avenue. In the middle is the walk with trees on either side, chiefly fragrant acacia. In the flower beds are the seasonal flowers. Beyond the trees on either side are one-way streets with pavements in front of the houses. The Alley leads to a park. The houses to the left of the Avenue lie in the "Polish Venice". The description is justified. The Prosna flows behind the houses and almost every home has its own rowing-boat. People here often held garden parties in the evenings. The garden would be lit up with the "gondolas" floating on the river. Not that there was much room for boating; only as far as the next dam, about a hundred metres in all. But they could boat and fish.

On the right was the new Polish Bank followed by the Municipal Theatre which was always under construction and so represented all kinds of queer architectural styles. From the Theatre balcony towards the park there was a magnificent view. Bands played here on Saturdays and Sundays. In winter they played for the skaters on the ice; in summer for the boats floating on the river. And then there was the Boat Race of the Boat Club.

Before entering the park, let us glance for a moment into the Wiejska Street (whose name was later changed to Pulaski Street) lying behind the right-hand side of the Josephine Alley. It was here, at the end of the street, that the lace factories were to be found.

I remember that after the San Remo Conference in 1920, when Great Britain accepted to Mandate for Palestine, it was decided to celebrate the occasion with a big public affair in the fields on the way to Meikow Village. A great platform was constructed, composed partly of flat wagons for goods carriage. All the work was done on a voluntary basis. Planks were supplied by well-known timber merchants whose yards ran the length of the Third of May Street. A huge crowd of almost ten thousand people filled the whole square. The programme was rich and colourful. A large choir was organized and was accompanied by the orchestra. Townsfolk and visitors from elsewhere delivered speeches and finally, the public made their contributions for the Redemption of the Land.

[Page 68]

It was an unforgettable scene. Women brought silver candelabras, took the rings off their fingers, men contributed gold and silver coins and watches. The enthusiasm was boundless.

In Kalish, there was a very happy scene one year on the 33rd Day of the Omer when members of Hashomer Hatzair in their hundreds marched through the streets with their banners, accompanied by the Band of the Jewish Sports Association as they made their way back from a hike.

There were also occasions of mass grief and sorrow. One of these was round about Purim 1921. Anti-Semitism was running riot in Poland under the leadership of General Haller. Jews were flung from railway carriages of trains in motion. In the streets soldiers cut off their beards. Jews became toys in the hands of rioters and murderers and were virtually put beyond the law. They were tortured and tormented and nobody said a word. To be sure, the Jewish carters and butchers of Warsaw displayed their bravery and showed the rioters what they could do, but the reports from all parts of Poland were very grave.

Kalish was quiet and there were no signs of anything wrong. But one day, I went to school and the streets seemed different somehow. The shops were open, and Jews were coming back from the morning prayers. But Christian youngsters were standing on the street corners, which was not customary, with sticks in their hands.

During the third lesson, the Headmaster instructed the Jewish pupils to go home. In the interval, we gathered together by order of our older companions from the upper classes and each one set out on his way. The streets were empty, and all the shutters were down. There was a pogrom raging in the centre of the city and it lasted for twenty-four hours.

The butchers opposed the rioters with organized force. A crowd of rioters gathered around the Jewish butcher shops in Nadwodna Street. When the Jews offered resistance, the rioters attacked one of the butchers, pulled an iron door out of its frame and crushed him with until they killed him.

After the dreadful pogrom in Lember, a Memorial Meeting for the victims was held in the Great Synagogue. Reb Noah was the Master of Ceremonies. The service was conducted within the building which, however, was not large enough to contain the thousands of people who came to mourn. There was absolute silence inside and outside. Reb Noah went up to the Holy Ark and began to weep, first quietly and later roaring: "Alas, what has befallen us!" following the Lamentations of Jeremiah. The silence inside and outside the building was so complete that the prayers could be heard at a distance. This was a day of great grief for the Jews of Kalish.

***

The landscape made a unique contribution to the romantic spirit of the city which was beautified by the river and its tributaries. The many bridges, the greenery, the trees and last of all, the extensive old park with all its delightful nooks and corners did their share. Much came from nature but the hands of men had no small share in it. Kalish folk walked about in the park from babyhood in prams under the shadow of the trees then into childhood, youth, maturity and old age. For the youngsters this was the place of their dreams. For adults it was a spot to rest and forget the troubles of the day. Everybody who comes from Kalish remembers this part of his childhood home with love.

[Page 69]

There were many entries to the park. The main way led from the Josephine Alley, with the Municipal Theatre to the right, the Avenue to the left and the Bridge... a bridge again in front of you. But no bridge resembled any of the others. Then came the Boat Societies.

You will find yourself standing at a meeting place of three roadways all leading into the park. Turn right with the Prosna. Walk on for a hundred metres and again you find a bridge and a big dam. Continue. The river is on your right and a green valley is on your left but you cannot see it for everything is a dense forest here. Only between the branches can you see paths, trails, benches and maybe statues in the distance.

The river grows wider. Now you can reach the ancient oak where the roadway runs down into the little valley; in the centre of which is a lake. In the middle of the lake is an island with a statue upon it. The spot it called: "Kogutek". The ancient oak is thick and lofty. They reckon that it is two hundred years old. It takes three men with outstretched arms to encircle the trunk. We know, for we have tried.

From the street of the square – from the statue in the island, there is a circus with a diameter of a hundred metres. All around are ornamental plants with benches beside them. During the mornings of the summer weekdays, when the park was not crowded, you could really enjoy sitting here, taking pleasure in the quiet, the singing of the birds and the beauty of nature all around you. Here Adam Asnik wrote his poems and musicians composed melodies.

In the early hours of the beautiful spring morning, you can see special kinds of persons walking here, sometimes alone and sometimes in groups. Those wearing green caps were called "frogs"; those in red caps were known as "beetroots". These were the pupils of the Government Gymnasiums. Somewhat later, other caps were also to appear: The pupils of the Jewish Gymnasium.

The Jewish Gymnasium was actually set up by a public Committee of parents who, for national or religious reasons, preferred an institution of this kind. The teaching staff was an effective combination and the Gymnasium swiftly achieved an excellent level. This was the first Jewish Gymnasium to last. Several earlier attempts had been made to establish a school of the kind in Kalish but without success.

For some time, there had been a Secondary School for girls. In spring 1914 while the Russians were still there, a Jewish pre-gymnasium was set up as a reaction against the numerus clausus exercised in Russian Secondary Schools. A vast number of young Jews registered to study there but the onset of World War I put an end to their good hopes.

You will see pupils walking about in the park. Now and again, you may come across a group headed by a teacher, all speaking pure Hebrew.

A little further along and to the right is the Orangery – a beautiful, well-tended spot with a greenhouse and lofty windows where plants from all over the world are grown. Here I saw my first orange tree together with other specimens of exotic sub-tropical flora. The whole area is full of beautiful flowers whose fragrance spreads far and wide. Opposite the Orangery is a typical Swiss Chalet built entirely of wood with stairs, balconies and characteristic ornaments. This is where the gardeners live and the central nursery is tended. Between the two buildings in the centre of the square amid the thousands of flowers is a sundial erected in the 19th century as well as beautiful statues. There is no shadow here so people come to stroll only towards evening.

[Page 70]

The park is large and has many lovely nooks. Here is a little artificial brook with a tiny flour mill on the bank. The water hurries by. There are benches on the hill. A romantic spot – and yonder is the "Mills". Here is the spacious Prosna. On the hill is a space with a parapet: it offers a panorama facing the boat jetty. And here is the Prosna, racing towards the "waterfall" which creates the Bernardinka Stream. Far, far beyond, is the "red" bridge (yet another!)

There is no end to all these lovely spots. But here is the "Ruin"; maybe the remains of an ancient palace or maybe an artificial structure. It is all of stone with numerous winding old stone stairs; one open space adorned with domesticated wild flowers. Steps lead to a second level. Here as well is a space with a concrete surface surrounded by an artistic stone parapet and a magnificent view. The "ruin" has a tunnel and from it a path leads to a modern "hydropathic" building: an institute for Medical treatment by means of artificial mineral waters. Here, the first medical examinations for gymnasia pupils were conducted.

The "new" park lies beyond the waterfall and the Sports Stadium. Groups of the various Youth Movements, particularly Shomer Hatzair, engage in their meetings at the "ruin" by the waterfall or in the wood. You will hear songs bursting out. The words are in Hebrew; still corrupt but Hebrew just the same. The songs resound afar. Then come the notes of the Okarina, beautifully played by one of our friends while another begins to lead them in singing.

***

There are many entrances to the park. One of the nicest is from Niecala Street. On the left of the 'red bridge' a roadway constructed out of great rough stone blocks leads to the hill on top of which is a building resembling a fortress of the Middle Ages. It has four towers at its four corners and the windows are barred. This is the District Prison on the Turek Road. The 'red bridge' used to be a regular starting point for many hikes and rambles outside the city. But let us forget the bridge. Here is an entry to the park through an avenue with a hill above it. In the avenue there is a roadway for the carriages of those who come to rest and recuperate in the park air. Here you will also see the carriage of the Russian Governor, driving with his family. This avenue is more than half a kilometre long with giant chestnut trees on either side. The branches meet overhead and make a natural roof. On sunny days, the blue sky gleams through the gloom while in the evening, the stars appear. There is cool shade on hot days and darkness at night.

[Page 71]

My late father used to spend much time here and gained inspiration for many of his musical compositions and melodies. It was here that the melody for the once popular song "Seu Ziona Ness va-degel" (bear flag and banner to Zion) was composed more than seventy years ago. More than one of his compositions was based on the Song of Nature in the Kalish Park. Almost every day, and for many years, he used to meet with Rabbi Ezekiel Libshitz, the rabbi of the city, at this spot.

When the two friends reached the Red Bridge, they were often joined by a third man: A short, tubby little fellow with a big head, fine blue eyes and a carefully tended beard. He did not shave, not because he was orthodox, but because tradition is a fine thing. Day-by-day he used to walk on foot to the city and back in order to attend to his affairs in the various institutions and banks. It was his habit to meet various worthies and citizens for friendly conversations or to discuss Zionist affairs. This was Reb Moshe Krakowski who used to cross the Red Bridge at least twice a day. Whenever he met the rabbi together with my father in the park, he would pause and then the conversation would indeed become lively. After such a conversation he would "hurry" home. Once again, he would cross the Red Bridge slowly, his back slightly bent and his hands clasped behind him. He would mount the hill on which stands the "Mediaeval Fortress" which was the District Prison. Reaching the hill, he would turn to the right and vanish.

****

That is the end of our ramble.

A dream rambles through something that once existed and has vanished. Deep in the soul the memories remain of a distant past which is near to the heart. Those we met on the road now rest in Paradise. They have passed away. The city stands with all its beauty and charm, but the Jews are no longer there. Their birthplace has been betrayed them. It has forgotten them.

But we remember. Let us hold them dear in our memory.

———

[Page 72]

Jews in the Commerce and Industry of Kalish

by Stefan Frenkel

To deal with the development of economic life in Kalish, it is necessary to survey the beginnings of the city's industry at the time of the Russian Occupation. At the beginning of the 19th century, the Minister Lubelsky did his best to improve the economic condition of Poland and it was he who supported the establishment of industrial enterprises. To this end, special privileges were given to industrialists and craftsmen from other countries who wished to settle in Poland. These included exemption from taxes for a number of years and exemption of the sons of the settlers from military service. The success of these measures was helped by the industrial crisis that ensued in Prussia following the Napoleonic Wars, which resulted from the Customs War and Industrial competition of Great Britain. Several tens of thousands of new settlers, chiefly Germans, came to Poland. There were also Czechs who settled in the vicinity of Lodz. At first, these newcomers were permitted to choose the domiciles they desired and for the greater part, they preferred to settle down on Government land. Similar industrial colonies were developed on private estates in Tomaszow, Ozorkow and Konstantinow.

At the same time industrial workers were recruited in Germany, France, Belgium and England. These included the well-known technicians Philippe Gerard as well as Fragette.

From 1821 onwards, the Customs policy of the country protected the local industry against Prussian competition while the Customs Agreement with Russia opened satisfactory opportunities for exports to Russia and China. The steam engine also played its part in developments. By the 20's of the 19th century, its influence could be felt not only in heavy industry but also in flour mills and textile factories.

After the November Revolt, i.e. after 1832, Russia abolished the Customs Agreement and the decline in exports led to a decline in manufacture. Many weavers moved over to Russian territory. Industrialists moved largely to Bialystok where they continued to manufacture. This state of affairs continued for close to twenty years because it suited Russian interests. In 1860 the Russians did away with the Tariff wall in order to facilitate the unification of Poland and Russia. Favourable conditions for the establishment and growth of industry were thus restored.

These conditions account for the commencement of industry in Kalish; but thirty years had to pass before the right entrepreneurs were found. Kalish was not the proper place for heavy industry because it was too far from the necessary raw materials. Beside this there was a high rate of profit in light industry. Less investment was required and the turnover was more rapid.

Another important consideration was the presence of skilled manpower.

[Page 73]

There was a shortage of the necessary experts in the town. Only two settlers of this type reached the city. These were Repphahn, who established the Kalish weaving industry and Mueller who set up a similar industry in neighbouring Turek. These two undertakings belonged to the type that preceded the Industrial Revolution. Repphahn's factory was rapidly liquidated whereas Mueller's enterprise continued to function for many years in Turek.

The embroidery and lace-making industries which were characteristic of Kalish before the war were established in the 1880's. Their development was conditioned by two factors: plentiful supply of water that was suitable for bleaching the fabrics and the close vicinity of the Russian-German border which facilitated contact with the west and the purchase of the raw material for embroidery (i.e. cambric) from England. Threads were purchased in England and Switzerland while washing and finishing materials came from Germany.

It was then the fashion to use embroidery on sheets and women's underwear. This fashion was widespread in Switzerland and Saxony. In 1886 the first factory for embroidery was founded in Kalish by Felix (Fishel) Frankel, a local Jew who had made money in France. He purchased the machinery in Saxony and brought embroiderers from there as well. These used hand-machines operating on the principle of the pantograph. The operator conducted an instrument over the design and the machine carried out the movement that the instrument indicated.

All this was done without the use of mechanical power but the embroidery differed in no way from handwork though the labour invested was far less; for 4.5 metres of material could be embroidered simultaneously. The embroiderer was assisted by several men who put the threads in place and fixed the needles in the frame. After the embroidery was finished, the material was sent for bleaching and was washed and bleached in primitive vessels. After drying, the various embroideries were cut from the roll, ironed, packed and prepared for dispatch. All operations, naturally, were performed by hand.

At that time, Meizner opened a similar factory in Kalish and , did the same a few years later. Before long, this industry was invaded by the machine. The washing was the first section to be mechanized. A steam boiler was built at the Frankel factory to operate the primitive laundering machines. Somewhat later a direct-current generator was installed and operated by the same steam engine while the factory was illuminated by electricity instead of kerosene. The dwelling-house was also illuminated as were the courtyard and the street.

At the beginning of the 90's there was electric light in the Josephine Alley where the factory was situated and it caused a sensation. Mechanization went no further in the Frankel factory where embroidering continued by hand. After Felix Frankel died in 1909, his son Raphael wished to bring in new machines but did not succeed in doing so before 1914.

Frankel and Meizner were large-scale industrialists who employed hundreds of workers. Their factories were professional schools. The men learnt their work from German experts who were first brought for the purpose. But the new workers were local Poles and Jews.

[Page 74]

The wages paid were relatively good. In the course of time, the more ambitious among them wished to become manufacturers themselves. The larger industrialists helped them. In particular, Raphael Frenkel helped many of his workers to open workshops of their own which grew and expanded as the years went by. His assistance took the form of selling those building plots on reasonable terms, granting credit and providing securities for the purchase of machinery.

The machinery brought at the beginning of the century was no longer hand-operated but mechanized and wove a roll of 9 metres. Production costs fell. In addition, a cheaper kind of stuff was used, and the number of stitches was decreased. The workers were employed on piecework. As a result, it proved possible not only to lower the price but also to expand the market. Naturally, hand-embroidery remained more expensive and was still in demand.

In addition, there were now automatic machines in operation which produced a width of 13.5 metres. Meizner among others brought these automats. Both quality and prices declined. The Russian market absorbed the new type of goods very well. By the time World-War I broke out, Kalish stood for the embroidery industry. However, the outbreak of the war interrupted its growth completely. Still, it was not the burning of the city that stopped this for it so happened that the embroidery factories were left untouched. The real reason was the loss of the Russian market; not only because the frontier was closed but also because of the change in the character of Russian consumption after the October Revolution, and the course of development taken by the

Russian economy. None but vital commodities were supplied to the population there; and those did not include either embroidery or lacework. The Polish market was unable to absorb the entire production of Kalish and meanwhile, the embroidery and lace fashions changed. The manufacturers began to adapt themselves to the market and produced new articles such as Valenciennes. Many machines were sold for scrap. Towelling was made in the large Flakovitch factory; curtaining, etc. were introduced. Little by little, the embroidery industry began to flourish again.

Kalish without Jews (anti-Semitic poster)

[Page 75]

In 1928, i.e. at the period before the major economic crisis in Poland, there were close to fifty large or small factories for embroidery and lace making in Kalish. Apart from this major industry, Jews were also engaged in other fields. Thus a stocking factory belonging to Marcus Holz was established in the 19th century and developed well. Jews were also active in the food industry. The agricultural surroundings maintained the flour mills. In 1928 there were more than 10 power-driven mills, most of which were in Jewish hands.

Naturally the developing industry required commercial and transport services. There were many businessmen, including Jews, who supplied the embroiderers with raw materials, not to mention a considerable team of agents and travelling salesmen.

Many Jews were also active in the field of credit. Before the war, the State Bank, the Commercial Bank and the Riga Trade Bank were all operative in the city. The two Jewish banks which engaged in all commercial operations were those of Landau and Mamrot. However, these could not withstand the competition of the large institutions and were liquidated before 1914. On the other hand, Polish commercial circles established a bank called: "The Kalish Mutual Credit Society" which in due course became the "Kalish District Bank" and existed for many years.

The Jewish merchants felt the absence of a Credit Institution of their own and in the 20th century, they set up a bank which they called: "The Second Mutual Credit Society of Kalish". This bank achieved a great deal for Kalish merchants but did not renew its activities after World War I and was liquidated.

During the 20's, two Jewish Cooperative Banks were set up under the Jewish Audit Society for the whole of Poland. These were the Cooperative Bank set up by the Jewish craftsmen and the Merchants Bank set up by the Jewish Merchant Society. Both institutions supplied considerable credits to Jewish businessmen. One should not ignore the activities of the Societies mentioned above, or that of the Society of Embroiderers and Lace Manufacturers, all of which looked after the interests of their members. Special mention should be made of Tsalel Halter, the adviser of all the Jewish Merchants and Industrialists in matters relating to the law.

The economic activity of Kalish Jewry developed well but the economic crisis which began in 1929 and continued for several years, checked this development. A general non-payment of debts set in, followed by bankruptcies, receiverships of factories, etc. The banks also suspended their activities and caused losses to the Jewish depositors. Shortly before World War II, Jewish industry began to flourish again but for only a short while. When the Germans came, they took most of the Jewish machines to Germany. The Jewish industrialists and the workers alike lost their lives in the Holocaust.

———

[Page 76]

The Lace Industry

by K. C.

The products of lace-making industry of Kalish achieved a worldwide reputation. They gained a wide clientele, particularly in the former Russian Empire which included Poland, Great Russia, White Russia, Ukraine, Georgia, Siberia, Central Asia, the Far East and Vladivostok. Lace reached the large and small towns, and these markets were relatively soon opened up.

A number of other cities in Russia and Poland, such as Moscow, Warsaw, Lodz and Wileika also tried to establish their own lace industries but were not successful. Kalish remained the only one to achieve this.

The lace industry actually came into existence in the following manner: Kalish was near the one-time Russian and Prussian frontier. After three months of residence in the city, any inhabitant of Kalish could receive a permit to cross the frontier to Skalmierzyce, Ostrow, Wielkopolski and Poznan and could visit Germany as well. There were also family ties between the inhabitants of Kalish and German residents. People visiting Germany would return bringing all kinds of goods with them. This led to the development of a flourishing smuggling trade.

Lace goods were also smuggled into Poland from Germany. The leading dealer in lace-wear was Etta Winter. She was apprehensive about putting her lace goods on the market for she was afraid that the customs officials would pay special attention to this and fine her, so she found a method of deceiving them. She brought two hand-machines for lace embroidery from Germany and after that, the goods smuggled in from Germany were put on the market as her own manufacture. Other dealers learnt from her and also brought machines; lace-makers were brought and taught the Jewish embroiderers how to make use of these machines.

In those times there were two kinds of machine in use: double and triple. The double manufactured quality goods, while the triple ones produced simpler wares. The machines were built with cast-iron frames and were four metres long and three metres wide. They were divided by two "wagons" which met and received the little needles in which the silk or cotton threads had been placed. In the front part of the machine was the model piece. The embroiderer followed the design with the aid of a pantograph and transferred it to the machine.

There were also special drills in the machine for making holes where necessary and the needles would embroider the edges of the hole. Each machine required three or four attendants: the embroiderer himself, his assistant and two needle-threaders. The machines were very expensive for those times, costing 1900 roubles. Special mechanics looked after the machines and a seamstress was also required to make repairs in pieces that had been spoilt by the machine.

The following raw materials and auxiliaries were necessary for manufacture: silk or cotton thread, material, needles, wax for waxing threads so that they would not fray and large frames. Quite a large room was necessary for setting up the machine. All this required considerable investment, but the merchants felt that this was a good business and enthusiastically engaged in building suitable premises, buying machines and producing the raw material for lace manufacture. Although the manufacture of the lace was a complex and intricate operation, the finished products proved to be cheaper than the goods being smuggled from Germany.

[Page 77]

The city grew rapidly. Within a short time, dozens of three-storey buildings had been built in all the streets and containing hundreds of workshops. The Chopin, Ciasna, Nowa, Zlota, Wodna, Majkowska and Babina Streets as well as others were transformed into an industrial district. The Frankel family built large factories in the avenues.

The inhabitants of the neighbouring towns and villages began to move to Kalish. They all made their way into the lace industry. Within a short time the goods had so improved that they drove the German product right off the Russian market. As the industry developed some of the embroiderers began to work at home. In the course of time they also became major industrialists.

All this led to the transition of hitherto unproductive elements to the life of workers. In addition, there appeared a new class of intellectual worker: clerks, bookkeepers, designers and travelling salesmen who went from end-to-end of Russia booking orders. The industrialists established ties with thousands of merchants and for thirty years there was no crisis. On the contrary, the industry expanded, developed and absorbed young and old. When Germany began to manufacture embroidery machines that were mechanically operated and the lace making industry of Kalish seemed to face severe competition, the local manufacturers promptly brought the new machines to their factories.

This industrial revolution came about in the years 1909-1910 and the whole industry swiftly moved over to mechanical operation. The old hand machines had done their share and were thrown away being replaced by the long and new machines. The distribution of work did not change. The small machines manufactured the most delicate materials and silk products for blouses and costumes while the eight metre long machines manufactured cotton embroidery for the mass trade.

The number of workers employed did not decrease. The machines were operated by motors brought from abroad. However, the manufacturers had to introduce a labour code and labour discipline in their factories. The workers had to become accustomed to this. The skilled hand-workers swiftly adapted themselves to the new machines. They even paid large sums of money to be given rapid courses in the methods of operating them.

Operating the power machines did not cause any unemployment but demanded more workers. Wages were attractive. A first-class embroiderer earned 25 roubles or more a week. A threader earned 6-10 roubles a week or more. The working day lasted for ten hours. The new factories were specially built for the power machines and their operation. Some of these were actually driven by electricity.

In 1913-1914, on the eve of World War I, the technical innovation of the automat was introduced and reduced the number of workers serving the machine. It replaced the embroiderer and only threaders remained. One mechanic could serve dozens of machines at the same time. But the benefits of this new technological advance were not felt for when the industry was at the peak of its development; World War I commenced in August 1914. The Germans took the city, destroyed it, burnt houses and smashed up many factories. The Russian market – the main customer – was cut off. And the German occupation itself brought about entirely new conditions.

[Page 78]

The industry adapted itself and worked only to orders. Many workers became unemployed and engaged in other occupations and trade. Some of the manufacturers liquidated the factories and turned their buildings into dwelling quarters since Kalish had been largely destroyed and there was a shortage of apartments.

In independent Poland, the Lace Industry continued to produce for the local market only. The Russian market had vanished. The pre-war period was forgotten. The hand machines had vanished entirely for they had been sold as junk. The small machines were also out of use leaving only the long machines and part of the automats. Little-by-little, the Lace Industry was replaced by the Velvet Industry which was initiated by the manufacturer Solomonowicz, while the curtain industry was established by Flakovitch.

Jews had worked for more than sixty years wisely and energetically and had spread the name of Kalish abroad throughout the world. Kalish lace was known in the U.S., England, France and Germany. The city grew on lace together with the Jewish and Christian population. Here are some figures:

When the Lace Industry was established there were less than 5,000 Jews in Kalish. In 1914, there were 15,000 and in 1939, there were more than 26,000. The Christian population grew in the same proportion. But, in 1939, both the Jews and their industry were brought to a sudden end.

The Trade Union Movement

by I. Klechevski

The Trade Union Movement in Kalish came into being during the German occupation of World War I. Later on under independent Poland between 1918 and 1939, this movement set its stamp on the life of the local workers.

To be sure, the beginnings of the movement go back to the turn of the century. The rapid growth of the lace industry which began at the end of the 19th century attracted thousands of Jewish and Christian workers to the city and brought them together under the same roof. Under Czarist rule, working conditions were very miserable indeed. The working day last 14-16 hours. The workers had no insurance whatsoever. The authorities did not permit unions to be established. Any attempt to organize this was cruelly suppressed by them.

In 1895 the P.P.S was established followed by the Bund in 1897, the P.S.D. in 1899 and the Poalei Zion in 1905. All these were political parties but they gave some shape to the union life of the workers. Conditions began to be established for union activity, suited, of course, to the conditions of those days.

[Page 79]

Between 1901 and 1903, these parties established circles of workers who aimed at changing the harsh working conditions. Worker exchanges were founded to settle disputes between the workers and the employers, though this was not in any way an easy task. But, in due course, a large-scale movement came about and attracted large sections of the workers in the lace making and other industries.

Attempts were made to obtain the introduction of a ten-hour working day. When the authorities learnt of this they conducted a series of arrests and these first attempts were nipped in the bud. The industrialists who had their contacts with the authorities helped the government in these measures.

In 1904-1905, during the Russian-Japanese War, Russian political life came to the surface and the first signs of the approaching Revolution were felt. The workers of Kalish also began to awaken. The spontaneous demonstrations of Polish and Jewish workers demanding political rights were also exploited for trade union organizations and were accompanied by steps to introduce a ten-hour working day and raise wages. The manufacturers fought the workers with the aid of the authorities. This in turn led to conflict but after a bitter struggle, the employers submitted to the pressure of the workers. A ten-hour working day was introduced,   and wages were raised considerably.

These changes were very daring for that period. A hand embroiderer earned between six and eight roubles a week in a 14-16 hour working day while a helper and threader earned 3-5 roubles a week. After the Revolution, the embroiderers earned 8-10 roubles weekly for a ten-hour working day while the helpers and threaders received 3-6 roubles a week or even more. The tremendous improvements were also made possible thanks to the feverish expansion of the lace making industry at this period. New factories were being built almost every day. Scores of new machines arrived weekly. The industry required an increasing number of embroiderers, threaders, finishers, designers, clerks and travelling salesmen. The Kalish product spread far and wide through the Russian Empire reaching thousands of towns and villages over a stretch of 12,000 kilometres and more as well as reaching China, Shanghai and other cities.

Kalish was lucky for the lace making industry took firm root there alone. Attempts were made to establish lace making factories in other Russian cities such as Wilieka near Vilna, Moscow, Lodz, Warsaw, etc. but none of these attempts reached the dimensions achieved in Kalish. All the pioneers of the industry in that city were Jews and even when the industry was fully established, 78-80% of the manufacturers remained Jewish.

After the 1905 Revolution, many active trade unionists of Kalish were arrested and transported to Siberia and other cities in all parts of Russia. Many of them escaped to Germany, England, France and the U.S.A.

The tempo of growth in the industry continued to increase and Kalish began to attract more and more workers and clerks from the towns and villages of the vicinity. The city grew and there was a constant shortage of skilled workers. This also caused wages to improve and there was no unemployment. Until 1910, lace making was a hand industry but thereafter, it became mechanical and power-driven. This transition also brought about a revolution for it required additional workers. The hand embroiderers learnt how to handle the machines and while the number of workers did not decline, output rose four-fold and five-fold.

[Page 80]

The shortage of skilled workers again led to a rise in wages. The machine embroiderer received 15-25 roubles a week for a ten-hour day while the threader and helper received 8-12 roubles a week. The improvement led indirectly to higher wages for workers in other occupations such as tailors, shoemakers, bakers, carpenters, house painters, mechanics, etc. This situation continued until the outbreak of war in August 1914 when the Germans conquered Kalish.

Within a few days, the Germans engaged in large-scale provocation and began to destroy the city. The centre of town was destroyed including many factories and several hundred persons were killed. The inhabitants began to flee for their lives and scattered over the whole of Poland and Russia. The manufacturers abandoned their factories and fled. It took a year before part of the population returned chiefly the homeless and began to rebuild the ruins.

It was impossible even to imagine the restoration of the industry. The manufacturers did not return – there was no raw material and above all, the Russian market had vanished. The Germans were not interested in reviving lace manufacture since that was a well-developed industry in their own country. So, those who returned tried to go over to other occupations promising a living. Some of the industrial workers began to exploit the stocks of raw materials and began manufacturing on a small scale and by primitive methods. Some engaged in smuggling and peddling, which was very widespread during the war and some became builders. Part of them proceeded to clothing industries such as shoemaking, tailoring, and textile manufacture and related occupations.

The class-conscious workers exploited the relatively democratic regime of the Germans and started establishing various institutions and unions. However, the German occupation authorities viewed these activities unfavourably and did not permit Trade Unions to be established. Only with the outbreak of the German Revolution, towards the end of 1918, did the workers begin to establish legal Trade Unions and cultural institutions. Labour Councils were set up to establish legal Trade Unions and cultural institutions. Labour Councils were set up whose strength derived from the participation of all political parties and all professions and industries. The parties that participated were the P.P.S., S.D., Bund and Poalei Zion. The Council established legal Trade Unions for the workers in lace making, clothing, leather, transport, domestic service, clerks, building, public works, railway workers, teachers, industries and services. The member of the Council was elected by the political parties – the large factories and the Unions.

When independent Poland was established in 1919, things began to improve. People came home and a period of prosperity began. The Kalish folk displayed their great ambition to restore their city. Large-scale building activities began which employed many workers and officials and the factories revived with a few exceptions. The majority of the lace manufacturers set their machines in operation again. The embroiderers, threaders, finishers and clerks returned to the factories. The embroiderers set up their "international" union participated in by Jewish, Polish and German workers who showed much solidarity. At the same time, there were other exclusively Jewish Unions in the town. Thus, the clothing industry workers, consisting of tailors, etc. had about 150 members but did not include all the clothing workers as a great deal of work was done at home. The union set out to settle disputes between workers and employers and supported the wage demands of the workers.

[Page 81]

Between 1925 and 1935, Kalish won over the Poznan clothing market and the branch became prosperous. Factory workers and home workers earned well. The city became a centre of clothing manufacturing. The Polish tailoring workers belonged to the Polish Craftsmen's Society which was essentially reactionary. With rare exceptions, they refused to join the Jewish Union.

The second Jewish Trade Union was that of the leather workers. This was set up as international with Polish and Jewish members alike but later became exclusively Jewish. About 100 workers were organized. They included: shoe sewers, shoemakers and harness makers. The union dealt with professional matters. This was not one of the occupations that gave a good income. Everybody who learnt something about the work opened a little shop of his own.

The third was the Clerks' Union which had some 150 members in its final years. Those active in it included members of Hashomer Hatzair, right-wing Poalei Zion, left-wing Poalei Zion, the Bund and the Communists. The Union engaged in independent cultural activities such as evenings for debates and literary activities. Most of the members spoke Polish. Extensive union activities were engaged in such as: fixing working hours, raising wages and proper behaviour on the part of the employers.

The fourth Jewish Union was that of domestic helpers and cooks and the membership was exclusively female. To begin with, it consisted of 70-80 girls who came from the small towns on account of economic distress. They had special working conditions. These were very bad and they had no contact with their environment and found themselves entirely subjected to the whims of their mistresses – many of whom were uncultured and treated the girls harshly. The Union did some important work. It helped to raise wages, insisted on fair behaviour towards the workers and a one-day rest during the week. The Sabbath day belonged to the worker. Some of these domestic workers moved on to other occupations and took a hand in public affairs.

The porters also set up a Union with the aid of the left-wing Poalei Zion and the participation of the Bund. The members were not professional porters and many of them engaged in this work only after the war. The Union numbered 40-50 members. The efforts of the porters and the carters were directed towards obtaining fair pay for their hard work and they did their best to get the authorities to permit them to move freely through the city in order to do their work properly. These efforts were an essential part of the Union's activities.

[Page 82]

During the final years, a Barbers' Union was also established with 20-30 members. There were workers in other occupations that only had a few members such as: printing, woodwork, building, public works and banking. Some of them joined the Polish Unions. The disputes of the members who did not belong to any trade union were dealt with by the political parties to which they belonged.

All the Kalish Trade Unions set up a joint council known as the "Central" the seat of which was in Lipowa Street. This Council was attached to the Central Committee of Polish Trade Unions which represented several million organized workers.

Apart from the Labour Trade Unions, there were also other professional associations in the city such as the Artisans' Society, the Socialist Artisans' Society (domestic workers), Poalei Emunei Israel (Orthodox Jewish Workers), Agudat Israel, Small Merchants' Society, Travellers to Fairs, Market Vendors and the Merchants' Society. All these institutions engaged in professional activities only and represented large numbers of persons gainfully employed.

Until 1914, Kalish had more than 50,000 inhabitants of whom some 15,000 were Jews. Some 9,000 of these Jews were employed in lace manufacture and the remainder in various other branches and occupations. More than three-quarters of the lace industry was in Jewish hands and more than half of the entire population made their living from it. To be sure, there were a number of other large enterprises in the city such as: Mold's Meat Industry, Rephahn's Textiles, Fibiger's Pianos and Fulda's Tannery but about 3,000 families or more made their living from lace manufacture.

After World War I, large flour mills were set up and many Jewish workers were employed there. Both the owners and the workers were organized.

The middle-class Artisans' Society was well organized and included almost all crafts. It had between 800 to 1,000 members and a representative of its own on the Municipal Council. It engaged in settling disputes between members and regulating labour rates; it helped to reach agreements and make contracts. It dealt with negotiations with Trade Unions regarding wages and wage disputes and fixed the rates for those who worked at home. It provided members with legal and material help and also advanced loans. The Artisans' Society was the most important position in Jewish Kalish. It was more progressive and also more respected than the corresponding Polish Society.

In addition, there was the Socialist Artisans' Society known as the Society of Home Workers, consisting of independent experts who engaged in work at home and also employed workers, mostly apprentices. This Society had more than 300 members belonging to all professions. The Market Vendors, Travellers to Fairs and Street Hawkers belonged to the Small Merchant's Society which had several hundred members. The Society obtained loans for those of its members who were in distress (on account of thefts, robbery or other misfortunes); persuaded the authorities to treat peddlers more gently, secured the cancellation of fines and punishments, provided legal aid and social assistance in cases of illness, misfortune, marriage of children and births.

[Page 83]

Apart from the large Unions, there were dozens of small societies in the city which were connected with professional activities such as Loan Funds or Credit Societies which engaged in discounting Bills of Exchange, etc. These societies helped wage-earners considerably in overcoming difficult periods. The Unions also engaged in such economic welfare work on a large scale.

The Jewish population of Kalish was proud of its professional organizations which were regarded as a model on a country-wide scale. They were the fruit of the toil of workers and craftsmen for a full century, yet they were wiped out as though they had never existed in the general extermination of Polish Jewry by the Nazis.

———

Our City

by Leon Solnik

The city of Kalish spreads around fresh green islands linked by ancient bridges and has grown around old avenues, spacious parks and gardens. The deep river breaks the urban area up into islands. The water dominates the spot together with the sun which tans the crowds at the bathing places and the breezes that cool them off so caressingly.

The young people develop their bodies in the large stadium and the football fields as well as on the river. The boat jetties run out into the water and serve as a refuge for boats and weary rowers. In winter, the main channel of the Prosna, the Kogutek and the Little Lake are blocked by ice and summon the younger generation to winter sports: skating and sleigh-riding.

As the day turns to evening, the younger generation crowd the huge Municipal Park which still remembers the days of Kasimir the Great. They fill the wood and the avenues and lawns not only along the banks of the Prosna but also in the centre of the city.

At the heart of Kalish, in the Old Market, rises the handsome and aged Town Hall with the shops all around it except for the main entrance at the front which is shaded as it is by a large portico supported on pillars. After World War I, the building was restored in the Renaissance style and it is the pride of the city.

Kanonicka Street runs to the ancient Church of St. Nikolai which links the vaults of the former walled city with the cellars of the one-time Asnik Gymnasium. This underground connection branches off to the gigantic building in the Old Market and to the Church of

St. Nikolai and has an outlet to Ripinek from the Old Market. The Jewish Quarter begins parallel to Kanonicka Street.

Zlota Street, known as the "Jews' Street" is constructed of narrow two-storey houses. Here on the left, the Great Synagogue can be seen with its Byzantine domes, separated from the street proper by a large clean lawn divided by gravelled walks and benches on either side. The lawn was separated from the street by a handsome stone fence on a low base-wall presented by Tikociner.

[Page 84]

Next to the Synagogue rose the 13th century House of Study at the entry to which was an ancient stone laver. Over the generations, this aged centre of learning sent forth rabbis and Jewish legal authorities whose name spread far and wide. A little to one side, rises the new two-storey House of Study – the only one that has survived.

To the right in front of the bridge are the old butcher shops. In Nadwordna Street next to the arm of the Prosna, are the other butcher shops. All these side streets together with Rosmark constituted the centre of the Quarter. Beyond the bridge Nowa Street opens which is crossed by Babina Street, Ciasna Street and Chopin Street and continues to Majakowska.

How close are the days when the Jewish population lived happily and tranquilly, not imprisoned in its own Quarter but mingling freely with all the population on good-neighbourly relations? The Jews had not only religious schools but also secular ones where the languages of instruction were both Polish and Yiddish. These were headed by the Jewish Gymnasium.

Various Societies maintained reading rooms and libraries. The Sports Association had a library and a reading room and played an important part in educating the younger generation. It also had a band of its own. There were producer and consumer cooperatives, Poalei Zion and other schools. Then there were the Trade Unions of the lace makers, needle workers, upper-leather sewers, shoemakers and transport workers. The Artisans Society maintained a vocational training school.

The Zionist Movement maintained a library in many languages and a reading room providing courses in Hebrew study and also participating in all elections.

The model Eliza Orzeszkowa School was housed in a building of its own. Tuition was in Polish. The Jewish Hospital with its numerous beds and full range of departments was also in a private building. Mention should be made of the Workers' Home which played an important part in spreading progressive culture and thought. It was situated in Ciasna Street. Apart from its three little rooms, it had a large hall which was used for lectures, meetings and performances. This was a very lively institution that was sensitive to all communal problems.

The premises of the Trade Union Centre had a canteen. It also housed a dramatic group which used to give performances in Kalish and the neighbouring towns. The Workers'

Sports Club "Stern" had its gymnastic and football team, a library, reading room and a band. Literary evenings were frequently held.

The Jewish Community in Kalish lived an autonomous national life of its own. All this has been eradicated. The Jews were murdered, their property pillaged and their homes destroyed. Grass grows everywhere. Even the old cemetery has vanished and is covered with new buildings. Only a small portion is left and is surrounded with barbed wire. Only a handful of Jews remain who passed through the inferno and survived in order to tell the world of the mass murder whose like has not been known in human history.

[Page 85]

Five Years of Communal Work. 1931-1936

by J. M. Heber

Herewith, we offer a first attempt to give the Jewish Community in Kalish a report on the activities of the Community Council during its five years of office. The Council decided to publish this Report in accordance with a resolution of the 1935 Executive. In submitting this comprehensive account, we have had the following purpose in mind: 1. To give Kalish Jews, who bear the burden of the Community, a clear description of the purposes for which the funds, placed at the disposal of the Council, have been expended; 2. To prepare statistical material for later community Councils so that they can learn what good actions deserve to be imitated and what actions should not be imitated. Let us stress here that this comprehensive Report marks the end of an epoch which has possibly been the most difficult and responsible in our history. Hence, it is a weighty undertaking and a contribution to the communal experience and life of our City.

In summing up and surveying our activities, it is first necessary to consider the conditions under which the work has been done. Let us pause to consider some of these conditions more particularly.

One of the main difficulties against which the Council has had to struggle consistently in order to keep its budget balanced was the weak and irregular flow in the payment of communal taxes. A large proportion of those owing taxes, and particularly persons of means among them, were in no hurry at all to pay. Furthermore, they demanded that their charges should be reduced to a half or a third. In most cases, the Council had to agree so our accounts have always been at a deficit.

The Council often sought for ways of influencing those who were in arrears but to our regret were not always successful. The compulsory collection also did not have the success it deserved. It was found that the crisis was stronger than all the laws and the tax-payers were in such a bad situation that they simply disregarded the level of tax imposed on them and were in no way alarmed by the "yellow form" of the Collection Department since they no longer had anything to lose. If the Council, nonetheless, succeeded in paying all allocations and wages of its staff to the last farthing, that has been its greatest achievement.

In considering the budgetary difficulties of the Community and the main reasons for this, we must re-examine the years 1932 when Kalish Jewry suffered a severe blow with the death of its great leader and guide, the learned Rabbi Yehezkiel Liebshitz, of Blessed Memory, one of the great luminaries of Polish Jewry, chairman of the Society of Polish Rabbis and Rabbi of Kalish for many years. During his years of office, peace and harmony prevailed in our midst and the majority of the Council conducted communal affairs firmly and resolutely to the benefit of all sections of the Jewish population in the city. His death has shaken communal life to its very foundations and we can still feel its effects. Our community cannot console itself for this irreparable loss.

[Page 86]

Almost all the charitable institutions without exception are in considerable deficit on account of the constant decline in income. This situation has led everybody to impose the principle of pressure on the community on the assumption that it has to help all who are in need. And although the demands from the community increase from day-to-day, we succeeded in surmounting the difficulties and obstacles, and to the best of our ability, largely satisfied the needs of the Jewish population.

In considering cultural institutions, we may state with assurance that if the fine, modern Talmud Torah, where 450 children of indigent parents study and are fed, continues to exist, this is thanks to the Community Council which regularly pays all allocations.

The Council has also elevated the Rabbinate to a level befitting a city like Kalish. The religious institutions are maintained, the Rabbinate has been paid a regular salary. Kashrut is under proper supervision. In particular there is the major Passover undertaking and a kosher kitchen for Jewish soldiers and prisoners and many other activities which swallow up a large part of the communal budget.

In setting out to sum up the activities of the present Community Council at the close of its period of office and on the eve of new elections, we look back with pride on our activities during the last five years. What has been done reflects credit on the doers and those faithful communal workers who helped. More than once our opponents brought us to the verge of despair but our strong feeling of responsibility gave us the strength and energy to bring the hard work to its close and pass it on to those who will be elected as the forthcoming representatives of the Community of Kalish.

Kalisher Leben (451) 28, 3rd Elul 5696, 21.8.1936

––––––––

Blaszki

(Błaszki, Poland)

51°40' 18°27'

by B. C.

There is a little town most of whose inhabitants were Jews. The place has remained but the Jews are no longer there. Those who came to Eretz Israel or emigrated elsewhere were saved. The rest suffered the fate of the six million.

From the account of friends, we have reconstructed the story of this place although the account is certainly incomplete. Whatever was told was written down. There are no reliable documentary sources.

The little town was fairly close to Kalish, only 28 kilometres away. On the one side was the Joszanka tributary of the Prosna which came from Joszema Village. This was a little stream whose water was drunk by the townsfolk. They washed and did their laundry there; they caught fish in traps and they built their ritual bath (Mikveh) over it. On the other side was the railway line. Between the railway station and the little town was the graveyard.

[Page 87]

There was a bridge over the stream. Then there were two main streets. Sieradz Street and Kalish Street which were the entry and exit. They met at the very large market-place which was divided into upper and lower sections. Every Monday and Thursday was market days. The Jews did not build stands in the market. They put boxes there and fixed covers over them. In the centre of the marketplace was a wheel pump, a rope and a bucket. In winter, they used to slide on the ice there. There was a big building in the marketplace, called the "Blaszkowianka" with shops below and above a hall for performances, a gymnasium and a bathhouse.

Only Jews lived in Kalish Street while in Sieradz Street, more than half of the inhabitants were Poles, chiefly craftsmen – shoemakers, carpenters and pork butchers. There was also a street of the Dutchmen. These were Christians from Holland and were chiefly shoemakers.

What did the Jews do? They made their living from the neighbouring villages by means of the market days. There were also Jews who used to exports eggs and had grocery shops. The trade in grain and seeds played a big part and the merchants were the important people of the town. But crafts played an important part too. Ready-made clothing for men was important. The goods were sold to the peasants at the market and were also sent to Poznan. Of the Jews, 15% were tailors. The hat-makers also went their goods to Poznan. Jews worked as tinkers, carters, watchmakers, porters, owners of handcarts, carriage drivers to the railway and on inter-urban lines and were also water-drawers. The line to the railway station, which was 3.5 kilometres from the town, was in the hands of Jews who owned open carriages. There were also goods carriers. Nor should we forget the bakers, barbers and barber-surgeons.

The latter, known as *feldshers*, were doctors to all intents and purposes. They carried out minor operations, dressed wounds and set fractures. In particular, Itzik Feldsher and Feivel Feldsher should be remembered.

When the Polish reactionaries began to encourage the anti-Jewish boycott, a Christian shop was opened next to or opposite every Jewish shop. The activities of the anti-Semitic Rozwoi Organization could be clearly felt.

It is estimated that until the 1920's, more than 400 Jewish families and 215 Christian families lived in Blaszki. Afterwards, there was an extensive movement from the village to the town and the number of Christians increased to 50%.

The Great Synagogue also contained a women's section. In the House of Study, there were several Minyanim (prayer quorums) and young men also studied there. Likewise, there were Hassidic Stieblech of the Hassidim of Gur – Alexander and Sochaczow. The secular minded Jews sent their children to the Polish elementary school and gymnasium. The observant maintained a "Bet-Yaakov" School for girls. There was also an Agudat Israel School. In 1919, a "Yavneh" Hebrew School was founded and became a model institution.

Jews were not permitted to study at the Tsarist School but teachers used to give lessons in the Hedarim (private Hebrew classes). In 1913 a four- class school was built and the Heder children used to visit it for half-an-hour a week in order to learn Russian.

[Page 88]

In 1907, Rabbi Isaac Meir Kanal was appointed rabbi and held the post until 1922 when he became Head of the Rabbinical Court in Warsaw. He accepted the post only after talks with representatives of all groups and was received with much honour. He brought Rabbi Fuchs, a member of the Mizrahi and an active Zionist to town. It was his practice to gather the younger generation in his home and familiarize them with Zionist ideas. He also used to teach Bible in the Polish School. One day, the Hassidim who were opposed to this practice, sent a boy to remove the Ikon (Holy Christian picture) in the classroom. The Ikon fell from his hands and broke. The rabbi was charged and imprisoned. He was so distressed that he grew ill and died.

Relations with the Christian population were characteristic. In 1910 during an important fair, a Jewish pickpocket who did not belong to Blaszki was caught while at work. The peasants beat him murderously and later crushed his throat under a wagon-wheel.

Following the declaration of Polish Independence in 1918, the Christians wished to conduct a pogrom. A meeting of the Town Council was held with Rabbi Kanal's participation. A number of the large estate-owners of the vicinity were also present together with the Priest. All of a sudden, shouts were heard and there was a state of alarm. A crazy Jewish lad was wandering around in the town and rumour spread that he had shot at the Poles. An anti-Semite went to the railway station and shouted: "The Jews are murdering Christians!" He had no answer. Peasants began to arrive from the neighbouring villages with their scythes in order to engage in riots against the Jews. The Municipal Council and the Priest took up positions at every entry into the town and prevented the peasants from entering.

In the same year, soldiers of General Haller's army arrived by train. The Jews at the station were busy sending off chickens and eggs. The soldiers began to beat them and they ran away looking for hiding places in attics. The soldiers chased them yelling: "Where are the Jews?" When they found them, they beat them and also injured a woman who had refused to tell them of their hiding-places.

In 1934 another attempt was made to cause an anti-Jewish riot. At a Friday market, a Pole went to Samuel Rockman's shop to buy boots. He took them and went on his way. It was already sunset, and the Jew locked up his shop. Meanwhile, the Christian showed the boots to his friends who decided that the Jew had swindled him. The man went back to the shop and when he found it closed, he began to smash the door. The Jews were already on their way to the Synagogue and the Poles began to beat them up. The Christian porters came out with knives in their hands. When a Jew went to speak to them, they declared: "We shall kill all the Jews". Many Jews were wounded.

[Page 89]

The Rabbi went to the Priest who calmed the crowd down. The Jews did not go to the Synagogue that Sabbath.

The Nazis concentrated the Jews of Blaszki in three places: Sarniaki, Losiec and Sikilow Podlaski. They encouraged flight beyond the frontier, and many ran away to Russia and the Warsaw Ghetto. The rest were either shot or sent to extermination camps. When they entered the town, the Nazis took ten hostages of the leading townsfolk, brought them to the Christian cemetery and shot them. In those days, the roads were crowded. Many Jews came to Blaszki in the hope of saving themselves, only to meet their death there.

Stawiszin

(Stawiszyn, Poland)

51°55' 18°07'

by Shraga Engel

The little community of Stawiszin lived its quiet life in the Kalish District, about 17 kilometres from the city. The 80 Jewish families made up 12% of the population. It is known that under the Polish Kingdom, Stawiszin had the status of a city. The ancient buildings and cemetery served to show that the Jewish Community had existed here for hundreds of years.

Together with the 80 families, there was a neighbouring village, Hutasz, containing another 10 which made a total of 90 in all. Together they provided a living for two slaughterers, a rabbi and a *shamash* (synagogue attendant), maintained a House of Study and a Hassidic centre for various groups. The men were organized in various traditional Jewish Societies such as the Society for Visiting the Sick and Burial, Reciting Psalms, etc. The women had a society of their own.

There was no special Jewish street or quarter. Jews lived in every second or third house and here and there they were more widely scattered. They had been living in that way for hundreds of years and had preserved their customs and character. For the greater part, relations with their Polish neighbours were satisfactory. The only important even which I remember was in 1918 when anti-Jewish excesses were the fashion. Some unknown person then broke down the synagogue fence at night. But, on the other hand, the townsfolk regularly came to enjoy our Simhat Torah processions and took part in the reception for a new rabbi. The young butchers and horse-dealers, who were on very close terms with the villages because of their business, told how their comrades used to defend them in fairs and markets elsewhere, while they also used to come to the aid of their neighbours if they were being attacked.

The Zionist Society was founded in 1916 by a group of young men. A special Society of Youths for the study of Torah was founded and the rabbi Tamarson and other scholars gave lessons in Bible every Sabbath afternoon. Gradually, they began to invite lecturers who were not very orthodox. In due course, the Society became definitely Zionist and women were also accepted as members.

[Page 90]

I would like to mention one simple but exceptional person. When jewellery was contributed to the Jewish National Fund after the Balfour Declaration, we went from house to house. I was secretary. We specifically left out the home of the late Abraham Gruenbaum, the only porter in town. But he came and complained. We went to him. In his clean and very modest dwelling, his wife gave us her gold earrings. Such people are not forgotten.

We have no details about the end of the community.

———

Religious life in the City

by Rabbi Dr. Meir Schwartzmann

Kalish prided itself on more than its great rabbis. Almost every Hassidic *rebbe* had his own Hassidim there. The Hassidim of Gur had several Shtieblech. One of these was known as the Shtiebel of the "Young Men" where the young, newly married men who were supported by their wealthy fathers-in-law, used to meet and study together.

The Hassidim of Alexander also had a big Shtiebel. I should also mention the Shtieblech frequented by the Hassidim of Sochaczow, Skiernewic, Kotzk, Sokolow, Parisow and Radomsk. Nor were they all.

Reb Velvel Mozes, one of the rabbis of the city, used to teach a special daily lesson in Talmud to the keenest students. A lesson was also taught by the Dayan, Rabbi Morgenstern, who was shot by the Germans in 1914.

Many youngsters from outside the city also studied at the Yeshiva and each of them ate on different "days" of the week at the homes of various householders. Apart from this, fathers taught their sons and fathers-in-law their sons-in-law. Every pious and observant home was a small-scale House of Study.

In 1914, matters took a turn to the worse. The Germans brought both economic and spiritual destruction to the city. The "free" wind that blew from Germany accelerated the process of mass secularization. The workers began to organize. There was an increase in the number of parties and organizations. The Houses of Study began to empty. The younger generation began to abandon the old-fashioned style of life. The Trade Unions inherited the Shtieblech and the party club premises replaced the Houses of Study.

This development aroused observant Jewry to action. Outstanding figures headed by Reb Abraham Mordechai, of saintly and blessed memory, the Rebbe of Gur, established the Agudat Israel which was first known as "Shelomei Emunei Israel" (The Entirely Faithful of Israel). Something fresh emerged in Jewry. Hassidic rabbis and rebbes, together with the rabbis of Lithuania and Germany, united in order to rescue Observant Jewry.

[Page 91]

In Kalish, the Agudat Israel was headed by Reb Joseph Moshe Heber and Hananei Rosenblum who established one of the strongest branches of the country in the city.

After the death of Rabbi Ezekiel Liebshitz, there was a dispute about the new rabbi to be elected. The Mizrahi and the Hassidim presented candidates of their own, each of whom was actually worthy of the rabbinical seat. In this struggle, the Hassidim of Gur were successful together with the Agudat Israel. The younger son of the Rebbe of Gur was elected to the office. This was Reb Mendele, until then the rabbi of Pabianice and brother of the later famed Rebbe of Gur, Reb Mendele was also elected President of the Rabbinical Association of Poland, thereby continuing the tradition established by his predecessor and maintaining the golden chain of the great scholars of Kalish. His opponents also accepted him fully. He was slain and hallowed the Name together with the members of his congregation.

The "Magen Abraham"

by Moshe Feinkind

Reb Abraham Abelle Gombiner, known as the "Magen Abraham" by Jewry suffered the fate of Jewish sages and lived in poverty and need all his life. That, as is known, is the way of the Torah.

He was born in the hamlet Gombin in 1636. In 1655 his father, Reb Hayyim Halevi and his mother, perished in that town at the hands of the "Confederates" under the Polish Hetman Czarnecki. After the Polish-Swedish War, those brigands finished what the Cossacks of Bogdan Chmielnicki did not do in 1648. Whenever these Confederates came to any town they slaughtered the Jews who lived there. A similar fate befell Poznan, Kalish, Lenczic, Piotrkow, Przedboz, Gombin, etc. Reb Abbele was nine years old and his younger brother was seven when he left home to study Torah. In Lissa, he had kinsfolk among whom he grew to maturity. He came to Kalish bearing heavy burdens. In those days Kalish was known as the centre for advanced students of Torah.

Reb Abbele began to teach Talmud to young men in order to make a living. His dwelling was a cellar in the house of Alrich where he dedicated himself to Torah by day and night in spite of his poverty. These facts are confirmed by Reb Joseph Samuel, Rabbi of Frankfurt, in the Haskama (Approbation) he wrote to the work: "Magen Abraham".

Reb Abraham Abbele was very modest and dedicated exclusively to his studies. For a long time the townsfolk were not even aware that they had an outstanding scholar in their midst. His knowledge and perspicacity were discovered in the course of a Halachic debate on a grave problem concerning Hametz (leavened food during Passover) which was discovered within the Community. The Rabbinical Court found it hard to issue any judgment for the problem was very difficult. Reb Abbele expressed his views among his acquaintances, from whom the community suddenly learnt that the simple Hebrew teacher was an outstanding Halachic authority. The Court adopted his decision.

[Page 92]

Thereafter, the Community appointed him Head of the Yeshiva and Dayan (Member of the Rabbinical Court). However, Reb Abbele refused to deprive any former Dayan of his livelihood and accepted the post only on condition that he was appointed: "Synagogue Dayan". He was known accordingly as long as he lived in Kalish. It was only when Reb Israel, son of Reb Nathan Shapira, became rabbi that he summoned Reb Abbele to be a member of the Communal Court.

Reb Abbele began to write his Commentary on the Shulhan Arukh before he was thirty years old. He used to write on torn paper bags. When some relevant thought occurred to him at night, he would write it on the wall with charcoal in order not to forget before morning. He continued to write even during the illness that afflicted him on account of his poverty. However, he never lived to see his work published though it had received the approbation of Rabbi Isaac, son of Rabbi Shalom Gombiner, Rabbi of Lissa in the year 1671. His brother Reb Judah Gombiner of Cracow went especially to Amsterdam in order to publish the Commentary but he died on the way and the manuscript was lost.

[Page 93]

After the death of Reb Abbele, his son Reb Hayyim set out to seek for the manuscript. The person holding it was commanded to return it by the Council of the Four lands. Two years later, the printer, Reb Shabtai Meshorer Bass, published the Commentary on his own account and it was printed in his press at Duerenfurth in 1692. There it was given together with the Shulkhan Arukh and the Commentary entitled: "Magen David" (Shield of David) written by Reb David Halevi of Lemberg, usually referred to as the "Turei Zahav" or TAZ. The name of the new Commentary was given as: "Magen Abraham"

(Shield of Abraham). Reb Abraham Abbele himself had called it "Ner Israel" (Light of Israel).

The publication of this new Commentary together with the already authoritative Commentary of the "Turei Zahav" immediately established the author of "Magen Abraham" as one of the leading Halachic Authorities of Poland and Germany. The rabbinic world began to respect him and accept his reasoning in their decisions. The Commentary is very succinct, clearly written, deeply logical and shows a consistency of thought. It deals with the customs of East European Jewry which were not mentioned by Reb Moshe Isserlein in his work: "Darkei Moshe", whereby the originally Sephardic Shullhan Arukh was adapted to the needs of the Ashkenazic Jewry. For this reason, we are not going too far if we claim that after Reb Moshe Isserlein, the Magen Abraham became the most widely accepted Halachic Authority in Poland.

So succinct was he in presenting his thoughts and views that Reb Shlomo of Cologne found it necessary to write an elucidation entitled: "Mahtsit Hashekel" (The Half-Shekel) which serves to complement the major work.

Reb Abraham Abbele also wrote a Commentary on the Midrashic Collection Yalkut Shimoni which he entitled: "Zayit Raanan" (Fresh Olive, printed in Dessau in 1704); a Commentary on several Talmudic Tractates of the Order Nzeikin (Amsterdam 1771) and sermons on certain weekly section of Genesis called "Shemen Sasson" (Oil of Gladness) which were published by his son-in-law Reb Isaac Meir Kaufman, Rabbi of Kutno.

Reb Abraham Abbele also wrote religious hymns which were recited in the Kalish Synagogue during his lifetime. Two of these hymns were published in his son-in-law's own books of commentaries but did not win the heart of the Congregation. They lacked religious poetic inspiration and the poetic language found among other hymn writers, and has, therefore been forgotten.

After a prolonged illness, Reb Abbele passed away on 15th Adar 5443 (1683) when he was not yet fifty years old. In his will, he left instructions that nothing more than his name and the name of his Commentary should be engraved on his tombstone.

The beginnings of our Old Cemetery go back to the year 1287. On the height within it lie buried the outstanding rabbis of Kalish and their disciples who are known as the Sages of Kalish. There the grave of the Magen Abraham was also placed. At the head is a simple stone bearing the legend: "Here lies Reb Abraham Abbele, son of Reb Hayyim Halevi, the Magen Abraham". This inscription was recently restored by the town scholar Weltsman. On the 250th anniversary of his passing, it would be proper to fence in the tomb of this holy and humble scholar and authority.

Kalish Leben, 9(79): 19th Adar I 5689, 1-3-1929

[Page 94}

The Gaon Reb Abbele Harif

by Mordechai Weiss

Reb Abbele Harif (the Keen-minded) was born in Lask in 1738 and was a member of a distinguished family. He served as Rabbi of Kalish for 42 years. Details of his period of office have not been preserved but on the other hand, there are several legends about his first year as rabbi.

The rabbinical chair of Kalish was far-famed. Rabbis who assumed office there had all had outstanding careers elsewhere. In spite of this, Reb Abbele Harif was elected to the post in 1767 at the age of 29 and had never exercised his rabbinical authority anywhere else.

There are various legends as to how he came to be elected. Here we shall only quote those that seem the likeliest.

Reb Abushel Lisser, Rabbi of Frankfurt, married a second wife in his old age. This was the daughter of Reb Nahum, one of the magnates of Lask. In the year 1767, a major dispute began between Reb Abushel and other rabbis regarding his approval of a divorce. Owing to this dispute, the Rabbi of Frankfurt became known throughout the Jewish world. In the course of that year, Reb Abushel returned from Lask, passed through Kalish and spent a few days there. The communal worthies entreated him to suggest a suitable candidate for the vacant rabbinical office. The rabbi recommended Reb Abbele, a youthful resident of Lask whom he had recently met. The leaders of the community accepted his counsel, prepared a Certificate of Appointment as Rabbi and sent two sages with it to Lask.

When the emissaries came to Reb Abbele's home, they hesitated to offer him the document for they could not imagine that such a young man should be worthy and fitting to become their rabbi. However, no sooner did they begin discussing Torah with him that they realised that Reb Abushel had been correct. When they told Reb Abbele why they had come, he refused to believe them until they presented the Certificate of Appointment to him. His wife also could not believe them until they left a large sum of money with her in order that she should be able to clothe all the members of her family in a fashion worthy of the Kalish Rabbi. In any case, Reb Abbele requested them not to say anything about his appointment in Lask in order that no mocking remarks should be made.

[Page 95]

Kalish welcome the new rabbi with much pomp and circumstances but the veteran scholars decided that they would not permit him to assume office on account of his youth. They, therefore, decided to heckle him with Halachic questions during his initial sermon until he would be so confused that he would not be able to answer them and would leave the City in shame.

However, Reb Abbele answered all their questions. As soon as he realised that these were not intended for purposes of clarification or for the sake of Heaven, but the men asking them were trying to trick him and trap him he said to one of the hecklers: "May the Lord cut off all smooth-speaking lips" and immediately began giving a sermon on matters connected with the Temple and Levitical purity which are not frequently studied whereupon all the scholars grew perfectly silent. And indeed, Reb Abbele completed his sermon very successfully and his appointment as Rabbi was confirmed. As for the man to whom Reb Abbele had applied the verse quoted above, he perished that very year; and this brought the awesome power of Reb Abbele home to them all.

However, there were still opponents to him. Reb Mordechai Parnass wanted one of his kinsmen to obtain the post and plotted against the rabbi. Reb Abbele, however, had a wealthy kinsman in Plotzk, a great scholar known as Reb Itshele. The latter wrote to Reb Hayim Parnass requesting him to cease persecuting the rabbi and enclosing a gift – a currency note of one hundred roubles. After that Reb Mordechai Parnass began visiting the rabbi and indeed became his friend.

When Purim came around, Reb Mordechai sent the hundred rouble currency note to the rabbi as a Purim gift. Neither Reb Abbele nor his wife knew much about currency notes. She went out next day to do her market purchases and paid with the note. However, the shopkeepers could not find change for this huge sum and they wondered how such a treasure could have reached the rabbi. The rabbi's wife swiftly returned home and told him what had happened. Reb Abbele feared that there might be some hint of bribery in this gift and at once sent to summon Reb Mordechai. The latter told him where the note came from and refused to take it back. Reb Abbele then sent it back to his kinsman.

In due course, the rabbi and Reb Mordechai Parnass made a match between their children. The kinsman of Plotzk then sent back another hundred rouble note, this time as a wedding gift to the young couple.

Reb Abbele Harif passed away in 1809 after having served as Rabbi of Kalish for 42 years. To this day, his name is mentioned with the utmost respect. And there are some who say: From Reb Abraham Abbele (The Magen Abraham) to Reb Abraham Abbele (Harif) there was none like Reb Abraham Abbele.

Kalish Leben 25 (107); 8th Elul 5689. 13-9-1929

[Page 96]

Rabbi Hayyim Eliezer Wachs

by M. Kalishai

Reb Hayyim Eliezer Wachs was generally known among the Jewish population by the name of his scholarly work: "Nefesh Hayya". (A Living Soul). The story of his life and his public stand and struggles display a natural leader who did not enclose himself within the four ells of Jewish law but lived a full and entire life and was strict rather than lenient. Some interesting information about him is found in the volume of reminiscences: "Poland" by the Yiddish journalist J.J. Trunk, the great-grandson of Rabbi Joshua Trunk, teacher of Nahum Sokolow who was famed throughout East European Jewry as Reb Shiele Kittner (i.e. of Kutno).

The fame of the "Nefesh Hayya" in Poland did not actually come from the genius displayed in the work but from its enlightened approach. The great rabbis of Poland were familiar only with the four ells of Jewish law and were not particularly well versed in everyday affairs. They lived simple lives after the fashion of scholarly teachers. This was not the case with the "Nefesh Hayya" who used to run his household after the fashion of the wealthy. He belonged to a rich family that came from Galicia and introduced this wealthy and enlightened style of life to the casual and rather impoverished atmosphere of the world of the Polish rabbis and Hassidic Tsadikim. This made a tremendous impression. He also sent his daughters to school. They could speak German and Polish and could read Schiller and Mickiewicz. The spoiled and prideful girls played the part of grand ladies rather than daughters of a rabbi and there was nothing in common between them and a simple Jewess like our saintly Aunt Saraleh. The rabbi of Kalish married off his children to the families of wealthy Polish Hassidim like Reb Isaiah Prives, Reb Jacob Engelman and Reb Itshe Blass.

"The rabbi of Kalish lived in a fine dwelling and lived the life of a wealthy man rather than in the usual style of the rabbi. He planted a flower garden in front of his house and went out every morning to tend the fine and beautiful roses which he grew. This was very exotic for a rabbi in Poland. There was something of a Jewish nobleman about him.

"He dedicated himself to the resettlement of Eretz Israel, according to the conceptions and possibilities of his period. He very much desired to improve the charity-ridden approach to the Haluka (collection and distribution of Funds for the Jews of Jerusalem, Hebron, Safed and Tiberias). He used to encourage wealthy supporters in Warsaw to build houses in Jerusalem. Since the constructive purposes of the rabbi were not sufficiently clear, these houses finally fell into the hands of the Haluka authorities. His plans for settlement in Eretz Israel were more modern than those of other Polish rabbis. He approved of Jewish settlement in the country.

"In Poland itself he did his effective best to convince his fellow Jews that at the Sukkot Festival they should only use the citrons of the Land of Israel. For some reason, the Polish rabbis did not approve of the citrons from the Holy Land. In their opinion, the Korfu citrons were more fully suitable (Kosher) for fulfilling the festival commandments. The Hassidic Rabbi of Gur, who afterwards wrote the work "Sefat Emet" (True Speech), was particularly unenthusiastic about the Eretz Israel citrons as was Reb Gershon Henech, the rabbi of Radzin who fought a bitter fight against the rabbi of Kalish on this account and wrote a polemic on the subject.

[Page 97]

The Rabbi of Kalish set out to defend his citrons with a lengthy "Teshuva" (Responsum) which is printed at the beginning of his work 'Nefesh Hayya'. But since the Rabbi of

Radzin knew only how to fight in a savage and insulting polemic style, the legal and theoretical differences of opinion were swiftly transformed into savage animosity.

The Rabbi of Radzin engaged in coarse and personal attacks on the Rabbi of Kalish, his fine living rooms and his roses. He claimed that all such rich men's habits belonged to the things proscribed under the rule that Jews should not follow the practices of non-Jews. He objected to the fact that the Rabbi's daughters were learning foreign languages and above all, that non-Jewish servant-girls were to be found in his home.

This opposition to non-Jewish servant-girls was a favourite theme of his. He wrote a long Teshuva on this in savagely polemic style including cruel and bitter attacks on Reb Hayyim Eliezer Wachs, the Rabbi of Kalish. This Responsum was also printed. Matters reached the point where the aristocratic Aunt Shifra-Mirel, who was his second wife, came in tears to her father and begged him not to permit the Rabbi of Radzin ever to enter his home again. That is, the home of her father Reb Shiele whom the Rabbi of Radzin often used to visit as a kinsman and friend.

The highly regarded and aristocratic Rabbi of Kalish had to leave the city for the following reason: Kalish was a frontier centre near Germany and contained many wealthy and progressive 'Maskilim' (Enlightened Jews). Berlin breezes began to blow in the city and the Maskilim wished to 'reform' the synagogue by placing the bema beside the Holy Ark and not in the centre of the building. The Rabbi of Kalish was sharply opposed to this. Finally, the Berlin-style reformers took the tried and tested means of deciding such disputes; namely: they found an excuse for denouncing the rabbi to the District Governor. The 'Nefesh Hayya' had to leave Kalish and move to Warsaw. Since he was known to be familiar with daily affairs and business problems, the richest Jews of Warsaw began to submit their business disputes to him for adjudication according to the Torah (Din Torah).

In Warsaw as well, he lived in a fine dwelling and ran his household in a lordly fashion. In due course he was elected Rabbi of Piotrkow.

Reb Hayim Eliezer Wachs was born in Tarnogrod in the Lublin District in the year 1822. He studied with the leading scholars of the day but followed his own course. One of the things that characterized him was that he never went to the Courts of any of the Hassidic Wonder-Rabbis. His second wife was the daughter of Rabbi Israel Joshua Trunk, the rabbi of Kutno who was one of the leading men of his generation in Poland and who was widely known as Reb Shiele.

When he was about forty years old, he became Rabbi in Kalish after having served as rabbi in Tarnogrod for twenty years. It was he who had the New House of Study constructed and gathered scholarly householders around him. He taught in the Kalish Yeshiva and handled rabbinical affairs firmly, not submitting to the Wardens and holders of vested interests (Takkifim). When he introduced the Eruv in the year 1878 (and thus permitted the carriage of necessary objects within the Jewish Quarter on the Sabbath), the Christians found it an excuse for riots. (See the article on the 1878 Riots and the story of the Eruv). He initiated regulations to encourage modesty of clothing and behaviour at festivities.

[Page 98]

But his national activities deserve a chapter to themselves. Apart from the Israel citrons which were a central issue in his life, he supported the Warsaw Polish Kolel (Community in the Land of Israel) and did much for it. He visited Eretz Israel himself in 1866.

His work 'Nefesh Hayya' is a collection of Responses on the four sections of the Shulhan Arukh which is the standard codification governing the life of modern orthodox Jewry. His work displays his deep knowledge and independence in the interpreting of Jewish law.

He became Rabbi of Piotrkow in 1882 and held that office until his death. He passed away in 1889 in the vicinity of Kalish and was buried in that city.

Rabbi Ezekiel Liebshitz

by A. K.

Rabbi Ezekiel Liebshitz was born in a small town of the Kovno District. His father, Reb Hillel Elijah, of blessed memory, was rabbi first of Suwalk and later of Lublin. Even in his youth, Reb Ezekiel was known to be an enlightened prodigy. He learnt several European languages and was ordained rabbi at an early age. Blessed with a clear and sharp mind, he studied incessantly and was, therefore, at home in world literature as well.

He began his rabbinical career at Yarburg in Latvia then proceeded to Boisk in Courland and later to Plotzk. From there he came to Kalish where he was rabbi for 25 years. He achieved renown in the rabbinical world with his work "Hamidrash vehamaaseh" (Theory and Practice). Large communities such as St. Petersburg, Tel-Aviv and London requested him to be their rabbi but he remained faithful to Kalish.

He served as President of the Rabbinical Association of Poland. This enabled him to take steps towards solving the grave problem of *agunot* (forsaken wives who cannot obtain a divorce under Jewish law). For this purpose he visited the U.S. where he was received by President Calvin Coolidge.

Rabbi Liebshitz was an outstanding Lover of Zion and was in constant touch with Rabbi Kook, of blessed memory and saintly memory. When the Jewish Agency for Palestine was established in 1929, he joined as a representative of non-party Observant Jewry and was elected a member of the Presidium at the Constituent Session. He was an ardent supporter of "Totzeret Haaretz" (all products manufactured or produced in Eretz Israel). During the final years of his life, he published an ardent Appeal in the world Jewish press calling for the use of Eretz Israel citrons rather than those from Corfu. He passed away in Adar II, 5692 (Spring 1932) at the age of 73.

[Page 99]

From the Memorial Notes of M. Carmel:

Reb Yehzkiel Liebshitz was an exceedingly deliberate person. It seemed as though he weighed and measured each word before he uttered it. His pleasant Lithuanian pronunciation sounded like fine poetry. A tributary of the Prosna flowed along the street in which he lived and trees grew on the bank. It was the rabbi's practice to take a walk in their shade every afternoon and his attendant, Moshe Baruch, would accompany him. All who passed, whether Jews or non-Jews, were enchanted by the spell of his personality. For indeed, he was honoured by all. His wisdom was accepted by all and people came for his advice on all serious problems whether private or public.

...When my father put on his Sabbath garb and took me to the Rabbi's home, I did not yet know the truth. Only when we arrived there did I learn that Reb Itshe Podaretzki had carried home the rabbi who had suffered a heart attack and had summoned physicians. But they came too late.

[Page 100]

In the large room the tables had been pushed aside. The rabbi lay on a poor straw mattress covered in black with large candles burning at his head. At the side sat women sewing the shrouds.

...The great synagogue was full to overflowing with all the three storeys of the Women's section and the galleries around. There was tense silence charged with grieving honour. It seemed as though the glass of the ancient candelabra was vibrating. The same silence used to be felt in the synagogue on the Great Sabbath (before the Passover) when Rabbi Ezekiel Liebshitz used to deliver his sermon which was a delicate fabric of deep thought and sarcastic remarks about communal worthies and affairs. The congregation would hold its breath in order not to miss a word he said. He used to speak and pause while a deep sigh of weariness would leave his lips; the weariness of one who bore the weight of the whole life and problems of the congregation.

Now his gentle voice will no longer be heard; only sorrow and sighing and bitter weeping and mourning ....

Torah and Prayer

by Aryeh Bornstein

I do not claim to indicate the full range of religious life in the city but merely to raise a memorial to several outstanding centres of Torah and prayer and tell a little about Torah students.

In a separate wing of the Great Synagogue was the House of Study of the "Magen Abraham". Householders prayed there all week round and also studied their daily passage of the Talmud. On the second storey were the lads and young men who studied on their own. Some of them studied all day long and were supported by their parents while others studied together in a group after the day's work. Every year they elected a committee of their own headed by their most mature members. Up there they also had at their disposal the Library containing all the relevant Torah and rabbinical literature. It was the largest in town and all who studied Torah made use of it. The after-work study was organized by Aryeh Knoblevitch, who passed away in Israel, Mordechai Roy and others. About four hundred young men participated in it.

The older of the young men used to guide and instruct the youngsters, all on a volunteer basis. When it came to the study of Torah, both the Hassidim and the Mitnagdim, who were opposed to Hassidic practices, took part on an equal footing.

The Magen Abraham Yeshiva was housed in the rooms over the House of Study. This Yeshiva was established by the young men themselves, headed by Pinhas Goldberg and Mordechai Kaperman. Boys studied there from the age of 11 until they were capable of studying on their own, after which they went over to the House of Study. About 100-150 pupils attended the Yeshiva. At its peak, the Head of the Yeshiva was Reb Mendel Wechsler.

[Page 101]

Reb Idel Traube founded and conducted the Etz Hayyim Yeshiva for more than twenty-five years. The Yeshiva Committee was headed by Reb Ezekiel Liebshitz. The Yeshiva Heads were Reb Hersh Yehuda Mamlok and Reb Katriel Stein, who are still with us. The committee maintained the Yeshiva thanks to contributions of members and individuals and did not collect any tuition fees. Students without means from small country towns used to eat on different days with various householders. There were Jews who preferred to pay money instead.

The Hassidim were concentrated in Shtieblech. Most of them were Hassidim of the Rebbe of Gur who had about ten Shtieblech in town. About thirty prayer quorums used to pray in succession in the two largest and from three to five in the smaller ones.

There was also a centre for Alexander Hassidim with several hundred in the congregation. The permanent warden there was Reb Moshe Wolf Traube. Then there were the Piltz Hassidim of several score only; the Skiernevitz Hassidim numbering between a hundred to hundred and fifty; the Hassidim of Strykow, of Radomsk and of Sochaczow, each with their own congregations.

There was the Society for the Study of the Mishna (Hevrat Mishnayot). Householders used to pray in the New House of Study. The Hassidic Rebbe of Zychlin and the Rebbe of Wola also lived in the city.

In addition, there was a branch, in actual fact a Contributing Committee of the famed Yeshiva of the Sages of Lublin. Its members were: Rev Velvel Mozes, David Perle, Shlomo Jarecki, J.M. Heber and Arieh Bernstein, secretary.

A particularly impressive occasion was the meeting of the Jews of the city after evening prayers on the Eve of the New Year at the crossing of the Nowa and Ciasna Streets when it was the custom for them all to wish one another a good New Year.

The Cantors of Kalish

by E. Krotianski

Kalish was highly respected for its synagogue Hazanim (cantors) and music. Not because there were so many cantors, on the contrary. During the last century there were only four or five cantors in the two principal synagogues. For it was the local practice to engage a cantor for life.

The old synagogue-goers still remember that the series began with Reb Srolke, a Lithuanian leader in prayer and scholar of impressive appearance. Some of the older folk still remember his works which were all impromptu, that is, sung spontaneously as he stood at his post. These melodies were not written down. In his old age he left to join his children in Eretz Israel.

Reb Srolke was followed in Kalish by Reb Noah Zaludkowski who possessed a powerful and lyrical baritone. He was an outstanding musician and great scholar. His prayers and choral singing used to arouse the congregation, particularly at the High Holidays. His "Avoda" on the Day of Atonement was famed far beyond Poland. From him we learnt his compositions and songs for four voices. He himself conducted the choir and usually sang his own works which were "stolen" by other cantors. After Kalish was burnt by the Germans during World War I, Reb Noah served as chief cantor in Rostow on the Don. When the war was over, he came back and remained in Kalish until his death. For 45 years, he prayed before the Ark in the Great Synagogue which had no regular cantor after his death because it was difficult to select a worthy successor.

[Page 102]

Kalish also had a modern synagogue in the Western style which was built by the wealthy local Jews in 1912. At the time, it had about thirty members with Raphael

Frenkel as chairman. The members included local Jewish magnates such as Dr. Zucker, Markus Holtz, Alexander Preger, Adam Schreier, Herman Gurny and Isaac Meisner. This was a lofty synagogue and was official known as "The New Synagogue" but Kalish Jewry named it "Die Deutsche Schul". In Russia a synagogue of that kind was called a Choir Synagogue. The building had the form of a little Temple, as in Berlin. It contained a large harmonium which the townsfolk called the "organ". The Hassidim boycotted it and held that Jews were forbidden to pray there.

Cantor Noah Zaludkowski   **Cantor Shlomo Kupfer**

The "Germans" soon advertised for a cantor. Before long they invited Shlomo Kupfer, the best student at Abraham Birnbaum's School for Cantors. He was a little man with an echoing and lyrical tenor. In his recitatives, the tones were weighed and measured and always fitted within the setting laid down by his great master.

The question of a conductor for the choir promptly arose. The Synagogue warden asked: "Why do we need a conductor? Mr. Cantor, don't you have hands?" And Kupfer had to explain that while the choir stood above and the cantor below there had to be a conductor between them, using his hands. Nor was that all. The conductor had to train the choir. Thereupon, an advertisement for the post of conductor was issued. The writer of this article, Elimelech Krotianski, who is the son of a famous cantor, was invited to conduct the choir. I set up a large choir of over twenty singers, men and boys. The outstanding soloists were Moshe Golombek, first tenor and now in America; Leizer Traube, first baritone; Isaac Bordowitch, alto; Welvel Tennenbaum, bass; Gershon

Messer, soprano and Wachtel, alto. These laid the foundations of the New Synagogue Choir.

The question of the repertoire also arose. The "Germans" desired the works of Lewandowsky. It stood to reason. If this was a German-style Synagogue, then the works of a Berlin conductor should be sung. However, Kupfer, who was a devoted follower of Birnbaum and Seltzer, wished that their works be heard. I myself came from the vicinity of Odessa, Yekaterinoslaw and Kiev and was very fond of Nowokowski, Dynayewski and Minkowski. I even made it a condition with Kupfer that if he did not include two pieces by Dunayewski in the service, he could go and find himself another conductor. Finally, we had to sing some of the works of all the above in order to satisfy everybody.

[Page 103]

However, I was not satisfied with my synagogue work alone and desired a wider field of action. With the aid of music lovers such as Mrs. Merantz, Mrs. Kletchevsky, Mr. Hammer, Mr. Ahronowitch (now Arnold), Mr. Leib Wolkowitch, etc. I succeeded within a single year in setting up two large mixed choirs. There was the Sports Club with 30 vocalists and the Choir of the Bund and Poalei Zion Members. Alongside the Sports Club, a Brass Band with twenty-five players was also established. In preparation for the opening of the "Hazamir" Society initiated by the banker Landau and Handwurzel, a String Orchestra was also established. Unfortunately, the District Governor dispersed the Society after the first concert as he refused to issue a permit for a Musical Society in the Hebrew language. In spite of this, the Hazamir Society organized several concerts at which extracts from the works of the classic composers were held. There were passages from Handel's oratorios, Handel's Halleluiah Chorus, Haydn's works, Mozart's Requiem, etc. Indeed, those years were full of musical activity in Kalish and song and melody could be heard in the Jewish streets. Those who could not afford a piano played the violin or the mandolin – but they all played.

Let us return to the cantors. After the death of Reb Noah Zaludkowski, the Great Synagogue remained without any cantor for a long time. After several auditions, a young man named Israel Boniufka, with a good tenor voice and a sound musical sense, who himself conducted a choir, was invited. From time-to-time he would sing Lewandowsky's "Lecho Dodi" and Sirota's "Retzeh" and would close with a finale by Koussevitsky.

Now began the competition between the synagogues. Two rival groups began to crystallize: the "Jews" and the "Germans". One party claimed that all the geniuses belonged in the "Jewish" synagogue while the other claimed the opposite. If you wished to hear a fine "Lecho Dodi" or a "Kedusha" with a finale in C – the highest possible – you would go to the German Synagogue. The dispute reached a point where Rabbi E. Liebschitz was told that women were singing in the German synagogue choir. He promptly ordered that the women should be sent away; but there was nobody to send. However, Cantor Bonofka did not stay long in Kalish. He wished to pray in a "modern" synagogue. Heaven helped in this and in 1933 he was called to pray in the New Synagogue in Lodz in place of Alterman. Thereupon, the competition between the two Kalish synagogues vanished as though it had never occurred.

Once again Kalish was left without a cantor. However, the German synagogue was also left without a cantor, though for different reasons. A strange epidemic spread among those who prayed there and they perished one after the other within a few years. The only ones left were Shimon Preger and Moritz Friedman. Cantor Kupfer was a realist. He understood that there was no sense in exhausting his throat for "Germans" who were already at rest, so he made his way to Leipzig and left German Jews for by this time he had achieved a reputation thanks to the records in which he effectively imitated Yossele Rosenblatt. From Leipzig, he made his way to Manchester where he is to be found until the time of writing. Not long ago, he wrote to me that the high C was still functioning in his throat.... After Kupfer left, the Synagogue Choir also came to an end. In due course, the Cantor Israel Kowalsky was engaged but served only for a short while and then went to England.

[Page 104]

Once again there was a cantorial competition at the Great Synagogue. Many hazanim came for auditions. Three came for one Sabbath. One was given the Eve of Sabbath Prayers, a second the Morning Prayers and a third the Additional Prayers. There were numerous gay occasions. One week the cantor Mottel Schwarzenberg arrived and remained another week for the High Holidays. The congregation took a liking to him and the competition was over. However, he never prayed without a choir. Negotiations about a conductor began again and after prolonged discussions I was summoned to conduct the choir.

The Hassidim protested vehemently against appointing a conductor of the Germans. Was it possible that a godless fellow, who for eighteen years had been a conductor in a synagogue with an organ, should enter the synagogue of the Magen Abraham? (Truth to tell, the harmonium was played only on Hanukkah and Purim and during vacation periods.) However, Noah Hiller, the vice-chairman announced at a meeting that the Hassidim were the very people whose duty it was to transform the godless one into a fit and proper Jew and they accepted his argument.

Now began Sabbaths that were really concerts. On Friday evenings, the synagogue was full from wall-to-wall. There was something new in having a conductor in the synagogue and above all in the music. On Sabbath Eve they could hear the works of Zeidel Rovner – "Emes Ve-emuno" and on Sabbath mornings came "Borikh Shemeih".

Unhappily, these were the final Sabbaths. On the New Moon of Elul 5699, September 1939, World War II broke out and destroyed both synagogues of Kalish together with all its cantorial music which had flourished for almost a full one hundred years. If a son of Kalish now comes to the city, he would have to search hard in order to discover where the two synagogues once stood.

Kalish, October 1947

In the Yeshiva

by Shlomo Yehiel Nobel

I can still picture before my eyes Kalish as it was from 1908 to World War I – Kalish of the Jews with the Jewish Street. On the one side was the House of Study of the Magen Abraham, of blessed and saintly memory, in Grabski Street. It had two floors. On the ground floor was a Prayer Hall where hundreds of Jews of all sections of the community used to pray. On the first floor was a large Study Hall – a true Bet HaMidrash, or House of Study seating about 300 young fellows of all ages – from thirteen to early twenties. They studied there from morning until late at night and their voices could be heard afar. On the other side was the New Study House.

In addition to the House of Study which I have mentioned, there was a Yeshiva with four classes. The head of our Yeshiva was Reb Yehiel Lasker whose Pupils used to make his life a misery with all kinds of tricks. The manager of the Yeshiva was Reb Yudel Traube who used to devote himself to his work from morning until late at night. He regarded us as his children because he had none of his own. His wife used to treat us very affectionately when we came to his home on Friday in order to receive slips instructing us to whom we were to go on Sabbath for examination in our week's studies; and on Sundays when we brought back the slips with the marks.

[Page 105]

The Jubilee of the Eruv

by M. Ben Menahem

The Story of a Pogrom

The Eruv we have in town is now all that it should be according to Jewish law and practice; and it is almost always in proper order. This is due to the watchful activities of three or four people who constitute a committee for the purpose. But, in the past, the Eruv led to a bitter quarrel between Jews and Christians. On the Jubilee of the Eruv, let us record what happened then.

Fifty years ago, the Rabbi of Kalish was the scholarly Gaon Reb Hayyim Eliezer Wachs who was honoured and esteemed by all. One of the matters to which he devoted himself was the establishment of an Eruv in town. Dozens of meetings were held in this connection. Everybody wanted to help the rabbi somehow in this holy task but the poverty of the community caused the matter to be deferred for a very long time. However, at length, the actual sketching and construction of the Eruv began. The Rabbi himself supervised the execution. When no more pillars were available, the Rabbi called on the wood merchants who responded favourably.

Work continued for months. The Eruv was spread around the urban area s it then existed: from the "Rogatka" as it was then called, beside the Christian Hospital as far as the bridges across the Stawiszin and Turek Streets. It was completed around midsummer of 1878.

In those days the Russian authorities tried to frighten the Poles away from politics. Those, after all were the years following the second Polish revolt. So they decided to exploit the Eruv for their own base purposes.

Within a few days the rumour spread among the Polish population that the Eruv was a piece of witchcraft. The rumour was spread by Russian agents. Reb Hayyim Eliezer Wachs, they claimed, had surrounded the whole city with an iron wire so as to bring the entire Christian population within the field of operation of the witchcraft. Oil was poured onto this fire of incitement against the Jews by the evidence of the wife of the Christian physician, Remarkevitz, who claimed that she had seen Jews throwing stones at a passing Christian woman. The doctor's wife was telling the truth but this was a Russian provocation. The supposed Jew was a disguised Russian provocateur.

[Page 106]

On Sunday, 3rd July 1878, when the Christians went to church, the priests delivered sermons of incitement against the Jews, particularly against the Rabbi and the Eruv served as the excuse. When the Christians left the church they proceeded to the Jewish Quarter in masses and began to riot.

They began thrashing every Jew who came their way – they pillaged Jewish property and wrought destruction in the Synagogue and Jewish Hospital. When they finished all of this, they gathered around the home of the Rabbi. Here, however, they met with the effective resistance of the House of Study students, headed by Tratel Green the butcher. The crowds had to withdraw.

Three Jewish children were killed in these riots while many grown-ups were injured while defending life, limb and property. It was estimated that goods to a value of more than 100,000 roubles were looted and stolen.

The Russian authorities in Kalish, who had planned and executed this fine piece of work, were very satisfied at the results but concealed the whole incident from the knowledge of the Colonel of Hussars who was a liberal and would undoubtedly have protested against the whole proceedings. And sure enough, as soon as he did learn about the pogrom he came to the town at the head of his regiment and put an end to this dreadful game. At his order, the Hussars placed many Heder children on their saddles to save them from the crazy crowd and to bring them to their homes.

Against their will, the Russian authorities had to approve of his actions and round off his humane measures. They imposed a fine of 120,000 roubles on the Christian population of Kalish and the vicinity.

However, the late Reb Hayyim Eliezer had to resign his rabbinical office in Kalish on account of the incident. That was the beginning and the end of the Eruv Pogrom in Kalish fifty years ago.

A Pogrom in Kalish in 5638 (1878)
(another version)

by M. Menahemai

The Jews of Kalish have had plenty of trouble during recent years and new trouble makes one forget old trouble. Little-by-little, the history of the city is being forgotten. The old folk depart without recording what happened to them and maybe they do not wish to tell their children about the troubles they saw. In either case, a large part of the history of Kalish, where every joy is mixed with tears, is being forgotten.

We shall describe on such incident fifty years after it happened. This was on the Christian Green Festival one Sunday in 1878. A tremendous crowd of Christians from the city and all around gathered to pray in the churches of Kalish. Their priests had summoned them in particular to gather on this Sunday and prophesized that there would be great events.

[Page 107]

The clergymen ordered platforms to be erected in the city squares, in order to be able to preach to the crowds who were waiting for them. But nobody knew what was liable to happen. So early in the morning believers in crowds began flowing to the City and gathering at the Churches and round the platforms in the open air. After prayers were over the priests mounted the platforms and in their sermons ordered the crowd to go and pillage the Jews. Nobody knows what the excuse for this incitement was, to this day. Some claim that it had some connection with a Liberation Movement of sorts in Poland. In any case the Order was carried out at once. A mob of more than 10,000 began dashing down into the Jewish Quarter with clenched fists, yelling all kinds of curses at the Jews.

With particularly savage rancour part of the mob burst into the Synagogue courtyard and broke open the doors. They dashed to the Holy Ark, where they began tearing Torah Scrolls. One of these had been written by the learned scholar who was the author of "Bet Yehudah." (The House of Judah). Many legends about this Torah Scroll were current among young and old in the City. The mob also smashed the Hanukka Lamp.

The Russian Army emerged from its aloofness at last, and made an end of the savage rioting of the heated mob.

This happened on 22nd Sivan. The local Rabbi, author of the "Nefesh Hayya", ordained a Fast in Kalish as a memorial for this Pogrom. Since many of the Torah Scrolls had been rendered unfit for use the Rabbi renewed the old Society known as "Tikkum Sofrim" (Corrections by Scribes) whoe first task was to engage in the restoration of the Torah Scroll written by "Bet Yehudah."

These events were recorded in the proceedings of the Tikkun Sofrim Society by Reb Israel Yaffe, who was the Cantor of Kalish in those days.

Dos Kalisher Leben 13 (41); 20 Sivan 5688. 8-6-1928

A Blood Libel in Kalish

by Hanski

The evil minds of the infamous Endeks never cease. The bloodthirsty rabble-rousers who can find nothing too evil to defame the Jews whom they regard as a bone in their throat are reviving diabolical stories from the darkness of the middle Ages.

Issue No. 37 of the black journal "Samo-obrona" describes in lurid colours how Jews use Christian blood for religious purposes: First, two weeks in the year, the rabbi takes the blood of a murdered Christian child and smears it on the doors of Christian dwellings in order that those who dwell in them may feel kindly towards the Jews; second, a solemn ceremony is carried out at every Jewish wedding in which the rabbi gives the youthful pair an egg to eat which which has been dipped in Christian blood; third, the Jews smear the eyes of their dead with Christian blood; fourth, at Passover, the Jews eat matzo that has been kneaded with Christian blood. The name of this kind of matzah is "Afikoman"; fifth, in order that Jewish enterprises may be successful, they take a letter from the rabbi containing Christian blood-stains. They bury this letter in front of the home of a Christian and that is enough to ensure them a good living.

[Page 108]

The writer sets out to show that Jews are born, wed, do business and die thanks to the blood of Christians!

Undoubtedly we would have laughed at all this farrago of ignorance and stupidity which might suit a circus clown who wants to make his audience laugh. But instead of laughing, we have to think it over very seriously.

This filthy gutter-sheet is sold in tens of thousands of copies, particularly among the masses. It fills the villages and is sent to all parts of the country in order to incite the base instincts of the mob who regard the printed word as holy truth. What are the writers and disseminators aiming at? The demagogues of that party must certainly know what they are after.

We ask the Jewish members of the Municipality, all the community leaders, and our chairman: Do you intend not to react this time as well? Are you just going to sit and wait for these vipers' eggs to hatch? Can you not see the Hitlerist incitement? Must you wait for the fruit to ripen?

We appeal to all representatives of the Jewish public: Do what has to be done to end this devils' dance which may go on and grow to - - -

Poznan was a centre of anti-Semitism but thanks to the energetic measures taken by the Jews there the pogromist paper: "Poznanski Prengiez" was suspended and its editor sent to prison. We await your announcement about the steps that will be taken to eradicate this dangerous poison.

Dos Kalisher Leben 2 (331); 25 Tevet 5694. 12-1-34.

———————

Kalish as a Family Name

by Joseph Milner

Kalish Jews pride themselves on the Magen Abraham. It is true that he was born in Gombin, a small town near Warsaw where there were no more than about 400 Jews. But he spent his life in Kalish. The date of his birth and death are not precisely known, though according to the leading Jewish bibliographer Professor Moritz Steinschneider, he was born in 1636 and passed away in 1683.

His work, thanks to which he became known as "Magen Abraham" throughout the rabbinical world of Ashkenazic Jewry, was printed in Duerenfurth in Silesia at the then renowned press of Reb Shabtai Bass, who was also referred to as "Basista" and also "Meshorer Bass". This Shabtai Meshorer Bass was himself the first Jewish bibliographer. He was born in Kalish in 1641 and died in Krotschin in 1718. His parents were killed in the 1655 pogrom in Kalish and he found his way to Prague. There he became a "Meshorer" or leading choirsman supporting the cantor in the Altneu Schul Choir. His exceptional voice secured him the family name "Bass". He continued studying of his own free will and became one of the leading Jewish and general scholars of the region, achieving a reputation beyond the boundaries of Poland. Jewish and general scholarly circles in Germany, Holland and elsewhere evinced considerable interest in his bibliographical work. Christian orientalists translated his studies into German and Latin. He settled in Breslau and spent four years trying to obtain a permit for a printing press. In 1687 he opened his press in Duerenfurth, a small country town not far from Breslau. His books were veritable works of art and drew the attention of booklovers throughout the world, Jews and non-Jews alike. The Jesuits also began to take an interest in him and finally had him imprisoned for publishing Reb Nathan Hanover "Shaarei Zion" (Gates of Zion) which they regarded as anti-Christian. He brought up his son Joseph Bass to share his love of books and the son continued his father's lifework.

[Page 109]

Shabtai Meshorer Bass passed away in Krotoshin which was a centre of Jewish learning where the Magen Abraham also died. There were a group of hand-setters in this city who were among the most famous in Jewry. After the persecutions conducted against him, Reb Shabtai persuaded the Monish family to open a Hebrew press in the city which later became known throughout the world. The Monish family were closely related to Professor Heinrich Graetz. Before the latter achieved renown as a historian, he was a proof-reader at the Krotoschin press of his uncle Monish. Dr. Max Nordau also used to pride himself on being a descendent of this family.

All persons with the name "Kalisch" or Kalischer" are connected with Kalish in one way or another. These two surnames are common among the Jews of Germany. Many Kalish Jews migrated to Prussia by way of Posen. Those who migrated to Kiew were all called 'Kulisher' without exception.

There were many Kalish folk among the Jews of Germany and in the Lodz district of Poland as well. Bertha Kalisch was born in Lemberg and is the only Galician who bears this name. She was a Jewish actress in New York who played in Yiddish and successfully presented the plays of Jacob Gordin. David Kalisch was a well-known German humourist whose parents came from that city, though he himself was born in Breslau. Isidor Kalisch (1815-1886) was a German poet. Ludwig Kalisch (1814-1882) was a German writer and literary man. Markus Kalisch, a scientist who took part in the 1848 Revolution, had to seek refuge in England. His parents came from Kalisch and later moved to Treptow in Pomerania.

In the 17th century there was a Dr. Moshe Kalisch in Poland who left medical works written in the Judeo-German of the period. Isidor Kalisch was a rabbi in Cincinnati from 1857. He was an outstanding scholar of the period who published important works on Jewish subjects and achieved a considerable reputation in America.

[Page 110]

Rabbi Zvi Hirsch Kalischer was born in Lissa in 1815. He served as Rabbi in Torun where he died in 1884. Reb Yehuda Leib Sheindels (Kalisher) was also born in Lissa in 1807. His son Reb Akiva Kalischer was a Dayan in that city. Reb Yehiel Mechel Kalischer, who also wrote a work called "Shaarei Zion" lived in the 17th century. Alfred Kalischer, an authority on Spinoza, was a university lecturer (Privat Dozent) in Berlin. Salomon Kalischer of Torun was a physicist in Amsterdam around about 1878.

In Russia there was a well-known ethnographer, jurist and historian named Michail Kulisher who was born in Lutzk in 1847. His son Joseph was an authority on economics and his other son Evgeni was a criminologist. In Russia there were many Jews bearing the name 'Kulisher' including famous physicians and journalists.

The Jewish Press of Kalish

by A. K.

During the 20's, a number of weekly journals began to appear in many Polish cities including Kalish. Much material was lost during World War II. Here we shall summarize what is definitely known:

Kalish Blatt, weekly 1922. The first to appear, edited by H. Solnik. On three issues were published.

Das Kalisher Wort, weekly, edited by S. Stern. Three issues.

Kalisher Tog, daily, 1925. This did not last long.

Kalisher Weker, 1931, weekly. Four issues. Organ of the Bund. Dedicated to Kehilla elections. In 1937 a special issue was published dedicated to the 40th anniversary of the Bund.

Kalisher Express. A daily local supplement of the Warshaver Express. It did not last long.

Kalisher Leben, weekly edited (most of the time) by A.J. Mamlok. Published with some interruptions until World War II. This was under Agudat Israel influence.

Kalisher Woch, weekly. It appeared with interruptions until World War II. This was under Zionist influence.

———

[Page 111]

1904-1920

by Peretz Walter

Before the revolutionary years the younger generation did not engage in any social activity. Most of them used to work at various kinds of embroidery. After work or on holidays they all used to stroll around the Town Hall which contained the Army Club where the Military Band used to play.

In the years 1904-1905 the period of the First Revolution, things began to liven up. Political strikes were held in Kalish too and were led by the Bund, Poalei Zion, P.P.S and the Social Democrats. The Russian Authorities engaged in large-scale arrests of the strike leaders. Every Thursday morning, they used to send off a transport of arrested revolutionaries to Siberia. Heart-breaking scenes took place in the streets when mothers saw their sons being exiled. More than one Jewish revolutionary perished on the way or was buried in frozen Siberia.

In 1909 or 1910, the authorities permitted "Hazamir" singing and musical clubs to be established in Poland. The Kalish Society set up an orchestra and a choir. The Club had a fine hall for premises and infused a spirit of life in the Jewish youth who used to come, sing folksongs and play musical instruments.

In the years 1910-11 the "Yiddishe Turn und Sport Verein" Sports Society was established and awakened enthusiasm in the younger generation who were proud of their shirts and caps in the national colours. Most of the youngsters were members. I remember a ramble to Opatowek, a distance of 7 miles from the city. The sportsmen marched together in the national uniform and the non-Jews showed their respect for the proud Jewish youngsters. Preparations for the Sport Festival lasted a whole year and it was very successful. The entire population, Jews and non-Jews alike gathered to watch the competitions and exercises.

In the course of time, the Society became a Cultural Centre for Jewish Youth. A Hebrew and Yiddish library was established and lectures in Yiddish and Hebrew were given from time to time. The Society continued to function until World War I. The Russians left the city on 2nd August 1914. The Germans entered on Sunday. The Jews received them with white flags and in a friendly fashion. But the Germans displayed their cruelty even then. They began shooting in the streets at 6 p.m. and many Jews and Christians fell.

The following day Polish and Jewish reserve troops who had been mobilized but not called by the retreating Russian Forces, returned to the city. The Germans ordered them to lie down in the street and shot anyone who raised his head. On Tuesday morning, the Jews were ordered to open their shops and anybody who refused to do so was threatened with punishment. After the Jews obeyed orders, the Germans began shooting again. This dreadful situation continued for several days and there were many more victims. The Germans who had occupied Kalish came from Poznan (Posen). The Poles placed crosses on their windows.

On the Friday, the Jews opened their shops and the Germans shot into them.

[Page 112]

They took people out of their houses, placed them against the wall of the Municipality and shot them. Towards evening they left the city and bombarded it with artillery all night long. On the Sabbath morning, German patrols returned, collected men in the Breslau Street and took them out of the city. There they were lined up and were told that every tenth man would be killed.

The Jews began to run away from the city but all the streets and roads were packed with refugees. Now the German soldiers killed more Jews and pillaged the abandoned Jewish shops. After that, they set the city on fire.

Jews began to return to Kalish only after several months had passed. Many did not find their homes. The shops had been looted or burnt. Poverty and need were widespread. A Relief Committee organized a "Teal-Hall" at the Jewish School where tea was served to the returning refugees. Young Jews served as volunteers in this institution. The Jewish Aid Society in Germany supported this Tea-Hall and actually ensured its existence. By this time, the Jewish population were virtually starving. The Aid Committee established a communal kitchen where bread, soup and potatoes were provided free. Long files of men, women and children used to line up there.

In 1915-16 the Germans kidnapped young people in the streets for forced labour behind the lines. As a rule these were Jews. The weaker ones who did not have the strength to work were murderously beaten and many perished. My brother Abraham Jacob was one of the few who returned unharmed.

In 1916-17 the Germans again permitted the public organizations to function. The Sports Society also renewed its activities at the new hall in Wieska Street. Sports groups were re-established and the library was re-opened. Lessons in Yiddish and Hebrew were organized as well as scientific lectures. Once again the choir was established and a dramatic circle was founded and produced plays from time to time. The Society also participated in the Olympiad of all the Jewish Sports Societies in Poland which was held in Lodz. The political parties likewise began to reorganize, particularly the Bund and Poalei Zion. Most of the young Jews belonged to the Sports Society. The "Tea-Hall" was renamed the "Arbeiter Heim" (Workers' Home). Here lectures were given and a Consumers' Cooperative Store was opened for foodstuffs and kerosene and sold its goods cheaply. A Workers' Kitchen provided good meals at cheap prices. The Aid Society in America supported the kitchen.

After Poland became independent, we set up the Childrens' Home where the children learnt and studied. The Poalei Zion party was the largest among the Jews and gained most of the votes in the elections to the Seim and the Municipality. The Party Club was in the Workers' Home. The Bund had its own club and so did "Zukunft". Other parties included the Zeirei Zion, General Zionists, Folkists, etc. Among the Polish parties there were the Endeks, the P.P.S which had no Jewish members and the Polish Social Democrats.

Each party set up Trade Unions. The Communists began to organize the workers who were engaged in clearing the ruins of the city. Their club was in Weiland House in the Josephine Allée. Every evening, meetings and debates were held in the Club. The subjects were the Revolution, brotherhood, improving the state of the workers and better bread; for at the time, the bread contained a high proportion of straw. A few days before Purim 1919, a strike was proclaimed in order to achieve these demands. In the early morning, the strike could be felt in the air and everybody knew that the matter would not end peacefully.

[Page 113]

In the morning I opened our (sausage) shop in the Jewish street. At nine o'clock my mother came and said that near the Police Station she had seen the Police Chief, a well-known anti-Semite, sharing out cigarettes to the unskilled workers of the communist Society. This friendship between the chief of police and the workers made my mother suspect that something unpleasant was going to happen. I went to the Workers' Home where I learnt that the Communists intended to arrange a demonstration but the P.P.S. was refusing to participate. The demonstration was to begin at 10 a.m. and would pass through the New Market and Ciasna Street, pausing at the Workers' Home because they wanted us to join the demonstration.

We promptly held a meeting to discuss the matter. Most of the members rejected participation because the P.P.S. was not taking part. The minority approved since the demands were exclusively economic, being for better bread, etc.

The demonstration began at the appointed time. When it passed the Workers' Home a number of members snatched the Poalei Zion flag on which revolutionary slogans were embroidered and went out to join. Other members also joined by themselves and so a group of the Poalei Zion marched in the communist demonstration. We sang revolutionary songs and many youngsters joined us on the way. The demonstration grew steadily bigger. When we passed through Ogrodowa Street near the Bund Club, they also joined. We marched on to the Gates of the Town Hall where the demonstration stopped and a representative of the communists gave a speech calling on the Mayor to improve the quality of the bread.

At this point we began to feel suspicious. During the speech many of the communist demonstrators vanished. They climbed onto the broken-down walls of the ruined hand-embroidery factory that had belonged to Meizner. When the speech ended, these ruffians began to throw stones at the Jews in the demonstration and beat their 'comrades' with long sticks. A panic began in our ranks, but we promptly understood that this was a provocation and that we had to go on marching. We reached Breslau Street and the building containing Burshin's cigarette shop where we saw a dreadful sight.

The ruffians attacked the Jews several of whom began to bleed at once. My companion Ragashinsky and I held fast to the flag which the rioters wanted to drag away from us. The flag fell to the ground for a moment. Two ruffians dashed to pick it up. I kicked one of them while Ragashinsky picked up the flag and ran away with it. Now I got the wooden stick out of the hands of the other ruffian and began to lay around with it on all sides, hitting them hard. I then started to run towards the Workers' Home. As I ran, a stone hit my head and leg. Blood began streaming over my face, but I continued to run. I suddenly saw a woman gatekeeper coming out of one of the houses and hitting a Jewish boy over the head with a wooden clog. I dashed over, plucked the wooden clog out of her hand and hit her over the head until she shrieked: "O Jesus". Nearby there was a Military hospital which had been a Commercial High School in the days of the Tsar. When the soldiers heard her shrieking, they came out and began chasing me. With the last of my strength, I reached the Bund Club where I hid in the attic. About an hour later, I dashed over to Havera Levitt who had a shoe shop and is now in Israel. She bandaged my hand and leg. Now I ran to the Jewish Street where I learnt that the ruffians had carried out a real pogrom. The policemen had "suddenly" vanished and the ruffians rioted without interference, looting shops and beating Jews.

[Page 114]

The next day the rioters tried again. They approached the Jewish butcher shops where they received what they deserved. The Jewish butchers were organized and went out to meet them with choppers and cleavers. There was a savage battle. One of the scoundrels was badly wounded but Moshe Anzel, son of a butcher, was stabbed to death. Joshua Rosenblatt was also severely wounded and later died of his wounds.

The riots continued for two days. The Polish press announced that the police had the Poalei Zion flag which bore revolutionary slogans against the Polish government. In this way, they wished to renew the riots. As remarked, the flag was in our hands.

The news of the riots startled the whole of Poland. The Jewish Deputies in the Seim submitted interpellations. A Committee of Seim Deputies was appointed to investigate the Kalish Pogrom. A few of the ruffians were given light punishments but the Police Chief who had organized the riots was not touched at all.

Two days after the riots, the first assistance of the Joint arrived. Baruch Zuckerman, representative of the "Peoples' Relief", reached Kalish. He lectured at the Workers' Home, calmed the Jews down, encouraged us and promised the assistance of America. The Kalish townsfolk in America also began to send help.

In those days the deputy, Dr. Rosenblatt of Lodz was in the U.S. as a representative of Polish Jewry. The Kalish townsfolk in New York gave him money to help the Jews of the city. At the time, all the Kalish townsfolk there had united in a joint committee which worked to help the Jews in their old home. This committee was joined by the Kalish Lodge, the Kalish Union and the Kalish Young Men's Arbeiter Ring, Branch No. 241.

In Kalish, a committee was elected for the fair distribution of these funds and I was appointed a member. We then received more than three thousand dollars from the United Relief Committee in New York and, in those days, it was a very considerable sum. The money arrived just before Passover and we distributed support for matzos and potatoes. We also allocated sums for the Jewish Hospital, the Old Age Home, the Rabbi's Yeshiva and the Children's' Home of the Poalei Zion and the Bund.

During those years, many attacks on Jews of the city were made by hooligans but the youth had learnt how to defend themselves and paid them back in their own coin.

Those are my memories until 1920 when I immigrated to America.

———

[Page 115]

The Clattering Machines (Extract)

by Simon Horonchik

The days and weeks dragged on, grey and heavy, like clouds bestrewn with spots which only faintly brightened on brief and lean Sabbaths.

Eizik Sheniak, a tallish fellow with a bent back who had taken Benjamin on to work as a threader, did have something good about him because he worked in the factory of Uncle Leib Hayyim, Benjamin could be sure of his weekly wage of several zloty. But, in all other respects, Sheniak was neither better nor worse than the average run of embroiderers. For a whole week he worked his hardest at the machine urging the threaders on and himself as well; toiling and busy from five o'clock in the morning until late at night. Before the Sabbath, he took the week's wage from the cashier, drank himself drunk on the Sabbath, wasted all his wages to the last farthing and came back to work on Sunday, fuming and angry, to start the race all over again.

Yes, he was no better than many other embroiderers, but no worse either.

The working day dragged on forever. The lamps had already been lit but it was still a long, long time before they finished. The hour grew later and later and the machine was already moving more slowly. The handle began to slip from the weary hands. The hands of the threaders were also as heavy as lead. Tirelessly, the fingers and eyes were closing by themselves. All their limbs were praying for rest.

Nearby, at the threading table, a girl was sleepily singing. In the middle of the day when the machines were clacking loudly, her song could not be heard at all. Now, with the more easy-going work of the late evening hours, a few words of her song could be caught from time to time. She was singing about the young men who had promised to write letters to her but did not keep their word.

> And remember how live did glow,
> And now it has gone out already –

The sad melody made something quiver inside Benjamin but he was so tired that his ear caught the notes indifferently – his heart did not respond at all and he wanted nothing but to be able to sleep.

Cold, turbid like winter rain after midmight, came some more of the girls' song.

> And remember how you promised
> Without a dowry me to wed.

By now the machines were keeping up a broken rhythm that seemed to support her, unlike their normal clatter in the daytime. At length, the work was done. Like all threaders, Benjamin removed the tools and parts, put out the lamps hanging above all sections of the machine and went home.

It was a clear winter night outside. His lungs had been breathing the dusty air of the factory all day long. Now they widened, deepened and he took long breaths while his eyes enjoyed the sight of the snow. Everything was while and the gas-lamps were burning. A solitary policeman wrapped up in his furs was pacing this way and that in the middle of the street.

[Page 116]

All of a sudden, Benjamin forgot the day that had passed so greyly and dustily amid the oil. The desire to live which had slumbered now woke up within him in a single instant and as though he wished to test his strength, he began to run. Not in order to get home more quickly but just for the pleasure of it. He was alive and he was young. Here he was, running like a foal, shaking his head and jogging his arms while the night watchman looked at him in astonishment.

The day was only beginning now at home after the work was over. Mother had prepared a herring for supper and all were eating it, slice by slice, with bread, gulping down tea at the same time. The little family sat around the table. His mother was praising little Simmeleh, telling how clever she was, bless her. She could be sent on errands to the shop and she bought whatever was needed and brought back the proper change.

Malka raised her head from the book she was reading so diligently. She told how something had gone wrong in their office today. A few cases of goods had been returned because of defects. Rosenblum, Uncle Leib Hayyim's partner in the factory, had raised hell.

Israel Noah, who was renowned as a nimble threader, asked Benjamin how he was getting on at work, whether he fell far behind the girl who was the head threader. Tranquilly and cheerfully, the family spent the evening together until Mother reminded them that it was time to go to bed.

But things were not always in order. Quite often, something disturbed the home. Mother, Simmeleh or somebody else became ill and expenses went up at once. Sometimes one of the embroiderers did not pay Israel Noah a fortnight's wage and the whole family promptly went short of food and fuel. They would all go to bed on half-empty stomachs and hunger would not permit them to fall asleep. In his restless slumber, Benjamin felt that he was now in the factory at the table with needles in front of him. He promptly felt afraid, wondering why his hands weren't busy. Thereupon, he began working, moving his hands as though he were threading the needles... It seemed as though Israel Noah also couldn't fall asleep on an empty stomach. He kept on waking up, then suddenly sat up in his bed and said drowsily in a frightened voice: "I must get up! Mother, what's the time?"

He then fell asleep again.

And just as though of set purpose, it was very cold indeed outside and the chill made its way through the thin walls of the miserable hut and took possession of it. The walls seemed to be covered by a layer of glass. The mother padded the bed next to the wall in advance with all kinds of clothes and oddities so that the children should not catch cold, God forbid!

At dawn when they had to get up, the room was so cold that all their teeth chattered. When they opened their mouths, their breaths formed a vapour just as though the cover were being taken off a boiling kettle. Mother gazed at the frozen window which looked as though some snow-white hairy skin had been stretched over it – a skin set with flashing diamonds. And the sighs left her lips, one after the other.

[Page 117]

Now the boys rose, dressed and wrapped themselves up in huge mantles that Malka had brought home for 'repair'. The mantles with their coarse unfinished embroidery were wrapped around their bodies several times. They put the lamp out; each took a chunk of bread left over from last night's super and went off to work.

Out in the open it might be the end of the world. There was a shrieking raging snowstorm, piling up heaps and heaps of snow-dust.

Benjamin and Israel Noah trudged along, bent and bowed like old men. Their necks were warmed by the mantle. They felt warm. The faint scent of soap, in which the embroidery threads were dipped before being threaded, now reached their nostrils. The smell made them sneeze and since their stomachs were empty, they began to feel nauseated.

They exchanged some words with one another. The words were very few and serious, only what was absolutely necessary. Within a few weeks, the hard labour and need had turned the boys into grave elders, practical men with heavy responsibilities on their shoulders.

Said Israel Noah: "Now we have a bad model which eats up lots of thread. We have to hurry." Benjamin, who was not yet a swift threader, remarked: "We always have to hurry anyway, every day."

And when they reached the parting of ways, each of them turned off in his own direction without a word.

When they reached the factory, they pressed the frozen palms of their hands against the glass of the lamps while their stiff and frozen fingers moved with difficulty until they thawed little by little. The embroiderer was better off. He swung the handle with his whole fist so he warmed up quickly. When he saw the threaders standing with their hands against the lamps, he gained the impression that they didn't particularly want to begin work. And he started annoyed: "Stop this business now. You've warmed up enough already!"

**

That was how the monotonous days ran on like long grey threads. The only ray of light for which their eyes looked out was the Eve of Sabbath and the Sabbath. Sometimes Uncle Leib Hayyim paid them a visit. He stayed a few moments in order to do his duty, to pay a debt and then promptly disappear with a promise to come another time. Sometimes his daughters came, Leah the married one or Esther with the red cheeks who was already grown up. The house seemed to grow brighter when they walked in. Mother became a bit cheerful, hid her wisps of white hair and invited the guests to sit down. As long as they were in the house, they seemed to bring a ray of light with them out of the happy home from which they came.

Yet, when they went, all the family felt as though they had been tricked. There was a sense of resentment at heart because they had come. The poverty here seemed worse, painful almost. It seemed as though the poverty was heavier than it had been before they had made their visit.

[Page 118]

The Sabbath passed and it was a weekday again. Somehow they felt as though Sabbath was shorter than any other day. Now the work-a-day week had begun. They wrapped themselves in the mantles and went off once more.

**

And now something happened which they had all dreaded and about which they had been speaking apprehensively. Aaronsohn, the manufacturer, brought machines. No longer would they need the embroidery machine with a handle and a man's palm and the pedals at his feet. Henceforward, engines and belt transmissions would set the machines moving.

A black dread settled on the streets and alleys in which the workers lived. The whole quarter was gripped in a deadly fear that their livelihood would be taken from them. Nor was it the embroiderers and threaders alone who began to be afraid. The fear also spread to the local mechanics that had learnt how to repair the machines, not in Saxony or in Switzerland but here in Kalish. They had been accustomed to break down one machine after another until they had 'grasped the principle'. Even Seidel the head mechanic grew melancholy. Some said he had told his wife to be a bit economical in her household and not to make so much noise with the big ladle.....

It became generally known that the new machines had already been brought to Aaronsohn's new building and were being assembled there. A mighty host of German mechanics, embroiderers and threading helpers had come with them and the new machines would start working in a few weeks' time; and there was a great outcry and alarm among the workers. The moaning and groaning could be heard in every home.

The wives of the embroiderers met in the shops. There was nothing else they could talk about except the black cloud hanging over their heads. Any moment now their husbands would be left without work and they wouldn't even have a mouthful of food at home for the children.

As soon as the shopkeepers heard about the shaky position of the embroiderers, they stopped their credit well in advance. And so the trouble came very close indeed and the necks could already feel the knife.

The dangers of the steam-driven machines were the general topic of conversation; in Benjamin's home, of course, as in all others. Mothers became dead afraid of the Germans and their steam engine, dead afraid of the days to come. Those Germans would deprive her household of their last crust of bread; she sighed and moaned all day long and she paid frequent visits to the home of her brother Leib Hayyim in order to hear what was being said there.

In one of the conversations, Benjamin remarked that the steam machines which did the work of human hands did not harm the workers but would benefit them only it would be necessary to get better working conditions as a result of the advantages which the machines would provide.

But Israel Noah insisted that the new machines were a calamity for the workers. They would increase unemployment and the manufacturers would grab all the advantage from them. So the only thing to do was to smash those machines by force.

[Page 119]

"And then they'll bring in new machines", said Benjamin. "We'll smash the new machines into bits as well until the importers get sick and tired and don't bring any more". And Israel Noah told a story. When he was still a little boy, he used to fetch missionary books from somewhere. He fetched them once and then fetched more. Jews used to try and persuade them not to bring any but he stood fast saying: "What do I know? They pay me so I bring them". And that was how things went on until one day Jews waited for him just outside the town; stopped his wagon and did whatever they felt they had to do to him and he then stopped fetching the "goods".

"The same with the machines", Israel Noah drew the parallel. "If it's impossible any other way, we can only rely on our fists." Abba was present at that conversation and had the same opinion as Israel Noah. "It's the only way" Abba added his opinion, "to smash the machines and make it tough for the Germans. And then they'll take their legs away from here."

Benjamin was not prepared to accept the view of Israel Noah under any conditions. But mother tended to agree with him except for one little change: "First we should go about it gently and go to Aaronsohn and make him realise quite clearly what a calamity he is bringing down on us with his new machines. And only if he turns us away, then we have to use force."

It was all they spoke about in the beer-houses on the Sabbath. Nota Makower had a beer shop. He had formerly been an embroiderer but had to give it up because of his health so he opened an unlicensed beer shop in his single room. That Sabbath afternoon, an unofficial Council gathered there.

Nobody was invited. They all came without having been called. Each one felt it necessary to discuss the business because he was worried at head and at heart. Since most of the Makower's customers were elderly embroiderers, skilled craftsmen whose name carried weight among the workers, the Council had something of the character of an official deliberation about the ways by which they could defend themselves against the danger of the power-driven machines.

Joel Pancher, who also came to down a glass of beer, said what Benjamin had said at home, that steam-driven machines were not the danger, but that the danger lay among the workers themselves. His words aroused a tremendous hubbub. The elderly workers, who looked like horses worn with toil, were angry at him. It almost seemed as though they would come down on him and give him a thorough working-over.

Hatzel Pins, who was one of the best of the craftsmen but still did not have any decent clothing and educated his sons at the Talmud Torah, jumped up to silence him.

Kreide, who worked at the Walberg Factory, was a tall, thin Jew with eyes surrounded by shadows and a high-pitched voice like a cock. He suddenly began declaring, nobody could say why, that the worst of the dogs were the manufacturers who had come up from the muck heaps. All the others present spoke, each one declaring what he had at heart and all speaking at once, yelling, fuming, then calming down. Then he began yelling again. Not a man paid attention to any of the others.

[Page 120]

When they silenced Pancher's arguments he swiftly cleared out. After they had all calmed down a bit, Meir Kalb, a dwarfish embroiderer with a greyish-black beard stood up and proposed that they should set up an Embroiderer's Society like Pancher wanted. But let them bring a Torah Scroll there and pray and have the teacher come and teach a chapter of the Book of Moses every Sabbath afternoon.

A little later, Feldberg the supervisor of Waldberg's factory came up to the beer house. At the sight of him old Propper vanished unseen. He was afraid that Feldberg might relate in the office that Propper was earning enough for a glass of beer as well. Kreide also began to feel uncomfortable. All the embroiderers became silent.

As they came down the stairs they agreed that it was necessary to call a meeting in some public place, the House of Study, for example. Makower, with the thinnest little beard, with glasses that had astonishingly thick lenses and ears that stack out on either side, suggested going to the Rabbi and asking him to summon Aaronsohn and persuade him to send the new machines back to the place they had come from and not to destroy the livelihood of a whole city full of workers.

Sure enough, the elderly workers met together and decided nothing and the whole business finished off with verbal argumentation. But the youngsters were different. They came together, it seems, in some other place and decided on taking real steps. A few days later, the Germans returning at evening from their work in the building where they were assembling the new machines, were attacked by a gang of youngsters and savagely beaten. Sure enough, the Germans were badly bruised but the next day the Police were busy conducting embroiderers from all the factories to the Chief of Police.

From factory-to-factory went the policemen, inspecting the young fellows and each and every one of them who seemed sharp or tough was arrested. All of them were brought together in one place and led to the lock-up under guard.

Fear and alarm spread everywhere. Faces grew pale; hearts began to thud and quiver like leaves in the wind. Gimpel's mother, the potato-seller, came running to the office and howled as she begged Rosenblum to persuade the Police to set her bread-winner free. Tevel Knop was also arrested because one of the policemen remembered him from the time when he had been a real tough.

Fear hovered over all the factories. Nobody was sure that he would be left alone and that they would not come to arrest him. Trying conclusions with the police was no trifle. There is a common saying: "keep your distance from the red collars". The members of the older generation who used to visit Makower's beer shop wished to disassociate themselves from the deeds of the young ruffians and prove that they did not like such tricks. A few of them went up to Aaronsohn, spoke out their frightened hearts and begged for mercy's sake that he should send the machines back.

Aaronsohn, so they related later, received them in the corridor. He called them idiots and cautioned them to be more careful in future and not to attack Germans. As for the fears that the Germans would rob them of their work, that was just so much nonsense for everybody was capable of learning how to work the new machines. He had no intention whatsoever of employing the Germans for any length of time but only until they had taught the local workers what had to be done. As soon as the local people learnt the business, the machines would be handed over to them while the Germans would go back home. And, in any case, the new machines did not manufacture the same things as the old ones. They only made muslin and applique embroidery. And all in all, said he, to finish off with, it was sheer idiocy to oppose the development of machinery.

[Page 121]

The messengers went back to the factory and told the workers what Aaronsohn had said. They could not quite make out what he meant and nobody knew whether to be glad or sad. But one way or another, they all became accustomed to the new trouble, accepted the existence of the machines, calmed down and no longer thought of revenge.

———

The Beginnings of the Century

by Morris Walter

These are the things I remember in Kalish near the beginning of the century: The Old House of Study, the Great Synagogue, the Shtiebel of the Alexander Hassidim, the Shtiebel of the Ger Hassidim, the New House of Study, and the cemetery, the Mikveh, the Slaughter House and the Slaughter House for poultry. The Jewish representative, known as the *Dozor*, was Berish Shimkowicz whose behaviour was not all it might have been. He was the *Shtadlan* or intercessor with regard to conscription and it was told that he used to get the sons of the rich exempted while he had the poor young men conscripted in their place.

The Chief Rabbi was Reb Samson Ornstein, a great scholar who was well versed in everyday affairs and knew several languages. The Dayan (assistant rabbi) was Reb Moshe Schlumper who was a scholar, quite capricious, a Mitnaged or opponent of Hassidism and who prayed in the House of Study of the Mitnagdim. It was his habit to be very stern and rude towards youngsters and he showed no particular respect for adults. The third rabbi, known as the *Moreh Horaa* (teacher and educator) was a noble-minded Jew who prayed in the Old House of Study.

The cantor was Yisroelke who was famous throughout the world. Of him I can only mention his way of praying. But I knew personally one of his assistants, Itschke Bass. Later, he was also the bass for Reb Noah and his mighty voice still echoes in my ear. In my day, Reb Noah Zaludkowski was cantor in the Great Synagogue where Reb Samson Ornstein prayed. Reb Noah was renowned as Noah Klager. One of his assistants, the cantor Katchka, went to America and became famous there.

[Page 122]

The Great Synagogue was used for meetings, weddings and in time of trouble as a gathering place. But only the wealthy had regular seats there. The next social rank, the learned householders who were not too rich but were respected, found their place in the New House of Study. There were definitely Mitnagdim but meticulously complied with all the commandments. The ordinary all-year-round Jews used to pray in the Old House of Study and their cantors were all *Baalei Tefilla* (prayer-leaders from among their own number). I can remember Reb Hayyim Sheinik, the *Shamash* or beadle of the Old House of Study who was the patron of any visitors and guests.

The following division reflects the various classes within the Kalish Community: Wealthy intellectuals; ordinary rich people; householders; scholars; everyday Jews and the Hassidim of Ger and Alexander.

All week long they were all busy making a living – the innkeeper, shopkeeper, artisan, porter, agent – but on the Sabbath they were all to be found in the synagogues. On Sabbath afternoons the scholars would refresh their memories of the Mishna while the ordinary folk strolled around the Market Square, pausing at Czenkalowski's shop, feasting their eyes on expensive imported dainties and tropical fruits which only the wealthy could afford, wines and sweets. That is how things were in those days.

The leading Kalish industry of lace-making had negative as well as positive aspects. There was no compulsory education, so children were taken to work for long hours and for a miserable pay. Since the families were large, the pay that the children received was an important part of the income. After a few years' work, the threader became an assistant at the age of 15 or 16 and his wages went up. But the result was the emergence of an ignorant generation.

Then came the days of Zionism and Socialism: Poalei Zion, Bund and Ahdut.

In 1898 the Zionist Club was in the Breslau Street. It had a Yiddish and Hebrew library and newspapers. There were debates on current affairs and Songs of Zion were sung in chorus. They used to say: "Next year in Jerusalem" from the very heart. They purchased shares in the Jewish Colonial Trust with full faith in the Jewish State. Young lads in the Yeshivot (Talmudical Academies) used to read profane and heretical literature in secret.

"Ahdut" was a Jewish Socialist Party. The Czarist regime prohibited even the reading of socialist literature. But the prohibitions led the students to spread this literature far and wide and to hold meetings. Two groups emerged: The radicals of "Ahdut" and the nationalists who were westernized Zionists. The orthodox combatted both groups alike for having lost their faith in Messiah. They called the Ahdut people 'shiftless lads and scamps' or rebels against God and State.

In 1903, I felt that there was no place for me in Kalish. The Colonel of the Gendarmes began to pay attention to me and informed me through a Gendarme they called "Hammer" that he wanted to have a chat with me because he wanted to take me under his protection as I was the son of a householder; so I was invited to come to his office. I decided not to go because I was nineteen years old, almost old enough for conscription to the army, which I hated; and because I suspected that he wanted to make an agent provocateur out of me for certain matters. A few days earlier, a provocateur of that kind had arrived from Lodz and we helped him find his way to the hospital.

[Page 123]

This is how it happened: One day a young fellow from Lodz aged about twenty paid me a visit. He introduced himself as a messenger from Ahdut in Lodz and wanted to meet the Ahdut members of Kalish. But we had been warned of his arrival in advance. Since I was a supporter of Ahdut, I told the members of his arrival. We decided to give him a lesson. I promised that I would arrange a meeting in the field near the slaughter-house.

The meeting was attended by several tough members like "Show me", the porter's son, "Klapper" and others, about twenty in all. We arranged ourselves in groups and started whispering to one another. When the provocateur arrived and asked: "what are those fellows whispering?" we answered him courageously: "They say you are a spy!" "What are you talking about?" "I think they are right", I answered. The signal was given; the lads surrounded him and gave him a thorough beating. He spent several days in hospital and then vanished.

The gendarmes summoned me because they hoped I would give away the names of those who had attended the meeting in the field. I had a frontier passport. So on Friday morning, I crossed the frontier. My uncle from America had sent me a ship's ticket. I parted with a curse and a vow never to return.

After a year of adapting myself to the U.S., like every greenhorn, my uncle Shlomo Feil brought me to the Kalish Fraternal Union (Kalisher Bruder Verein). At my very first meeting I was unfavourably impressed by the undemocratic character of the Society: The secret rapping at the door; the official greetings and the almost military ceremonial; the "by-laws". For instance, only a Russian Polish Jew could be admitted to membership – the Fund was the Holy of Holies, the cemetery was "the ground". These were the things discussed at every meeting. They all repelled me but there was no choice. This Society was more liberal than the "Kalisher Lodge". So I remained in the Society.

When I proposed that we should also interest ourselves in general Jewish affairs, the Treasurer, Mr. Levi, protested that we wanted to use up all the funds and Galewski, the President, accepted his opinion; and that was the end of it. Monotonous years passed without any change. Only during World War I did I succeed in establishing a Relief Committee for Kalish and in associating our Society as well in the Relief, which resolved that all the Societies had to contribute to the Relief Fund.

In 1918, young immigrants arrived and with their aid we established the Kalish Young Men's Society. It was set up at the home of Abraham Wolkowicz with the assistance of M. Friedman, the three Waxman brothers, S. Kapp, M. Beatus, J. Kott and I. When the Young Men joined the Workers' Circle, I left. I could not accept the attitude of the Bund towards Zionism.

That year, the General Relief Committee for the Kalish Poor was founded with the aid of: Sigmund Galewski, President; Sam Kapp and myself for the Young Men: Joseph Kott, Joe Frashker and Morris Friedman. Participants of the Committee in Kalish were: Eliezer Friedman, Yehiel Tenzer, Yehiel Grinspan, Peretz Walter, M. Kletchevski and Levenberg.

I attended the inaugural meeting of the Non-Party Relief, which resolved that its purpose was to assist aging embroidery workers in Kalish. Its non-party character was stressed as a primary condition and its name also clearly expresses this.

[Page 124]

When it was decided to plant the Martyrs' Forest, the task was joined in by the Shalom Aleichem No. 30 Lodge, the Walter Family Circle and the Relief. Within three years, we collected close to $10,000. In 1958, the Jewish National Fund arranged a trip to Jerusalem for the Memorial Days. I participated in the delegation of Kalish Folk from the United States.

[Page 125]

Society
and
Culture

The Jewish Political Parties

[Page 126]

Eliezer Birnbaum writes on the establishment of Tseirei Zion in the year 1917. Jewish life was just beginning to revive in the city. A number of young members of what can be described as the middle class were seeking social progress though not necessarily along the lines of the workers who already had their Poalei Zion, Bund, etc. The new Society had its centre in Warsaw. In Kalish, they had about 50 members to begin with and started with courses in Modern Hebrew. They also organized a choir of their own and actively engaged in all Zionist activities. Within a year, they had about 100 members and fully supported the United Zionist list in the first Seim elections of the new Poland. In those days, interparty relations were friendly and differences were largely restricted to official debates.

When the split came about in the *Poalei Zion* movement, the Tseirei Zion joined Hapoel Hatzair of Eretz Israel and established the "Hitahdut".

*

H. Shurek describes the early years of the Left *Poalei Zion*, from 1915-1919 when a number of young Zionist workers moved away from the general Zionists and established their *Poalei Zion* cell. As they had no club of their own, they joined the "Tea Hall". In due course they elected an Executive which sympathized with them so that it gradually became their centre. After the Germans left Kalish in 1918, the Committee changed the name of the club to "Arbeiter Heim", which engaged in extensive cultural and other activities and also had a dramatic group and a choir.

*

L. Makowsky gives an account of the "*Yugend*" Youth section of the Left *Poalei Zion* and its activities in Kalish between the two World Wars. It was a large organization and took an active part in labour, communal, cultural and sports life. Most of the members were themselves factory workers. One of their chief activities was evening classes at which they provided youngsters with an elementary education, teaching them writing, arithmetic, history and geography. "*Yugend*" was never recognized by the authorities and, therefore, conducted its activities under the guise of a Sports Organization. Now and again, one of the members was arrested for a few days and after a thrashing, was released. The Association used to hold a summer camp of its own every summer.

*

Hayyim Brand describes his activities on behalf of *Poalei Zion*. He came to Kalish as a Polish soldier in 1920 and was impressed by the first meeting of the *Poalei Zion* which he attended. At the time, the Branch was setting up party groups in the Jewish Trade Unions and taking the first steps towards the establishment of a kindergarten which, later, developed into the Borochow School. When he left the army the Kalish Branch appointed him as secretary. *Poalei Zion* had already been in existence since 1916 and during World War I it established a Consumers Cooperative and a Bakery. Various other institutions providing the necessary minimum of staple foods were also to be found in town. Lectures from then Warsaw Headquarters included, among others, Rubashow, now Zalman Shazar, third President of Israel. There was a Popular University giving two lectures a week. Political economy was studied every Saturday morning while current affairs were discussed on Friday nights. The Sections in the various Trade Unions used to meet once a fortnight. The Textile Workers Union had to hold double meetings to enable all members to attend. *Poalei Zion* increased its strength at every election campaign.

[Page 127]

In elections to the Sick Fund Council the main opponent was the Bund. Poalei Zion obtained 5 seats and the Bund only 2.

The chief fields for public activity were: Municipal affairs; work for the unemployed; anti-Jewish persecution; the Ghetto Benches at the Universities for Jewish students; the various British White Papers on Palestine, etc.

The Borochow Youth played the leading part in demonstrations. Between 1918 and 1922 there were no international 1st of May demonstrations following the attack on the demonstration in 1919 described elsewhere. In 1922 all groups agreed to share in a common procession. The Bund first demanded that Eretz Israel slogans should be prohibited but had to give way because the Polish communists supported the stand of the *Poalei Zion*. Defence groups were organized in advance along the line of the procession which was attacked by Polish students with clubs. The defence groups dispersed them and indeed, several were taken to hospital. However, two members of *Poalei Zion* were stabbed. There were, of course, no police in sight.

Poalei Zion conducted successful activities in the following unions: Porters, Food Workers, Clerks, Leather Workers, Needle Workers and Textile Workers. The most active group in the party were the Borochow Youth who also maintained the Stern Sports Club.

*

S. Ziezwinski briefly describes the successful *Hitahdut* party with its reading room and library, lectures, meetings and discussions which were devoted entirely to Zionist problems and the realities of Eretz Israel. The party actively supported the Cooperative Bank and worked to help the artisans and small merchants. Many members came to Eretz Israel between 1933 and 1939. Younger supporters were organized in the *"Gordonia"* Movement.

*

Saul Zalud gives a detailed and affectionate account of *Hashomer Hatsair* which originated as a Jewish National Scout Movement in Galicia and had reached Warsaw and the larger towns of Poland by the end of World War I. In Kalish, the senior gymnasium students were the first to join but were rapidly followed by others including the lawless gangs of youngsters who were part of the debris of the war. Some of the wealthy Jews of the city placed their summer estates at the disposal of the youngsters to serve as camps. Afterward, they went on longer hikes and rambles. Kalish was particularly fortunate in its membership. The leaders organized courses in various subjects including philosophy, the theory of relativity and radio-techniques. The local branch produced the first working crystal-set radio in the town. *Hashomer Hatzair* became a movement which seemed to provide everything that the youngsters found lacking in home, school and surroundings.

[Page 128]

Actual immigration to Eretz Israel, which the Movement called *Hagshama* (fulfilment), began in the early 20's. Sets and libraries of books were sent to the early settlers, workshops of various kinds were gradually established and when *Hachshara* (training for Eretz Israel) became official Zionist policy in Poland, *Hashomer Hatsair* took an active part. In Eretz Israel and Poland, the Movement became more political and there were splits but the nucleus in Kalish profited by becoming more mature. Looking back after almost half a century, the writer concludes that the efforts spent in and on this Movement have more than justified themselves by the results in the new Israel.

*

Z.K. describes the General Zionists who made up the greater part of the Movement which arose at Herzl's call in 1897 and succeeded the *Hovevei Zion* that had functioned in Kalish from 1882 until about 1894-5, as described in an essay by Shmuel Zvi Weltsman. (It should be remembered that Rabbi H.E. Wachs, the rabbi of Kalish, had been one of the guiding and initiating spirits of this Movement.)

Though the Jewish National spirit was widespread, it remained virtually unorganized before World War I and only became efficiently unified as an outcome of the Balfour Declaration of 1917. Activities included supporting the Zionist Funds, disseminating the Shekel, supporting the Youth Movements and combatting assimilation. In 1927, when the "Al Hamishmar" wing of the General Zionists gained control in Kalish, there were about 600 members. Hebrew study groups were widespread. The Youth Movements began to become popular with the worsening economic situation and emergence of active anti-Semitism in 1928 and a branch of *WIZO* (Women's International Zionist Organization) was established. As elsewhere, the final years were marked by intra-communal struggles, chiefly with the Agudat Israel.

*

I. Kletchevsky, in recording the activities of the Bund, tells of the guild structure that had emerged of itself among the Kalish embroiderers, and the entirely exposed position of their helpers and threaders. As a result, it was far easier to organize the latter than the skilled workers and master craftsmen. The first steps in this direction were taken by Jewish members of the P.P.S. (Polish Socialist Party). The Bund as such began to be known at about the turn of the century and had established itself by 1902. By 1904, there were 4 meeting centres in operation. The manufacturers took active steps against known Bund members which led to grave disputes and the injury of two manufacturers. By spring 1905, the Bund had enlisted the support of most Jewish workers in the city who engaged in active demonstrations before the 1905 Revolution. The Kalish prison was assaulted and taken, the authorities disarmed and the political prisoners released.

[Page 129]

Russian reinforcements killed several demonstrators and wounded many more. Hundreds of Bund members were arrested and exiled to Siberia. Though the workers' conditions improved, however, Bund leaders and members were persecuted and the Bund had to go underground again. It was revived only during the German occupation in 1916 with a membership of about 60. A Clubroom was opened in 1917 and the Bund emerged as a political party of the Jewish workers. It began organizing unions, set up a consumer cooperative, a club and a kindergarten.

After the war, its influence began to increase. It had two representatives in the Kalish Town Council, one of who was chosen as town clerk. A report in the Labour Almanac of 1920 gives the following information: There were 125 political members; 2 town councillors (536 votes); it largely dominated the Needle Workers and the Leather Workers' Trade Union; the Zukunft Cultural Society (315 members); the Children's Home (62 children); the Einigkeit Workers' Cooperative (160 members) a Youth Organization (50 members) and a Youth Club (100 members). In the second Municipal Elections the Bund obtained more than 1000 votes and the same two representatives returned. The Town Council supported the Jewish schools. However, these friendly relations did not last long.

A Peoples' University established in 1917 continued to function until 1927, from October to May, and lectures were attended by 500 persons regularly. Towards the end of the twenties the Bund also began to participate in the affairs of the Kehilla and its representatives were elected to that body.

*

P.A. records the *Poalei Agudat Israel* who first organized in 1910 as the *Poalei Shlomei Emunei Israel* and finally adopted the new name in the twenties when a Hebrew anthem was composed for them to which the famous cantor, Yossele Rosenblatt, composed a tune. Kalish, indeed, was one of the first three cities in which the Organization was established. One of its main purposes was to ensure employment for Jewish workers who were not prepared to work on the Sabbath day and to help train fully observant youngsters for the industrial life of the city. By the early thirties, however, it was taking an active part in hachshara activities for Eretz Israel and members were immigrating to Eretz Israel by the mid-thirties. A *Bnot Agudat Israel* for young women was established in 1928 and had about 400 members.

*

Issachar Kott gives a brief account of the *Poalei Zion* (Z.S.) known as the Right Poalei Zion whose members engaged in *Hehalutz* and Hebrew activities besides conducting activities in Yiddish and supporting the social struggles of the Jewish workers. Lecturers from Eretz Israel, speakers from other towns and local members all lectured at the Popular University. The Party operated within the Kehilla and influenced the Artisan's Organization and all the Zionist Labour Parties collaborated in the League for Labour Eretz Israel. It collaborated with the Polish workers and took part in May Day demonstrations. Many of the members came to Eretz Israel.

[Page 130]

*

Jacob Bienstock gives an account of the way the left-wing parties operated underground in Tsarist Russia when he was a member of the Poalei Zion. He himself had a Hassidic upbringing in the home of his father, an Alexander Hassid, and in his childhood he constantly envisaged the coming of Messiah and the return of his family to Eretz Israel where they would all till the soil.

In 1905-6 the left-wing parties were illegal but had their regular meeting places as described in the section on the Bund. Each party sent its best spokesmen to the meeting places of the others in the hope of winning adherents. The Poalei Zion were divided into 'circles' each of ten members. It was his own task to provide literature for two such circles. On one occasion when he was at the Bund section with his pockets full of illegal pamphlets, he began trying to explain the principles of Marx and Borochow to a Bundist. Suddenly he looked around and saw that the other had vanished and the whole stretch of pavement was empty. Looking to the left he saw the Chief of Police and three mounted policemen riding very slowly by with whips in their hands. He went walking on for several dozen paces then stopped and stared at the Chief of Police who stopped and stared back. As he was wearing typical "Jewish" garb, the other suspected nothing wrong and in a few moments spurred his horse and galloped off with his men.

After the parties were legalized, following the Russo-Japanese War, he used to prepare the flags, banners and slogans of all the left-wing parties to their satisfaction. Before the 1st of May 1906, he worked very late preparing the Poalei Zion flag which he thrust under his vest. On the way hope he was stopped by police who wanted to know what he had in his pocket. A red flag, he answered. "Show us!" they ordered. He produced a red velvet bag and showed it to them. "What do you keep in it?" "Bombs". "Open it and show us the bombs". He opened it and displayed his tefilin and prayer book. Thereupon they let him go.

*

Gershon Wroclawski describes the Club of the *Zionist Youth* and the *General Zionist Hehalutz* which united during the final years and had several hundred members. Their whole ideology was summed up in one word: Eretz Israel. Thanks to this organization, there are several dozen more Kalish folk in Israel than would otherwise have been the case. There were both summer and winter camps. Instructors were trained at the latter.

The older members used to proceed on hachshara before going to Eretz Israel. At first their parents were opposed but gradually opposition faded away. Israel Bienstock and the writer headed activities including fund-raising until the last. The writer managed to bury the Hehaluz flag in the Club courtyard during November 1939.

[Page 131]

*

H.B. describes *Betar* which was commenced in February 1929 by a group of 8 youngsters who were soon joined by others including a group of twelve and thirteen-year olds. When they numbered 60 or so, they hired premises. When Jabotinsky visited them the following year they were headed by Binam Grausalz. By this time there were some 600 members who were given a sports and para-military training. In 1930, Kalish sent a delegation numbering 30 to the 1ˢᵗ Betar Assembly in Warsaw; and the first members then left on hachshara. Boxing was introduced in 1933 and members engaged in "*Aliya Bet*" (immigration to Eretz Israel without the certificates demanded by the Mandatory Government). *Brit Hahayal*, consisting of ex-soldiers, was founded in 1932 as was *Brit Hatzohar*, the Zionist Revisionist Party. The Movement participated in the boycott of German goods in 1936. The Rowing Crew won 1ˢᵗ prize in 1937. The Betar groups met 3 times a week for courses in Jewish history, Zionist history, drill, singing and dancing and talks on discipline, etc. As the members grew older they graduated into the Revisionist Movement.

*

Benjamin Zvieli gives a brief account of *Hahalutz Hamizrahi* and *Hashomer Hadati*. The former consisted largely of observant young workers more-or-less parallel to the older Mizrahi, while the latter was a Youth Movement. Both alike, they engaged in hachshara with a view to proceeding to Eretz Israel, a step which was taken in due course by groups and individuals. *Hashomer Hadati* was set up in 1932 and not long after, the "Torah Vaavoda" (Torah and Work) training kibbutz was established in Kalish and participated in by observant young people from all over Poland, almost all of whom proceeded to Eretz Israel later on.

———

Seeking for the Way

by Hayyim Stein

Those bright years of the youth movements in general, those years when aspirations awakened and there were so many longings for a lofty purpose, were the most joyful period of our lives.

Kalish, like the other towns of Poland, had almost all the parties and youth movements to be found among the Jewish population. We remember the nights full of significance and the thirst for study when we used to attend lectures and engage in debates without ever growing tired. In those days, we we were wide-awake to all that was going on in the world at large and within Jewry in particular. Like a baby sucking insatiably, we longed and yearned to know everything that was going on and developing in the world. And of course, we were primarily concerned with our own part of it.

[Page 132]

That part was broken up into many sections. On the one side were the Bund and the Fraction as the communists were called, who opposed Zionism; on the other were the two Poalei Zion movements and in between were the Zionist youth movements which regarded Aliya to Eretz Israel as their ultimate purpose. Those Olympian heights attracted us in particular. There was something of the daring of youth in going against all the accepted social and family practices and proceeding to fulfil great ideals. Not that it was easy for it involved tremendous effort and a capacity to stand against all those who deplored the "hot-headed craziness of the youth."

I could tell a great deal about those days when it was hard for me to get away from parents who crowded around me and entreated me to "deliver" their children from the danger called Aliya. I had to calm them down and reassure them. But they did not always come with requests. Sometimes I had to wander through the streets of the town for hours in order to escape the platoons of parents who were waiting for me at the entrance to my home. The days of Hachshara and finally also the days of Aliya, which were so unforgettable for the Movement, were a source of tears and anger for parents and kinsfolk. We required strength and a firm will in order to break away from loving arms when we saw angry tears instead of a farewell smile.

This life with all its glory, grace, pain and heroism shaped the Youth Movements. The world around us was all but forgotten and the only thing we were concerned with was shaping the rosy dreams of tomorrow. We had no small help from educators and men of goodwill among the adults, although their help did not always benefit us. For they themselves lived a hopeless grey and monotonous life where nothing but local communal affairs put any spirit into them. Zionist and Mizrahi circles had the function of collecting money. There were many among the Zionist and Mizrahi who wished to go there themselves but they did not have the financial resources and had to provide for their impoverished families as well.

Here I wished to mention a person who was popular among the youngsters. This was Yurek Klinger, an enlightened but very unfortunate man. All of us can remember the negligent way he went about, the shaggy hat on his head and his ridiculous physique. He came to every Youth Club whether invited or not. He lectured and debated – he learnt and taught. He was aware of everything that was going on within the Jewish street.

Here I have been told a great deal about him. Under the German occupation, he appeared as a Volksdeutsche and in that way he helped the Jews risking his life for others. The Nazi caught him in the middle of his activities and killed him. May his memory be blessed.

Then there was another person who served us as a model. This was the elderly Shabtai Seidorf, representative of the Jewish National Fund who got on well with everybody. He regarded the Fund as something really holy.

[Page 133]

He reckoned he was the oldest Zionist in Kalish and enjoyed telling stories of bygone days.

There were many exceptional characters in our city and indeed, there is not enough space to list them all. Intensive Zionist activity of every kind was engaged. The movement was represented on the Kehilla Executive and the Town Council.

When Bialik visited us, it was a great festival. All the Youth Movements and Zionists were there to welcome him. The pupils of the Hebrew Gymnasium lifted his carriage up on their shoulders and brought him into town that way. The leading Jewish lecturers and speakers visited us and always had an attentive and intelligent audience. The *"Hehalutz Hamerkazi"* (Central Hehalutz) Movement consisted of youngsters who did not find their place in the other movements for reasons which do not need to be described here. But one thing was clear. Most of those who sought a way to be Halutzim pure and simple found their place in its ranks.

———

The "Lamifal" Training Kibbutz in Kalish

by Edzia

Kalish was a Jewish city which had known many Halutzim during quite a long period and was less surprised by us when we met than we were surprised by the city. It was an outstanding centre of light industry, particularly lace and embroidery. There was a Jewish working class with a full labour consciousness which, at the same time, longed for aliya to Eretz Israel. It expressed these yearnings among the older generation by belonging to Zionist Organizations and among the younger groups through membership in youth movements. For a long and continuous period, the city had been living a lively Zionist youth life and a widely-known Shomer Hatzair group had existed there only a year or two before our arrival.

The first "Lamifal" section which arrived in June 1933 met the last members of the previous Hachshara Kibbutz in a little apartment of two rooms at 95, Gornoszlonska Street. But before long, we remained alone facing the difficulties of adaptation; and this at a time when, in general, local Zionist activities, youth movements and our own movement were all at a very low level. But, within a month, there were about sixty of us.

Some of us made our way into industry and the Jewish needle trade occupations. The Jewish manufacturers looked at the Halutzim with eyes of pity, you might say, as though they felt it was only for the sake of Zion that they were prepared to keep us in their factories. Still, they were not afraid to exploit our lads thoroughly in bringing materials to the machines, packing and other work. The girls took piece-work home from the lace industry. They spent hours on hours removing the black threads that joined the lacework. We called this job: "drawing the consequences".

Another part proceeded to agriculture, working for a Zionist with a large kitchen garden growing tomatoes for industrial purposes. Some of the girls also engaged in this work while others tied up sacks and transported them to the flour mill.

[Page 134]

Here we first began to take part in the life of the workers, their organization and the struggle for working conditions. At the kitchen garden near the city we met with the tyrannies and oppressive regime of the Polish peasant at the hands of a certain Leibush, the foreman of the owner. It is unnecessary to add that the peasants regarded us as queer fish. They could not understand this lunacy of abandoning good homes in order to hunger together with them. Two not particularly large rooms and a small kitchen served us for everything: bedroom, dining room; meeting hall and reading room. We exploited the height of the rooms and constructed bunks in tiers.

We paid no particular attention to food. We reckoned that that was something incidental while the idea always came first. Our partial unemployment and the low wages of those who were working caused difficult conditions. The light did not always burn for the bill was not always paid in time. But, cultural activities were well developed. Many groups were operative, particularly in learning Hebrew. They worked under very difficult conditions, reading a great deal in our rooms and talking a great deal.

...When new members began knocking at our doors, we hired a large apartment in No. 15 Piskozewie Street. This was a spacious hall in an unused factory. Modest provisions were made to divide it into sleeping rooms, dining room, a workshop containing a carpenter's bench, shoemaking utensils and a sewing machine together with a kitchen and conveniences of a sort. These conveniences consisted of a half-closed room containing two basins. In those days we were always saying: "I'm next" about the turn for washing. What was lacking we made up for by taking a bath once a week in the Community's kosher Mikveh (ritual immersion pool) which was specially warmed up for us. We did away with the bunks but slept two in a bed. The dining room had an iron stove that was heated with coal. To be sure, it was a poor object but it served as the focus of social life. A radio set was obtained. Hunger and poverty continued to reign supreme, but we silenced them with tempestuous dances and overcame the cut-off electricity with romantic songs.

This was the third year of our training yet there were scarcely any immigration certificates to Eretz Israel. Most of the boys were called to the army. We hired a private dwelling containing small rooms which we painted very carefully. There was also a carpet of a kind on the floor. Here we had a reading room and even a shower bath with sprinklers and hot water.

In the courtyard was a vegetable garden and one milk cow on which the love of the whole group was concentrated. We were helped to set up this 'small-holding' with the aid of a group of Zionist supporters who also helped us with our Immigration Fund.

– And Aliya came at last!

[Page 135]

Cultural Life

by Meir Packentraeger

Kalish, with a Jewish population of close to 30,000 never had the slightest reason to be ashamed of its cultural achievements in the fields of journalism, theatre, art, etc.

In 1919 the first Jewish Weekly, "Die Kalisher Woch" was founded in Kalish on the initiative of local writers and journalists. This was the organ of the General Zionists and was edited by M. Abramowitch and Shlomo Brish. The weekly quickly became popular and several thousand copies were sold. Its writers included not only the editors but also Zalman Kaplan, Hershel Solnik, Mordechai Shmuelevitch, M. Wieroszewski and others. From time-to-time, a poem by Rosa Jacobovitch was published. Shlomo Brish published sharp and effective light articles in which he dealt humorously with local communal workers and institutions.

In the same year, a second weekly appeared. This was "Dos Kalisher Leben" edited by I. Mamlock, a gifted journalist and editor educated in the Yeshiva. He raised the level of his weekly and his own weekly article was wisely written and was full of choice and apt quotations from Jewish sources. He was also the correspondent for the Warsaw "Moment". Other contributors were Jacob Alberstein, Shlomo Rubin, Moshe Flinker and Meir Packentraeger.

An orthodox Jewish paper also appeared for some time. In 1930, Jacob Alberstein began publishing a daily "Der Kalisher Express" which had to suspend publication before long. In 1926 the Kletzkin Publishing House in Warsaw issued a volume of stories by Hershel Solnik entitled: "Fun alten Kloister" (From the Old Close).

In connection with a jubilee issue of "Maccabi" in 1939, Zalman Kaplan wrote in "Der Kalisher Woch" about the beginnings of the Sports Movement in the city:

"It will not be in any way paradoxical if I say that the beginning of these festivities is connected with a Singing Society called "Hazamir" with which the Sports Movement began. It happened in 1912 when the youth were very busy in the successful lace industry and wished to provide themselves with a place for social meetings. In those days there were no secular societies at all. But the Kalish industrialist, Handwurzel, displayed a highly developed social sense when he headed the Hazamir Society.

The conductor Krotianski had a choir and a symphony orchestra under him. The rules and regulations of the Society were submitted to the authorities for approval. Everything would have been in order was it not for the Tsarist regime which did not show even the slightest interest in permitting any communal activity whatsoever. Within a few weeks a Government Order to close down the Society was received. This compelled the young people to move in a different direction and the idea developed of founding a Sports Society.

Mr. Handwurzel was very dejected after the failure of "Hazamir" and did not wish to help in setting up the new Society. But it was necessary for us to gain the approval of the authorities and the only way to do this was bribery. We adopted this course and were assisted by the influence of the banker Hermann Landau and our friend Handwurtzel who finally allowed himself to be persuaded to take the necessary steps. And so the Sports Society was established and included all the members of Hazamir.

[Page 136]

The same Hazamir group also carried on the cultural work of the Society. In the course of time, these members engaged in interesting literary and musical evenings and staged operettas of a good artistic level by Goldfaden and others.

Although the Society engaged mainly in sport, it also did a great deal in other cultural fields. To our regret, the Archives of the Society have not been preserved, otherwise we could have had a very interesting picture of pioneer activities during the twenty-five years.

There were only a few writers and journalists in the city. They concentrated on the two local Yiddish weeklies and each of them contributed whatever he could to Jewish cultural life.

Undoubtedly, the leading figure in the group was the poetess Rosa Jacobowitch who published a volume of poems. She began writing almost together with J.L. Peretz and at the time described how she already had forty years of literary activity behind her. All the writers of the city used to be in and out of her home, reading their work to her, listening to her opinions and accepting her advice. Hershel Solnik was a regular visitor. Mention should also be made of the poet Mordechai Shmuelewitch and of Israel Rubin who wrote a great deal for the theatre and the variety stage. His one-act plays and sketches were presented successfully by the "Comet" Light Theatre of Kalish. All the townsfolk of those days remember his verses: "What do I get out of it?" the melody of which was composed by the conductor Krotianski.

Of the journalists I shall mention Moshe Flinker, M. Abramowitch, I. Mamlock and Shlomo Brish. None of them have survived and no one knows where they are buried. Professional troupes from Warsaw often visited Kalish and appeared at the Theatre which was managed by Levin. The Comet Theatre was established in 1932 on the initiative of the poet Moshe Broderson.

Cultural Activities. 1918-1939

by S. Baum

When Poland was liberated in 1918 and the Polish-Russian War broke out, there was no organized communal life in Kalish whatever because all the parties had been abolished. It was then that the Sports Society: "Yiddisher Turn un Sport Verein" was founded and the social forces of all the parties gathered around it; for it provided the only opportunity of establishing and maintaining Jewish cultural activity. A library was founded which gave young Jews their first impulse towards knowledge and culture. Courses were arranged for the study of Polish, Hebrew and other languages. Lectures were given three times a week on science, politics and health which interested all sections of the Jewish public. Sports attracted their own people. When you entered the Sports Club you were welcomed by noisy and pulsating activities. The liveliness when the Committee was elected goes without saying. Each party did its best to increase its membership and the propaganda and contests were very obstinate.

[Page 137]

Little by little the branches of activity developed. In 1921 Mr. Witkowski proposed that a Brass Band be founded. Members were promptly recruited and they began to study the instruments they were to play. The Band appeared for the first time three months later and promptly achieved popularity. It held concerts, took part in gymnastics and sports displays, in rambles and hikes and also responded to invitations from Sports Club in smaller towns such as Zdunska-Wola, Blaszki, Sieradz, Wielun and Kutno. When we came to one of these places, we brought a holiday with us. All the Jewish residents came out to welcome us, old and young, religious and non-religious. We were appreciated by everybody except the anti-Semites. Whenever we went out on a hike and on any other opportunity, they attacked us and threw stones at us.

I shall describe on such incident. After a sports display, our football team played a Polish team and God gave us the victory. We saw at once that there was going to be trouble. We arranged all our members in ranks headed by the Band and marched away to our Club in the Pulaski Street. When we reached the District Court building, we were attacked by the hooligans, but we repulsed them and went on marching. When we reached our own street, a large crowd came up against us and began to fight. We swiftly hurried the children, women and the band into the house where our members grabbed the Indian Clubs used for exercise and dashed out to do battle. And it was a real battle. The injured were taken into the Club and additional volunteers promptly took their place. The hooligans received a thrashing which they remembered for a long time to come.

In 1929 Mr. Witkowski left Kalish and I took over the band. After that, a symphony orchestra was also established as well as a choir which was conducted by Mr. Krotianski. A motorcycle section was added to the Club and had a large membership. At every display, public appearance or hike, they rode their cycles and made an impressive appearance. Later, a dramatic circle was established and successfully produced both plays and operettas.

In the years 1933-34 a large group of members broke away from the Sports Society and found the Maccabi Sports Society which restricted its activities to sports alone. This was immediately followed by the Hapoel Sports Club whose committee consisted of Simeon Baum, Gad Goldman, Mordechai Blaszkowski, Laszczewski and Piotrkowski. The Club developed and about three months later, it held a successful first display. A dramatic circle of the Hapoel was also established and successfully presented important dramas.

In Kalish, there was also the Haoved Society for Workers and Craftsmen which engaged in cultural activities and organized courses in Hebrew.

[Page 138]

'Turn un Sport Verein'

by Isaac Kleczewski

The 'Yiddishe Turn un Sport Klub' served as the cradle of the cultural, sports and political life which was engaged in so intensively in Kalish until the Holocaust.

The Yiddishe Turn un Sport Verein was founded in Kalish in 1911 and derived from internal Jewish needs. Industry was in a state of rapid growth and the city expanded at a gigantic rate together with it. The mechanical lace-making industry was growing fast and attracted a new population. A large part of the young men who had been studying in the Yeshivot were looking for some way of changing their lives. The growth of industry was accompanied by a shortage of workers and poverty was gradually diminishing. The day's work, to be sure, lasted ten hours but the wages were satisfactory.

The members of the younger generation used to gather in separate circles and groups either in the lovely park or on the banks of the Prosna or in the dance halls. Naturally, this state of affairs did not have a good effect. The youngsters as well as responsible community figures could feel the absence of some public institution which would serve as a gathering place for the youth and improve their style of life.

At the time, Poland was responding to the slogan of "a healthy mind in a healthy body" and this finally crystalized in the idea of establishing societies for the physical development of the younger generation.

The industrialist, Meizner, placed a hall in his factory at the disposal of the prospective Society while steps were taken to obtain a permit for it. For until it was legally approved, nothing serous could be undertaken. And, after several weeks of effort in various directions, the rules and regulations of the new Society were approved by the authorities and it began to forge ahead. Youngsters began to flow to it. Fresh gymnasts joined every day. In the daytime, children also came to the Club premises to engage in drill, gymnastics and various kinds of sports. All steps were on a voluntary basis and the need for guidance by professional sports instructors was soon felt. A German was invited to serve as teacher and conducted the exercises in German. Hundreds of young people belonging to all sections of the Jewish population attended the inaugural meeting.

As the Society began to develop the question arose as to whether it should restrict its activities to sports only. For the desire to engage in cultural activities seemed to grow of itself. As a result of the discussion, a choir was founded with Krotianski as choir-master. Sports competitions were held every year as well as regular rambles, swimming lessons and hikes in the countryside around Kalish. Each of these activities attracted hundreds of young people so that the Society came to include almost the entire younger generation.

The Society added a fresh, enjoyable and interesting dimension to the life of the Jews in the city. But precisely when it was reaching the peak of its activities, World War I broke out. The Germans invaded the city and bombarded it; the population fled in all directions and everything was ruined. In 1915-16, the Jews began to return and life gradually grew normal under the German occupation. The younger generation promptly renewed the activities of the Society and concentrated on them. This state of affairs continued until Poland became independent in 1918.

[Page 139]

Within a few years the Society had become a non-party organization for training youth. A brass band was founded and conducted by Witkowski. The younger generation began to display considerable achievements in sports and the members of the Society were constantly among the first in all sports competitions in the city. In spite of the gradual appearance of political societies and organizations of all kinds among Jewish youth, this Society maintained its position as a non-party Sports Organization and its activities continued to provide a model and an example for all the townsfolk. It maintained this position until 1939 when the Germans again invaded Kalish. This time, it was not the buildings of the city but the entire Jewish population which they destroyed with the wonderful youth of Kalish among them.

———

Rowing Club K.W.30

by S. Pinczewski

Rowing Club K.W.30 was founded in Kalish in order to enable the Jewish youth to take an active part in water sports while permitting older members and their children to enjoy the jetty and the excellent fleet of boats which the Club possessed. In due course, this Rowing Club became the social centre of local Jewish intellectuals with activities that spread far beyond those originally envisaged.

Year-by-year, on the anniversary of the opening of the Club and at every rowing competition, the members gathered en masse with their families and guests. The Club arranged parties at the end of the year and at Purim, as well as dances at its Club premises from time-to-time. On occasion, these were held in the larger chambers of the Town Hall or the Musical Society. In addition, there were satirical evenings and lectures on sports and general themes.

It should be added that this Club K.W.30 was an independent body and the only one of its kind in Polish Jewry.

The Municipality granted the Club a stretch of its own on the banks of the Prosna which was buttressed with planks and poles. Handsome wooden buildings were constructed and painted in gay colours. They contained cloakrooms as well as a large covered area for the boats. Each member had a locker for his belongings. Year-after-year, there were improvements at the jetty and the training installations. Architect L. Comber, a member of the Club, planned new buildings for training halls and cloakrooms. The finances were very satisfactory and nothing held up building except the approval of the plans.

[Page 140]

There were seven boats of excellent quality, both racing and semi-racing, which were purchased in Poland and abroad. They were among the best of their kind in the country. In addition, there were several dozen good rowing boats. Of the 250 members, about 100 were active sportsmen; several scores of whom made up racing teams, both male and female. Jewish students spending the summer holidays in the town were allowed to use the Club and its equipment for a nominal fee or even gratis. Apart from the jetty and buildings, the Club had its winter premises in the Josephine Allée. This contained six rooms, a library, a reading room which received many newspapers and a billiard and table tennis room. The rooms were always full to overflowing with members even in the summer.

The boat racing which was chiefly engaged in Poland required teams of four in racing boats. These needed close and well-time cooperation of our rowers and coxswain for at least two years. In Kalish it was very difficult to ensure this. It was hard to build up several teams of this kind or to assure the proper combination of members in each team. In addition to this, unsatisfactory team construction was another difficulty. Under the conditions in which the Jews lived, the crews were bound to break up from time-to-time when one or other of the members left Poland or moved to another city.

Two years before the outbreak of World War II, the Kalish Club began to discuss a plan for sending a crew of four together with their boat to the Boating Competition in Tel-Aviv. It was decided to carry out this plan in 1940. The committee felt sure that the trip would serve to advance the sportsmen of K.W.30; would have a good effect on the boats men of Tel-Aviv; would encourage everybody to make greater efforts and would increase the number of sportsmen, both in Kalish and elsewhere. However, those circumstances which were to make an end of Kalish Jewry prevented this project from being realized.

The Budgetary Session
of the Kehilla Council, 1930

by M. M.

A meeting of the Kehilla Council took place at 6.30 p.m. on Sunday, 16th February in order to consider the budget. Proceedings were opened by the chairman, *Mr. Isaac Oder* and *Mr. Margulies*, the secretary, read the minutes of the previous meeting in Polish. *Mr. Eisenberg* then read them in Yiddish. Mr. Eisenberg stressed that there were certain discrepancies between the minutes in both languages and that a Jewish Community ought to be simply ashamed at keeping such minutes in its archives.

Mr. Traube demanded that the agenda should be amended to include a motion on easing the distress of the poverty-stricken masses and another on the competence of the Executive in signing promissory notes whenever it sees fit to do so.

Mr. Eisenberg: "It is not parliamentary procedure to add any more items to an agenda that has been prepared." In view of the urgency of the matter, he nevertheless demanded that first there should be a discussion of ways of easing the distress of the impoverished Jewish masses and only afterwards should the budget be discussed.

[Page 141]

After an exchange between *Messrs. Eisenberg, Traube* and *Oder, Mr. Stein* was given permission to speak out and support the proposal to deal with the distress of the masses on account of urgency. *Mr. Stein* stated inter alia that the previous year several hundred Jewish unemployed had enjoyed Government support while this year, only thirty-odd were receiving it. He therefore thought that it was the duty of the Kehilla to save the Jewish unemployed from ruin and starvation.

Mr. Sheps: we cannot permit a motion which allows the executive to sign additional promissory notes even before they have given us a detailed report for 1929.

Mr. Kohn remarked that as far as the left are concerned, there were only unemployed while for the others there were also persons who were not making a living. In his opinion it was first necessary to discuss the budget and only then to deal with other questions.

Mr. Eisenberg insisted that first there must be a discussion of the unemployed and those without any livelihood since these were vital and urgent matters and the budget should only be discussed afterwards.

The question which item should first be discussed was put to the vote and the majority called for a prior consideration of the budget.

Mr. Kohn demanded a reconsideration of the resolution regarding the slaughterers which had been adopted at the previous meeting. (commotion in the *Gallery*: *Voices*: "the slaughterers still have plenty to eat...we demand a discussion of the unemployed question").

Mr. Gutfreund categorically opposed any reopening of the issue of the slaughterers.

Mr. Eisenberg: "If we reconsider the decision taken at the last meeting, there will never be an end. The same scene will recur at every meeting."

Mr. Stein thought that in order to reconsider a resolution, it was necessary first of all to obtain signatures. Only then could the question be discussed at the next meeting.

When the matter was put to the vote it was resolved to re-examine the question of the slaughterers. During the renewed discussion on this matter, it was resolved inter alia that the chicken slaughterers should be paid 4,680 zloty per year while the other slaughterers were to received 7,800 zloty.
Mr. Gutfreund: "I protest vigorously at the cancellation of the resolution passed at the last session."
The discussion of the budget then began. The secretary, *Mr. Margulies*, read out the following list of allocations for the year 1930:

	Zloty
Talmud Torah	12,000
Mikveh repair	7,000
House of Study	2,700
Old Age Home	1,000
Talmud Torah	8,000
Eliza Arzeszkowa Orphanage	5,000

[Page 142]

Boys' Orphanage	1,500
Girls' Orphanage	1,000
Jewish Hospital	2,000
Hachnassat Orhim	1,500
Coal for the poor	2,000
Fire Brigade	300
Immigration	1,500
Linat Hatsedek	3,000
Gemilut Hassadim	1,000
Rescue Committee	3,000
Completing New House of Study	10,000
Hebrew Teacher in Government School	2,400
Jewish Gymnasium	4,000
Magen Abraham Yeshiva	1,000
Etz Hayim Yeshiva	1,000
Bet Lehem	500
Poor women in childbed	200
Two Scholarships	500

TOZ	300
Evening classes at the Artisans' Society	1,200
Unemployed	3,000

Mr. Eisenberg: The item of the Mikveh is fictitious because nobody knows what is going on there. Of all the allocations, 90% are given to religious functionaries and only 10% for all other purposes. If you were employing Jewish workers there would not be any Jewish unemployed at all (applause from the gallery). For the Old Age Home, there is actually 450 zloty instead of 1,000 and that includes the Matzot. The Eliza Orzeszkowa actually receives 1500 zloty instead of 5,000 and that also includes the Matzot. The same applies to the other institutions.

Mr. Eisenberg paused in particular to consider that Linat Hatsedek which is one of the most useful and important institutions but was drowning in debts. Since 1927, it had hardly received anything from the Kehilla. The Medem School should get 3,000 zloty, the Peretz, Shurek and Borochow Schools and the popular university should receive 10,000 zloty together.

Mr. Sheps sharply criticized the budget remarking: A total of 2,000 zloty were allocated for heating but luckily we have had an easy winter. What would we have done if the temperature had gone down to minus 40 degrees? What would the poor have done? The Kehilla has also allocated 200 zloty in good cash money for poor women in childbirth. Isn't this a sheet scandal? A city where 19,000 Jews live is not in position to allocate anything more than 200 zloty for those poor and exhausted women... The entire budget is artificial!

Mr Stein (ironically): Five budgets have already been discussed by the Kehila in this automatic fashion... You could print another five copies and then you would have a budget for another five years. You pass resolutions and don't carry them out so what is the point of passing them? You are not fit to represent us decently – you had better resign!

[Page 143]

He then went into details regarding the Linat Hatsedek saying: "If the Kehilla allocates 3,000 zloty on paper, it actually receives no more than 25% of the amount. Since the Linat Hatsedek is about to set up its own pharmacy which will cost several thousand zloty, we propose that the Kehilla should participate in order to speed up the establishment". With regard to the allocation to the unemployed, he demanded that payment should be made in money and not in goods.

Mr. Stein then dealt with the emigration budget of 1500 zloty and demanded that the Kehilla should distribute 5,000 zloty for this purpose. Since we could expect a constant worsening in the economic situation, it was clear that the stream of emigration would increase and he, therefore, proposed that the Kehilla should allocate 10,000 zloty for this purpose. He also demanded that the Kehilla pay the Gemilout Hassadim Fund the allocation for the years 1927, 1928 and 1929.

Proceeding to the problem of the unemployed, *Mr. Stein* stated that those primarily to blame for unemployment were the Jewish industrialists who were boycotting Jewish workers. He demanded that the Kehilla should require the Jewish industrialists to abolish the special boycott of Jewish workers.

Mr. Ader noted: No additional burden can be placed on the budget which is inflated in any case. If we overload it we shall be unable to do anything.

Mr. Goldstein: When the Kehilla received a letter from the Starosta (District Commissioner) nobody thought it necessary to call a meeting of the Executive. That means that some things are kept secret from the members of the Executive. As for the grants given by the Kehilla, they are not shared out on any correct scale.

A resolution was submitted to pass the budget *in toto*. The resolution was adopted. The allocations were also approved *en bloc*. A vote was held on Mr. Eisenberg's proposal for the allocation of 10,000 zloty to various schools. The proposal was rejected. Mr. Stein's proposal for the allocation of 10,000 zloty for emigration requirements was then put to the vote and rejected.

Mr. Eisenberg: "In the future when we have a clear majority in the Kehilla, we shall pay you back as you deserve since you are causing us trouble for you have all united against us. We express our lively protest and resolve to leave the meeting".
The secretary, *Mr. Margulies* read the supplements to the budget but there was so much noise that it was impossible to hear anything.

The noise grew louder from moment-to-moment. Someone turned out the gas. Benches were overthrown. There were shouts, yells, confusion, curses, and threats against the Kehilla. It was impossible to calm the public.

The chairman closed the meeting at 9.30 p.m.

Dos Kalisher Leben 3(131); 2 Shevat 3690, 28-2-1930

———

[Page 144]

Results of Elections
to the Kehilla Council, 1936

by A. K.

The elections to the Kehilla Council held on Sunday, 6th September this year ended with the following results:

List 1. Agudat Israel, 488 votes, 3 seats: Joseph Moshe Heber, Hannanel Rosenblum, Wolf Tosk. Deputies: Moshe Karman, Isaac Redlich, Simha Wiederschall.
List 2. The Rebbe of Wole, 200 votes, 1 seat: Noah Hiller, deputy: Jacob Waldfreid.
List 4. Bund, 333 votes, 1 seat: Michael Eisenberg. Deputy: Leib Hirshbein.
List 5. Zionist Labour Block, 242 votes, 1 seat: Zelig Kempinski, deputy: Ber Gross.
List 7. Poalei Zion, 366 votes, 2 seats: Sam Wolkowitch, Jacob Kenia. Deputies: Aaron Joseph Wolkowitch and Isaac Traube.
List 8. Revisionists, 166 votes: no seat.
List 11. Small Merchants, 240 votes, 1 seat: Hayyim Perle. Deputy: Joseph Schachtel.
List 12. Popular, 45 votes, no seat.
List 13. Religious Worthies, 5 votes, no seat.
List 14. Religious Block, 432 votes, 2 seats: Lipman Mansfeld, Nissan Goldhammer. Deputies: Jacob Shapira and Isaac Kohn.
List 15. Alexander Hassidim, 344 votes, 1 seat: Isaac Oder. Deputy: Isaac Solomon Rosenwald.
List 16. Poalei Agudat Israel, 205 votes, 1 seat: Abraham Hersh Goldberg. Deputy: Mordechai Isaiah Perle.
List 17. National Religious Block, 666 votes: 3 seats: Professor Asher Bakalar, Berish Shaviska and Henekh Sitner. Deputies: Jacob Lustig, Raphael Gruenbaum and Gustav Markowski.

What have the Kehilla elections taught us?

The Kehilla elections were participated in by almost 4,000 of the 5,000 persons with voting rights, that is, 80% of the Kalish Jews entitled to vote. The results are instructive. To begin with, we have seen the victories and defeats of several organizations, bodies and groups which claimed to be the representatives of Jewish Kalish and their leaders and spokesmen. Yet, in the light of the recent results in which public opinion expressed itself, we see clearly who is fit to represent the Jewish public here and to speak in its name and who has no right to do so.

The election results proved the political maturity and healthy instincts of the Jewish public which is unaffected by cheap phraseology in spite of the so-called 'press' of a certain kind whose whole purpose was to degrade honest and worthy leaders. For months on end they did their best to blacken the reputations of communal representatives of long standing and of the Orthodox majority in the Kehilla headed by the chairman, Mr. J.M. Heber. Yet, the Jewish public distinguished between destructive activities and beneficial and honest measures for the good of the public and gave its main support for List One.

[Page 145]

If we remember that List One went alone to the elections and received 488 votes while List 17, the block that included the Zionists, Misrahi, Hehalutz, Great Synagogue, Artisans, National Artisans, Small Merchants, Travellers to Fairs, "Jewish State Party" and others as included in their own lists, obtained only 666 votes, we must reach the conclusion that List One gained a tremendous victory, both numerical and moral.

If we bear in mind the fact that the systematic incitement did not affect the results of the elections at all, we can describe the latter as a victory of truth over falsehood. We can also view them as a barometer of Jewish society which has proved its political awareness and maturity and has functioned worthily at this hour of grave political decision. That is our consolation in these bitter times and from this, we shall draw the courage to hold out until better times..

Dos Kalisher Leben 31 (454); 27th Elul 5696 9.9.1936

————

The Jewish Hospital

by Dr. P. Beatus

Adam Hodinski, the honoured historian of our city, states that the Jewish Hospital was founded in 1835 from the contributions of the Jewish residents. This date is not quite accurate. The Hospital was founded in 1837. The Council of the Institution set up a small provisional hospital consisting of one room in a building belonging to the Jewish Community and placed it under the charge of Dr. Michael Morgenstern. The treatment of the poor patients in the city was also entrusted to the hospital's director.

On 26th March 1836, Dr. Morgenstern presented a report to the aforesaid council. From this and from all the reactions which this report aroused among the authorities, it is easy to understand that in 1836 there was no hospital in existence as yet and its foundation took place during the first period of office of the Committee of the Institution in Kalish and the main Committee in Warsaw. Official recognition of the Committee of the Jewish Hospital was registered on 9th December 1835. The hospital itself was not built from the ground up as had been done in Warsaw, Lublin, Radom and other cities, but was housed in a reconstructed building purchased in 1837 which was situated in the Piskozhewska Street.

The hospital was built from contributions made by the entire Jewish public which were paid to the Kehilla. Here, however, I must return to the 13th century when the Jews of Kalish were permitted to build a synagogue on grounds belonging to the Canonical Church (the Church of Holy Mikolai) and were charged with an annual tax, the payment of which was to be secured from income of the Kehilla deriving from slaughter (Shehita) and from the four inns belonging to the synagogue. This tax was not paid regularly and after the Order was abolished in 1810, the debt amounted to 14,967 zloty. The Priest, Ignaci Prszebilski, head of the Church Community of Mikola the Holy, imposed an attachment on the funds of the Kehilla aiming at the Hospital Fund as well.

[Page 146]

Ludwig Mamrot, chairman of the Hospital Committee, began to take measures for the cancellation of this step. The hospital archives record that in 1840 the case was heard at the High Court of Appeal in Warsaw and the Funds of the Jewish Hospital were released from the attachment.

In the continuation, we read that the Kalish Municipality thereupon commenced a long trial against the hospital demanding payment of taxes amounting to 232 zloty. A Government Committee, to be sure, recommended that the Institution should be exempted from taxation but the Municipal Council was not prepared to renounce its claim so easily. On April 1st 1837, the claims of the Municipality were dismissed in virtue of an Order issued by the Governorate of Kalish.

This was not the only conflict which the hospital had with the Municipality. There was a matter of land tax. The plot on which the hospital was built had been purchased on perpetual leasehold. The vendor undertook to pay the Municipality a tax of 1 thaler and 20 groschen twice a year; and after the sale, the purchaser was to pay 5% of the estimated value. In accordance with this agreement, the Municipality demanded the sum of 1,838 zloty from the Hospital Committee. The trial regarding this payment had not yet been ended in 1848 and litigation still continued in 1868. Finally, the amount was divided and paid off in installments. In 1863 the Central Committee requested that in negotiations with the authorities, use should no longer be made of the expression "Hospital for the Fully Faithful" (Starozakonani) but "The Jewish Hospital".

From what has been written above, we learn that the Municipality was never the owner of the hospital and even evinced a hostile attitude towards it.

In 1871 the Hospital Committee requested the Municipality to repair the bank of the Prosna that lay within the hospital grounds. The Municipality replied negatively explaining that the plot and the ground were the property of the Jewish Community and Jews alone were being treated as patients there. Hence, the Municipal exchequer was not required to meet this outlay of 81 roubles and 20 kopeks which was not considerable and could easily have been collected from the numerous wealthy Jews of our city. In October of the same year, the Municipality wrote to the curator, Maurici Mamrot, that since winter was approaching, they requested him to repair the banks of the Prosna within his property otherwise he would be held responsible for any damages that might result.

Can there be any further doubt that the Municipality is not the owner of the hospital? However, there are two reasons for its claim: One is: During World War I, the German occupants entrusted the Jewish Hospital to the Municipality and did the same with the "Hospital of the Holy Trinity" in accordance with German practice. The second reason is: Registration in The Land Registry has only recently been completed. The contract of purchase was signed by Mamrot and Redlich who were acting on behalf of the Kehilla; but that fact is not mentioned in the contract.

[Page 147]

And so, it came about that the Municipality built an additional wing to the hospital without asking any permission from the owners of the land. The Kehilla conducted its own health service properly and we find evidence of this in the 1839 Report of Czetirkin, Inspector of Health Services, who wrote as follows: "The Jewish Hospital is excellently arranged and the noble efforts they make in their care for the sick in spite of their limited resources are worthy of all praise."

It was the Kehilla which supplied all the needs of the hospital. Now all the implements and equipment have been transferred to the "Hospital of the Holy Trinity" while only patients suffering from internal and venereal diseases, mostly Christians, are admitted to the Jewish Hospital. Is it reasonable that a Jew should be able to find a place only with difficulty in a Jewish Hospital? The Kehilla appealed to the Court and lost. It was decided that the hospital was communal.

Since there had been no registration in the Land Register, the hospital has passed into the possession of the Inter-Community Association which regards it as municipal property.

Our hospital was founded on the initiative of the Jewish population and was absolutely religious in character. Evidence of this is the synagogue built there in the year 1885 by the heirs of Jeanette Apt. The Kehilla alone is capable of ensuring the religious character of the institution which was established on behalf of one religious grouping within the total population. In the course of the hundred years that the hospital has been in the hands of the Kehilla, the Municipality not only did not help it but actually harmed it.

Yet, there is another reason for the Municipality's haste in proclaiming the hospital to be public property. After the Germans had burnt Kalish, the Prussian General Bessler prepared a plan for improving the city. According to this plan, which is to be found in the Warsaw Archives, all the houses in Nadwodna Street on the left bank of the Prosna were to be demolished and replaced by gardens. The authorities approved the plan and the hospital would also be demolished. If it should be municipal property, the Municipality would not have had to pay any compensation to the Kehilla.

At the beginning of the 20th century, we proposed the building of a modern hospital. The Silberstein heirs contributed a plot of two morgen of land in the Udzialowa Street for the purpose but the Municipality impounded this property as well.

[Page 148]

A DECADE

[Page 149]

Kalish in 5687 (1927)

Our history has been enriched by one more year.

Another year is over with all its happenings, both good and bad. We have grown more mature and that enables us to learn lessons and draw suitable conclusions. Together with Jewry as a whole, Kalish Jewry has to make a summing-up at the close of the past year in the fields of culture and economics alike. Let our more satisfactory achievements serve us as an example in order that we may double them in the future. And let our errors serve as warning to our leading personalities in order that they may not repeat them. Let us briefly survey the departing year before we bid it farewell.

Culture

We would have done better if we had chosen "Lack of Culture" as our heading or if we had left a blank space. For if we propose to discuss this subject at all, we shall blush with shame at the ostensible cultural achievements of our city.

There is not a single Jewish society or association party group which does not feel that it has the holy duty of promising its members, in the very first lines of its programme, that it is going to do wonders in the field of culture. All the parties, right and left, orthodox and other, promised their members that they would provide a series of informative lectures which would help to satisfy the general longing for and aspiration towards information and science in general and Jewish knowledge in particular. Surely this was a field in which every group could show its capacity and prowess and talents. How regrettable that none of these possibilities was realised. Nothing more was achieved than a few beginnings at the most.

During the whole of the past year not a single important lecture was delivered and not one scientific lesson was given in the fields to which we referred. All we heard was petty party skirmishing and the settling of private accounts which spoilt the members for anything useful; and that was all.

A somewhat more serious approach and a little goodwill might have given rise to tremendous results. If the leaders of the Societies take this to heart, the error will not be repeated.

Education

The education situation in the community is more or less satisfactory. There is a network of hadarim and schools. Every party or current spares neither money nor effort and they all do their best to ensure the proper education of the younger generation. Obviously, each party does what it can to inculcate its own approach and methods but this does not worry us much. Every Jewish father endeavours to send his children to the institution that is closest to his own point of view.

Besides the hadarim and elementary schools, we also have a gymnasium with eight classes, the "Havatzelet" School for girls and the Trade School. In the course of their existence these institutions have rightly won the approval of the public. However, two matters in this field are not satisfactory.

[Page 150]

To begin with, a certain section of the parents do not appreciate these schools but send their children to Christian schools which are alien where their Jewish souls are spoilt and they become estranged from their own people. This is partly due to insufficient explanation and propaganda but it is something that can still be put right.

The second mistake is that fourteen hundred children are sent to government schools where they are almost forcibly estranged from us. We shall suffer from this mistake before long when this young generation grows up to be entirely assimilationist and absolutely without any contact with us.

However, we have done our duty on all occasions and opportunities and from our columns we have warned the public, rebuking them for the great wrong done to our little ones. The correction of this mistake lies in the hands of our communal worthies who have both the power and the resources.

Commerce

In our city, wholesale and retail trade together with handicrafts to some degree are dependent on the village purchasers. They in turn are dependent on the crops which fix the peasants' purchasing power. During recent years the peasants and farmers have become accustomed to using better quality products and now their purchases depend entirely on their income.

Last year the crops were unsatisfactory and obviously the farmer's purchasing power fell off considerably. But at the beginning of the harvest, when the peasant hungers for goods, he disregards such considerations and buys whatever comes his way. And so the last year can be divided into two parts: During the early months trade was almost satisfactory but during the rest of the year it was almost at a complete standstill.

However, the local tax commissioner completely ignored the state of business and last year the tax press squeezed hard. If the appeals of most of the merchants are not satisfactorily considered, they will simply have to shut their shops.

The three Jewish economic organizations should have done far more in order to make the tax authorities realise the real situation of the merchants and in that way save trade and commerce from collapse.

The Lace Industry

The Lace Industry, which was once the backbone of Kalish economy and a decisive influence in the rapid development of the city has ceased to be important since the war and has hardly any influence at all. All efforts to sign a Commercial Agreement with Russia have been unsuccessful although Russia, before the war, was the main customer of the local Lace Industry. So for the time being and until trade with neighbouring countries is restored, our industrialists must rest satisfied with the local market.

The result is that the machines work for only six months a year and in only a few factories. The absence of any steady demand has compelled the lace manufacturers to unite or at least not to compete with one another. They have set up a common fund to which each manufacturer makes a certain contribution per kilogram of finished product. When the branch is at a standstill, the manufacturer receives seventy-five zloty per week for each machine standing idle.

[Page 151]

The Fine Lace Industry has recently begun to develop in our city. Hundreds of these machines are now operating here. But as long as the Tariff War with Germany continues, there is no hope of better prospects in this branch. In any case, it is clear that when a Trade Agreement is signed with Germany, the government will have to take this manufacture into account in order to prevent the Polish market from being flooded by German lace.

In some measure, this industry has solved the problem of unemployment for the present and the government must take this into consideration.

Flour Mills

The second branch of industry in which Kalish stands out and of which it is proud is its flour mills. Kalish plays an important part in the food supply of Poland through its flour industry. The grain that is ground here reaches the whole of Zaglembia from Kattowitz on the one side and as far as Bialystok, Vilna and the Russian frontier on the other.

This development of the industry and the numerous mills secure the living of large numbers of Jews. It also supports quite a few grain merchants who sell their goods by the railway wagon and market merchants who also supply the grain to the mills.

Last year the crop was not satisfactory and the grain trade was almost at a standstill. Most of the corn was imported and the large mills managed without difficulty. This was not so easy for the small mills, including dealers and agents who have nothing to do because all transactions were signed directly with the mills.

The market dealers have no business because next to no grain was bought from the villages. To sum up, the flour mills did not have a bad year though the trade in cereals underwent a crisis.

The export of bran and chaff to Germany, which always served as an important factor in regulating the price of flour in Poland, has recently been prohibited. More precisely, a customs duty of 7.5 zloty per cubic metre has been imposed. This duty has stopped exports completely. It would only be proper to abolish it. Poland has never been in a position to consume all the bran and chaff it produces. Now, in view of the tremendous surpluses and the fall in prices, the millers will have to find themselves some compensation by raising the price of flour and it is clear that the government is not interested in that.

Product Assistance

Kalish has done a great deal in this respect and is certainly not behind other cities in the country. Here we have two Cooperative Banks which largely help the Jewish merchants. Their tremendous development is the best proof possible of the confidence they have gained in local mercantile circles.

[Page 152]

The second institution which has gained the confidence of the public is the "Gemilut Hassadim Fund" also known as the Relief Committee whose loans are granted without interest. Thousands of families who would otherwise have had to apply for charity have recovered thanks to the assistance of the Relief Committee and that is certainly a tremendous achievement.

*

Those in brief are our achievements during the past year. As remarked, let us hope that the errors will serve as a warning and not be repeated while the achievements are doubled and more.

May a New Year begin with all its blessing.

Kalisher Leben 12, New Year's Eve 5688, 25-9-1927

Kalish in 5688 (1928)

We are on the threshold of a New Year to which we look forward with hope and faith. To be sure, it is only the faith of the Jew that gives us the strength to withstand our distresses and look ahead to better times. Today, at the end of 5688, let us sum up the debit and credit sides of Jewish life in Kalish.

We shall register the important events and preserve them in our memory in order to forestall the evil that may come and in the hope of doubling the good in so far as we have done good deeds. May these words be a thanksgiving offering to those individuals who worked to help the Jewish public in Kalish and may those who neglected their public duties give ear and magnify their efforts so as not to lag behind their good colleagues in the year to come.

The greatest impress on the public was made by the local government elections. The Jewish statesmen of the city became ardently enthusiastic and we even feared that we would never achieve any joint Jewish list at all. However, political common sense proved victorious and the large and influential parties presented a common list. Thanks to the joint stand in the elections of such parties as the Agudat Israel, the Zionists and the Small Merchants, we won a complete victory. List No. 16 gained the largest number of seats as it had fondly hoped.

Still, it is true that if their votes had been supplemented by the lost votes of List N°8 and the surpluses of List No. 17, the number of Jewish councillors would have been still greater. But we shall never be short of personal ambitions and it seems that we shall never succeed in surmounting them.

The satisfactory results of the victory were soon seen. The successful election of our candidate to the office of Alderman will certainly ensure a satisfactory and beneficial policy in the Town Hall for the good of Jewish Kalish. And we may certainly say that our work was not in vain.

[Page 153]

It is possible that sceptics do not yet see the "golden mountains" of the new policy. Let us remind them of the Polish proverb that "Krakow was not built in a day". It would be a good thing if several of our local hotheads were to remember this.

*

The Town Council is opening its term of office while our Kehilla (Jewish Communal Council) is preparing for elections because its term of office will soon be over.

According to information from the District Offices, the elections must be over by December 2nd. So the Kehilla Executive and Council will do well before giving up office to publish a report of activities during their four-years at their posts.

We are very well aware that when things were taken over from the Parnassim (wardens) it was necessary to begin everything from the beginning. And indeed, the organization of the business of the Kehilla is a great achievement and will be remembered in favour of the Executive who did not flinch from responsibility but transferred the Shehita (ritual slaughter) to its own control. A beginning has been made with the construction of the Talmud Torah Building but when will it be finished? In addition, the Mikveh has been improved and the allocations for certain institutions have been paid. Yet, it must be stated that the Kehilla is not sufficiently interested or maybe not interested at all in the education of the younger generation.

Thousands of Jewish children are being educated according to principles which are alien, almost hostile, to everything that is Jewish; yet the Kehilla disregards this. Surely it is in a position to help by opening an afternoon school for children attending the government schools? That will save Jewish children! In addition, the children at the

Talmud Torah are taught unsystematically and without any useful purpose. For what is a Jewish child trained to do after he leaves the Talmud Torah?

Why do we not remember the old Talmudic statement that any study of Torah which is not accompanied with a handicraft leads to idleness? Let us hope that this defect will be corrected in the new building.

*

We have heard a great deal about the restoration of the synagogue but see no signs of any steps being taken. Every year allocations are made for the Relief Committee, yet they are not given a penny. Surely it would be better not to allocate anything and finish, as is the practice with "TOZ" and various other institutions.

And we have another question to the Community Executive: What is the point in electing a Council and calling on it to approve the Budget if it is not invited to hear a Report on activities?

*

Large numbers of Jews find a little help in the Cooperative Bank. The tremendous progress which the Bank has made during the last year marks an institution of which Kalish Jewry may well be proud. Nor is it a matter for pride alone. The Bank has really saved thousands of shopkeepers and craftsmen who have been delivered from the moneylenders in the streets only thanks to the help it has given. For the Bank's affairs are in full order and show us that all currents which represent the general public in it are capable of working together harmoniously. We have only to wish it continued success and expansion in the same way as it has grown until now.

[Page 154]

Just as the Cooperative Bank has worked for the benefit of the masses of craftsmen and small shopkeepers, so the Merchants' Bank has helped the industrialists and larger merchants. This is a relatively youthful institution in our city but it already enjoys the recognition and esteem of the bigger businessmen and manufacturers. It was easy for us to learn what is going on here. At the general meeting of the Merchants' Bank we heard a report on its activities. No better proof of the confidence of the public, which is so justly vested in the Bank, can be found than its tremendous turnover during the past year. The Institution was established thanks to the initiative of a few individuals and owing to their obstinacy and persistence; we now have a Bank of which we may be proud.

These institutions with all their local activity are incomparably helpful to merchants, manufacturers and craftsmen alike. Yet, at the same time, the Gemilut Hassadim Fund is a necessity for thousands of families whom the Banks cannot help. The slight assistance they are given they receive from this Fund, or, as it is called, the Relief Committee. It is superfluous to write about all that this institution does, for everybody can see the results. Yet, it is our duty to remark that the Jewish public of Kalish has not yet shown any adequate appreciation for it.

Admittedly we must point out again that in spite of our repeated reminders the Management of the Gemilut Hassadim has not yet found time to engage in a drive for contributions; and if no one demands, nobody gives. It follows that both sides are equally to blame, the Management and the public alike. It is our duty to give a warning. If the Fund does not expand its activities it will deviate from the purposes laid down by its founders and will gradually be transformed into nothing more than a very large charitable institution.

This is how things appear: one the one hand, efforts are made to help Jews to hold out while, on the other hand, the pressure of taxes is increasing to unimaginable dimensions and may well take the food from the mouths of many Jewish families. The Income Tax rates are now being fixed and the fate of every Jew will be sealed. The Jewish economic associations must stand on guard, carefully preparing all the material that is submitted to Committee members in order that the latter may be able to work properly. If this is not done, all the outcry of those who are badly treated will be useless later on; particularly those who have been wrongly assessed by mistake.

The Jewish economic societies displayed ample activity last year and then something became perfectly clear. As the influence of the political parties on the masses declined, the influence of the economic organizations grew greater.

[Page 155]

We shall not try to explain this development now. Yet it is clear to us that a large part of the change is due to the disappointment of the public. The political parties deceived them more than once by promising mountains and valleys without fulfilling any of their promises. Let this serve as a lesson to the Economic Societies which have gained the hegemony over the Jewish street. Let them be more careful in their methods and act according to the rule: Say little but do much!

*

The condition of cultural activities in our city is a miserable one. There is not even a single serious organization or society to engage in our cultural and educational problems without narrow political and party interests.

We regret that most of our Jews in Kalish have no understanding of what may be the most important issue of all. We always see the same sad sight. While one drags right the other drags left; and the ordinary Jew, the all-year-round Jew remains perplexed and confused and does not know what to do. Finally, he pays no attention neither to one nor to the other and meanwhile he sends his children to the Government schools. As a result, the younger generation of Jews gradually become a weak limb of the nation, assimilating little by little. At the same time, the party leaders to right and left can hear mocking laughter at their pretended concern for Jewish culture, but by now, they are unable to improve matters. We can see how, when it is a matter of sharing posts, honours, etc. the leaders of all the parties can reach an immediate understanding, but when it is a matter of what may be the most important issue of all, they cannot find a modus vivendi. These gentlemen should remember that if they do not pay careful attention to this matter they may be left without a Community to control.

*

It is notable that while many institutions only exist for the seat and the rubber stamp, a youthful institution like "TOZ" has already achieved much. Here we shall not refer to its financial resources. If the Jews of Kalish were to help it properly, its activities would naturally be wider and better. In spite of this, "TOZ" has maintained summer holiday camps for three hundred children during two seasons. The children receive good food and proper pedagogical and medical supervision. We can only hope that "TOZ" will be well supported and helped to rebuild an orphanage for winter – its immediate objective.

*

The above is a brief summary of Jewish life in Kalish during 5688. There is much to improve. Let those who can improve matters take the necessary steps. We ourselves shall continue to support every just cause, we shall be a platform for every just complaint and help to realize every good idea. Maybe we shall at last achieve the old saying: May the year with its curses end and the year with its blessings begin.

Das Kalisher Leben, 27 (55). New Year's Eve 5689. 14-9-1928

———

[Page 156]

Kalish in 5689 (1929)

Let us now try to sum up all the joys and sorrows of Kalish Jewry during the past year. If we paint ourselves the necessary picture, we shall be able to prepare a report and learn lessons for the future from it.

To be sure, we were full of hope at the beginning of the year and were certain that things would begin to go well. For it was hard to assume that we would still have the strength to bear any more spiritual and economic crises. But it seems that there are no limits to trouble and distress and people can be relied on to reveal the strength to withstand them as they come.

The parting year which was so tragic for Jewry throughout the world because it ended with the savage disturbances in Eretz Israel, was certainly not happy in any economic respect for Polish Jewry. In this regard, we underwent a great shock. This unhappy situation also reigned in the economic life of Kalish, particularly in local industry which is largely in Jewish hands. There were certain branches in which competition was almost savage and the merchants and dealers took bills whose dated payment were deferred almost indefinitely.

The transformation that came about in the whole country regarding the date of payment of promissory notes naturally did not miss Kalish. As a result, there were quite a few cases of bankruptcy and the closing of businesses in the city. By now, the situation has begun to settle down and those factories that have surmounted the crisis are secure, more or less. They are doing their best to make a profit and are even succeeding.

The economic situation of the city suffered a severe blow through the bankruptcy of the Bank Kupiecki. This was a popular institution headed by outstanding business and social personalities. As was natural, the presence of those leaders ensured that the masses would be able to trust the institution. Undoubtedly the merchant, or anybody else, deposited his savings in this bank because he believed in the responsibility of the management. The community was struck by the news of the failure like thunder from the bright blue sky. After a year of waiting, the depositors have not yet seen a penny of their savings. Those "trustworthy" leaders are to blame for this delay.

It is not surprising that this unforeseen financial collapse of a Jewish institution has also give rise to uncertainty about other Jewish institutions of this kind in Kalish. The public has begun to think and hesitate. But the healthy instinct of the masses ensured their trust in the Cooperative Bank and we are happy that we have learnt that the popular instinct was not wrong. From this incident we have learnt a very significant lesson. An institution does not need noisy publicity nor does it have to be headed by "stars". It is better if it is a popular institution managed by simple people for then it can be trusted.

While we are dealing with our local financial institutions we should mention the important part played by the Gemilut Hassadim Fund among the craftsmen and small merchants in general for it saves them from destruction and economic extinction. In the process of pauperization which the Jewish masses are undergoing, the Gemilut Hassadim Funds are a true salvation. Yet, at the same time, we must note the complete indifference of our well-to-do circles towards this useful institution. This attitude of theirs is almost a scandal. It may cripple the existence of the Fund and deprive hundreds of Jewish families in our city of a crust of bread.

[Page 157]

Jewish Economic Societies

During the past year there have been several domestic revolutions, and changes that have taken place in the leading positions. In the first line came the Merchants' Society where Mr. Shelak was elected chairman. He was also chosen as Adviser to the Lodz Chamber of Commerce. This change came about as a result of the bankruptcy of the Merchants' Bank whose directors were also the heads of the Society. After the changes in the management, the Merchants' Society regained the confidence of the Jewish public. It is now a very useful economic body that does a great deal for its members.

The second change came in the Society of Artisans whose previous management had taken a very arrogant personal line. Its dictatorial methods gave rise to dissatisfaction and the General Meeting elected ordinary people without any labels that had been prepared in advance. Truth to tell, the struggle in this Society is not over yet. Things are not yet entirely in order but even in this case we can rely on the healthy instincts of the members and believe that they will elect the leaders they deserve.

On the other hand, there has been no change in the Small Merchants' Society. The heads of this Society are concerned first and foremost with the heavy burden of taxation and the problems of making a living which always worry the numerous members. There is no room for personal intrigues in the life of the worried small merchants who have to manage from day-to-day. In general, those responsible for the activities of this Society stand firm and defend their members' interests wherever this is necessary.

Yet, what can be the supposed strength of these three economic organizations against the Sword of Damocles named 'taxes' which always hangs over their heads?

In this respect, our city is worse off than others and the tax machine grinds mercilessly here. With all our efforts to make things somewhat easier, we have failed. So it was with the Assessment on Turnover and so it is now with the Income Tax Assessment, which is at present under preparation in our city and is terrifying the remnant of the merchants. That is what economic life is like in Kalish today.

*

There have been no improvements in our social life either. The Kehilla, (Community Council), whose terms of office is long over, did not do anything serious in the year 5689. Indifference, somnolence, helplessness all marked the activities of our representatives. They did nothing! They showed no initiative and took no positive steps in the fields of charity or culture. The Kehilla does not have the necessary cooperation and harmony for public well-being. Our wardens and bosses do not even dream of worrying about the education of thousands of children, some of whom receive a 'supposed education' in the choking atmosphere of the Talmud Torah whose new building is still under construction...Most of them are drawing away from their people and their own language in the official schools while nobody says a word. The quarrels about the Dayan (Assistant Rabbi) and Cantor have continued for a long time but nobody has even given a thought to really serious communal activity.

[Page 158]

Even the hospital has been neglected and that has caused much distress and bitterness. Yet, we have not seen any real steps in this field either. The party-men are out for party victories all the time to the discredit of the other sides. So, sure enough, scarcely anything has been achieved during 5689.

*

Matters are different in the Local Authority. In the Jewish 'Group' there you can find harmonious cooperation. Our representatives do their best to exploit every opportunity and every possibility for the benefit of the public. We owe this largely to our Alderman. Thanks to him the Relief Funds of the local government and other sources were opened to us in order to make Jewish poverty a little easier. In general, ever since Mr. Heber has entered this post, the degraded position of the Jew in the Municipal institutions has faded away little by little.

To be sure, there is nothing to be enthusiastic about. We know that much water will still flow down to the sea before our rights become an actual fact. But this is not restricted to Kalish alone. In this respect we have to take part in the struggle of all Polish Jewry.

*

Cultural activities among the Jewish population have not improved at all. The regrettable situation we recorded last year is still to be found. All this field of action has become stamped with the party credos and there is no genuine concern for cultural education.

In this respect, the situation is so regrettable that there is simply nothing to report. Let us hope that matters will improve next year and that there will be more positive developments.

Yes, in the field of physical education, Jewish Kalish developed well during 5689. A number of Jewish Sports Clubs were established and are developing satisfactorily. In addition, the 15th birthday of the Yiddish Turn and Sports Club was celebrated on a lavish scale.

*

So here is a brief summary of public activity in Jewish Kalish. In general, it was a very difficult year both economically and socially. The positive lessons to be learnt from this year's developments are very few. Let them serve as a warning for the future.

May the year 5689 with all that happened during it be relegated to the past and may the coming year bring happiness to us and to all of Israel.

Kalisher Leben, 28 (110); New Year's Eve 5690. 4-1-1929

———

[Page 159]

Kalish in 5690 (1930)

We stand on the threshold of a New Year. Let us try to sum up Jewish life in Kalish during the year that has passed.

To tell the truth, we did not expect miracles but the realities were far worse than we had anticipated. The economic life of the whole country reached a very low point and it is not surprising that Jewish trade and industry fell even lower. Jewish Kalish shared in the grave economic crisis. Factories were closed or worked only part–time. In general, no buyers were found for their goods. The crisis was made even worse by the fact that the Jewish industrialists received no government credits and credit from the street did not permit manufacture on any reasonable basis of calculation. The Jewish merchants and craftsmen found a little consolation in the meagre amount of credit provided by the Cooperative Bank.

However, this institution was also hit by the general situation and is now in a state of convalescence. We shall not go seeking for the causes of this situation. Larger institutions were shaken last year and actually collapsed while our Cooperative Bank held firm. To be sure, banking activities were diminished this year but we were not in a position to increase them. Still, we have to strengthen the Bank for by doing so we shall all grow stronger.

The Artisan's Society underwent an internal crisis during the year. Control went back to the 'veteran' leaders though there have been changes in the external representation. The near future will show whether this is going to help.

Yet, whatever our economic representatives may do to make the crisis easier, they cannot change the situation for the roots of the distress lie in the tax system which crushes trade and industry. Our Kalish, which in this respect is under 'close supervision', is simply being levelled flat under the burden of heavy taxation. Our only hope lies in recent rumours of tax cancellations for several years and a radical change in the Income Tax system. For the time being, we live on hope, and we very much hope that these will not end like similar election promises.

A result of the present crisis is the tremendous increase in the number of persons applying for loans to the Gemilut Hassadim Fund. This institution is the real barometer for the Jewish economic situation. To our regret, we witness a complete contrast between the desirable and the actual situations. The greater the numbers of applicants, the fewer are the supporters. The number of weekly contributors to the Fund grows less and less every week, and the management are not in a position to satisfy the increasing number of applications. It is the sacred duty of our local Jewish population to support this Fund which is at present the most useful thing we have.

In our Kehilla there is domestic peace. The members of the executive are finding ways not to fight. They always discover the golden mean which satisfies all groups represented. The only time there was anything like a quarrel was when several wardens wanted to appoint two additional Dayanim. However, common sense prevailed and for the time being it is not an urgent issue. That is what our communal representative institution is like. Silence no disputes, indifference, slumber without effort or action. Does this idyll give evidence of fruitful public activity? We shall not answer this question here. But, it is generally agreed that our wardens could be doing considerably more.

[Page 160]

Kalish saw one satisfactory development with the restoration of the Great Synagogue. It is true that those who prayed there were literally risking their lives because bricks and pieces of plaster had begun to fall on their heads. Thanks to the energy and insistence of the members of the new synagogue committee, the interior has been restored and renovated. Apart from the assurance regained by the congregation, they now have an aesthetically satisfying House of Prayer as well. We should add that the vast financial resources which were needed for the restoration were collected by the committee from the local Jewish population; and that is a happy situation which should be noted.

*

Jewish cultural life has been marked by complete neglect. During the past year, no activity in this field could be noticed. Good will, to be sure, was shown and even a strong desire to found a Cultural Society. But ideas alone are not enough. The non-establishment of such an institution is the sin of the local Jewish cultural representatives. We must on no account neglect this matter. We shall go on demanding the establishment of a Jewish Cultural Society in Kalish until it has been established.

On the other hand, our educational institutions are fairly satisfactory. We have a first-class Trade School conducted according to the most up-to-date pedagogical principles, with a staff of excellent teachers. In spite of this, it is rather backward. This is due to the masses of Jews who still refuse to understand how important the school is for the coming generation of craftsmen. The Jewish public has to get used to the idea of vocational training in every way possible and raise a new generation in this school for its own benefit.

The Jewish Gymnasium does not require any publicity at all. The Matriculation Certificates which it issues every year and its large number of pupils are the best evidence of the excellent education which it provides.

But the Jewish public have not done their duty for the Gymnasium. They have not taken steps to provide it with a building of its own suited to the needs of such an important institution. The time has come to bring bricks for construction. Our community has to do this job as a matter of sheer self-respect.

*

Mention should be made of the political maturity shown by the Jews in the last elections to the Seim and the Senate. At many public meetings, a firm and absolute demand was made to establish an all-inclusive National Election Block. We know beyond any shadow of doubt that if two lists are presented the local seat is certain to be lost. So, even if the leaders of the parties in Warsaw do not reach an agreement on this, our own region must present a united list of its own, headed by a generally respected leader of the community.

[Page 161]

*

This balance sheet is not at all a cheerful one. The path of the Jewish Community is strewn with thorns. Still, we tread it restored and full of faith. May this be our consolation. The year is passing and we are now waiting for better times. May they come indeed!

Kalisher Leben 37 (159); 19ᵗʰ Elul 5890. 12–9–1930

————

Kalish in 5691 (1931)

The year 5691 was difficult for Jews in every respect. The terrible world crisis which has affected so many nations and countries penetrated deep into Jewish life and shook our well–based positions. The year marked by the economic ruin that ran riot throughout the world and hit the Jews the hardest of all. As a result, all other problems of Jewish life became of secondary importance and our thoughts were dedicated only to finding a refuge from the crisis and easing the distress. Yet, in spite of this, we shall try to sum up the important events of our Jewish world.

*

This was first and foremost the year of elections. Elections were held to the Seim and the Senate. The Jewish parties all acted separately and a deep abyss appeared between them. This division and struggle grew even deeper in the recent elections to the Kehilla in which the Agudat Israel and the Zionists chiefly contended against one another. The atmosphere of those days still continues and to our regret, there is no likelihood that these two elements will extend their hands to one another for the sake of Jewish interests which call for unity and intensified work together at this critical hour.

The Shehita (slaughtering) fees scandal exacerbated the quarrels and division. It was found that the Kehilla had been deceitfully robbed of many thousands of zloty. The Zionist wardens actually threatened to bring slaughterers of their own.

During the past year, the Jewish representatives in the Town Council and the Jewish Community as a whole fought a bitter fight for the existence of the Jewish Hospital. There were certain groups that wished to liquidate this institution entirely, or at least to merge it in the Polish hospital; thus restricting its activities to a minimum and ensuring that in due course it would be entirely forgotten. Our journal, "Kalisher Leben" was the first to sound the alarm. We awakened Jewish public opinion and conducted a campaign to ensure that the institution should remain a Jewish Hospital in all respects.

The Jewish Council members and various communal figures conducted stormy consultations. The Jewish public protested at mass meetings. Finally, those who wished to destroy the Jewish character of the hospital and close it down, had to give way to the pressure of the Jewish public opinion which proved to be firm and united on this matter.

[Page 162]

In connection with this campaign, Doctor Edward Beatus published a series of articles in the "Kalisher Leben" in which he proved by historical facts that the Jewish Hospital belonged to the Jews and that Jews alone had the right to own it.

*

The economic crisis also led the Town Council to cancel its allocations to Jewish charitable institutions. Naturally, this decision shook those bodies which are undergoing a severe crisis. As a result, such an important institution as the nocturnal First Aid Station of the Linat Hatsedek Society was closed down. That is a tremendous loss for the Jewish community. Let us hope that the latter will have the sense to assess this night service at its proper value.

We should also note that this year, after great effort, part of the building of the Talmud Torah has been completed. Now, at last, several hundred pupils of the Talmud Torah will be able to study in spacious and airy rooms and not in dark and filthy premises.

*

This year, the economic societies showed special activity. The paralysis of trade and the bad times in the economy in general compelled the public to associate in economic societies, just as people cling to wooden planks and boards after shipwreck. This year, "Guilds" of all occupations have been established in the Artisans' Association which is particularly important for each separately and for all of them together.

The Merchants' Society and Small Merchants' Society have also shown considerable activity. Mention should be made of the 5th Anniversary celebration of the latter Society at which its considerable achievements were well displayed.

Last year the authorities closed down the other Association of small merchants (at Warszawska 24) and its members then re-organized as a section of the Merchants' Association.

This has also been a fateful year for the Cooperative Bank which was so strong in the past. At first, it seemed that this Bank, which is the pride of all Jewish Kalish, would finally overcome its difficulties and once again be what it had been. But apparently, it could not regain the confidence of its clientele. Finally, it was declared bankrupt and is now about to be wound up. It has been replaced during the past year by two new Credit Institutions. One is the Small Merchants' Cooperative Fund which supplies credit to its members, most of whom are small merchants. The other is the Credit Cooperative founded by Zionist figures whose members are mostly the large and medium merchants.

Naturally, these two banks have not progressed as rapidly as the Cooperative Bank did at first. This is because of the present economic crisis and above all, owing to the loss of trust on the part of the clients after the collapse of two major Jewish credit institutions in our city. But the persons heading the new institutions are such that in the course of time these will come to enjoy the full confidence of the Jewish public once again.

[Page 163]

*

In the cultural field there is now a deathly silence just as there has been for so long a time. Nothing whatever is being done. On the contrary. There were a few stout–hearted people who wished to set up a Cultural Society with the purpose of satisfying the cultural requirements of its members and the Jewish public. But the institution has also collapsed and is now in the process of liquidation. This fact proves for maybe the 100th time that in our city the Jewish public has no cultural needs at all; and in addition, it lacks suitable personalities who are capable of interesting the public in any cultural matters at all.

For a long time there was a struggle within the "Yiddishe Turn und Sport Verein" as to whether its flag should be blue–and–white or green–and–white. Finally, it was resolved to change the flag from green–and–white to blue–and–white.

Mention should also be made of the Central Hehalutz which celebrated its fifth birthday this year.

Among those who passed away in the year 5691 were the devoted leader of the Artisan's Association, Abraham Rubin who was one of the founders and editors of "Kalisher Leben"; Reb Wolf Feiffer, the veteran communal head, warden of the Great Synagogue and most honoured communal worthy; Reb Noah Zaludkowski, the beloved cantor of the community who was honoured by all and Leon Margulies, the veteran Secretary of the Kehilla.

*

We are on the threshold of a New Year, concern in our faces, our skies overcast, while the future of the Jewish people seems to be very black. The grave economic crisis and the terrible poverty have created a spirit of depression, without a single ray of light allowing us to hope for a better morrow. But let us hope that the New Year will disperse the gloomy clouds on the horizon and bring with it courage, faith and hope for a better future.

May this be the end of a year with its curses and the beginning of a year with its blessings.

Kalisher Leben 37 (210); New Year's Eve, 5692. 11–9–1931

———

Kalish in 5692 (1932)

The year 5692 was marked by the effects of the general crisis which spreads all over the world and has impressed a special stamp on the Jewish masses.

The process of economic pauperization of the Jews has gone ahead with giant strides and is affecting a steadily increasing number of victims. The extent of the effects of the crisis on the Jewish population can be seen from the following fact: At the time of Passover, measures initiated by the Kehilla - 70% of the Jews in the City registered for help.

[Page 164]

The crisis has been particularly severe for large numbers of small merchants and artisans whose earnings have declined to a minimum on account of both the general poverty and the high taxes imposed upon them by the authorities. Their situation during the past year has been particularly bad on account of the ceaseless attacks and pogroms which have so greatly affected the fair and market travellers in the Poznan region which is the source of livelihood for a large section of each group. Only after the intervention of the local economic organizations and the central bodies in Warsaw did all these attacks come to an end.

The grave economic crisis also compelled the local Jewish economic organizations to engage in urgent measures on behalf of their members. It must be said that the Merchants' Association, the Small Merchants' Association and the Artisans' Association have achieved a great deal. Anybody checking on the work done, the meetings held and the various measures of intercession must confess that these bodies have done much to ease the fate and conditions of their respective members. Particular activity was shown by the Market dealers' section of the Small Merchants' Society which did a great deal to help calm things down at the fairs and markets.

It is not surprising that in such a grave economic situation the state of public and communal institutions is also bad and there can be no improvement in communal life such as might have come about in better times. In spite of this, let us sum up our more important institutions.

One happy development during the past year was the opening of the new Talmud Torah Building for hundreds of pupils who had been studying so far in unhygienic and absolutely unbearable surroundings. The new building enables them to enjoy pure air and study in healthy surroundings. The building consists of two and a half storeys and cost 120,000 zloty, which were provided by the Kehilla budget and very large contributions from private individuals. Here, mention must be made of the struggle between the Talmud Torah Committee and the young men studying in the Bet Hamidrash, who demanded the best structure for themselves and for that reason, engaged in sabotage which the Committee could overcome only with difficulty.

This year, the Linat Hatsedek Society has opened a pharmacy in order to help the impoverished Jewish population to purchase remedies. This pharmacy was established with great effort and several thousand zloty were invested in it. Owing to this investment, the Society had to suspend its First-aid night service but succeeded in resuming it after a while. During the past year, the Linat Hatsedek Society was particularly active. In addition to the pharmacy, it also opened a dispensary for examining the sick poor. The work of the Society is particularly important during these difficult days of crisis for it provides cheap medical aid for poor Jews.

The Polish Territorial Conference of the Linat Hatsedek was held in Kalish on the initiative of our local Society and was attended by several dozen delegates from all the cities of Poland. Discussions on the problems of providing medical aid for the Jewish population continued for two days.

[Page 165]

*

Mention must also be made of the changes that have come about in Jewish sport affairs. Hitherto, there had been two Jewish sports clubs - Hakoah and the Turn und Sport Verein. The former used the blue-white flag and the latter had a green-white flag. More recently, certain members of the YTSC demanded that their flag should also be blue and white. This led to a severe struggle between the two parties which took the form of meetings and discussions in the press and in public. Finally, after several tempestuous gatherings, it was decided to adopt the blue-white flag. Soon after, it was decided to liquidate both clubs alike and combine them in one large Maccabi Sports Organization. This unification came about and today there is one Maccabi Sports Club (that is, apart from Stern Labour Sports Club).

Mention should also be made of the struggle among the Jewish boating society members which was formerly called "Jewish Boatmen's Society". Several members of the Club demanded that its name be changed to "K.W.30" in order that the Jewish part of the name should not be constantly in the eyes of the Poles.

There were debates at meetings and in the press as well. Finally, the gentlemen of the Boating Club refused to be convinced. They changed the name of the Club and by doing so deserted from the field of Jewish sport.

*

During the past year, a great deal has been written about the foundation of a Charity Fund which is an urgent necessity in these hard times. Finally, an Inaugural Meeting was held and an Executive was elected whose task was to initiate and organize the new institution.

To our great regret nothing more has happened. The organizers began very noisily but the entire matter has gone to sleep. This is not the place to analyse the reasons for the failure. Yet, the attempt as such was distinctly praiseworthy and no harm at all will be done if it is tried again.

To finish our summing up, we must also draw attention to the great loss which the Jews of Kalish have experienced by the death of their Rabbi.

Reb Ezekiel Liebshitz, of blessed memory, passed away suddenly only three months after the Community had celebrated the semi–jubilee of his occupation of the Rabbinical Seat in our City. His passing has given rise to considerable grief throughout the world for he was one of the most outstanding figures in contemporary Jewish life. Yet, the loss to Kalish Jewry has been particularly heavy. As long as Reb Ezekiel Liebshitz held the rabbinical office, which was a matter of twenty–five years, there were no quarrels and disputes within the community. Since his death, opinions are divided with regard to the election of his successor. Some wish to place his son, Reb Eliezer on his seat while others propose other candidates. The Kehilla wished to defer the dispute and, therefore, decided to put–off the election of the Rabbi for three years during which period there would be no rabbi in Kalish.

A little later, there was a dispute regarding the slaughterers which would assuredly not have broken out if our rabbi, of blessed memory, had remained alive. The opposition within the Kehilla wished to bring pressure to bear in order to obtain their demands and brought slaughterers of their own to the city that began competing with those of the Kehilla. In general, there had never been such a sharp struggle between the majority and the opposition in the Kehilla as there was now and it is impossible to say how far matters may go. In any case, it is clear that this quarrel does not benefit our community at a time when the Kehilla has to handle many grave and responsible tasks.

[Page 166]

It should also be noted that the Kehilla has taken over the registration of population which was hitherto in the hands of the Rabbinate. This was decided after the demise of the rabbi when doubts began to arise about the place where the registers should be kept. It is an innovation in Kehilla life for the registers are held by the rabbis in most of the cities of Poland.

Finally, we must record the passing of the wealthy Reb Abraham Abele Friede who was born in Kalish and lived in Cape Town, South Africa for many decades. For the past eight years he had provided lunches for the hundreds of pupils of the Talmud Torah. This was a worthy enterprise and was greatly appreciated. His passing has occasioned much grief.

*

As we see, the balance sheet for 5692 is not particularly happy. On the contrary, it is a grim one yet, what lies ahead seems to be grimmer. There is a spiritual and general dejection in all fields of Jewish life and at the moment, there are no signs at all of any ray of light promising us a better future.

But we are a people who have always lived by our hopes. Let us hope that this New Year will finally restore us and that the sun will shine upon us too from out of the dark and menacing clouds.

Kalisher Leben 40 (265); New Year's Eve 5693 30–9–32

Kalish in 5693 (1933)

The terrible world crisis which has already been continuing for several years could be felt in particular during 5693. It is unnecessary to add that the worst sufferers here were the Jewish masses who had always lacked firm ground under their feet so that every economic crisis and shock injured them first and foremost and dragged them under the surface. But this year, there was some slight amelioration for small merchants and artisans who suffered so greatly from the heavy burden of all kinds of taxes.

The "Ryczalt" arrangement offered a kind of rationalization of the tax problem for it set the tax payers free from the Assessment Committee which never gave any consideration to the citizen's capacity for payment. Yet, there is no assurance that this arrangement will continue in the future as well. The economic organizations are already gathering all their forces in order to take steps to ensure that it is maintained.

[Page 167]

The departing year was overshadowed by Hitler's barbarity which shook the world and alarmed World Jewry through the cruel persecution of German Jews. The Jews of all countries organized in United Committees in order to combat savage and evil Hitlerism. A united committee of this kind has also been established here and the leading communal workers and public figures participate in it. Its function is to provide for refugees from Germany and conduct a boycott of German goods.

Our local Jewish population was greatly concerned at the anti–Semitic press. Our columns regularly report the regrettable fact that Kalish has become a centre for anti–Semitic journals which are sent throughout Poland from here. This press oozes venom and infects the Polish population with a dangerous Jew hatred. It may lead to very regrettable results indeed unless effective defence measures are taken ahead of time.

During the year 5693 various public festivities were held including those of the Mizrahi, Betar, the Tailors" Society and the Maccabi. This Sports society has already undergone several transformations including the union with Hakoah and the struggle regarding the blue and white flag. It is now a well–established society with a wide range of activities. This year, Maccabi celebrated its 20th anniversary and on this occasion dedicated its flag and inaugurated its private jetty for boating and swimming.

The "TOZ" society again began to be active in Kalish during the past year. It is unnecessary to explain its functions or describe what it does to the Jewish masses. These are matters of general knowledge. So it is gratifying that the local branch of "TOZ" has been summoned to renewed activity under the direction and supervision of well-known and experienced communal figures.

Here, it is our duty to record the far too frequent crisis at the Talmud Torah which comes about at almost regular intervals. It is clear that this state of affairs derives from the economic crisis on the one hand and the indifference of the Kehilla on the other. No attention was paid to the situation by the Kehilla until there was a public scandal and the teachers were compelled to declare a strike and close the classrooms. The "Kalisher Leben" kept on sounding the alarm and at length, the Kehilla agreed to pay the Talmud Torah allocation every week thus ensuring the existence of this popular institution where more than 400 children are studying and gaining an education.

The question of the rabbinate also began to move at last and this painful problem, which caused prolonged tension, is no longer on the agenda even though we do not yet know the end of the matter. However, we can safely say that we now regard the problem as solved. Let it be said in praise of Kalish Jewry that the discussions, etc. about the rabbinate were conducted in a tranquil atmosphere, that the mood is calm and people are patiently waiting for the decision of the Rabbinical Court in this matter.

On this occasion we also mention the Artisans' Society which is doing its best to restore itself to health while continuing its regular activities. The new executive has rented more spacious premises as befits the society's prestige.

[Page 168]

Each union and guild belonging to the Society will have a separate room for its members in the new premises. The executive is also doing its best to set up a secretariat worthy of the name that can serve the numerous members. Steps are already being taken to merge into the Society those gild and sections that have been on their own until now.

The Small Merchants' Society has a very positive balance sheet to show. Its wide-branching activities can be divided into sections and sub-sections. First of all, it succeeded in getting rid of the danger that menaced the market travellers. The executive devoted special efforts to the protection of their lives and property and now there no longer are any disturbances at fairs and markets. The executive also succeeded in removing the brothers Larenti from the roads where they had been terrorizing the market travellers and extorting money from them. These brothers were arrested thanks to the efforts of the Society, brought to judgment and sentenced to six months imprisonment. The market travellers could breathe more easily.

The impoverishment of the Jewish masses, the steadily increasing unemployment and absence of any livelihood induced the Small Merchants' Society to hold a large-scale convention of Jewish economic bodies with the participation of outstanding communal workers in order to establish an Economic Council which would remain on guard and take steps to ensure that the Small Merchants and Workers are not driven out of their economic positions, and also to struggle against the boycott of Jews by others.

This initiative is evidence of a healthy and consistent line of activity which is worthy of all blessing.

*

At the boundary between the old year and the new, we sadly part from the one that is departing bearing with it the whole weight of worries and concern. Yet, as we stand on the threshold of the New Year 5694, we are imbued with the ancient and constant faith in the everlastingness of Israel and with this hope, we welcome the coming year.

Kalisher Leben 37 (315); New Year's Eve 5694. 20-9-1933

————

Kalish in 5694 (1934)

This year 5694 continued to be overshadowed by the general crisis experienced by the whole world which has so greatly influenced the impoverished Jewish masses. In our city, with its 'declassed' population where 80% of the Jewish inhabitants have been transformed from lace manufacturers to 'merchants', 'businessmen' and men who live on air, the crisis is naturally felt even more strongly. It is not surprising that the number of needy Jews applying for public help is steadily increasing.

It certainly cannot be said that our communal worthies have shown themselves indifferent towards the situation or that they have not tried to improve matters. Those who took most interest in the position of our pauperized groups were the Small Merchants' Society which, last year, called the Jewish organizations together in order to set up an Economic Council to safeguard Jewish small merchants and craftsmen from being extruded from their economic positions and withstand the boycotting of Jews.

[Page 169]

We very much regret that the efforts of the Society, headed by their chairman Perle, were nothing more than a voice crying in the wilderness. In spite of all their efforts, the Council has not come into being.

As remarked, Kalish Jewry suffered last year from the grave economic crisis in spite of which the Jews of the city proved their patriotic feelings when they were called upon to contribute to the National Loan. They made the greatest possible efforts and did their civic duty, responding to the call of the Government and participating in the Loan with their very last pennies.

The lion's share in the success of the National Loan campaign can be attributed to the efforts of the "Kalisher Leben" which ceaselessly called on the Jews to do their civic duty. We stood on watch all year round, reminding our readers each month to pay their monthly contribution. Mr. Minkowsky, the chief commissioner for the National Loan, gave particular thanks to the "Kalisher Leben" for the devoted and patriotic measures by which it helped to make the Loan a success.

The activities of the Linat Hatsedek Society were renewed during 5694. All its departments are now in operation for the benefit and convenience of the local Jewish population. It would appear unnecessary to list the difficulties placed in the way of this important Society's renewal of activities which called for goodwill, effortful measures and above all, the regaining of public confidence. Thanks to the dedicated and unwavering labours of the new executive, the Linat Hatsedek has regained its former position of honour and esteem in the public eye.

Last year, the "TOZ" Society engaged in intensive activity. Apart from the regular and systematic day–to–day work in its special branches, it also carried out a large–scale summer holiday programme and a hundred poverty–stricken and weak children were sent to summer resorts, regaining strength in a satisfactory fashion. Each child gained an average of 3 kilos.

The Municipal Elections were held during last year in accordance with the new elections system which reduced the Jewish prospects of obtaining as many representatives as they would have gained under the former proportional representation system. In addition, the election campaign among the Jews themselves had a very bad effect because it became a source of chaos such as we had never known. The inner divisions in our own society together with the new district election system had the result that the Jewish representation in the elected Town Council was reduced to a minimum.

The year 5694 registered a black page in the history of Jewish Kalish through the shameful denunciation of the Kehilla. The members of the opposition denounced the majority in the Kehilla and thereby did something that has no parallel in the history of Jewish communities throughout the world. All sections of the Jewish public rejected the denunciations whose results were very sad. Owing to the checking and frequent examinations, the Kehilla activities were suspended and the work of the various departments was interfered with. The first victims of these irregularities were the worthy Jews who had become victims of the crisis and whom the Kehilla was unable to help.

[Page 170]

The denunciations also unfavourably affected the implementing of the rabbinical court decision with regard to the rabbinate. It is as clear as the sun at midday that in the situation that came about there was no possibility of carrying out the decision fairly or accurately. A group of politicians and trouble–makers who are always happy to engage in conflict refused to understand this fact and began a struggle against the Kehilla seeking every opportunity and excuse to impair the good standing of those who head it.

In spite of these base intrigues and the incitement behind the scenes, the Jewish public believe that the Kehilla will succeed in restoring peace for the personalities who head it hold Government offices and have gained the full confidence of our Society by their many years of public activities. This does not apply to a handful of professional politicians. The community knows that the interests of the local Jews and the safeguarding of peace can be entrusted to the present leaders.

*

There was darkness around, emptiness and chaos, division and splitting apart while despair consumed all around. Here, in addition, came the distress of Jewry as a whole: Hitlerism, Algeria, the stopping of Aliya to Eretz Israel, other decrees in that country and many many more.

This is the situation of the Jewish people between the old and the new years. But we are an ancient people who have withstood many hardships. Our faith in the eternity of Israel is not shaken and we believe with certainty that we shall outlive our enemies and all the evil and hardship. Now, as well, in preparing for the New Year 5695, we are imbued with absolute faith in the bright future of the Jewish People.

Kalisher Leben 35 (364); 27 Elul 5694. 7–9–1934

Kalish in 5695 (1935)

It is very difficult to try to sum up Jewish life in this country and particularly in our City with our joys and sorrows, struggles and battles, hopes and disappointments which can all be included in the one significant word: Chaos!

This year is engraved particularly deeply in our memory on account of the unbearable economic crisis on the one hand and the backwardness and spiritual distortion on the other. But, nevertheless, it has also given rise to several bright spots for the despairing Jewish masses.

Mention should be made first and foremost of the Small Merchants' Society which engages in lively and constructive activities for the benefit of its 800 members and intercedes with the government regarding the disturbances against Jews at the Poznan and other fairs. Its Gemilut Hassadim Fund plays an important part and has saved hundreds of families of small traders from absolute collapse. During the coming year this society is planning to celebrate the 10th anniversary of its fruitful existence. This will be a true festival not only for the society and its members but also for the Jewish community as a whole.

[Page 171]

The foundation of a branch of ORT marks a special chapter in our history. It is unnecessary to waste words on the importance of ORT whose function is to spread the knowledge of handicrafts and agriculture among Jews. Yet, we have to note that certain members of the executive wish to give this institution a party colour. Now this is an absolutely incorrect approach since the ORT Society in our town must remain just what it is everywhere else; a broadly–based people's movement and not a market for party bosses. We believe, however, that the ORT leaders, who are well aware how important their objectives are, will take steps to build the Society on a lasting and healthy foundation.

Let us also mention the Linat Hatsedek Society which functions very effectively. We can only hope that it will continue to operate properly with all its important and useful departments for the good of the general Jewish population here and without distinction between classes and currents.

Last year, the Jewish population took an active part in connection with the National Loan bearing 3% interest which was proclaimed by the government and very widely publicized in our columns.

A deep and sorrowful impression was left by the death of Marshal Pilsudski who was so greatly beloved by the entire population of the Polish Republic. News of his death cast a heavy cloud over the citizens and gave rise to deep sorrow among the Jewish population which found its expression in our pages. We gave fitting expression to the downcast mood of the Jewish population here and to our deep grief at his death.

During the year that has just ended, elections were held for the Seim. These did not arouse much interest among the Jewish population because no Jewish candidate was presented in our electoral zones. In spite of this, there were several short–sighted leaders of Jewish parties who did not join the Kehilla's Election Committee for reasons of personal prestige, but opened separate 'shops' of their own.

There was a certain development in the painful questions of the rabbinate which has made the differences in our community so much more acute on account of the attitude of certain party fanatics. Yet, as remarked, there has been some progress and it may be hoped that this painful question will be settled in the near future to the satisfaction of the entire Jewish Community here.

At this moment, when the parting year bids farewell and the new one begins, we stand full of hope and expectation for better times and wish to believe that all that is bad and corrupt will vanish with the departing days and be forgotten. Hoping for a better morrow which must finally come, we welcome the New Year with the old and new cry: May the year with all its curses end while a year begins with all its blessings!

Kalisher Leben 33 (412); New Year's Eve 5696. 27–9–1935

———

[Page 172]

Kalish in 5696 (1936)

The year 5696 has been a difficult and bitter one for Polish Jewry. It was a year of harsh experiences and sad developments, economic decrees, anti–Jewish disturbances and blood–thirsty riots. All of these, besides the savage anti–Semitic incitement, unbridled as it was, and the acute economic boycott, have exerted a bad influence on the three and a half million Jews of the country and have given rise to a mood of despair and helplessness. The heaviest blow was the anti–Shehita decree which deprived masses of Jews of their livelihood and all of them of the possibility of eating kosher meat.

The savage boycott which aims at depriving the Jews of a living was felt in our city in particular. Here, hundreds of Jewish families made their living exclusively at fairs and markets in the vicinity of Poznan. The unchecked incitement carried out there by the local anti–Semites deprived them of every possibility of continuing to attend these fairs since the Poles robbed them of their property and beat them murderously.

In order to deliver those Jews from inevitable catastrophe, a delegation from the Small Merchants' Society of Kalish appeared before General Slawoi–Skladkowski, Prime Minister and Minister of the Interior and described the terrible situation of these market men who are doomed to starvation on account of this venomous animosity towards the Jews. This appeal had a good effect. The Prime Minister promptly published urgent orders which enabled the Jews to maintain their economic positions and continue to attend the Poznan Fairs.

This delegation which, incidentally, was the first Jewish body to appear before the Prime Minister, also achieved the result that the local markets would not be placed outside the city. The Prime Minister issued suitable orders on this matter too and they were transmitted to the relevant institutions. Thanks to this, a thousand families of market peddlers in our city were saved since their livelihood was in danger on account of the paving of the New Market.

Last year, the Society also engaged in several festivities. These were the installation of the flag, the 10th anniversary and the completion of the writing of its own Torah Scroll. These festivities were very successful. Here as well we had an opportunity of seeing the many–sided activity and productive effects of a purely economic organization on every branch of communal life.

This year saw the 1st anniversary of the passing of Marshal Pilsudski who is mourned by the entire population and in particular by the Jews for we can feel the great loss and the change in the attitude towards us that has recently come about in the country. And so the Jews mark the anniversary with true grief and sorrow.

[Page 173]

This year there was a general meeting of the Gemilut Hassadim Society which has already completed ten years of activities on behalf of the Jewish population. It is the duty of every Jew to support this Fund in order that it should be able to respond to all those who apply to it requesting a loan.

Here we must also mention the Annual General Meeting of the Cooperative Discount Bank which was schemed against this year by several individuals who wished plain and simple, to smash this important Credit Institution. Yet, in spite of all these attacks, common sense prevailed and the victory found expression in the fact that the general public and the members declared their full confidence in the present management which has achieved so much.

Mention must also be made here of the heavy loss which the Jewish Gymnasium sustained by the death of its Director, Samuel Helling who was one of its founders and builders. We are consoled by the fact that he has been worthily replaced by Dr. Moshe Freilich, the well–known pedagogue and educational worker who is the right man for this responsible post.

Mention should also be made of the Linat Hatsedek Society whose departments for pharmacy, dispensary and nocturnal first–aid service, play such an important and useful part for our Jewish population. This is an institution which has to be supported by the entire Jewish public.

As in the other towns of Poland, the year left us something by which to remember it. This was the Kehilla Election which, to our regret, so clearly displayed the great disunity among the local Jews. There were 17 lists competing in the elections whereas in 1931, namely five years ago, there were 8 lists only. The only positive achievement of these elections is the representation of the Small Merchants' Society and the Artisans' Society on the Kehilla Council.

The newly elected Kehilla representatives are now called upon to elect the Kehilla Chairman according to something more than purely party considerations. If we really want the Kehilla to be headed by a man of good will who is prepared to take positive action on behalf of the Jewish masses, let us not elect a tailor's dummy but a man with a sensitive Jewish heart who is known to us thanks to his many years of activity and his readiness to sacrifice himself for the sake of the people.

If the Kehilla representatives understand this, if level–headedness is stronger than the short–sighted instructions of the parties, we shall see a sensible policy which is the fruit of a successful and cautious appraisal of the situation. That would be a pleasant parting gift of the year that is leaving us.

Standing as we do at the crossway between the old year as it withdraws and the New Year as it approaches, it is our fervent aspiration that all the distress and suffering which have descended on the Jewish people from every side may at last come to an end. May we see the fulfilment of the verse: "And may all the wickedness vanish like smoke".

Filled with a firm and unshakeable faith in the divine promise of a radiant future for the People of Israel, we take leave of the departing year while, at the same time, welcoming the New Year of 5697.

Kalisher Leben 32 (455); New Year's Eve, 5697. 16–9–1936.

[Page 174]

Dos Kalisher Leben weekly newspaper

[Page 175]

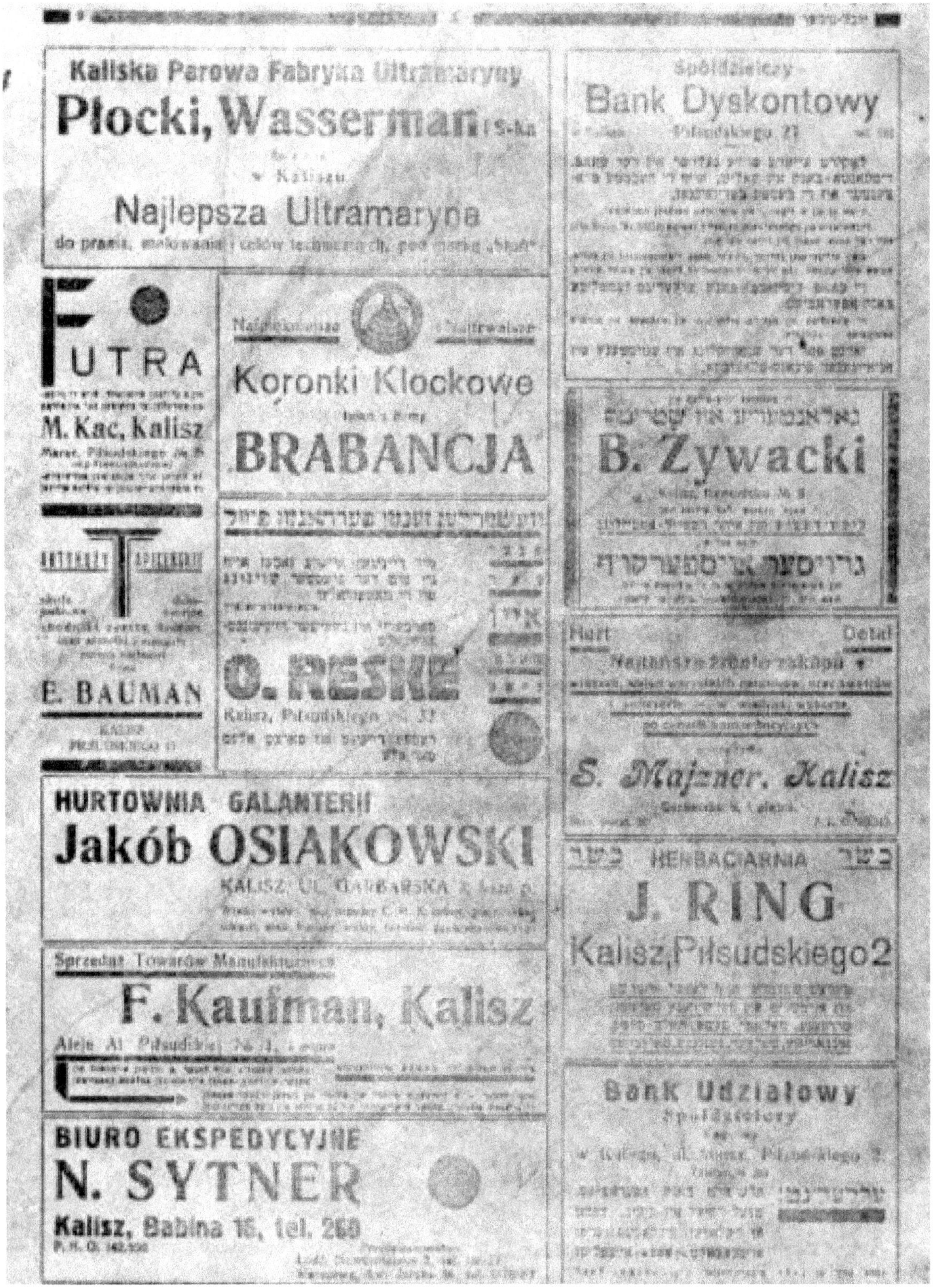

[Page 176] Blank

[Page 177]

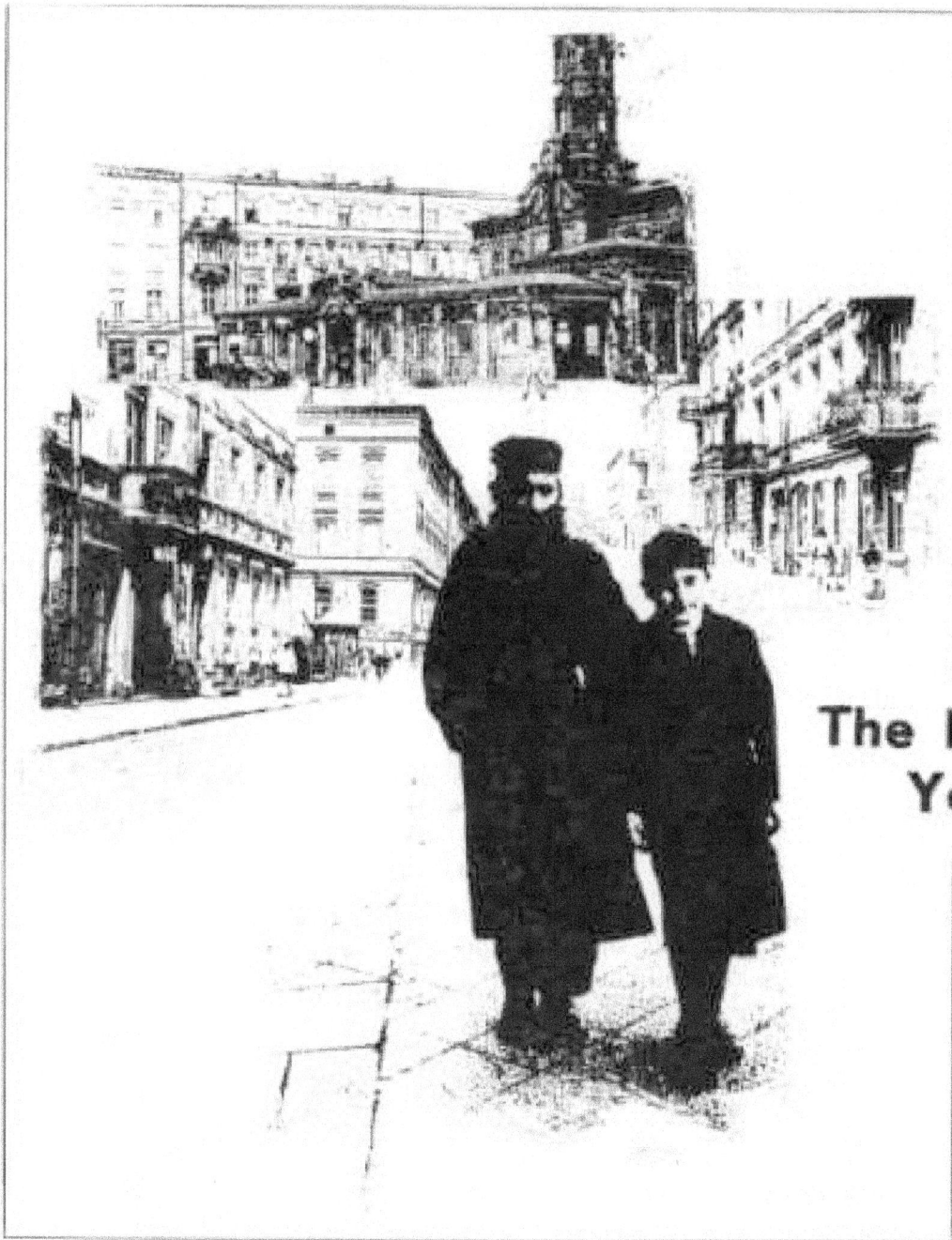

The Final Years

[Page 178] Blank

[Page 179]

The Attacks on the Market Dealers in Grodzisk

by K. W.

It is unnecessary to describe the miserable position of the Jewish small merchant. There is no exaggeration in the Talmudic saying: A poor man might as well be dead. This applies to the petty merchants, the market hawkers and the poor persecuted and tormented travellers to fairs. These three types, or more precisely the single type – for the petty merchant is also a market hawker and a traveller to fairs – are struggling for their lives and their very food, exhausting themselves with toil and all gateways to help are locked before them.

We have already had occasion to write more than once about the distressing conditions and trouble which the fair travellers have had to face in their daily struggle for bread, particularly in the fairs and markets of the Poznan District. There, they cannot even be sure of the small stock of goods they have with them nor of their lives either. But the trouble they have recently faced in Grodzisk passes all imagination. Last Thursday there was a fair in Grodzisk. As usual, Jewish merchants went there each one with his handful of goods. They all arrived at midnight.

Thirteen lorry-loads arrived in all containing what little Jewish property there was. When the first lorry arrived, there were cries of: "Out with the Jews!" When the other lorries arrived, they were met by a large gang of ruffians armed with knives, bayonets and bludgeons. A few ruffians kept guard over the lorries to make sure they could not get away while the rest attacked the Jews, murderously beating and stabbing men and women alike. The shrieks and cries of the helpless people are indescribable but there was not even a sign of a policeman.

It should be noted that the Police Station remained locked up all night long. The ruffians rioted until the morning by order of their leader.

One of the Jews named Feivish Messer who lives at 14, Dobrzecka Street and is the father of six little children was very savagely stabbed. The depth of one of the wounds in his head is 20 millimetres. He is now lying in hospital in a grave condition.

When the ruffians attacked them, the Jews fled in all directions – men and women alike – abandoning their goods and seeking a hiding place in a cellar. But when the scoundrels found that they were hiding, they hurried there and began to beat them with sticks and stab them. Several people from Kalish were gravely wounded. The ruffians tore the women's clothes and beat them savagely.

There was a Kalish girl among them. The scoundrels tore off her clothes and wanted to drag her away. By chance, a Jew from Kalish named Getreuman was nearby. The girl shrieked: "Jew, save me!" He risked his life and got her away from them, emerging only with slight wounds.

The ruffians caught one Jew and began beating him murderously. When the Jew saw that his end was near, he fell on purpose and pretended to be dead.

[Page 180]

The ruffians took him and flung him into the water which, luckily for him, was shallow. After they had gone away he emerged and was saved.

The ruffians now approached several of the lorries, claiming that the Jews were hiding in them. The Polish drivers were afraid that they might actually find the few who had hidden in the lorries which would be very bad for them too. So they told the ruffians that they were Christians and would they possibly permit Jews to hide themselves among them? The ruffians inspected their papers to make sure that they really were Christians and that saved several Jews from a beating.

The market-dealers all came together in one restaurant when they ran away. The ruffians went in and demanded that the owners should expel the Jews in order that they should settle their accounts. But in the restaurant there were also some brave fellows from Lodz who were not cowards at all. There were also a number of Christian merchants whose goods, which were displayed in the market, also began to be looted. All those in the restaurant united, charged very noisily out onto the street and began to defend themselves in lively fashion. They caught the leader of the gang and kept him until the morning when the first policeman appeared.

When the police station opened at 7 a.m. a delegation of merchants marched in and a file was opened. It turned out that 162 people were injured in the riots. There were many wounded; two of them gravely. These were Feivish Messer who was wounded in the head and Moscovitch whose leg was broken. Among those slightly wounded were the following: Abraham Weger, Moshe Tamberg, Shechter, Brenner, Jacob Shapiro, Rosenblum, Katz, Mera, Shlomo Lifshitz, Mr. Wolf Getreuman, Sadalski, Mrs. Tsadek and Levi.

Kalisher Woch, 33: 26th Heshvan 5692. 6-11-1931

———

The Dreadful Fate of the Market Travellers

by A. Avenavitz

The worldwide economic crisis that has shaken the position of entire nations has particularly affected the Jews who, even in normal times, made their living from the air, facing all kinds of distress and disturbance, wandering here and there, staff in hand and earning their bread with much toil.

This hopeless crisis affects everybody: millionaires, industrialists, large banks which go bankrupt overnight, etc. In this confusion, the Jews go out to their bitter daily struggle, using all his senses, exerting all his limbs, doing every kind of hard work for the sake of his bread of affliction.

There are heavy clouds on the horizon. The life of the small Jewish merchant is particularly gloomy. These petty merchants, these market dealers and fair travellers live in a kind of hell. Most of them live in tiny crowded, airless dwellings with many children who grow up under unhygienic conditions. On one wall is a shelf for goods. Some keep their goods in boxes, crumpled and scattered about. There is always noise and dashing hither-and-thither at home. Here the wife goes off to Lodz – there the husband hurries to an acquaintance to obtain security on a bill of exchange so that he can get a loan of several zloty without interest at the Gemillut Hassadim. When the sun rises all the family including the children come out to load the handful of wares on a handcart. The peddler places himself between the shafts, the children push and the wife orders: "start!" and off he goes to market.

[Page 181]

They fix the cart-cover, spread out the handful of goods and stand there all day long looking at the neighbouring stalls and yawning. Towards evening, they go back home. The cart is not particularly light and there has been no turnover.

And so it goes on, day-after-day. The Treasury sends orders for payment. The husbands run out to Joseph Moshe of the Small Merchants' Society and the wife runs after. First, they tell Tsomber what they want. A long time passes. He pushes them in and he pushes them out. He tells them to come tomorrow as the director is at a meeting in the Kehilla now. In short, you get sick and tired of everything. The handful of goods is sold at a public auction and the peddler goes out penniless.

While the poverty at home is shrieking in every corner, the family gather together and decide: the brother-in-law will be a guarantor on a bill – they will borrow some money – they will go to Lodz to buy some goods and henceforward, the "former merchant" will be a fair-goer. And they begin to prepare for the journey.

About ten such "travelling merchants" hire a cart. The wife orders: Pack the goods properly so that they don't get wet! They all climb onto the wagon and off they go. They travel along the high road, uphill and down dale, through the forests and past the fields. They pass through hamlets and villages. They are weary and exhausted. Every hour of the journey feels like a whole day. At length, in the middle of the night, they come to a fair somewhere in the Pozen District. And you can already hear the noise and tumult. The "merchants" from other towns have already arrived and there are also ruffians who have discovered a new living for themselves. They block the approach to the market place and the merchants have to pay them a tax or compensation.

And then, a while later: Hurrah! Out with the Jews! They use knives, beat them with heavy sticks, break their bones and run riot. Sweat mingles with blood; the cries mount to the skies. There is no salvation. They run off and hide in dark cellars. The goods are abandoned. Yet, they wish to save their lives which are just as hopeless and free for the first murderer.

That is how the small merchant lives – the man who travels off to fairs. His is a bitter life of anguish and distress.

Kalisher Woch, 43. 26ᵗʰ Heshvan 5692. 6-11-1931

[Page 182]

Competition

by M. Warshawski

One of our biggest troubles is the plague of Bills of Exchange and promissory notes. We are well aware of the "great" capital and the disposal of the Jewish shopkeeper. We are quite familiar with the "ample" credit that the Jewish merchant enjoys. The "reliability" of the Jewish merchant is generally recognized… and in this situation, the system of Bills of Exchange becomes a very harmful phenomenon. Half of the trouble is in the branch of ready-made clothing, clothing and drapery where the shopkeeper gives his note of hand to the wholesaler yet that as well is at a considerable risk which exceeds profit. For no one can be sure that the Bills will be met when they are due, particularly when the term set for payment is 9 or 10 months in the future.

Yet, the gradual infiltration of the system of payment by promissory note in the food and grocery branch is a graver and entirely abnormal development.

This branch operates almost exclusively for cash. Sugar, flour and baked goods are all paid for in ready money since the profit on these commodities is a minimal one so that the wholesaler has to be paid in ready money. To our regret, however, the purchasers are also beginning to settle their debts with the shopkeepers by bills.

In the past, cases were known where the shopkeeper bought the Bills of Exchange and sold for cash. Nowadays, it is just the opposite. The shopkeeper has to pay cash while the individual customer, who has already been buying on credit for many weeks, settles his debt with a Bill that is due in several months' time.

This harmful method of trade was introduced by two or three of the local grocery dealers whose situation enabled them to grant such credits to the customer. The trouble is that the system is taking root in the entire branch and can undermine the existence of hundreds of grocery shops.

This unhealthy development must be considered by the Grocery sections of the two Merchants' Societies in town. They must both take joint measures to eradicate the evil and make an end of the unparalleled and disgraceful competition.

Kalisher Leben 11 (81); 3 Adar II, 5689. 15-3-1929

[Page 183]

The Only Way Out

by Yedidia

When we survey the economic position of the Jews with open eyes, we feel very sad at heart. Not a single Jew can count on the passing day and he does not know what awaits him tomorrow. In the past, we used to be described as "Luftmenschen" – people who live on and from air – but the truth was that we knew how to make a living from it for everything around us was firm and secure.

Ever since the War began, our situation has deteriorated completely. The property that had accumulated for generations lost its value and vanished within a few years. The speculation times began. Everybody made a great profit and there was so much profit that the actual capital began growing less and less. When the profits reached their peak people also began to sober up. Everybody suddenly saw that actually there was nothing left for them.

Then came a time when it seemed as though life was becoming normal again. We all began working energetically and trading energetically. But the good time did not last. A major crisis was on its way.

The reason for the crisis was the loss of the Russian market. In Poland, trade and industry had chiefly been directed eastwards. When this market was closed to us all the Polish wares were flung on the local market. Every industrialist, every merchant began hunting for customers and offered the best possible terms. Yet, business was at ebb because of the lack of turnover. How were people to make a living? They ate up other people's property. Bills of exchange solved the problems that arose from the financial crisis. There was an inflation of promissory notes and almost everybody went bankrupt since nobody had as much as a shoelace of his own. Here I see a man who is still regarded as well-to-do in his own town. He is going to hunt for a loan hoping to keep up his 'position' in that way. His poverty is not yet generally known. He lives in a fine apartment and is well dressed in public, yet at home, everything is black.

Every able-bodied young man delivers himself by stealing across the frontier and going to Belgium where he does any kind of hard work that the Belgians themselves are not prepared to do. But very few are fortunate enough to improve their position in that way.

The situation in the little towns is far, far worse. People wander about like ghosts – their faces dark and their eyes extinguished. You can no longer recognize the shtetl which Shalom Ash described with so much artistry. In the past the young people went to the big towns where they found work but now there is no point in going there. Cooperative stores have been opened in the villages. The peasants come to town only in order to sell their produce and they take their money back with them to the village where they buy all they need in the Cooperatives. The shopkeeper in town has no turnover but he has to pay his taxes even when he is unable to pay. The Treasury squeezes and makes its demands and where does it bring us? Where is this development leading us?

[Page 184]

It is unnecessary to say that this state of affairs leads to certain collapse from which we can see no salvation.

There are many who say that we have already seen bad times and we have survived them. To this I answer: Read the history of Israel in exile and you will see that we have chiefly been oppressed in the spiritual land. The various nations set out to break our spirit but were unsuccessful because our spiritual level was higher than theirs. But we did not face problems of livelihood for we always made a living. Trade was largely in the hands of Jews. It may have been hard to make a living, true! When they closed us away in ghettos, we waited patiently for better times and preserved our strength.

But nowadays, we are not suffering from spiritual oppression. The authorities permit us to develop both religiously and nationally. Yet, is that enough when our wives and children want to eat? When our sources of livelihood dry up, our bodies follow? No evasion will help us now. We are in a state of despair. All our other requirements fade away. Man is transformed into a wild beast that wishes only to stop being hungry and does not care about tomorrow. That is why the danger we now face is greater than it was in the Middle Ages. Then we were victorious thanks to our spiritual superiority. But now, we are very weak economically and, therefore, we are bound to collapse.

Yet, the will to live, the struggle for existence, is part of human nature. Every man is entitled to live and make a living and we Jews are also living beings who do not wish to give in and leave the stage of life. We wish to continue to exist. There is only one way out: we must help ourselves!

The days have passed when the Jew was ashamed to do any kind of work because it did not befit him. Nowadays, everything befits him and Jews do everything. Therefore, let the Jew do any work he is capable of doing and he is capable of doing anything and without any excuses. Anybody who gives his work not to his Jewish brethren but to others is sinning against his people and himself.

Let the stamp of treason towards their people be set on all those who claim to be honoured and respected Jews while their factories are working on the Sabbath; and whose brethren hunger for bread while they sit at ease on their balconies during the Sabbath day. We face the danger that the Jewish Sabbath of which we have sung so much is going to be profaned in the course of time whether we wish it or not, for hunger is stronger than death.

Nor is it a matter of factory workers alone. It applies to the household help, to the watchman of the house. Let Jews do all these kinds of work. You have no people in the world who employ the members of another people for such work. Is this the practice of the Germans, the English and the French even though their situation is far better than ours? Why, they certainly prefer to give work to their brethren and they do not look for any special other people to do so.

It is our duty to give preference to the Jewish worker for that is the demand of our will to exist. It is time to forget the old saying that: "it's good to go to the Synagogue with a Jew, but that is all" for otherwise there will not be any one with whom to go to the Synagogue before long. The Jewish People are being destroyed and we have to rescue what we can before it is too late.

Kalisher Woch 6: 12th Tammuz 5669. 19-7-1929

───────

[Page 185]

Kalish Miniatures

by Baal-Davar

We Have to Wait

Well, well, everybody knows how the official institutions rush to fix something up when the applicant is a Jew. You might suppose that if the Jew has certain rights and privileges in the country his affairs will be attended to as swiftly as possible. After all, he has his rights because he sacrificed his health for the country! But nothing like it is the case, it turns out, most§ certainly NOT. Whether he has rights and privileges or doesn't have any, the Jew is always treated the same way – let him be patient and wait!

A poor war invalid (it stands to reason that only a pauper has the 'luck' to be an invalid) who lives in Chopin Street was granted a concession to sell cigarettes. By dint of much toil, he managed to hire himself half a shop. The invalid submitted an application to the Excise Department. Since so-and-so is renting him half his shop for the sale of cigarettes, he requests the Excise Office to send a Committee to the said shop in order to decide whether the spot is suitable for the purpose in accordance with regulations.

After he submitted his application the poor fellow began to wait. (After all, did he have any choice?) In due course he reached the conclusion that he was waiting too long. Meanwhile he was paying rent to the shop-owner and the man had to make a living after all. He thought it over and went off to the Office to ask why the matter was dragging on like that. They told him: "It will take some time yet and you will have to wait".

Gentlemen, maybe you know how long?

Lemon!... Lemon! ...

I was strolling about in the New Market (and how long is it going to remain new?) thinking about Jewish livings which have as much reality as snow in July and the good luck of Jews in general and of the fair hawkers in particular. I surveyed the 'tables' which were loaded with 'goods' that were worth, say four times fourteen farthings, and out of which 'the Jew extracts a living' and from which the authorities milk any amount of taxes, turnover tax, income tax and what's the name of all the other taxes?

Surely, I said to myself, the miracles that are happening nowadays are far greater than those that happened to our forefathers in the days of long ago?

Such were my golden meditations at the sight of the 'exhibition of goods' which is called the New Market and suddenly, as though a bomb had gone off, the air was rent apart by the chorus: 'Lemon! Lemon! Lemon! Lovely wares! Ten farthings a piece..."

I woke up from my thoughts and turned towards the voices, startled. The 'merchants' thinking that I wanted to buy something, swooped upon me from every side with their lemons in their hands. In particular, there was one pretty girl who would not let me be. She had a white peasant kerchief around her head out of which peeped a pile of pale yellow curls and dimples, in her cheeks. She pushed a fine big lemon at me and said: "Buy some good wares. Nobody has goods like mine. Buy cheap. Ten farthings each".

[Page 186]

When I had long left all those lively lemon sellers behind, I could still see in my mind's eye the young dealer with dimples in her cheeks. In my ears echoed her voice: "Lemon! Lemon! Lemon! Lovely fruit! Ten farthings ..."

Another Novelty

When I heard that there was a novelty in Kalish, I dashed off to have a look at it. My imagination worked feverishly for I wanted to guess what it could be. I tried to imagine something fresh. A communal worker who had some kind of Jewish education... A wealthy Jew who contributed to Jewish needs...or, maybe one of the local preachers of morality who had decided to behave in a moral fashion... or, maybe a nationally conscious Kalish Jew who was not ashamed to speak Yiddish; and other extravagances of this kind occurred to me.

When I reached the spot I saw a large placard which proclaimed in huge letters: "Novelty". I pushed my way through the crowd surrounding the plate glass window of the new shop, my heart throbbing. Behold, said I, I have reached my destination and I shall now see the novelty...

And now imagine what I saw there? Stuffed fish... Fish well peppered...Fish cooked at home... Just fish! *There* is a novelty for you.

Kalisher Woch 5 (43) 12th Shevat 5691. 30-1-1931

My City

by S. Rubin

Kalish, you are indeed a city of cities! Your boundaries are steadily spreading, the ruined streets are being rebuilt and are improving too – 'skyscrapers' are appearing, plate-glass windows are flashing, there are large and many-coloured electric signs. The map of Poland has no reason at all to be ashamed of you. So I always think to myself when I go for a walk. Yet, in spite of all the efforts to make our city look like a metropolis, in spite of the development and the appearance, our city lacks the melodious dynamism, the rhythm and tumult of the streets and squares of the big city.

It is almost impossible to believe that in these multi-storeyed buildings scattered over such a large area there is a population of 70,000 souls. There is little movement in the streets. Everything is slumberous and apathetic, no less than in the little country towns.

In our city there are public halls, cafés, fine cinemas and other places where people can enjoy their leisure in the evenings. But all of these places are empty and everything is boring.

[Page 187]

The public is not alive. They waste their time. They spend their evenings alone with their own selves out of the natural habit of people whose time has passed, of young men from country towns who have nothing to do in the evenings except to play dominoes. The difficult economic situation has set its stamp on everything when some money is still to be found in their pockets. All the week round there are few who go there. Don't we have some better and more pleasant ways of spending time after work during an ordinary weekday?

I sit in a fine well-lit café. The marble top tables stand like silent witnesses of the hard times. Here we miss the regular visitors who used to fill the place with a friendly and comfortable atmosphere. No, the public is not alive today. Patiently it consumes the difficult hours of its evenings waiting for better days which may possibly come with the spring.

It is 10 o'clock in the evening. Where can everybody be? Is it possible that the centre of the city can empty itself so completely and so early? What has happened to the regular strollers taking their ease along the Pilsudski Boulevard?

My friend offers me a philosophical explanation. This is a characteristic result of the crisis we are experiencing. The porters of the houses lock the entries at 10 o'clock so people hurry home in order to save the few farthings they might otherwise need to pay for having the door opened. I laugh aloud but he insists: "And you have to laugh. It's a very miserable joke. I know many people like that."

There is ample light from gas and electricity in the street shining on the dead and empty pavements. At long intervals, a noisy car dashes past with a resounding blare of the horn, reminiscent of the existence of what was once called "life". It comes from who knows where and must doubtless be hurrying to some place or other.

Like passengers whose ship has sunk at sea, the carriages wait at the street corners. But there is not a person to be seen. The drivers yawn widely, gaping aloft at the cloudy skies and tease one another from time-to-time in their own special driver's slang.

One young fellow whose blood is hot within him cannot bear to remain on his seat. Down he comes and starts dancing with some old josser as much as to say: "Well, my lads, if there aren't a customer, then to hell with them and let's dance at least!"

Their boots beat hollow on the pavement. It is 11 o'clock at night. A taxi passes by and the carriages look even poorer than before. The drivers must really envy the motorized magnate very much indeed.

A couple of drivers spread their arms and beat themselves over the shoulders to warm up. They are cold and miserable and give the impression of trying to beat the melancholy out of themselves. They must surely be longing for the days when they used to drive faster than eagles to the railway station, there and back.

Kalisher Leben 111 (123); 14th Adar 5690. 14-3-1930

———

[Page 188]

On the Bridge of Kalish

by Observer

I stand on the Zlota Street Bridge looking down on the Prosna and I see a vision: How good if the municipality were to widen and deepen the river here, strengthen the banks with concrete, build arched marble bridges, pave Babina Street and Nadwodne Street and cover the walls of the houses with marble. How enchanting it would be when the sunshine would be reflected from here by day and the moon by night? Why, this would be a little Venice!

Or another scene: A fine Saturday evening with the moon shining bright. Young Hassidim coming out of the Shtieblech after their Melave Malka (Speeding-the-Sabbath festivities). They go to the bank, sit down in gondolas, row the length of the streets and sing one melody after another; the tunes spreading all over town. Pious women light Close-of-Sabbath tapers in the windows. The gondolas are also lit up and the lights are reflected on the hill and in the water under the shining moon.

Gradually, Jews gather on both banks of the Prosna. Their happy mood rises high. Everything is well arranged thanks to their municipal representative who is here among the musicians. The chief player holds a little Psalm book and sings: "They that go down to the sea in ships" - - - "The sea saw and it fled"; and "Then Moses sang". And the choir sings songs of the departing Sabbath and the songs and conversation go on till after midnight and the proud parting with a final: "a good week".

So my vision went. Suddenly I remembered that the municipality intends to block the branch of the Prosna that runs along Babina. In general, it has more important budgetary worries. And back I come to the grave Jewish situation.

Across the bridge Jews scurry about with worried faces. One is hurrying to pay a bill that has already protested, another looks for a loan without interest and a third begs for an execution order to be deferred. Nearby, Jewish porters stand beside hand-carts and coils of rope, waiting for work. Jewish drivers stand by their broken-down carriages with their lean and hungry horses, waiting for a journey or "someone". Beside them stand Jews buying and selling old clothes, worn shoes, and a broken alarm clock. A little further along sits a Jewess selling soda water and peas. Opposite stands a Jew shouting: "Buy bagels, chocolate and sweets"!

My eyes survey the scene and I feel like asking: "Is the stream of history going to sweep all this away sooner or later? And what will remain here then?"

Kalisher Leben 38 (120); 11th Kislev 5690. 13-12-1929

[Page 189]

During the First World War

by Katriel Stein

I was nine years old when World War I broke out. My parents then lived in Kalish where they owned a 'restaurant'. I was educated in Blaszki with my grandfather Reb Yoel Wangczewski, of blessed memory. He was known there as "Black Yoel" and was a well-to-do and respected Hassid who engaged in communal affairs. He was a member of the Community Council and of the Municipal Council and always sought ways and means of helping his people.

I remember how such dreadful words as 'War' and 'Mobilization' were hanging in the air. The chief thing done by the soldiers who passed through the little town was to steal liquor, drink themselves drunk, pour the rest out on the ground and set it alight. Several shops were burnt down. Where Kalish lay, on the horizon, there was something grey like smoke rising up into the sky.

At last my parents arrived after all kinds of adventures and mishaps. My father related that on the first day, the townsfolk looted the railway station. The Russian soldiers had already withdrawn and the city was left without any rulers or protectors. So the Jews welcomed the Germans as redeemers, particularly since they spoke German and could understand one another. The German soldiers willingly purchased from the Jews and behaved politely.

Suddenly there was a storm of bullets. Machine guns could be heard chattering all night long. The men said Psalms and put heart into the fainting women. Quiet was restored only in the morning. The Germans put up posters declaring Martial Law and gave permission to go out and purchase food during three hours. Between the shots, people peeped out like mice from their holes.

My grandmother Rachel, may she rest in peace, hired a cart with two horses and went off to Kalish in order to fetch back the members of my family. But they had already left the town. All the property they took with them was loaded on a baby carriage. By the Sabbath most of the Jews of Kalish had fled to Blaszki. Rabbi Kanal announced to all the townsfolk that this was an emergency that deferred the Sabbath and all those who had vehicles went off to Kalish to fetch the refugees back.

The little town filled up with refugees who were housed in the synagogue and all the public institutions. The large square was also full to overflowing. Many found refuge with their kinsfolk. The rest went on to other villages and small towns.

That Sabbath the Germans mishandled eight hundred Jews who were collected from the entire city. They were ordered to count to ten and told that they would be shot. This trick was repeated several times without any shooting. The last time a messenger arrived with a letter of reprieve for them.

[Page 190]

Parts of the dwellings of the city were destroyed but the industrial section was less affected. Some say the reason was that the machines were German and the purchasers still owed money to Germans for them. In Blaszki itself, they ruled firmly but without any cruelty.

One winter morning in 1918, young Poles marched into our courtyard in civilian clothing, with rifles on their shoulders. What is this? I asked and they answered: "Nasza Polska! (Poland is ours!) I had gone to sleep as a German citizen and woke up as a Polish citizen. They went over to the German soldiers and demanded their arms. The Germans, who had claimed that they were going to conquer the world, very quietly handed over their weapons. The Poles also stripped some of them of their uniforms and boots.

When an ultimatum was served on the garrison, the Germans decided to fight a last battled and trained their artillery on the Church. On that Sabbath, Rabbi Kanal headed a deputation and requested them not to destroy the town whose Jewish inhabitants were certainly not responsible for what had happened.

That was the end of the German rule after World War I.

On the Island

by L. Shurek-Halevi

This happened in the year 1925. Since all these years have passed, it is good to revive the scene of the events in my imagination. It was the Island we knew so well in the Prosna.

Let us stand facing the bathing cabins, our eyes towards the Prosna current coming from Piewonice. To the right is the floating bridge by which we passed over to Prochowski who was a tall and a very decent Christian. From him we used to hire boats and kayaks. About a hundred metres further on stood a little booth with a jetty for better boats beside it. Two hundred metres further along the right-hand bank going against the current could be found the Kazimierczak's Restaurant, which was at the service of the boatmen.

From Kazimierczak's restaurant the way leads to the Cross. Here the bank is very pleasant with high grass and shady trees and it is easy to reach the boats. At this point the river is deep and wide and many people used to come to bathe here, naturally free of charge. Near the bank stood a wooden cross and so this bathing beach was called the Beach of the Cross.

Now let us return to our starting point. On the left was the magnificent waterfall and next to it a narrow bridge enabling people to pass to the bathing cabins and in later years to the Stadium. Behind the bathing cabins stretched the great meadow in which natural pasture grew. This was the place where the army conducted its training and where there were also horse races and athletic exercises of the Kalish Sports Clubs.

[Page 191]

At the end of the meadow the Prosna becomes quite shallow for about a hundred metres and has formed the Island we know so well, opposite the Cross. And now to the story proper:

Several hundred young fellows devoted themselves to the Talmud at the Kalish House of Study. Most of them belonged to poor families who ate on regular 'days' with the worthies of the community. They used to eat their breakfast together in the cellar at the corner of Zlota and Garbarska Streets where they were provided with a bran soup, cabbage borsht and a slice of bread.

Between three and six of them used to sleep in one hired room while some of them slept on the benches of the House of Study. Those were the conditions under which they studied Torah for its own sake.

Now Kalish had good swimmers but it should be noted that excellent swimmers in no small numbers were to be found among the Yeshiva lads who lived under the miserable conditions we described above. Almost every afternoon when study was over the lads went to the river bank in order to swim and play in the water.

I remember one nice looking young lad named Aaron who came from the neighbourhood. He could tread water. Sometimes he would fold his arms on his chest, smoke a cigarette and keep still in the deep water. From the bank we could not see any movement on his part. Some of the lads used to go as far as the Cross because bathing was free there.

One summer day after exercising in the meadow, a number of us went to the Island. All of a sudden, we heard yelling and shouting. The Yeshiva lads were bathing not far away. A large crowd of young Christian scamps had flung their clothes into the water and then began to fling the lads themselves in. We dashed over and intervened. I was the oldest of our group and I knew the local street slang very well, so I tried to turn the whole thing into a joke. But I did not succeed. Our situation grew steadily worse. I knew the Polish temperament well from experience, so I began in this way: "Look, there are only a few of us here and there are hundreds of you. Aren't you ashamed to attack us? You choose one of your fellows to wrestle with me and put me on my back. Then you'll be the honourable winners, or maybe the other way around"?

I should add here that in 1922 I had taken a course in boxing with the Warsaw Maccabi under the guidance of a Hungarian Jew who was an excellent trainer. I had regularly watched all the wrestling matches and had not missed even one of them. I had also won the boxing championship of D.O.K. Poznan.

The young Poles approved of my suggestion and burst out roaring and dancing savagely yelling: "You'll see what a goulash we'll make of this Jew!" And they chose a hefty young fellow as their champion. Their voices mounted to the skies.

[Page 192]

In brief, within less than a minute, I had sent the fellow flying over my head and brought him down. He remained sitting, unable even to yell. There was silence. His friends led him aside. I stood tense, waiting for developments.

A handsome young Pole, well built, came over and asked me if I would be prepared to wrestle him as well. I answered that his proposal was not in the agreement but still I was ready if he wanted it. On the other side of the Prosna stood many Poles, yelling: "What are you playing at with the Jews over there! Kill them and have done!"

My new rival was a better sportsman than the other and also demonstrated a greater degree of culture. A large circle was marked out. The first victim had already recovered and helped to keep order. This encouraged me for I was beginning to regret my tough tactics and the success that had resulted.

The second wrestling bout began. During the first few seconds neither of us allowed the other anything and the match was conducted according to all the established principles.

All of a sudden, the other fellow hit me in the nose. "What's this?" I asked and he answered: "We are going to box".

There is nothing much to tell. My Jewish sense of honour woke up and my blood began to boil. I started to pummel him mercilessly. Blood began to flow from his nose, his eyes and his mouth. Now I began to feel sorry for him.

There was no guessing the continuation. My victim was already completely finished. I did not wish to end the fight as drastically as I had finished the first one, so I played with him a bit. He fell and then rose to his feet. I did not exploit the opportunity but he refused to give in.

The yells grew louder and louder. They were no longer shouting "Kill that Jew!" but: "Don't give in!" They wanted to encourage him with their cries.

But then he fell flat on his back. The Poles could not bear that. To this day I do not know how many louts between the ages of thirteen and nineteen came dashing at me with thin, soft branches that had been prepared in advance and began whipping at me. My blood began running down my face and from all parts of my body. I saw that I was in a very bad situation. I could not defend myself and could expect the worst to happen. Honour is a very honourable thing but now I had to get away. Where? To break the ring, jump into the water and there I would again be strong and secure. I hit out with my arms and kicked with my feet, broke the ring and reached the water.

By the bank, I saw several boats with oars. Now I could teach them a lesson I thought to myself. The grandson of Reb Benjamin Hayyim Wolkowitch doesn't leave debts unpaid! I grabbed an oar and began to swing it around my head. Once again, blood began to flow but now it was their blood.

[Page 193]

A ring formed again and I stood in the centre swinging the oar like the vanes of a windmill. I was like an animal at bay in the forest, standing wounded and bleeding, surrounded by dogs that wanted to bite but were afraid to with a few trying to get behind and hit there from time-to-time. My position was a little bit better but far from satisfactory.

At this moment there came shouts: "Help! Help! Help! Man drowning!" The attention of the mob was diverted to the drowning man. All of them ran to the bank and I was alone at last without needing to defend myself. I felt fine. I knew I had emerged the victor.

Meanwhile, hundreds of people were standing on both banks of the Prosna and the shouts did not cease. "Hello! Hello! Over there! Help! Take a boat! Help!"

I stood about fifteen metres from the river. The yells awakened me from my thoughts. I ran to the water. Several people were already swimming. Two of them wanted to save the drowning man. A boat set out from the other bank with several youngsters and a sergeant.

As I learnt afterwards, one of the rescuers was already dragging the drowning fellow ashore when the latter suddenly gripped his rescuer and they both began to go down. The rescuer succeeded in getting loose but now the other two were afraid of the drowning victim. At that moment, I saw a few fingers above the water. I dived in and swam to the drowning fellow under the surface, seized him and came up together with him. I held him with his face upwards and made for the shore with the other arm as I had been taught.

Once again came the shouts, this time: "Bravo! Bravo! A real champion!" Half-way ashore, the boat caught us. The sergeant pushed an oar over to me and in that way we reached the bank. They stretched the drowning fellow out on the pasture and began getting the water out of him. Within a very short time he began to breathe properly and came to himself.

One of the men, a municipal official then turned to the crow with these words: "Gentlemen! As a Catholic I feel very bad and am quite ashamed at what I saw here today. I was bathing at the Cross and saw all that happened on the Island. Just imagine the drowning man is a Catholic and a poor swimmer and he risked his life and wanted to cross the Prosna in order to help in beating up peaceful citizens who have done nothing wrong. You all saw what happened. It was this gentleman, who is a Jew and whom you attacked unfairly and beat till he bled, who risked his life to save the drowning man. Now, because of that, I request of you that henceforward there should be no attacks on bathers on the Island. Otherwise, bathing will be entirely prohibited there".

After that, the lads from the House of Study continued to bathe on the Island for several years and nobody interfered with them.

———

[Page 194]

The New Year

by M. Packentreger

In a chilly twilight during the month of Ellul, the sound of the Shofar bursts from the House of Study and spreads tremulously through the Jewish streets. Reb Mendele Baal-Tokea (the Blower of the Ram's horn) a squat Hassid with a tufted reddish beard, is testing his Shofar in preparation for the New Year. In the corridor of the Great Synagogue, the aged cantor, Reb Noah Zaludkowski (or Reb Noah Klager as they called him in town) is teaching his choristers a new version for the awesome 'Unetaneh Tokef' prayer and for 'Upon the New Year this is inscribed' and also a new melody for the cantor's personal prayer: "Behold me poor in deeds". The sweet voices of the lads ring out like silver bells through the twilight hour and spread far and wide.

On the pavement nearby, Jews pause; Jews with beards and ear-locks, wearing black silk kapotas and black Jewish peaked hats, listening to the prayers that go to the heart.

Slowly and deliberately, the town is preparing for the Days of Awe. Through the heat of the day, immersed in God-fearing thoughts, slowly paces Reb Itshe the slaughterer, passing along the Hospital Alley. He is a lofty Jew with a pink and fleshy face surrounded by a reddish beard going down to his middle and a woollen scarf around his neck. His slow and thoughtful pace is evidence that this year he is preparing to sing the Morning Prayers in the Synagogue. The woollen scarf is there to safeguard his voice lest it should be affected by some draught, Heaven forbid, that might make him hoarse.

Wandering cantors and Hassidic prayer leaders have come from distant towns and villages in order to be tested in readiness for the services in the many synagogues. They have been waiting a whole year for these Days of Awe.

In the Great Synagogue and the smaller synagogues, the sale of seats is going ahead already. Wealthy Jews and everyday Jews have already provided the places for themselves, their wives and children. In the plate-glass windows of the stationery shops, all kinds of many-coloured New Year greeting cards are signalling the passers-by. The shops have filled up with purchasers, all selecting their greetings.

Every day the railway is taking a different group of Hassidim who are setting out to spend the festival days with their particular Rebbes. The coaches are full of long-bearded and ear-locked Hassidim wearing black robes.

As is his fashion, year-after-year, Reb Leibish Hersh, the bookseller, appears in town during the days before the New Year. A tall withered-looking Jew with a short and small goat-beard, dressed in a torn and dirty kapota, wearing muddy and old knee-boots, sells fringes, prayer-shawl bags, prayer books and festival prayer books. Everybody knows him. When the congregation leaves the House of Study, each of them does a good deed and buy something from him. Leibish Hersh is smiling. His goods are being sold and, please God, he will be able to go home the day before the New Year with a good profit.

[Page 195]

The eve of the festival approaches. At dawn, as day comes grey on the horizon, a dense dust-cloud rises on the long earthen trails? Out of these clouds, suddenly and simultaneously, appear the wagons of peasants coming to market. On their ladder-carts the peasants have brought vegetables, poultry, ducks and geese for the Jews of the city. Now they reach the market place. The old peasants come stiffly down from their seats, hitch up the horses, hang a nose-bag around the neck of each and light up their long pipes which are stuffed with home-grown machorka. Little by little, the noises of the market begin. Horses neigh, cocks crow and geese cackle. A white mist hovers in the air and rolls along the ground. From the cart of one peasant comes leaping and flying a white fowl with a red comb, beating her wings and fluttering down to the ground. The peasant runs, puffing to catch her, but she evades him between the carts and wagons. At length, he grasps her by the leg.

Now the Jewish housewives appear in the market carrying white woven baskets in order to purchase a fowl or goose. They puff at the feathers and feel the fat with their fingers. Quite often, the transaction doesn't come off. Just as the housewife is about to pay the peasant his price, one of the market women snaps up the bargain from under her nose. The housewife stands her ground, yells her fill and goes on to another peasant to buy a bargain there.

It becomes late. The market grows empty all of a sudden. The last of the shopkeepers close up their shop and fasten them with iron bars. The apprentices take the new clothes from their masters' workshops to the homes of the worthy householders; those new clothes that have been specially prepared for the festival. Of course, they expect some beer-money. Jews go off to the mikveh with bundles of underwear under their armpits.

The sun slowly moves westward. Its last gleam lights up the windows. A silent melancholy fills the Jewish streets and alleys as they await the Day of Judgment.

Jews with scoured heads, beards and ear-locks still wet with the mikveh water, wearing their black kapotas have already begun pacing slowly towards the synagogue. Lights have already been lit in the houses. Little flames quiver yellow and their pallid radiance spreads into the street.

In the streets of the Jews, everything is silent. There is an awesome solemnity in every corner. Silently, like a shadow passing, Mordechai Meir, the water-carrier, moves through the synagogue alley, a short Jew with an astonishingly camel-like head planted like a block of marble between his broad shoulders. His large black eyes are melancholy and a thin little beard sprouts on his chin. He also wears a new kapota and on his legs are shining knee-boots smeared with pitch. He stops every householder in the street and wishes him a Good Year. The Jews greet him in return and say: "Reb Mordechai, beg for a good year for all of us! And may you not need to carry water to the houses in your old age!"

[Page 196]

"Amen" he answers with a God-fearing look on his face.

From the Hospital Alley comes Moshe the Fool with a large winter hat covering his head and ears, great knee-boots on his legs. He hurries along panting and sweating, shouting hoarsely: "Jews, pray for a Good Year for all of us!"

Night descends on the city. From the illuminated synagogues and shtieblech come the chants and melodies of the evening prayer. Jews are praying in fervent devotion, begging for the atonement of transgressions. And after the prayers, the entire great assembly bursts into the streets, men, women and children all wishing one another a Good Year. Long-standing foes make it up and forgive one another.

Next day, the sun rises high. Girls with well-braided plaits walk through the streets. Jews wearing their prayer shawls stand in the synagogues praying. Here and there the shofar can be heard together with the warm appealing outpourings of the prayer leaders. In the shtiebel of the shoemakers stands Yankel, the old cobbler covered head, shoulders and body by his prayer shawl, beating his fist against his chest like a hammer "for the sin that we have sinned". When he reaches the verse: "do not fling us away in old age", he bursts into bitter lamenting tears as though the great calamity were already taking place. The tears pour from the dim eyes of the old man as with his hands raised on high he repeats the words: "do not fling us away in our old age". And his tears roll one by one down onto the open pages of his yellow-leaved prayer book.

The Ninth of Av in 1914

by H. Solnik

For several days, the air has been heavy with signs of war. The faces of the Russians seem to be veiled in mystery. There is lively movement in all the government institutions. They are packing up, vacating the premises. The railways are carrying everything away. Silently and secretly. The officials work and run to and fro diligently. No citizen hears a sound from them. Everything is wrapped in deepest secrecy.

There is a hurried mobilization. Parents moan and groan, brides and young married women sigh from their hearts. Pale startled young men part from their families as though they were ascending the gallows. Confused and perplexed they look back again dropping another tear and calling: "be well!"

People murmur something as they hurry to the banks to take their money out but the banks are closed! They refuse to pay. Heavy burdens press down upon each heart. Everybody is buying food. People are hoarding. The hurried alarmed folk can feel that something is approaching. Nobody trusts anyone else. There is no more credit. Do you have cash? Buy and pay. Everybody has an unvoiced fear of the morrow, of the passing day, of the approaching moment.

[Page 197]

We live on the frontier and are on the verge of war. "What is going to happen to us?" – "Oh stop it – nothing. You pass the threshold and go into the room without excitement. The parlour is a long way from the corridor".

People think a great deal but do not know what they should do next. Thoughts are as heavy as lead. A true nightmare. "What's the news?" everybody asks. There are guesses. Hints. People whisper a secret in your ear: "The Russians have withdrawn". "What! Just abandoned us without any defence?"

*

Sunday, the 9th of Av. A confused mood. The sad familiar melody. The quiet moans of the God-fearing congregations and the light-hearted mischief of the boys. We stand together on the pavement of the Old Market, the snow-white teacher, Sinai Blei, may he rest in peace and I. It is an hour or two after the singing of the lamentations. The shops are closed. It is Sunday, the 9th of Av and there is a grave-like silence. Thoughts of the 9th of Av mingle with war thoughts. There is no sign or trace of a policeman or a soldier.

"Where have they all gone?" Old Blei asks me. "It's really queer, frightening – there is something in the air", I answer. "There is a new epoch coming. Will it be for the better? No one can say yet".

Out of the Breslau Street (now Pilsudski) a soldier pedals a bicycle into the market place. About ten metres behind him comes another, then another, and another and yet another. For a moment all the senses seem to blur. Germans? Yes.

Slowly and steadily they pedal glancing to either side. Behind them a large force is marching, all armed and at a quiet and rather terrifying pace. From the pavement opposite us a number of people welcome them by waving their hats.

We gaze at one another. What has happened? Out of sheer astonishment, we stand as though frozen, not uttering a word. Our hearts tell us that something great is taking place before our eyes, tidings of a threshold that has been crossed.

Home! Some secret sense commands us.

That silent entry into the town with light furtive thief-like paces has depressed us and awakened harsh forebodings. Nor do they keep us long in our expectancy.

[Page 198]

My Eyes Perceive You

by Meir Packentreger

Like a priest preparing to serve in the temple, I remove the shoes from my feet when I come to speak of Kalish my birthplace. My very fingers weep when I remember what Hitler's hordes did to our fathers, our mothers and our children. My ears still hear their weeping – the entreaty of the martyrs being led to slaughter.

I can still perceive you, Kalish my city. The streets, alleys and the closed-off entries. The Houses of Study and the Synagogues. The Old Market, the stalls and the shops. The streets of the Jews and the Jews chasing and toiling for a livelihood. The hawkers tossing about at night in covered carts as they go to the markets at Kozminek and elsewhere. The burly carriage drivers taking passengers to the railway station. Here they are, quarrelling – one dragging a passenger from another – fighting with shafts tugged from the carriages, hitting one another over the head. Blood flows. There is a commotion and then silence again. They have made up – they have reached an agreement and then drink together as though nothing ever happened.

Now I hear the shouts of the beigel sellers proclaiming their wares: "Fresh egg cake! Ten groshen each! Jews, buy fresh cakes without holes!" And here comes the voice and melody of Torah from the Old House of Study beside the Great Synagogue. A Yeshiva lad sits swaying and studying his Talmud text. His voice vanishes in the noise of the street and its tumult. The hawkers are louder than everything else there is. And now comes the chant of the Talmud Torah boys: "*Vayedaber* – and He said...*Adonoy* – God-...*leMoshe* – to Moses".

These are the pictures that still quiver so clearly before my eyes.

———

Daily Life

by Gershon Wroclawski

When I look back on the last years of the city, I see Endek men standing in front of the entries to Jewish shops and preventing all Christian customers from coming in. The market has been divided: here Christians and there the Jews. The boycott is at its height. The first to be broken are the small merchants, the peddlers and those who travel to the fairs who are not permitted to enter the markets in scores of towns within the Poznan District.

When the fairs are closed off, the Jewish craftsmen, particularly the little men, find themselves with nothing to do. The Endeks put up their notices even in the Municipal Park: Entry to dos and Jews prohibited! We enter in groups; we fight them in the park and around the shops. Yet, how can we help? There is a spirit of gloom all over these days.

[Page 199]

Yet, it had not always been like this. I remember other times which bring a smile to the lips and sometimes a twinkle in the eye. There was a kind of tranquil innocence about the life of the Jews as I see them again with the eyes of a young boy.

Here are the alleys, open and concealed, scattered here and there. There are only Jews in the streets. The only non-Jew is the Shabbes goy, the gate-keeper. Further on is the wooden bridge. There are couples strolling, apparently innocently but they have secret intentions. You can see it in their eyes. Strolling would be good and pleasant if only the non-Jews didn't set their dogs on them. The couples turn around and enter the park.

The park was a paradise for those feelings of love which had to find release and things happened there which did not lead to the slightest suspicion of even one single Jewish maiden...

And now come voices from the House of Study. My eyes rest on the stand where I once helped my father when he prayed as leader of the congregation. And do you remember?

Once upon a time a foreign painter came and painted the whole House of Study, free of charge.

As for the House of Study itself, it is an absolute market-place between the afternoon and evening prayers. They discuss everything. Politics, trade, who is rich and who is poor and what's happening in general. After the midday meal on the Sabbath, Jews fill the House of Study, their voices ringing as they study Midrash. But after study, they begin a comprehensive and careful discussion of communal affairs, of the Mikveh to which my mother sent me to immerse a glass and whose special scent then filled my nostrils.

And I also see young fellows studying most melodiously and loudly while between the pages of the Talmud text are hidden letters which were certainly not written by any male hands.

When the Sabbath was about to begin, the town became very happy. The shopkeepers locked the doors of their shops and hurried off to welcome Queen Sabbath. The father went off to the Mikveh with his sons while the mother and daughters cleaned up the house, polishing lamps and sooty pots. There is fresh smell everywhere.

Father has brought a guest home from the House of Study and loudly hallows the Sabbath. The voices of the Jews and their melodies can be heard all over town while the fragrance of food spreads far and wide.

After the afternoon sleep of the Sabbath the fathers examine their offspring to see what they learnt during the week while the mothers sit with the "Tse-ena Ure-ena", the women's Yiddish Pentateuch on their knees; some reading it and others simply glancing at it now and then.

As the Sabbath ends the girls take possession of the street with the lads after them. The world goes on after its old-established fashion.

All this has departed together with the picturesque individuals whose very names are enough to bring a way of life back to you: Feivish Poiker, Leibish Hoiker, Joel Piatek, Mordechai Smatek, Mendel Trik, Moshe Bik, Leibish Brand, Yehiel Tanz, Abraham Koch, Mendel Fluch, Michael Floi, Joseph Shtroi, Mordechai Ston and Moshe Han.

[Page 200]

Mordechai Ston, the gravedigger, used to frighten everybody yet even worse was his son-in-law who could joke only with his knife. There is no light without shadow and no community without its bad and its fools. And if Moshe was asked who died today he would answer: "one man and two Jewesses".

All that innocence and all that innocent badness has been destroyed. It is as though it had never existed.

Oppenheim House

by Benjamin Zvieli

There was a special style of life about Oppenheim House which stood at the corner of Pilsudski Street and Pilsudksi (formerly Josephine) Boulevard; a two-storey corner building with Jewish shops all around it.

Here on the corner was Reb Shlomo Herszkowicz's delicatessen shop called "Zloty Rog". Next to it was the iron and building-materials stores of Reb Eliezer Lipshitz and nearby the textiles shop of the brothers Braun and the Kollektura of Weltfried, the Orbis Travel Agency and the drugstore of Solnik, a brush shop and the sausagery belonging to Beatus, a clothes shop and, at the end, Daum's Pastry Shop.

On Sundays when all the shops were closed in front, commercial life continued behind in the courtyard. The neighbours who often used to help one another out with a loan, used to sit at the back doors between customers, chatting about Torah or the latest news or reading the Haint, Moment or Nasz Przeglond. Up above on the second floor all along the gloomy corridors running from end-to-end of the building were wooden doors leading to private rooms, offices and workshops. Here is Dzialowski the glazier, small and hunched who is always uttering wise sayings and quoting the words of our sages, of blessed memory. Here is portmanteau maker, a sign painter and a barber looking for new customers.

At the end is the door leading to the Mizrahi Synagogue and Club with its two large rooms. On the Sabbath Day it was always chockful and its congregation included outstanding figures that held official positions in the Kehilla or were exceptional by reason of their own personalities. Among them was Reb Eliezer Oppenheim, owner of the house and the timber store in the courtyard, the almost permanent head of the Mizrahi; the testy Reb Mordechai Hacohen Shapira and Reb Moshe Krakowski, both of them scholars and enlightened after their fashion; Reb Shlomo Herszkowicz owner of the "Zloty Rog" with whom every important person visiting the town stayed as a matter of course; the aged Reb Shmuel Weltsman who owned the large book store in Ciasna Street and who was a historian and bibliographer, always busy writing his book on the History of the Kalish Community. And here is Reb Simeon Widewski, a fleshy man who is both learned and wealthy; the modest and gentle Reb Feivel Lipshitz who is an expert Hebrew grammarian and scholar; Reb Alexander Ziskind Moses, the crippled son of the Rabbi Reb Welvel Moses who reads the Torah on the Sabbath and boils and erupts at every imagined or actual misdeed; Reb Shlomo Kalman Parzenczewski who allocates the order by which the congregation are summoned to the reading of the Torah and then says the relevant blessings; lame Reb Joel Sitner who always proclaims every event and every action and last but by no means least, Reb Mordechai Mendel Weintraub, a Hassid who loves the Land of Israel with every bone and sinew in his body. He has a hoarse voice and shares in countless prayer quorums all the time. Ever since he visited Eretz Israel he sits at the third close-of-Sabbath meal in the twilight singing Sabbath melodies to Sephardi tunes he heard in Jerusalem. Between the afternoon and evening prayers on the weekdays, he produces the Haint or the Moment from his pocket, goes over to the Bema and reads an article on the Land of Israel aloud as though those were the words of the living God. When it is time collect for the Jewish National Fund he is always hard at work making sure that the prescribed amount should be raised.

[Page 201]

And here is Reb Joseph Moshe Fisher and his brother Reb Getzel, Reb Jacob Hyman, Reb Israel Braun who sings the Additional Prayers (Mussaf) on the Days of Awe and the short and lively figure of Rabbi Jacob Littman (Avtalion), a fiery orator and the head of the Tahkemoni School.

On Sabbath and festivals, the shops in Oppenheim House are closed and locked but in the Mizrahi Synagogue they gather and sit like brethren over a glass of liquor. To one side is a little wooden barrel and the pump produces foaming beer whose sharp tang spreads all through the Synagogue.

I can still hear their voices ringing in my ears.

———

The Old Bridge in Kalish

by Joseph Sieradzki

Kalish lies on the banks of the Prosna and as long ago as the year 1264, Jews were dwelling on both sides of the river. Indeed, ancient Jewish houses are still standing here and there, including worn old paving stones. Long-established householders lived in Babina, the Jews' Street.

Over the water hangs an aged wooden bridge which is the chief artery of Jewish life in town. On the one side of the river are old and new houses while on the other are the butcher shops, the fish market, the vegetable market, the Kehilla building, the Mikveh, the Jewish Hospital, the little synagogue of the tailors and many Jewish religious societies. On one side is a pharmacy and on the other, an inn. From the time it was built until the time of our destruction, this bridge saw the life of the Jews in Kalish. If any trouble came down on the Jews and there were riots, the bridge was broken. As soon as things became quiet, it was repaired.

[Page 202]

All kinds of boots have crossed the bridge. Here passed the conscripts in the Russo-Japanese War. In 1905 the Cossacks crossed it; in 1914 the Germans; in 1918 Haller's Poles whom they called the Hallerchicks and in 1939 Hitler's brutes.

And here is a day of Jewish life in the Kalish of the past. From the little wooden houses slowly shuffle elderly Jews with bushy beards and large prayer-shawl bags under their arms. On the bridge they meet and enter the Hospital Synagogue for prayer. These are butchers, wagoneers, tailors and cobblers. They are the first on the scene in the early morning.

Business is also done on the bridge. A wealthy butcher sells meat to poor butchers. They shake hands on it and do their trade by word of mouth according to a margin of profit. And the fish-sellers do the same. Carts full of meat and fish cross the bridge. On this side of the bridge the lean horses stand and the wizened wagoneers and on the other, in a long row, the porters with ropes looped around them and handcarts. All of them are waiting to earn a few coins and keep their households going.

On the bridge the unemployed also stand including bakers, shoemakers, tailors, hat-makers; and it is indeed sometimes called the 'labour exchange'. From time-to-time a small factory-owner or a master craftsman comes and chooses himself a few workers for the day. The others go on with their arguments. One group wants to immigrate; others want to stay here and struggle shoulder-to-shoulder with the Polish workers. These call for a revolution; those for gradual improvement. All of a sudden somebody mounts the bridge parapet, flings communist leaflets among the unemployed and shouts: We demand work and bread, down with the capitalist governments, long live the revolution!" Another lad has tied a little red flag to a stick and there you have a demonstration all cut and dried on the bridge. Off they march towards the Town Hall. The police disperse the unemployed with rubber truncheons and tear-gas.

Then the bridge is taken over by members of the underworld. Their own private trials begin as they start thrashing one another. After that, they make it up and go off to the inn near the bridge to have a drink together.

And now come the hawkers with the sacks who make the rounds of the courtyards shouting: "Old clothes! Old clothes!" On either side of the river, they spread out the 'wares' that they bought in the courtyards and sell them to the tailors and hat-makers. This is also a way of making a living.

Here stands a youngster next to a large basket full of flat hard cakes, hoarsely proclaiming from morning to evening: "Hot egg-cakes, hot egg-cakes!" A woman sells cold water in glasses. A little old crone sells hot peas from her bowl. And now suddenly a black wagon appears with black horses slowly driving across the bridge by a Jew with a long white beard. Those summoned to weddings and funerals have to cross the bridge because the synagogue stands nearby. Jews accompany the departed as far as the synagogue. There they wash their hands and then go back to daily life.

Towards evening, the bridge is taken over by the ordinary people, the needle and thread fellows and their like. They come out of their close rooms to breathe a little fresh air. The children play in the dirty gutter and the women sit along the banks talking from shore-to-shore. The men stand beside the parapets and discuss politics. The Kalish match-maker hurries from group-to-group, tall and long-necked, suggesting matches. The bridge is his anvil. Here he has hammered out many a successful match. Young men and women meet on the bridge and along it pass peacefully more than one couple who wanted to get divorced.

[Page 203]

The Café Goers

by J. Holz

The picture of Jewish social life remains incomplete if we do not mention the cafés and restaurants, those who went there and sat there and the atmosphere they established. The Jewish public, the intellectuals, the middle class and the class-conscious workers all spent pleasant hours in cafés. Current affairs of any kind, from a chat about fresh news to scandal all the days of the year which the observant Jews gets rid of after his prayers in the synagogue or shtiebel or in the corridors leading from them, provided the material for café conversation. All the local sensations spread from these tables as a rule.

There were certain cafés where Jews concentrated. For the greater part, each of them had its own particular style and clientele.

After World War I the best known was the Mayer Café whose cakes were renowned. It was situated in the main market at Milstein House which was built after the war. In those days it was the meeting place of the Polish gentry, the Polish and Jewish middle class and the professional men and intellectuals. As through a mist, I can see the large plate-glass window and the darkish hall beyond. My father used to take me there. If my memory does not mislead me, it was a male institution. I do not remember women at the tables. It would seem that the presence of women in cafés was not yet acceptable to people of good taste.

[Page 204]

On market days when the squires and estate-owners of the neighbourhood used to gather together, there was far more noise outside the café than inside. Agents and factors, chiefly Jews, used to wait for them on the outside. Those Jews would glance in to find the men they were looking for. Religious considerations and the withdrawn and distant attitude of the Poles did not permit them to sit together with their Jews at the tables.

At that time there was also the Shaub Café which was similar apart from the billiard tables which also attracted Jewish youngsters. Until World War II the most successful café was the Udzialowa in Wiszniewski House on the Josephine Allée. This was the meeting place of doctors, lawyers, engineers, industrialists, businessmen and a large group of snobs of both sexes. Many of them had regular tables here; their own social groups and meetings at regular hours. The coffee hour, with or without milk, was from 12 noon to 2 p.m. The ladies usually arrived first and the men came in on their way home from work. Between 5 and 7 p.m. it was the same thing except that people sat around longer, there were more people and in general the mood was livelier.

The most crowded time was on a Sunday before noon and in the early afternoon. The regular habitués included people who provided a kind of permanent background. Here you would find Dr. Alexander (Olesh) Danziger with his wife Maria Janka, the oldest daughter of Reb Bezalel David Halter. This corpulent old man with his tranquil face, constant sense of humour and considerable shrewdness, used to attract many people to his table. Bronek Silber (Dzims) the impresario of the revues and representative of the 'Muse with the tucked-up dress' was a treasury of jokes and japes and his name went ahead of him throughout the neighbourhood. And here you could see Elvira Holz who never grew old and was surrounded by her circle of admirers.

The Udzialowa Café was the place for the lawyers among whom Zygmunt Neuman was outstanding for his humour and liveliness. Here too the lawyers Mieczyslaw Danziger, J. Perkal, Leon Sitner, J. Prager, Stanislaw Frenkel and Kacenel were regularly to be found. The engineers were represented by the architect Leon Tzomber, member of the Town Council on behalf of the Jewish Artisans, Stefan Pinczewski, A. Fisher, Jacob Holz and Kazimierz Danziger, Leon Danziger, Manager of the Merchants' Bank and member of the Town Council was also a regular visitor.

At 12 noon the millers came in, namely: the brothers Leon and Moritz Kowalski with their representative Moniek Semiaticki, Fisher Gottfried, Nowak and Scheinfeld.

The lace-making industry was represented by Jacob (son of Isaac) Adler who had been paying court for decades to Xenia Seidorf (known as Sidonia). The merchants are displayed by Leon Semiaticki, Chairman of the Zionist Association and of the Cooperative Bank. He usually came together with Leon Szubin, the Bank Manager.

[Page 205]

There are usually a couple of doctors to be found here. Among them would be Drs. Trachtenberg, Plotsky, J. Beatus, Lubelski and Zeid. The younger ones included Berek Goldstein, Pabek Neuman and others.

The only non-Jews regularly fond here were the particularly courteous waiters Andrzei and Leon. The atmosphere was Jewish. Conversations touched on all possible subjects from international affairs to verbal onslaughts on others. There were also certain tables reserved for certain subjects. During the six week-days the Poles were a distinct minority here. On Sundays they were as much as half for then they brought their families with them.

Entirely different was the Café George at No. 3, Pulaski Street. This was the café of the young folk, first of the members of Hashomer Hatzair and afterwards of all the other Youth Movements from right to left. However, the Hashomer Hatzair was always a majority. They had discovered the 'Institution' in 1920 and had made it their own. The café cannot be thought of without 'Auntie' who ruled the roost here. This elderly spinster was always grumbling, but was very fond of those who came regularly to her café. We grew up and became mature before her eyes and afterwards we visited her as husbands and wives and fathers and mothers of families. Here the activities of the

Movement were planned as was Aliya to Eretz Israel. Here we began our first flirtations, assignations, casual and more serious love affairs.

Auntie knew who had been there, who had gone out and when he would return. She was a post office for various purposes. She knew exactly what to give each visitor and never made a mistake. In those days the constant visitors included Abba Seife, Shlamek Buzhwinski, Duciu and Lutek Krassucki, Olek Poznanski, Genia Krassock and others.

Guests included the active Maacabi leaders whose club was not far away. When they returned from the club they would enter the café. Among them were Heniek Oppenheim, Mottek Oppenheim and his wife Marina, née Temkin, M. Jarecki, Zeif and others.

When I entered the Café George after the war in 1945, Auntie received me most cordially and asked me whether I still liked a 'Stepanka' with my coffee. Her professional memory had survived and defeated the War.

———

We Are Taking Steps

by Alexander Poznanski

Anybody who wishes to know how far we Jews are from true autonomy can do no better than read the regulations governing the elections to the Councils and Executives of the Jewish Kehillot. And if anyone is interested in the powers and possibilities of action of the Kehilla, let him attentively read the minutes of the recent sessions of the Kehilla in Kalish.

We entered the election campaign enthusiastically. Many of the deeds of the Kehilla Executives until now were shameful and we wished to make an end of them.

[Page 206]

The elections ended with the victory of the Progressive Jews. The Council members elected are people who in the course of their communal activities have proven that they know the functions of a Jewish representation quite clearly and are capable of overcoming all the obstacles on the way towards a secular and democratic Kehilla.

With the same dedication as was evinced by our supporters during the campaign, we have now gone to work in the Kehilla. But to our regret, the activities of the recently elected bodies are being slowed down by the third party. (And when we come to speak about interferences in activity, let us not forget those quarrels of a personal and party character which burst out and have become permanent even among us ever since the 19th Zionist Congress).

The election of the Executive – the actual controller of the Kehilla – which should have been completed at the 1st Meeting of the Council has now been deferred to the second month under articles 14 and 64 of the election law: and there is no end in sight. People who have already been approved as Council members are found to be ineligible. It is absolutely impossible to understand the steps taken by the authorities and the effect of these measures on the Jewish community is painful. When the Kehilla liberates itself from the burden of the Executive, all its activities in respect of current needs are brought to a standstill. The old Executive should have gone long ago. Do they expect any initiative at all during the transition period?

The Block which I represent had to face a choice: either to do nothing and wait explanatory letters, confirmations, and elections and so on or, in view of the tragic position of the Jewish population, ignore all formalities of procedure, take over the administration of the Kehilla and begin working. We chose the second alternative. That is the reason for my urgent proposal at the last meeting of the Kehilla with regard winter relief. The Council found my proposal of real interest, adopted it unanimously and resolved to carry out the programme and elected an organizing committee.

Will the Council succeed in providing relief in these difficult economic situations of Jewry? Most definitely and certainly! The will to live of the Jewish community is powerful and it will not fail at this tragic moment. We cannot rely on any help from the outside. Therefore, let everybody respond gladly and willingly to the summons of the Kehilla. Our self-help will determine the fate of many Jewish families. Do we have to seek the means to awaken Jewish generosity?

You, worker at a job or Jewish craftsman, will you refuse to contribute one day's work for your hungry brother? In spite of the boycott, will you, Jewish merchant, refuse to aid your starving brother who was also a merchant only a short time ago? Jewish mother and housewife, will you not save some of your meagre food at least once a week so as to contribute what you can spare to the Relief Committee?

I am convinced that the first Relief Action of the New Kehilla will be crowned with success.

Kalisher Leben 35 (458); 28th Heshvan 5697. 13-11-1936

[Page 207]

19, Ciasna Street

by I. Holz

Dedicated to the precious memories of Abba and Bella Seife.

In accordance with the meaning of its name in Polish, this was really a narrow street which always had a smell of sewage. On either side of the street stood houses of two or three storeys. They had no style whatever. Sometimes they were ugly, crumbling with old age and the dust of generations, and the plaster peeling off.

What caught the eye in these houses were the broad double gates through which the peasant carts used to rumble to find a resting place, particularly on Tuesday and Friday market days. Behind the gateway was the 'heart' of the house that is, the courtyard surrounded by all kinds of buildings and wings.

In 'our' house there was a courtyard that was just like a lengthy pipe paved with shapeless cobblestones in which ran runnels of sewage. It took considerable skill to cross these runnels, particularly during floods caused by rain or simple overflow from cess-pits.

On the left-hand side of the courtyard was Biezwinski's workshop, a locksmith who was well-known in the city. On the right was a succession of apartments in the wings standing one behind the other and full of poor families, each with any number of children. These inhabitants engaged in petty trading or some in selling all kinds of trifles on the stalls of the Municipal Market. At night they often used to sleep on their little carts in order to go off to markets in the neighbouring villages and small towns early in the morning. There were also two shtieblech of different Hassidic groups in this courtyard. On festival and Sabbath nights their melodies used to compete with one another and strangely enough, the competition often blended well.

At the end of the courtyard, in a building which had formerly served as a factory, was the Hashomer Hatzair Club. The entrance and staircase were perfect archaeological specimens. The wooden stairs were warped and dry with age. They creaked and groaned at every step and functioned by sheer force of habit alone while the peeling walls rounded off the melancholy scene.

A high door with a rusty lock in it was the entrance to the club which carried the picturesque Russian name "Izba" (cabin). We were young then so we paid no attention to the entry-way, the stench and the ugly surroundings. We were busy re-shaping the world and our eyes were raised on high all the time.

The big room was actually a hall in which the ceiling was supported by many pillars as in every such room intended for machinery. At the end, behind a wooden screen that ran the width of the chamber, were two tiny rooms. One served for the secretariat and for meetings of the local leadership, the other for the meetings and activities of the groups. The problems with which we dealt were grave and difficult. The arguments and debates were lively and tempestuous. We were indeed young.

[Page 208]

The walls were decorated as the times required, changing according to festivals, holidays and Zionist events. The photograph of Herzl was never missing.

There was a feeling of cleanliness and beauty in there. Whenever you came you would find either Hasia, Yutka, Genia or else Rhuda with a broom in her hand. It was noisy and cheerful. There was always a great deal of hubbub. There was dancing, particularly the Hora and sometimes danced until very late at night. We also had a wall newspaper with notes and remarks on current affairs. It always caught the eye with its beautiful arrangements and its drawings. I also remember the slogan "Hebrew speak Hebrew" set out with the aid of little electric lamps.

We were well organized, between four and five hundred youngsters of both sexes, full of high standards and ideals. It was a most intense and stormy period in our lives. There is no going back to that period. But one may and can refresh one's memory.

————

No. 3, Nova Street

by Bluma Wroclawski

The house, in which I was born, grew up and lived until the outbreak of World War was like any other house, and yet, there was something special about it which makes my heart ache.

There were dozens of inhabitants in the house and apart from the non-Jew, they were all Jews. Who was he? The janitor, of course. Each tenant had his private world and goings-on and together, they constituted a panorama of Jewish life.

To the right of the gate there was a large shop belonging to Pazanowski and selling second-hand clothes. The enormous courtyard was full of stables and cowsheds. On Fair days, the courtyard would fill up with wagons before dawn. Farmers would bring geese, poultry or butter. The inhabitants of the house would go down to buy the goods. Artisans used to live in the house; factory workers and a water-drawer. There was a bakery in the house, a pastry-cook's shop and a laundry. The Rebbe of Zychlin lived there as it was near to the big synagogue.

A water pump stood in the centre of the courtyard. The water-drawer, Moshele, was a short, heavyset man with crooked legs. He would lift his ware pail-by-pail and pour them into the barrels of his clients.

[Page 209]

There was a traditional atmosphere about this courtyard. On Friday evenings it would become very quiet. All the tenants who had been rushing around each day to make a living now seemed to have changed their very image. Suddenly they turned into Jews praying to God, wrapped in their prayershawls.

The days before Passover were happy and noisy ere. The children would light a bonfire and there was no end to their delight. Women would throw parcels of *Hamets* (leaven) from the windows to be burnt. The children were delighted to fulfil the Commandment.

But as the hour of the Seder drew nearer, the courtyard became very still. Everybody would be sitting around with a grave air trying to impart certain splendour to the ceremony, and anyone who prolonged it deserved to be praised.

Once the Passover was over, the grey days returned to the courtyard, worries and problems, making a living, taxation and various hardships. This went on until the Feast of Succoth.

There were sixteen booths to adorn the courtyard and one of them was particularly impressive – that of the Rebbe of Zychlin. The Rebbe would only enter his Sukkah after all the other Jews had settled in theirs. I can clearly recall his impressive figure in his silk kapota, his white socks, and the shtreimel on his head. He would chant the Kiddush in a loud voice and all the inhabitants of the courtyard would cray: "Amen" after him.

On Yom Kippur, the fear of the Day of Atonement could be felt in the courtyard. At the time of the lighting of the candles, rivers of tears would flow from the eyes of mothers. Voices were heard mourning and weeping. When the meal was over, the fathers would bless their children and go down to pray. The following day they would stand wrapped in their white shrouds, praying and weeping all day long.

But their prayers were not heard. One day in September 1939, Gestapo men came and took all the residents of the courtyard at No. 3, Nova Street; old people, women and babes in arms to the buildings of the Shrier market. They walked with small parcels on their backs, driven by Nazi whips. It was the beginning of the end.

A Lag Ba'Omer March

by M. B.

In the early hours of the morning, groups of young people could already be seen wearing their uniforms, hurrying to the premises of their various organizations.

At seven o'clock precisely, all the youth organizations had already gathered at the starting point in the large courtyard of the Zionist Organization buildings at No. 21 Josephine Boulevard

By 7:15, they set out on their journey headed by Mr. David Wolkovitch. The "Hashomer Hatzair" band played marches. It was an impressive trip.

[Page 210]

The fine weather and the sunshine contributed to the very effective parade which passed through the Josephine, Pilsudski, Warzawska and Turek streets towards Winary. The following Youth Movements took part in the trip: Histadrut Zionit, Hehalutz Hamerkazi, Hashomer Hatzair, Hebrew Gymnasium, Hehalutz Hatzair and Gordonia.

In the Forest

Once they reached the Winary Forest the various movements parted. Each had its own corner of the forest in which it set its tents and organized its own plan as had previously been arranged.

An outsider would have noticed that discipline and order prevailed in all the youth movement camps. There is no better proof than the fact that the Hora dance was not sufficient for them, though the man in the street tends to believe at times that it is all they do. Oh no! National Zionist work is carried out among them and is of immense value. They change the character of the Galut Jew from its very foundation in both physical and mental aspects. They prepare him for a life of freedom as against his fettered life of today. This sort of educational activity can only succeed if it is begun while the children are still very young.

In a number of camps, speeches were made on current affairs and in particular on the closing of Aliya to Eretz Israel. Y. Litman of Brit Trumpeldor and H. Palach of Hehalutz Hamerkazi addressed their listeners making impassioned speeches. They pointed out that the closing of the gates would be of no use for we would continue to immigrate and penetrate through the cracks. All day long the road to the camps was busy. Carriages, cars and bicycles kept bringing visitors. Many "pilgrims" were drawn to the forest at Winary. The guests were estimated to have numbered several thousand. This public was varied and belonged to all sections of the community. The majority were the parents of the young members of the Youth Movements. They were now given an opportunity of seeing part of the work of the movements to which their children were so devoted.

[Page 211]

The March Back to Town

At 7 p.m. all the Movements prepared to march back to town. As soon as the order was given, they started homeward. The marchers were in high spirits and never stopped singing. They were accompanied by a large audience all the way.

At 8 p.m. they approached the town. About 2km away, they were awaited by hundreds of people whose numbers grew constantly. The public cheered the marchers and three flowers at them. The roads through which they passed were crowded with people. Everybody watched the marchers with a sense of pride and satisfaction. They passed through Babine Street, New Market, Ciasna, Nova, Zlota, Pilsudski Streets and Josephine Boulevard to the courtyard of the Zionist Organization.

At the end of the ramble, an impressive parade took place and the various Movements then went off, each to its own premises.

Kalisher Woch 10: 23-5-1930

———

Lag Ba'Omer Rambles

by Roshem

In their customary fashion, the Zionist Youth Movement have kept up their tradition of rambling out of town this year as well. At 7 a.m. the Brit Trumpeldor left to the sound of their band, displaying their blue-white flag along the road to Lissa and wearing their brown uniforms. They were joined by the Brit Trumpeldor youth of Stawiszyn. Mr. Grausalz headed the youngsters who made a very nice impression.

At about the same time, the Hashomer Hatzair, Hehalutz Hamerkazi, Gordonia and Hehalutz Hatzair left for their traditional march to Wolitza (Lissa). This march had many participants and the column was a long one. The walked to the sound of the bugle and the drum. Although very small children took part, the marching was exemplary. In the morning, the weather was not very good but this did not affect the proud and steady marching of the young people. It is interesting that they chose the Lissa forest for their trip, although it was six kilometres away from town.

[Page 212]

When the hikers reached the forest, each Movement marked off its own area with string, put up tents and set out to carry the plans which had been prepared previously. The youth enjoyed themselves, engaging in sports activities and games. They also discussed current affairs under the guidance of older members.

Visitors kept coming to the forest all day long and the youngsters with the blue National Fund boxes called on them to donate.

The first to return at dusk were the Brit Trumpeldor. Their band began playing as soon as they approached town. In town itself, a large crowd of parents and children awaited them and the streets were full of spectators. An hour later, the second set of marchers arrived. Its members carried torches and sang Halutz and Shomer songs. As soon as they approached the town, their band began to play and continued until they reached the Hashomer quarters.

Kalisher Woch 18; 15-5-1931

————

The Herzl Assembly at a Hashomer Camp

by Bar-Saba

The 20th of Tammuz. A really hot summer day. The sun has been beating down since dawn and it is very hard to bear the heat. The sky is crystal-clear; no clouds mar the pale blue horizon. Nature must be preparing herself, putting on her best holiday garb in honour of this holy occasion. The camp is noisy. A hundred *kfirim* ("Lion Whelps") are hastily getting ready in couples. The atmosphere grows tense.

Then suddenly – silence. Attention! The bugle blows a halfnote and then spreads sadly. The blast ends in a long call – today is the anniversary of Herzl's death.

One minute more and a great band of Jewish children wearing white shirts and Shomer ties, stand ready for parade; the leaders at their head. The flags are down at half-mast, waving in the wind. – Attention!

The head of the camp reads the Order of the Day. The Hebrew words are pronounced in the Sephardi fashion, echo in the silence of the Polish countryside. For a split second you can imagine to yourself that you are in Eretz Israel.

It seems as though Herzl, the figure standing on the balcony of the Congress House in Basle, must be looking down on the youngsters who have gathered in this place and smiles his gentle and fatherly smile.

The children's eyes are bewildered, pensive, dreaming.

[Page 213]

"Am Yisrael Hai! Amcha Yisrael Yibaneh!" (Israel is alive. Your People of Israel will be rebuilt.)

An enthusiastic Hora dance is the response to the Order of the Day. The circles of dancers move as though they are in a spell.

"Shomrim Yivnu Hagalil" (Shomrim will build up Galilee!) The words ring out for the first time in the forsaken Polish village. The driving force of the youth can be felt, the iron will is there.

"Anu Nivneh Yehudah! Anu Nivneh Hagalil!" (We shall build Judea! We shall build up Galilee!)

Evening. The sky has grown dark. Newly harvested sheaves of rye like around in the field. A row of cherry trees can be seen in the background. On the border between the field and the row of trees, Herzl's picture has been set on a special stand. Sheaves have been placed on either side of the picture and agricultural implements are laid before it. Everything is lit up by two campfires. They throw a rosy glow on the picture and on the "Whelps" that pass in a file. Hundreds of Jewish children march past without a sound, turning their heads to the noble face of the leader.

The tune of "Tel-Hai" is quietly played on the violin. The sad notes harmonize with the surrounding. Suddenly – an explosion! A white flame bursts aloft in the field. The "Kfirim" have lit the bonfire which has been prepared for this purpose. A moment later, they have all gathered around the bonfire and the head of the camp begins his speech.

He reviews the generations of Jews in the Diaspora and speaks of those who fought in the past for the Freedom of Israel; the Hashmonaim, the Maccabees, the martyrs who went to the flames in Spain, Benjamin Zeev Herzl, the Pioneers and the Shomrim. He ends by saying that the 20th of Tammuz has turned from a day of mourning into a day of rejoicing; rejoicing for the achievement of creation throughout the years; for each footstep that brings us closer to the aim set out by the leader.

The bonfire burns higher. Its flames are very high.

This is the gift of youth: Arms entwined, heads set back, shirts are out of pants and skirts awhirl – they are dancing. Dance! Dance with all your heart! Dance with body and soul! "Mi Yivneh? Anu Nivneh!" (Who shall build? We shall build!)- sparks from the bonfire and the moon in the sky is red. The hours move on. It is already midnight while these children of Israel still dance their victory dance on the 20th of Tammuz.

Kalisher Woch. July 1929

[Page 214]

The Gymnasium

by Micia Jedwab–Katsir

For many years the main and side entrances to the gymnasium were in the gloomy tunnel–like gateway. Wooden steps led to the two upper floors. Most of the classrooms faced onto Kilinski Street. The scenes in the courtyard were more interesting. The courtyard was large, paved and surrounded by tall buildings. We spent the breaks in the open air. On marketdays part of the courtyard was full of peasant carts. The unharnessed horses cheerfully chewed their hay and oats. The scent of the hay told us about the clear air of the fields in the distant villages.

The first floor was arranged like a proper school: Class rooms, a hall for the breaks between lessons, the teachers' room, and the principal's room which we used to pass almost on tiptoe. At one end of the corridor on the second floor were classrooms, while there were private apartments at the other. The poor tenants always grumbled and rebuked us about our bad behaviour. They could not understand how studying youth could yell and sing during the breaks. But in its final years, the gymnasium bought up all those dwellings.

The Jewish gymnasium at Kalish was the property of the Jewish Society for Secondary Schools which were headed by Dr. Braude. The language of instruction was Polish. We usually began the school year with prayers at the synagogue in Krotka Street. Two–by–two we used to march there through Babina Street at the beginning and end of the school year and also on Polish national holidays. On those occasions we marched through the main streets and aroused the admiration of the Poles.

The Gymnasium Building

[Page 215]

The School Committee was largely Zionist and that set a stamp on the education. The matriculation examinations were usually conducted in a very solemn atmosphere but that was not the case with the Hebrew examination which was characterized by a cheerful national spirit.

The head was Mr. Helling whose principles determined the school spirit. Most of the teachers came from Galicia, which was the cultural centre of Poland in those days. Each one is worthy of mention, but I shall restrict myself to Mr. Zimmer, the youngest of the teachers and the one closest to us in spirit. He left his post at the gymnasium and proceeded to Eretz Israel and that strengthened the spiritual ties between us.

My own teacher was Mr. Bakalar, an excellent pedagogue and the one–time secretary of Bialik who imbued us with a love of Zionism and Hebrew literature. Thanks to him we came to love Bialik and Tschernichovsky. On his initiative, we wrote a letter to Bialik and received a reply which was framed and graced our hall. Bakalar led us into the world of ideals when he told us about his Zionist activities in Pinsk where he was born.

They used to set out in boats on the river Pripet and there they organized their Zionist activities which were prohibited by the authorities. He was proud of each one of us that went up to Eretz Israel as a Halutz or a student. It may be largely thanks to him that all the surviving members of his class have gathered together in Israel although the war scattered us in many countries.

I cannot mention all those who fell but must speak of Judith Lefkovitz or 'Drina' as we called her. Her father was the gymnasium dentist and an active member of the committee; a Zionist from Lithuania who gave his daughter a Zionist education as well. Drina was a thorough–going idealist. She completed her studies at the Warsaw Institute for Jewish Studies and also completed her studies at the university. She then returned to Kalish in order to teach at the gymnasium from which she kept in touch with those of us who had already gone to Eretz Israel. She fell as a heroine when she slapped the face of a Nazi while defending her Jewish self–respect and became a symbol of the young Jews educated in the national spirit at our gymnasium.

———

The Jewish Theatre and Amateur Groups

by W.K.

The first group of Jewish actors who came to town in 1908 was "Landsman's Troupe". Those were the years of the reaction which followed the 1905 Revolution and the presentation of Yiddish dramas on stage was forbidden. Permission to appear was achieved thanks to bribery. The advertisements announced that this was a German–Jewish theatrical troupe. But sometimes the Governor himself came to the theatre and found that what was being spoken on stage was not German at all. When that happened, no excuses helped and the audience had to disperse.

[Page 216]

 Under the German occupation, Yiddish performances were allowed and Jewish actors used to appear in town. After the liberation of Poland, the well–known and popular Leizer Levin, who was generally known as 'Geler' or 'Ginger Levin', engaged in the theatre as his hobby. He continued to be active in this field until the outbreak of World War II and used to bring us excellent theatrical groups such as 'Vikt' and 'Young Theatre' as well as well–known actors.

Scene from a Play

The first group of amateurs was founded in 1912 by the actor Rakow who also served as its producer. In 1915 a Dramatic Circle was established by Ephraim Zimmer, Moshe Jedwab, Zalman Gottfreund and Jacob Reich who presented Gordin's 'Brothers Luria'. In 1917, Mondze Klechewsky and Ginger Levin revived the circle as part of the Turn Verein activities. They presented King Lear, the Brothers Luria, Shulamit, etc. and had a least thirteen amateur members who were later joined by three younger people.

Following the expansion of Jewish communal life in the Polish Republic, dramatic circles were founded by all the parties and in the schools for further study associated with the Arbeiter Heim. Peretz Hirshbein, the dramatist, visited Kalish in 1920 when three Dramatic Circles presented his plays.

The Poalei Zion Amateur Group was managed by W. Jacobovitz and D. Neugarten and had a least ten acting members. The plays presented included: Bimko's Thieves, The Broken Hearts, Hertzele the Aristocrat, Shlomke the Charlatan and The Slaughter by Gordin. The Bund Circle was managed by Stark and Matuszak.

In 1925 the 'Sambation' and 'Azazel' Little Theatres were very successful in Poland and the establishment of a Little Theatre of the kind in Kalish was proposed. The organizers were Tenzer, Leszczinsky and Sieradzki. By agreement with Jacobovitz and Neugarten of the Poalei Zion Amateur Group, it was decided to ask the poet Moshe Broderson to undertake the artistic direction of the new Theatre, Broderson came to Kalish, met the amateur actors and accepted the post offered. Jacobovitz, Neugarten and Kaplan were to be the stage-managers.

[Page 217]

That was the start of the 'Comet Amateur Little Theatre'. The first programme was given the familiar Kalish phrase: "Wos well ich hoben darfun?" (What's in it for me?) as a title. The text was by S. Rubin and the music by the conductor Krotianski while part of the material was written by Moshe Broderson.

The performances were very successful and were repeated eight times in all. Broderson was enthusiastic about the execution. The second programme was entitled: 'Lomir sich iberbeten' (Let's make it up) and the third: 'Hallo Charleston'. Texts were provided by Broderson, Rubin and Kaplan. The "Comet" also went on tour and was very successful in Poznan, Turek, Kolo, Sieradz, Zdunska-Wola and Wielun.

Actors of the "Comet" troupe were: W. Jacobitz, Z. Neugarten, W. Shlomowitz, H. Englander, H. Jachimowitz, H. Rosenzweig, L. Rabinowitz, Nissenbaum, W. Lubelski, A. Leder, Helfgott, Beckermeister, Tondowska, Scher, Berkowitz, etc. But in spite of the material and moral success, the receipts were not enough to cover the outlay on orchestra, conductor, costumes, scenery, etc. The troupe broke up in 1928. Some of the members left town; several of the women started raising families, etc. But Kalish folk will continue to remember their "Comet".

Hehalutz

by S.R.

S.R. describes the changes within the centuries-old community of Kalish which led the younger generation to find their way to various youth movements including Hehalutz immediately before World War I and during the two decades that followed. Aliya to Eretz Israel began to be thought of in 1924 when many young people registered to proceed to the homeland on foot. However, a major crisis came about in 1926 and 1927, and many of those who had gone to Eretz Israel came back bitterly distressed and disappointed. Yet, those were the years which marked the beginnings of Hehalutz, whose members started off by studying Hebrew and singing Hebrew songs. Apart from Hashomer Hatzair, this was the only Youth Movement in the city which called for actual Aliya under all conditions.

The new group had no club of their own but met every evening in the Municipal Park. At one time they also used to gather at the Poalei Zion Club and later in the Hashomer

Hatzair quarters; but the meetings in the park, held in all weathers, remain unforgettable.

When the late Daniel Levy joined, the Kalish Hehalutz was transformed from a sentimental group of youngsters into a serious body aiming at and preparing for Aliya, going through the full channels of Hachshara. Hehalutz never became a mass movement in Kalish but it exerted considerable social and public influence. It provided the channel through which many young people from Kalish and elsewhere proceeded to Eretz Israel and became part and parcel of the new life there.

[Page 218]

Map of the City

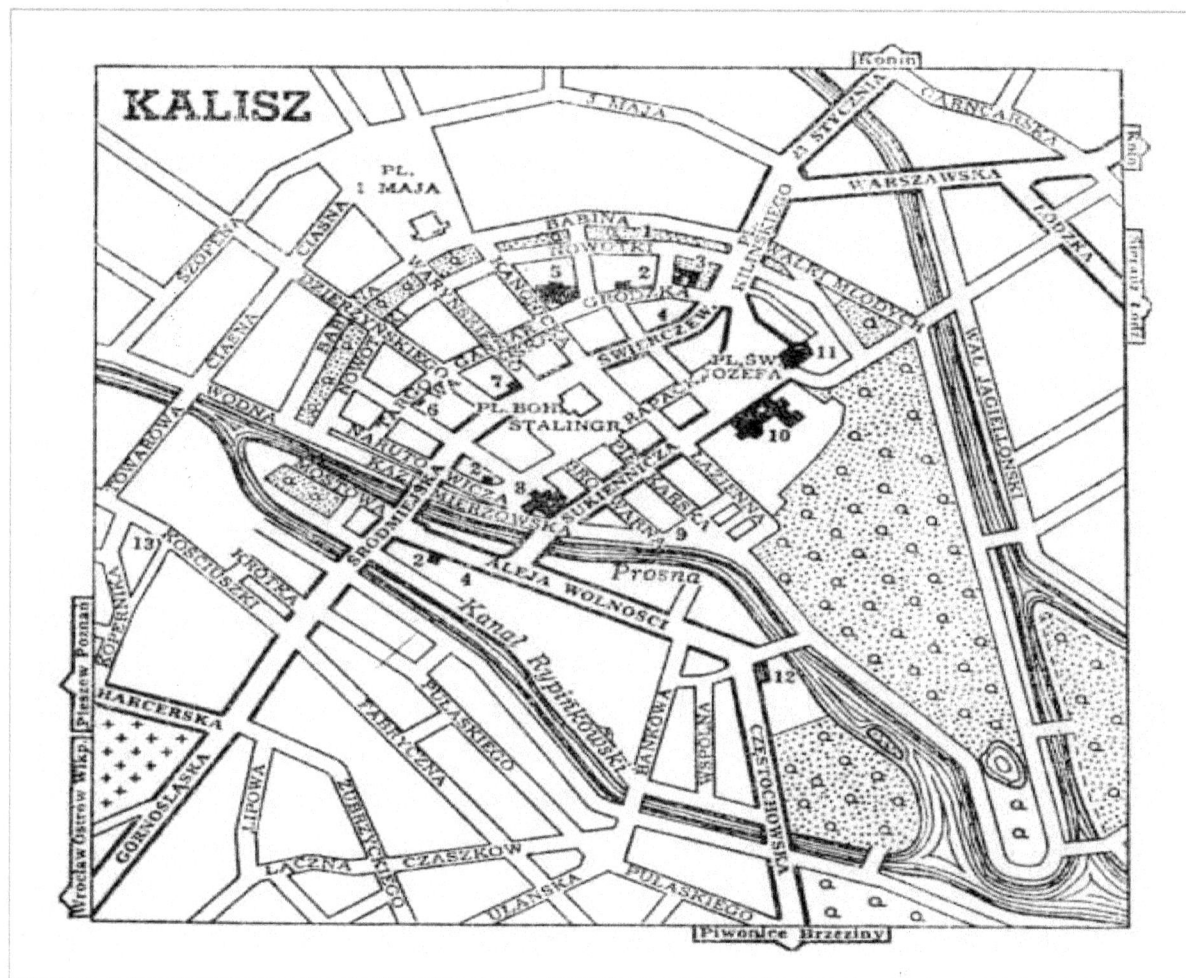

Key to Numbers:

1. Bus Station
2. Hotels
3. Adam Asnik Secondary School
4. Post Office
5. Holy Mikolai Church
6. Local History Society
7. 'Orbis' Offices
8. Franciscan Church
9. Parking places
10. Stanislaw Church
11. Kolegiata and 'Dorotka' Tower
12. Municipal Theatre
13. Municipal Museum

Changes in street names:

First of May Square – The New Market. Nowotki Street – Nadwodna Street.
Srodmiejska Street – Wroclawska Street. Heroes of Stalingrad Square – The Old Market.
Dzierzinski – Nowa Street. Freedom Boulevard – Josephine Boulevard.

[Page 219]

The City Remains Solitary

by Baruch Tall

Before me lies the map of the City of Kalish. At first sight, it is a simple plan: dust a few lines criss–crossing one another, other lines that are more or less parallel with circles and segments of circles here and there. Only the townsfolk will know how to decipher this map and breathe the spirit of life into it.

In the centre of the city stands the New Town Hall which was erected on the ruins of the building that the Germans destroyed in 1914. From the early hours of the morning the building is thronged with citizens and residents who come to find a birth certificate, pay taxes or hunt up an address.

In the corridors can be seen Jews in their traditional dress holding round little 'Jewish hats' in their hands waiting for some spokesman or counsellor who can help them reduce the burden of taxes.

The clock in the Municipal Tower strikes the hours according to which those shops in the Town Hall Square, which is called the Old Market, are open or closed. On festival days and national holidays crowds gather here, a military band plays and speeches are delivered from the balcony of the Town Hall.

Three lively streets have their beginnings at the Town Hall Square. The first is Wroclawska or Breslau Street. After its first half it is known as Gornoslonska Street. Here the handsomest shops in the city can be found – banks and an iron bridge over the Prosna. Halfway along is the starting point of the Josephine Boulevard and at the cross roads on the corner is the Exchange. There you see merchants and middle–men buying and selling goods, foreign currency and land. The great majority are Jews. The corner is like a beehive, people seem to be milling around aimlessly but in actual fact, many make a living here.

On the Sabbath, the whole appearance of the street changes. Most of the shops are closed and locked while the Exchange also seems to have vanished.

This street leads to the Railway Station. There are few buses and poor roads. The railway line is the main link between Kalish and other cities.

A single bus–line leads from the Old Market to the Railway Station, but few people make use of this means of transport. Most of the residents go to the station in a carriage or a 'risorka' (a horse vehicle taking passengers at a fixed rate along a fixed route). Most of the carters are Jews and the central station for the risorkas is in the 'Ross–Mark' or Horse Market.

The second street, starting from the square is Zlota or Gold Street which continues as Nowa or New Street as far as the Maikow Fields. This is the spinal cord of the Jewish Quarter.

In this street lies the Great Synagogue with the House of Study behind it. All the shops belong to Jews. During the six week-days, the streets are thronged with merchants, customers and simple idlers standing at the street corners discussing ways and means of making a living and politics and whispering the latest news to one another...Here there really is a small-scale 'Jewish Commonwealth' living, breathing and working according to the rules it has set itself.

[Page 220]

On Sabbaths, festivals and other regular seasons, the street is quiet. Early in the morning the householders can be seen wearing their prayer-shawls under their coats as they proceed with measured paces to the synagogue or to one of the many shtieblech to be found in the district.

In the afternoon, lads and lasses wearing Sabbath or festival garb come out to stroll or meet, attend a lecture or a discussion at the Hashomer Hatzair Club in Ciasna Street or the Left Poalei Zion Hall across the road. The residents know one another, rejoice in one another's joys and share in their sorrows. A wedding in the street makes the neighbours happy while a funeral, far be it from us, grieves them one and all.

To be sure, Jews live in all parts of the city but this street, together with Babina, Ciasna and Chopin streets which cross it and are inhabited by Jews (the only Poles being the janitors) are the heart of Jewish Kalish.

The third street is Kanonicka Street where most of the inhabitants are also Jews. Halfway along it is an aged building that looks as if it is about to tumble down. It contains the offices of the Kehilla or organized Jewish Community. Next to it is the Mikveh or Ritual Bath Building.

The Church of Holy Mikolai somewhat disturbs the harmony here. It is not the habit of the Jews to walk along the pavement next to the church.

Kanonicka Street leads to the New Market at the centre of which is the Fire Brigade Building. The bells ring. There is a fire in town. From every side, large and small, old and young come dashing. "Es brennt!" (Fire! Fire!). Voluntary Fire brigade members arrive, harness horses to the engines – there is ample commotion. It has happened more than once that by the time the Brigade arrives the fire has burnt itself out and nothing but charred and smoking walls are left.

The New Market is the place at which hundreds of Jewish peddlers make their living. They bring their goods by hand-cart early on Tuesday and Friday mornings and arrange their stands in level lines along the centre of the Market Place.

Peasants from the surrounding villages fetch their produce: butter, cheese, eggs and chickens. Jewish housewives go about between the stands poking at chickens, bargaining and buying what they need for the Sabbath. The peasants put the money in their hip–pockets and disperse among the stalls. From the Jewish peddlers and hawkers they buy clothes, shoes, caps and kitchen utensils. The 'mutual trading' goes on until noon. On Fridays in the winter, the Jewish peddlers do their best to clear their stalls early and hurry home for fear of profaning the Sabbath.

Between the Babina and Nadwodna Streets there once flowed slowly a branch of the Prosna which crossed the Nowa and Zlota Streets passed along Kanonicka Street and reached the Municipal Park. After the Nazis exiled the Jews of Kalish, they blocked this branch and paved its banks with gravestones from the Jewish cemetery.

[Page 221]

The 'Jewish' section of the river has vanished from the map. Together with it, as though symbolically, has come the termination of the Community of thirty thousand Jews who lived in this part of Kalish for so many generations.

People who have visited the city during recent years relate that it stands as before. Poles have taken possession of the Jewish homes. Only buildings where the plaster is falling from the walls still stand as memorials for a vibrant Jewish community that has been exterminated.

When a son of Kalish looks at the map, he sees once again, with the eyes of his of his spirit, the streets and squares of those days; the Jews walking through those streets on weekdays and Sabbaths. His heart sorrows and his soul grieves for the Jews of Kalish who have been cut off, and for the City where they were abandoned.

[Page 222]

The Organization of Immigrants from Kalish & District in Israel

The people of Kalish were always very sociable and wherever there were a few persons from Kalish, they would organize. There is a tradition that in the days of the Turks, there was a Hatzer (courtyard) of Kalish Jews in the Old City of Jerusalem. Menahem Shklanovsky records that when he came to Jerusalem for Passover 1924, he stayed at the home of Moshe Haim Waxman. The Kalish townsmen gathered there and discussed the possibility of organizing.

In 1925 Gad Zolty, Isaiah Leib Sowa, Menahem Shklanovsky, Moshe Yitzhaki and Shmuel Toporek, all from Kalish and Blaszki, met at the home of the late Eliyahu Berlinsky in Manshieh, Jaffa and set up a Kalish Club. They used to meet each evening and arranged cultural evenings as well as assisting members to find employment.

People from Sieradz, Turek and Warta also used to attend the meetings and gatherings. This Club functioned until 1928.

In 1929, there were further immigrants from Kalish and the Society organized once again. The oldest member, the late Hirsch Weltz, used to help members of the Society. It was a time of unemployment and the shop of Nahum Shurek served as an address and meeting-place. One day, about fifty members met at the home of the late Moshe Goldenberg and decided to start a 'Society of Immigrants from Kalish for Mutual Assistance'. The Government approved the Society which began with an initial capital of £P.10– and began granting loans of a pound or half a pound. The yearly turnover did not exceed £P.100. Membership fees were fixed at 4 piastres a month. At a later date it was decided to raise them to 5 piastres. A new immigrant was given £P.2 to help him buy a bed and the very basic necessities. The Committee looked after social cases. General meetings were held in various places.

Meetings and gatherings of part of the members were usually held in private dwellings. The Committee applied to the Kalish Kehilla and asked them to allocate some money in support of the local relief activities of the Society. The Kehilla allocated a sum of 1,000 zloty and informed the Society that 500 zloty had been sent. For some reason, the money was never received. The Committee tried to obtain help from townsfolk in the United States but received no reply.

Apart from the actual Committee, a Council of Patrons also existed. It was composed of the late Joel Solnik, the late Joseph Mamlok and the late Raphael Meir Shklanovsky.

When the Society expanded, a collector had to be appointed and the late Jacob Wartski was appointed to this post. In December 1932 shares of 1£ were sold to members who bought them on an instalment plan and also to tourists from abroad.

In 1934 the Committee decided to raise the membership due to 50 mils. As there was no fixed address, the Society decided on the homes of a number of members which would serve as its meeting place and address for the payment of dues. Activities continued as before.

[Page 223]

We can learn just how small the resources were from the following figures: The turnover of the Mutual Assistance Fund amounted to £P. 22 in the year 1931; £P.13 in 1932 and £P.53 in 1933.

All activities ceased during the 1936 disturbances as well as World War II. In 1945, former members resumed the activities of the Society. The first members to begin were: J.D. Bet Halevi, Chairman; Mendel Sieradski, treasurer; Yehiel Heber, secretary; Eliezer Birnbaum and Menahem Shklanowsky.

When the first of the European survivors arrived, they needed help. The sums provided in those days were: £P. 5; £P.7.5 and £P.15. Six hundred members were then registered. A Ladies' Committee was also formed for special relief work. These were Mesdames:

Bet Halevi, Avrunin, Birnbaum, Shklanovsky, Maroko, the late Leah Sieradzki and the late Hanna Gootschell. Memorial services began to be held for the martyrs of the city.

In 1946, upon the arrival of the first immigrant ships in Cyprus, the Committee mobilized for special relief work and co-opted Mesdames: Bet Halevi, Birnbaum, Avrunin, Shklanovsky, Maroko, the late Hanna Gottschell and the late Leah Sieradski. The ladies collected food and clothing and sent parcels together with money to Kalish immigrants in Cyprus and the survivors in Poland. The Cyprus relief work continued until the immigrants came to Israel.

That year, the reconstituted Kehilla in Kalish asked for ritual and religious objects. A few members met at the home of the late Joseph Mamlok and sent prayer-shawls, phylacteries and mezuzot with the assistance of the Committee. During the years 1946–1949 including the War of Liberation, most of the members were busy in defence work of various kinds. But they continued their activities and helped to organize branches in Jerusalem and Haifa as well as assisting the new immigrants who came to the country.

In early 1949, the Chairman of the Impartial Kalish Relief in the United States, Mr. Joseph Arnold (Aronowitz) arrived in Israel. At a Joint Meeting of the Committees, a Central Committee was elected consisting of: Eliezer Birnbaum, Haim Mendel Naparstek, Mendel Sieradzki, Shimshon Green, David Sinaderka, the late Shlomo Shimshoni, the late Fania Rogozinsky and Abraham Zohar. It was then decided that all money coming to the country from abroad should be sent to the Central Committee which would distribute it according to the following key: 3 shares to Tel-Aviv; 2 to Haifa; 1 to Jerusalem and for the rest of the country. The same key was used for Central Committee membership. Monies from the local collections were to remain with the various branches which were to send detailed reports to the Central Committee. At the same time, the Gemilut Hassadim Fund began functioning again and was named for those who fell in the War of Liberation.

The wish to commemorate the martyrs began to make itself felt. In 1950, S. Avrunin and M. Shklanovsky proposed that a special Forest be planted in memory of the dead of the City. In May 1954, even before the Jewish National Fund announced the planting of the forest, a circular was sent calling for the allocation of 50 dunams for the purpose. The sum if IL.500 was borrowed from the Gemilut Hassadim Fund as an advance payment to the JNF. In February 1952 the Forest Committee was elected consisting of Messrs. S. Avrunin, Abraham Zohar, M. Shklanovsky, M. Sieradzki, G. Wroclawski and Meir Maroko. Each member was called on to plant one tree in the Kalish Martyrs' Forest. At the same time we contacted fraternal organizations in the U.S.A. and they also commenced activities.

[Page 224]

In May 1952 collections began in Israel. Mention should be made of the main collectors: Esther and Shmuel Avrunin, Leah and Eliezer Birnbaum, Bluma and Gershon Wroclawski, Abraham Zohar, Gad Zolty, Moshe Yitzhaki, Shoshanna and Meir Maroko, Neha and Haim Mendel Naparstek, Melech Shurek, Yonah and Menahem Shklanowsky, Leah and Mendel Sieradzki.

In March 1953 Joseph Arnold, Chairman of the Forest Committee in the United States, visited Israel. He informed the Society that he had donated 1,000 trees to be planted as a wood in the name of Aharonovitch and Sandziewsky families. This wood was to form an inseparable part of the forest in memory of the Martyrs of Kalish and District.

In April 1953, close to one hundred members went out to plant trees in the Forest. The inhabitants of Israel planted some 20,000 trees while those from the United States planted an additional 10,000.

In November 1953, Mr. S. Avrunin went to the U.S. on a family visit and met the Committee for the planting of the Forest in Memory of the Kalish Martyrs. With the help of Kalman Aharonovitch he met the late Gedalya Yoffe. He persuaded him to leave a sum of money in commemoration of his name and the name of his wife. The Fund for the Forest succeeded in raising a sum of $4150 in the United States until November 1954.

In 1954, the Committee visited the planted area and found that the trees were not growing well. In April 1955, Walter Morris and Kalman Aharonovitch, members of the Forest Committee in the U.S. visited the forest together with members of the local organization and found that the condition of the trees had not improved. It was decided that a protest should be sent to the JNF. In 1958, a final meeting was held between the JNF representatives and the Committee who demanded a new site for the Kalish Forest. After a prolonged and exhausting negotiation, the JNF agreed to allocate another planting area to the organization. The site was to be chosen by the Forest Committee.

In April 1958, the organization applied for and received permission to erect a Memorial Stone in the Forest. The cost amounted to IL.900. In 1960 it was unveiled. Care of the forest was then passed on to the Committee of the Organization and Mr. S. Avrunin was elected as representative to the JNF. In 1961 it was decided that the square in front of the Memorial Stone should be extended and Mr. Joseph Arnold made a personal contribution for the purpose. Money was also donated by the Committee of the Kalish Organization in Australia. The extension was carried out by the JNF.

In August 1961 members of the Organization went to the Forest with their families. The excursion was filmed and the film has been shown on various occasions.

In 1952 the Jerusalem branch fixed 22nd of Sivan as a Memorial Day (before National Memorial day was fixed by the State). Several hundred members went up to the Vault of the Holocaust on Mount Zion and unveiled the tablet commemorating the Martyrs of Kalish and the neighbourhood. The late Rabbi Jacob Avtalion delivered a eulogy.

[Page 225]

In 1953, the Israel Legation in Warsaw received a Torah Crown, a salver and a hand through Kalman Sitner, now of Kibbutz Ein Shemer. These were brought to Warsaw by two men from Kalish. Upon his arrival in the country Abraham Friedman of Kalish brought two Torah Scrolls with him. These were handed to the Organization. One was donated to a synagogue in Marmorek Street, Tel-Aviv, by the Organization of Kalish and District. The second Scroll was donated to the Haifa Branch. That same year, Simeon and Batya Green left on family business to the United States. The Committee gave S. Green a mission concerning help to new immigrants from Kalish arriving in Israel.

After meeting in different house of committee members week–after–week, the members decided that a home should be found for the Organization and it was resolved that a Club of the people of Kalish and the neighbourhood should be erected. Here is an extract from the Protocol Book:

"At the meeting of the Committee of the Organization of Kalish and the District which was held at the home of Mendel Sieradzki on September 1st, 1955, it was resolved that a 'Kalish House' should be constructed. All members voiced their readiness to donate money and raise funds for this Kalish House. The building is to serve as a Cultural Centre and Museum and shall have a Hall for meetings and for the Committee of the Organization. Meir Maroko was elected secretary of this undertaking".

A building committee was chosen. Meir Meroko, Eliezer Birnbaum, Gad Zolty, Avraham Zohar and Menhem Shklanowsky were the members. A circular was sent to the Committee of the Organization in the United States. At first, the local members were not certain that we would be assisted by the United States members because of the Martyrs' Forest. The first to be convinced was Mr. Joseph Arnold who donated the sum of IL.2,000. The founders in the country and in the United States, as well as individual members, donated through the Relief. In 1955 the building containing the Kalish House was erected by the initiative and help of our member, Eliezer Birnbaum. It was dedicated with impressive ceremony in the presence of guests from the Diaspora.

We would like to mention the Israeli founders:

The late Rabbi and Mrs. Jacob Avtalion; the late Hannah Gottschell; the late Fania Rogozinsky; Esther and Shmuel Avrunin; Leah and Eliezer Birnbaum; Ruth and Mordechai Bloch; Joseph Gottschell; Bluma and Gershon Wroclawski; Haya and Avraham Zohar; Haya and Gad Zolty; Ruhama and Moshe Haimovitch; Sarah and Moshe Yitzhaki; Shoshana and Meir Maroko; Neha and Hayyim Mendel Naparstek; Bella and Moshe Shurek; Yonah and Menahem Shklanowsky and Leah and Mendel Sieradzki who are happily all with us at the time of writing.

[Page 226]

From the estate of the late Gedalya Yoffe, a request was received for completing the Kalish House and establishing a Library in his memory and in that of his wife. Members donated books as well and there are now over 650 books in the Library. At a meeting of the Organization Committee, Mr. Joseph Arnold was elected Vice–Chairman of Kalish House. Mrs. Paula Arnold was elected Honorary Chairman of the Ladies' Committee for construction of the building.

In 1956, Rabbi J. Avtalion passed away. At a meeting held after his death, it was decided to plant a small forest of 500 trees in his name at the Rabbi Gold Forest on the way to Jerusalem. In 1957, Mr. Joseph Sieradzki and his family came to Israel. Together with them, they brought another Torah Scroll, salver, hand, two wooden crowns and a Shofar which had survived from the Kehilla of Kalish. These religious articles were not in a good condition and expenses were involved in bringing them over from Poland. Leah and Eliezer Birnbaum undertook all the expenses involved in the repair of these articles and dedicated the Torah Scroll in memory of their parents. The Scroll and the vessels were given to the Synagogue in Marmorek Street in the name of the Society of Kalish and its District.

At the Dedication of Kalish House in Tel–Aviv

The Gemilut Hassadim Fund and the Hannah Fund have developed very well. The Hannah Fund was started by the husband of the late Hannah Gotschell, Mr. Joseph Gotschell, on the first anniversary of her death with a donation of IL.8,000. Her sister, Mrs. Esther Malka Ziegel donated the sum of IL.1,000.

[Page 227]

The Birnbaum family donated a further IL.200. The yearly loan turnover in the Hannah Fund amounts to IL.22,000. The turnover of the general Gemilut Hassadim Fund indicates the extent of activities: 1956: IL.1,222: 1957: IL.8,502; 1958: IL.11,411; 1959: IL.15,147; 1960: IL.18,228; 1961: IL.20,566 and 1962: IL.25,567. In 1959 the General Meeting elected Mr. Dov Zilonka to the Financial Committee.

On 22nd Sivan a yearly memorial is held at the Kalish House for the Martyrs of our city. A memorial plaque has been put up in the House with the names of the founders and donors. In 1959, a meeting of onetime Kalish members of "Hashomer Hatzair" was held there sponsored by Dr. Saul Zalud. In 1961, a meeting of Graduates of the Kalish Hebrew Gymnasium took place there.

It was decided in 1957 to contact members in the United States and France in order to issue a Memorial Book for Kalish and its martyrs. Material, pictures and information from people who had lately arrived in the country were collected. This material was sent to the United States.

However, the work did not progress there. It was then decided that the activity should be shifted to Israel. At a meeting with certain members from Kalish, namely Baruch Tall, Dr. Saul Zalud and Joseph Holz, it was decided to put out a Kalish book which was to contain all material dealing with the community and the neighbourhood. A special committee would see to the publishing of the book and a special budget would be provided for it.

In 1959 the following members were elected to the Publication Committee: Baruch Tall, chairman; Abraham Zohar, secretary; Dr. Saul Zalud, treasurer; Joseph Holz, collector of material; Gershon Wroclawski; Eliezer Birnbaum; Mendel Sieradzki and Menahem Shklanowsky, Secretary of Organization. The committee contacted members in the Diaspora and requested the return of material from the United States. The Book Committee in the United States agreed to publication in the country and material began to arrive. At the time, Messrs. Yitzhak Kletchewsky and Yehiel Greenspan from France were visiting Israel. They gave the committee the material which they possessed about the city. While the material arrived from the United States, material was also gathered in Israel. Evidence was taken from survivors of the Holocaust and the committee set to work.

Members suggested including Arthur Szyk's Edition of the Statute (or Privileges) of Kalish. In 1960 Leah and Eliezer Birnbaum went to the United States on a visit and were empowered to bring back the material. Eliezer Birnbaum contacted members in the U.S.

and began to search for the work of A. Szyk. Abraham Bandel devoted himself to this with all committee members headed by the Chairman, Joseph Arnold. When the pictures were discovered in the Jewish Museum in New York, the members helped financially. They also undertook to ensure that the work would be printed only in the Kalish Book. The Birnbaum family brought the illuminations to Israel. Shmuel Brand, the graphic artist, was co-opted to the Editorial Board and is responsible for the attractive and artistic design of the work. Ninety-five-percent of the material has been written by people from Kalish and it has been printed at the "Avalon" Press by Yaakov Krzepicki of Kalish and Meir Anavi (Traube) who helped in the layout.

[Page 228]

Every year, a gathering of Kalish folk is held in the different towns. The Tel-Aviv gathering is held during Passover; the Haifa gathering at Tabernacles and Jerusalem is held during Hanukka; the Feast of Lights. On the Memorial Day for the Holocaust, there is a tradition pilgrimage to the Martyr's Forest of the Kdoshim. Members from the whole country participate. In 1962 a "Mattan Beseter" (Secret Relief) Fund was established at Kalish House to assist needy members in secret. The major part of the Fund comes from the donations of friends in the United States. The Committee has assisted sick members financially, has looked after their welfare and encouraged them. In 1965 there was a special Drive at which IL.7,000 was collected.

In 1962–1964, after several decades in the United States, the family of Hava and Israel Shurek, who were active in the U.S. Kalish Organization, arrived in Israel. The Roth family as well as Nahum Lenchitsky who were active members of the Organization in Australia, also came to settle here. They promptly began to help the Organization in Israel.

In 1966 a General Meeting was called. In accordance with the Regulations, a new committee was elected with a council of 25 members. The following committees are appointed by the Council: Financial Committee; Relief Committee; Cultural Committee; Kalish House Committee and Audit Committee.

Council of the Tel–Aviv Organization of Kalish and District Landsleit
Standing: l. to r. **Gad Zulty, Nahum Linch, Yonah Shklanovsky, Melech Shurek, Dov Zielonka, Moshe Yitzhaki, Hava Shurek, Shmuel Avrunin, Eliezer Birnbaum, Meir Anavi, Shoshanna Anavi, Yitzhak Nissenbaum, Moshe Haymovitch and Moshe Rubinstein**
Seated: r.to l. **Hela Rosenfeld, Leah Birnbaum, Menahem Shklanovsky, Baruch Tall, Abaham Zohar, Esther Avrunin, Gershon Wrotzlavsky, and Ruth Linch**
Not in the photograph: **Abel Rosenfeld, Mendel Sieradzki and Arieh Kviatkovsky**

[Page 229]

The Committee of Kalish Landsleit in Jerusalem

In 1944 all persons from Kalish living in Jerusalem and the surroundings were invited to a General Meeting in order to organize and elect a Committee. More than one hundred persons participated and elected the First Committee consisting of the late Shimshoni, chairman; the late Heiman; the late Dr. Noah Braun and happily still with us: Dr. Solnik, Klein, Noah Bimko, Mrs. Doba Bet Halevi and Mrs. Masha Lavi.

The Committee was required to organize economic and social aid in absorbing the new immigrants who began to reach Eretz Israel from Kalish, first in the army of General Anders and later from Cyprus. The early steps of the Committee consisted chiefly of collecting and sending clothes to Cyprus, providing financial support for those who needed help on arrival and helping them to find work and housing. One of the Committee's most important measures was the Mutual Assistance Fund in Jerusalem which provided loans when necessary, for newcomers to make their first arrangements in the country.

In 1952 a national convention of Kalish Townsfolk in Israel met in Jerusalem. Those present went up to Mount Zion and lit candles in memory of the Kalish victims of the Holocaust, unveiling the tablet in memory of the Kalish Community which was one of the first to be set up in the "Martef Hashoa" or Vault of the Destruction. On this occasion there was a discussion of ways and means of strengthening the Organization and providing more help for newcomers from Kalish.

The Memorial Ceremony on Mount Zion was recorded and sent to the Organization of Kalish Landsleit in the U.S.A.

Activities of the Committee Members

Mention should be made of the productive activity of all members of the Committee who worked as devoted volunteers to help all who needed help during the first period after their arrival in Israel. Special mention should be made of the Piotrkowski family who served as an example and model for the others. Mrs. Piotrkowski in particular was the vital spirit of the local Committee.

Meetings were held between Kalish Landsleit in Jerusalem and various guests from abroad who came to visit the country. The Jerusalem Committee was particularly active in planting the Forest in memory of the Kalish Martyrs in 1955 as part of the Martyrs' Forest in the Jerusalem Corridor. When the Memorial for Kalish Jewry was set up in the Martyrs' Forest in 1960, the Committee played a very active part particularly the Chairman, Mr. Carmeli.

[Page 230]

During recent years, activities have decreased because some of the original Committee Members have left Jerusalem while others have passed away and have not been replaced by new arrivals.

On 9–6–1966, a General Meeting of Kalish Landsleit in Jerusalem was held with the participation of members of the Central Committee and the Committee for the publication of the Kalish Book who came from Tel–Aviv. After a Memorial for the Kalish Martyrs, a report was given on the activities of the Book Publication Committee and the methods of distributing it among those that came from Kalish.

———

Committee of the Jerusalem Organisation of Kalish & District Landsleit

R to L: **Zvi Lavi, Noah Aloni, Judith Carmel. Moshe Carmel, Michael Klein, Joseph Rosenbaum**

[Page 231]

The Kalish Landsleit Organization in Haifa

The Haifa branch of the Organization was founded in 1925 and the first committee members were: Samson Green, Arie Nussbaum, Zvi Knobel and Elijah Winter. The chief purpose of the committee was to help people from Kalish and aid them in finding work. Activities were interrupted in 1936 and renewed only in 1944 when reports of the destruction of Polish Jewry began to arrive. Messrs. Samson Green, Elijah Winter, Fishel Katz, Yehezkiel Salz and Fingerhut decided to help Kalish survivors. Together with Mesdames Batia Green, Bracha Knobel, Leah Salz and Renia Katz, the committee collected clothes and money which were forwarded to Kalish and reached their destination.

A Mutual Assistance Fund was also founded which aided immigrants from among the survivors to the sum of IL.7 each. Pauline Arnold visited Eretz Israel at that time and her contribution encouraged activities.

In 1947, larger numbers of survivors began to arrive in Haifa. The committee members received them and helped them with money and work. In 1950, Messrs. Israel Friede, David Sinaderka, Naphtali Ziege, Judah Kott, Mrs. Brandwein and Mrs. Parzenczewski jointed the committee while Messrs. Fuerstenberg, Baum and Meizner served as an Audit Committee. A Gemilut Hassadim Fund was founded the same year and with the assistance of friends in the U.S. it was enabled to loan IL.50 per family. With the assistance of the National Committee of Kalish Landsleit, the amount of the loan had been increased to IL.500. Monthly assistance 'in secret' is also provided where necessary.

Committee of the Haifa Organization of Kalish & District Landsleit
Standing: r. to l. **Ezekiel Saltz, Simeon Baum, Israel Friede, Moshe Fuyara, Samson Green, Elijah Winter and Fishel Katz**
Seated: l. to r. **Shoshanna Becher, Bella Katz, Bella Winter, Sarah Fuyara, Leah Baum and Leah Saltz**

[Page 232]

Mission to Poland, 1946

by Joseph Arnold

To my wife Pauline

In April 1946 the Relief called on me to go to Poland in order to extend aid to the Kalish survivors. On 5th May I flew to Paris where the World Conference of Polish Jewish Federations was being held. I participated actively in the deliberations and talked in detail with the delegates from France and Poland. The urgent need for immediate relief became perfectly clear to me.

In Paris I visited the Orphanages which were housing the World War orphans. I went there in the company of the Jewish artist Naum Aaronson. I shall never forget a talk with a seven–year–old orphan. When I asked him how he was he answered: "Yes, everything is good, the teachers are good, I don't have to be afraid of the Nazis any more... but what use is it all if I haven't got my father and mother?"

I held a special meeting about the Relief with the Federation of Jewish Organizations which was headed by Marc Jahrblum. Since the sums allocated by the Relief for Paris had already been used up, I added 30,000 francs of my own. During my two visits to Paris, where I stopped on my return, I visited the Foreign Ministry where we were promised 5,000 entry permits for Jewish emigrants from Poland.

Apart from my mission on behalf of the Relief I also served as the representative of the American Federation of Polish Jews. When I arrived in Warsaw on 20th May, I attended a meeting of the Central Committee of Jews in Poland where current affairs were discussed. At this meeting, I presented the contribution of the American Federation of Polish Jews for the Children's Homes in Poland amount to 4 million zloty. After I visited two orphanages in Otwock and saw their condition, I added to the contribution on behalf of the Relief.

With a heavy heart I visited Kalish. I think I must have been one of the first Jews from Western countries to have visited the city after the war. I arrived in the middle of the night, did not sleep at all and went out into the streets as soon as it was light. To tell the truth, the city had hardly been touched compared with other cities in Poland. But Jewish Kalish had been almost entirely destroyed. I was received by the tombstones of our parents with which the Germans paved the streets. Indeed, it was a dreadful feeling to tread on the tombstones of parents and ancestors whose graves had vanished. The Poles all around were walking freely while I hesitated to put my foot down for fear that I might be obliterating the name of a Jew who had lived here; he himself, his father and grandfather...

I wanted to visit the Old Jewish Cemetery but it had vanished. They used the tombstones to pave streets and buttress the banks of the Prosna. Nor had the New Cemetery escaped. About a quarter of its tombstones were still in place. The rest had been desecrated.

[Page 233]

Before this shock was over, I was shaken when I went out to search for some survivor of my own family. Nobody was left. I wandered through the streets trying to find some Jewish communal building that was still standing. The Great Synagogue was a pile of ruins. The large House of Study had vanished with the hospital and the various Kehilla Institutions. Poles were living and working in the surviving homes and workshops. The people had revealed the hiding places of the Jews to the Germans and had been given their reward. They had murdered and had also inherited.

I met a handful of Jews who had come back to the city in the hope of finding survivors of their families. They had found nobody at all and now they were wandering around mournfully, planning on how to leave the soil of Poland forever, soaked as it was in Jewish blood. They were afraid to demand their property back for fear of re–awaking the fury of the Poles.

One Jew told me that he had entered the former home of his parents. There he found a Polish family who stared at him as though he had come back from the dead. "What, are you still alive? And we thought the Germans had cleared the Jews out of Kalish! What a pity!" When I heard this story I kept away from the bakery of my murdered parents which now belongs to Polish owners. But I did find a grain of consolation in the story these Jews told me about my sister Hannah Rackman. Before she was shot, she slapped the face of a German officer who tried to take her only child from her.

When I visited Kalish I found 290 starving, ragged and tattered Jews there without any means of livelihood or work. And from whom could they ask for alms? Between 30 and 40 of them lived in a single room and slept on the bare floor. Luckily 900 parcels of clothes and food had just arrived in those days from the Relief and another 70 from the Aid Committee in Eretz Israel. These two shipments had really given life to them.

I immediately established contact with the Local Committee in Kalish. At several meetings we discussed Relief programmes, Jews who wished to emigrate and those who proposed to remain. I gave the Committee the contribution of the Relief and help activities began at once. The Committee bought two houses that very day. In one large house they opened a Relief Kitchen, a Hostel for the homeless, Cooperative Workshops and cultural institutions. Workshops were set up in the other house.

However, it turned out that plenty of building materials were needed to restore the houses which we had bought. I went to Dr. Koszutski, the Mayor, who promised to supply the necessary materials. Then he described the distress of the non–Jewish population to me and I thought it advisable to make a contribution to the Municipal Charitable Fund as well!

We viewed the help in setting up workshops and cooperatives as an important step towards making the surviving Jews productive once again. When they began to manufacture and earn a living again, they would find it easier to forget the horrors and at the same time they would prepare for Aliya to Eretz Israel or emigration to some other country if they so desired.

Next day I set out for the New Cemetery which is some distance from the city. Although it was not the month of Ellul, many joined me and we travelled in a long procession of carriages. With me I had a large wreath on behalf of Kalish People in the United States. After the "El Maleh Rahamin" prayer, I said a few words to my companions and promised that we would not forget the martyrs and would help those who had remained alive. The common grave of the Kalish martyrs had been dug by Jews after the liberation of Poland. Masses of the Jews of the city had been shot by the Germans in the neighbouring forests. When the Jew came back from their hiding places and slave camps, they brought the murdered martyrs to a Jewish grave.

[Page 234]

Upon our return from the cemetery, we held a meeting of all the Jews in town. I asked for their opinions and requests in order to get to know what they were thinking. A few of them spoke. In all their words I could hear uncertainty, fear of the morrow and a desire to live. How sorry I am that I did not note down their words! For it would have been a very interesting document. What most of them said amounted to: "Jews of America, get us out of here. We cannot live here – we cannot breathe. The air is poisoned with anti–Semitism. We want to go to Eretz Israel but if that's impossible, we shall immigrate to America."

There were a few who proposed to remain in Poland for terrifying reasons. "We are tired of being fugitives and wanderers and we know how hard it would be for us to start a new life in Eretz Israel. So we want to live the rest of our lives in the place where we find ourselves".

In my reply I said: "Our help will branch in several directions. We shall help every man who wants to go to Eretz Israel and every man who, for personal reasons, wants to go to some other country. And we shall not abandon those weary ones who propose to remain here." I felt the necessity of allocating a considerable sum to building a wall around the cemetery, the only Memorial of a flourishing community that had been destroyed.

Within a few days the number of Jews in Kalish rose from 290 to 1060. The new arrivals were Kalish Jews mostly from Lodz, Cracow and Lower Silesia. They had heard that a Kalish landsman had arrived from the United States and came to receive and give greetings from and to relatives and friends. A certain number were repatriates who had only just returned from Soviet Russia. Most of them stated that they had no intention of remaining in Kalish. They had only come in the hope of finding some kinsfolk still alive. When they were disappointed, they wished to run away wherever they could; as long as they could get a considerable distance from the common graves.

It was clear that many more would be added to this thousand during the coming months and I told myself that we must not rest until each one of those who had been saved had found a place in Eretz Israel or some other country. But, meanwhile, these Jews would be spending weeks and months in Kalish and how could they live in a city where the hatred of Jews could be felt? So I interviewed the Chief Police and in the name of former inhabitants of Kalish who were now in the United States, I requested safety and protection for the survivors. The Chief of Police promised to ensure the safety of the Jews.

I ended my visit to the city with a contribution to the local Red Cross on behalf of the Relief. Then I proceeded to Lodz through Zdunska Wola where I found a Jewish community of 190 souls and helped the local committee as best I could.

[Page 235]

In Lodz I found another 190 people from Kalish, all in direct need. The Funds of the Relief were already exhausted, so I had to take a loan in order to provide immediate help for those who wished to proceed at once to Eretz Israel or to other countries or to remain in Poland.

I met the representatives of the writers and journalists in Poland. They also needed urgent help to ease their distress. In Lodz I also met a delegation of the Borochow Kibbutzim directed by the left-wing Poalei men, Joseph Rotenberg and Abraham Kagan. At the time the kibbutzim provided a place for repatriates and agricultural training centres, preparatory to Aliya to Eretz Israel. They asked me to visit at least one of the kibbutzim in Lower Silesia but to my regret, I was unable to do so. This kibbutz bears the name of the heroic Abraham Diamant of our town. They also required considerable aid.

Shaken to the very roots, I left Poland and proceeded to Stockholm. With the assistance of the World Jewish Congress, I made contact with twenty people from Kalish, some of whom had been brought there from Bergen–Belsen by the Red Cross immediately after the collapse of Germany while others had come from other camps thanks to the head of the local branch of the World Jewish Congress even before the defeat. Hillel Storch had ransomed a "consignment" of Jews at a very high price and with the help of a local physician. I learnt that rescued sons of Kalish were to be found in the hospitals but to my regret, it was already impossible for me to visit them. I promised them the help of the Relief and the promise was kept as soon as I returned to the U.S. Some of them proceeded to Eretz Israel while others immigrated to other countries.

On my way back, I stopped in Brussels in order to redeem a Jewish child from a Christian house; but when I arrived, I learnt that the child had already been redeemed. At the Brussels office of the W.J.C. I recognized the directors of the left–wing Poalei Zion Children's Home headed by A.J. Kibble of Kalish. I also met with the camp survivors of Austria among who were also several Kalish people. For them I left the last $200 of my own that I had on me. The official funds had already been expended long before.

And I returned to the U.S. with a clear sense of the debt that is owed to these survivors.

The Financial Report of the help given by the Relief in the course of my mission is as follows:

Paris Orphanage: 500 suits of clothes, 200,000 francs. Kalish people in France: 1,200,000 francs; Children's homes in Poland: 250,000 zloty. Aid Committee in Kalish: 9,500,000 zloty. Kalish Municipal Charity Fund: 25,000 zloty. Wall built around the cemetery: 1,000,000 zloty. Zieradz folk: $100. The Zdunska Wola Committee: $500. Borochow Kibbutzim: 400,000 zloty. Kalish folk in Stockholm: 800,000 zloty. Children's Homes in Brussels: 10,000 francs.

[Page 236]

The Story and Activities of the Non–Partisan Relief in the U.S.A.

The First World War saw our hometown of Kalish demolished. Most of the buildings had been shelled or set on fire by the Germans. The Jewish population fled and the economy of the town was entirely destroyed.

In the years 1919–1920, when the refugees returned to their town, they found its rehabilitation a very difficult task. Only those people who had no alternative and were unable to immigrate began rebuilding their homes under very difficult conditions. They laid the new foundations for commerce and industry. But there were large sections of the population, particularly among the youth, who could not see opportunities of making a satisfactory living and decided to immigrate. Those who did not have relatives in the United States or money for a ticket, immigrated to Germany and with great difficulty established themselves there. A few joined the Halutz Movement and immigrated to Eretz Israel. But the majority of those who left chose to immigrate to the United States. And so it came about that between the years 1921–1924 there was a considerable immigration of Kalish Jews to the United States.

The social integration of the newcomers was difficult. It is true, of course, that each person established contact with the existing Societies and Fraternal Organizations according to his individual preference and social flair.

It appeared as though the activities of the Organizations of former Kalish residents were insufficient for the 'newcomers'. In 1928 the idea of founding a new society for Social Aid was aired. This Society was also to look to the old home town which everybody regarded as their source and origin.

The Society for Social Assistance (Frein fuer Socialer Hilf) was founded at a ball given by Branch 244 of the Arbeiter Ring (Workers' Circle) in 1928 when the young new immigrants came together. They decided that for actual social welfare (sickness and unemployment) they would remain in the Organizations they belonged to. The new Society, however, would deal with cultural assistance to institutions in the Old Home.

Before leaving Kalish we had witnessed the rise of secular Jewish schools and the financial difficulties which its founders, etc. faced. We, therefore, made up our minds to devote all of our assistance to these institutions and we were not in touch with other organizations. Our first President, Joseph Aronovitch (Joe Arnold) stated at the time that the Jewish school also served as a soup kitchen for hungry Jewish children. It was there that the child received a glass of milk, a roll and a plate of soup; for where there is no bread, there is no study. All the members of the Committee agreed with him.

The Society supported all secular Jewish schools in Kalish no matter what their parties for close to six years.

In 1934 we decided to extend our activities. There was a permanent economic crisis in Poland. Jewish artisans and market travellers were being pushed out of their unsteady employment. The Jewish labourers were also out of work and tried their luck at peddling, or else depended on assistance from elsewhere. The various professional societies and the managements of the Jewish schools asked us to extend our assistance.

[Page 237]

At the close of the Day of Atonement, we gathered at the shop of Joe Arnold. The following took part: Mendel Mansfield, Yohanan Yaakov Heber, Shmaaya Wartski, Yehuda Aharon Brockman, Wolf Zivush, Peretz Walter, Sam Oscar and Leizer Zolty. It was unanimously decided to found a non-political Aid Society of ex-Kalish folk whose name would be: "Umparteisher Kalisher Relief" (non-partisan).

We suggested that an impartial committee to be founded in Kalish which would contain all trends and professional societies. This body would receive the relief funds from us. The people of Kalish agreed to our suggestion and the Committee was active until the outbreak of the war.

During the first twenty months of our work we mainly assisted kindergartens and schools, some of which were attended by the children of our sisters and brothers. By the beginning of 1936, however, we extended our activities.

Our organizational basis grew wider. All the landsmanshaftn of New York and the vicinity joined us. We also established contact with other mutual aid organizations which existed in Kalish. We assisted the Market Travellers Section which was affiliated to the Society of Small Merchants and founded the Gemilut Hessed Fund of the Society, the Moshav Zekenim (Old Age Home), and the Society of Artisans, the Societies of the Weavers, Porters and Coachmen. With our aid, the Society of Food Workers with its two sections of butchers and bakers set up co-operative workshops for its unemployed members. In the years 1936 and 1939, we also sent food and parcels to help needy families at Passover.

Once the Jews really began to feel the organized economic boycott of the Polish reactionaries, a company was formed in town for the encouragement of craftsmanship and farming among the local Jews. We immediately responded to their plea and helped bring a change to the dislocated sections of society.

The four years preceding the destruction were years of considerable assistance in all fields of life in Kalish. We wish to enumerate the organizations with which we were in touch and the names of the persons who contacted us in the names of these organizations:

1. *The Society of Food Workers*: Hillel Englander, Chairman; Avraham Diamant, Secretary; Fishel Sieradski, Treasurer; Hirsh and Joseph Klein.
2. *The Society of Artisans in Poland, Kalish Branch*: Dov Neuhaus, Chairman and B. Arkush, Secretary.
3. *Gemilut Hassadim of the Kehilla*: H.I. Grzybowski, Chairman; Yaakov Katz, secretary.
4. *Moshav Zekenim Home*: Maria Zuker, Chairman; and Ben–Zion Wartski, Treasurer.
5. *Gemilut Hassadim of the Small Merchants' Society*: A.L. Brzezhinski, Chairman; H. Boiman, Secretary and Joseph Heber, Treasurer.

[Page 238]

6. *Market Travellers Section of the Small Merchants' Society*: Haym Perle, Chairman.
7. *The United Distribution Committee for Aid Funds from America*: Abraham Wolkowitch and Yehiel Tenzer; Left Poalei Zion, Michael Eisenberg; Bund: Hayyim Perle; Small Merchants' Society: Zelig Kempinski; Artisans: Israel Mansfeld; Knitwear.
8. *The Society of lace Workers*: Yehiel Tenzer, Chairman; Sam Wolkowitch, Secretary; Eliezer Wartski, Kasriel Lev and Aharon Joseph Wolkowitch.
9. *The Society of Transport Workers*: Avraham Tobias, Chairman and Shaia Markovitch, Secretary.
10. *The Society for Craftsmanship & Farming among Jews*: Advocate Joseph Perkal, Chairman; Dr. M. Trachtenberg and S. Feiner, Vice–Chairman; Dr. S. Peristein, Secretary; S. Kass, L. Tubin, Y. Lustig, H. Perle, A. Posnanski and Selig Kempinski.

We also supported the Joint, U.J.A., HIAS, Red Cross, etc.

We assisted Jews that had been expelled from Germany and whom the Polish Government refused to re–admit and were kept in the Zbonszin Camp. Some of them were from Kalish.

During the war we did not suspend activities and supported the general War Funds and the Jewish Assistance Organizations: Joint, HIAS, ORT, Passover Aid, The Federation of Polish Jews, The Red Cross, the Jewish War Appeal, etc. We assisted the Kalish folk who reached Teheran with the Polish Army through the World Jewish Congress. We realized the significance of our help from the numerous letters we received from them.

When the war ended, we found out that our Kalish brethren were dispersed all over the world and were in great need. Our brethren in France, who had been fairly prosperous, were now displaced persons and homeless. Many of them came back from Germany, from hiding–places in France, from the Maquis. There were Jewish children in Christian homes and in monasteries and homes had to be found for them. Polish Jews too began swarming to Paris, among them Jews from Kalish – people from Kalish who had just emerged from underground bunkers, travelled hither and thither on immigrant ships together with partisans and people from the camps. Some of these immigrants were taken to Cyprus by the British. Transports of Jews returned to Poland from the U.S.S.R. entirely destitute.

There was no time to waste on methods of assistance. The members of the Relief Committee were, at that time: Joseph Arnold, Chairman; Milton Mansfield, Peretz Walter, Becky Prashker, Lottie Lishow, David Tiger, Leizer Zolty, the late Pinhas Greenwald, Israel Glovinski, I.I. Heber, Hershel Arkush, Israel Diamant, Kalman Aronovitch, H. Okonowsky and Y. Shurek, Secretary. We realized that quite apart from immediate help, we had to provide constructive assistance and for this purpose, we must rely on progressive forces in the countries where our brethren were residing.

In 1945, we announced that we were starting a $25,000 drive. That year, we sent parcels to France and Belgium. When the town of Kalish was liberated we sent ordinary food parcels, Passover parcels and clothes to our brethren there.

[Page 239]

When the first representative of Polish Jewry, Dr. Joseph Tannenbaum, went to Poland, we sent Kalish the first $3000 and we immediately began preparing for the trip of our own envoy, namely our Chairman Joseph Arnold, one of whose tasks was to organize constructive assistance.

Joseph Arnold's trip to Europe has a special article devoted to it in this volume. On our behalf, he distributed a total of $41,000 in Poland, France, Sweden and Belgium, to organizations and private persons. We would like to note two outstanding points in his activities on this trip: In Poland and France, special organizational institutions were set up for our townsmen whose function was to prevent political feuding and personal misunderstandings. He also saw to it that some of the money was used for constructive purposes: namely, the Co–operative workshops which were then set up and the pioneer

Kibbutz named after Abraham Diamant. Indeed, his trip was acclaimed both among our own people and in the circles of the Polish Government.

The assistance we gave to refugees in Cyprus also merits a special chapter. Apart from the considerable financial help, we maintained a lively correspondence to encourage them in their national purpose.

We began activities in 1947 with a deficit of $13,000. The days of wartime prosperity were over for us but we maintained activities in all fields.

We continued supporting people in the Displaced Persons' Camps in Germany, Austria and Italy and in the Kalish Institutions of France and Cyprus. At about the same time, a group of refugees reached Oswego, New York. We sent them some assistance and also a special delegation: – Joseph Arnold, Israel Diamant, Max Smollin and others.

Here we wish to quote some figures on our activities in 1947: We sent $4000 to Poland; $800 to Cyprus; $1700 to France; loans to people who left the camps to the amount of $450. To camps and Training Kibbutzim in Germany and Italy, we sent hundreds of parcels to a value of $2500.

For this purpose, we had help of the "Ladies Auxiliary" of the Relief. They helped a great deal in local activities; preparing for major appeals; collecting advertisements for our Yearbook; preparing our traditional joint festival celebrations, etc. Their activities contributed a great deal to the success of the occasions and added a charm and beauty of their own.

In 1955 the activities of the ex–Kalish townsfolk in Israel were resumed and the renewed society of "Irgun Olei Kalish Vehaseviva" was established. The Relief responded to a request from the Organization and immediately helped them found a Gemilut Hessed Fund which is still active and has branches in Tel–Aviv, Jerusalem and Haifa. We regarded these funds as very important for we were aware of the hardships an immigrant had to encounter at every stage of absorption in a new country.

During this period, the idea of commemorating our destroyed Kehilla was taking shape. This, it was decided, was to be done by the erection of a building in Israel which would serve as a social centre for all Kalish folk throughout the world. The Relief initiated a meeting of all friends and organizations. Sam and Golda Prashker suggested holding a gathering at their home and expense. The participation fee was $100 and the entire income of $25,000 was donated to this purpose. To our great regret, the plan could not be carried out immediately owing to the needs of the rescued brethren. But a few years later, the house was indeed built in Tel–Aviv with the active assistance of the Chairman, Joseph Arnold and many members. The Kalish House in Tel–Aviv has now become the focus for all our active members and all visitors to Israel.

[Page 240]

The Relief responded to a request by the Organization to plant ten thousand trees in Israel in "The Forest of Martyrs of Kalish and its Vicinity"; a section of the large Martyrs' Forest which the Jewish National Fund planted in the hills of Jerusalem.

The Relief has been publishing a Year-book since 1942. This contains historical material and current reports of its own activities and those of organizations of Kalish folk in Israel and elsewhere. The first editors of this Year-book were: The late Jacob Kaner and the late Shmuel Margolis. It is now being edited by the writer Menashe Unger.

The Relief Committee, the Committee of the "Kalish Martyrs' Forest" and the Committee of "The Kalish Book" hold a yearly memorial service for the dead of the city. This service brings together all ex-Kalish residents in the United States.

The Relief takes part in the activities of the Committee for the "Kalish Book" which will serve as memorial to the creative work and lives of the Jews of Kalish.

The Relief holds a banquet each year which brings the people of Kalish and their friends together again and enables them to spend an evening in the atmosphere of the Old Home. During this banquet there is fund raising for the funds of the Relief.

These varied, productive activities have been possible thanks only to the devotion of many ex-Kalish folk in the United States. Each individual dedicates his time and money to the aid work and regards his activities as a holy task. For lack of space, we are unable to name all of them. We shall, therefore, only mention the most active members of the Relief who have given life and soul to these good deeds for many, many years: Joseph Aronovitch (Arnold), Chairman; Pauline Arnold, Jacob Arkosh, Hershel Arkush, Sam Oscar, H. Okonowsky, the late M. Beatus, Abraham and Fella Bedel, Glowinsky, the late Pinhas Greenwald, the late Z. Gollawsky, Yeshayahu Goldberg, Israel and Sadie Diamond, the late Yohanan Heber and his wife, long may she live, Shmaya Wartski, Moshe Walter, Samuel Wittkower, Perez Walter, the late L. Zolty, I. Sachs, the late David Tiger, the late H. Yoffe, Mrs. L. Lishay, the late M. Mansfield, Max and Marie Smolin, Mrs. Piedzanek, the late Noah Perle and his wife Frania, long may she live, Sam and Golda Prashker, Wolf Tsivush, A.S. Klaper, the late N. Kahn, Sam and Janet Okladek, the late Michael Kempin, Shmuel and Yasha Roth, Israel and Hava Shurek.

Throughout these years, the secretaries of the organization have been: Paul Walter, Kalman Aronovitch and Israel Shurek.

[Page 241]

We are happy to have some of the original members still continuing with the good work to this very day. They are: Joseph Arnold, President; Abraham Bandel, Chairman; Pauline Arnold, Secretary; Sam Okladek, Financial Secretary; Peretz Walter, Israel Diamond, Treasurer. Members of the Executive are: Jenny Okladek, Max and Marie

Smolin; Yasha and Shmuel Roth, Hershel Arkush, Sam Beyrack, Sadie Diamond, Nahum Medina, Jacob Levy, Ludwig Walter and Paula Bandel.

The idea of commemorating the memory of the Martyrs of Kalish struck roots in our hearts. When the Israel Knesset called for trees in memory of the murdered millions, we too responded. At the same time, the Appeal of the Organization reached us. This is why a large United Committee was set up for planting "The Forest of the Kalish Martyrs".

The committee members in New York were: Joseph Arnold, Chairman; Sam Beyrack, second Chairman; Kalman Aronovitch, Secretary; Mortis Walter, Treasurer; Lena Friedman, Secretary; Israel Shurek, Financial Secretary; Hershel Arkush, A. Bandel, M. Duel, I. Diamond, M. Friedman, Shia Goldberg, A. Krotowsky, A. Lubelsky, A. Miedzinsky, S. Okladek, Mrs. S. Piedshank, Samuel Roth, S. Rakowsky, H. and I. Shurek, M. Smolin, S. Weingarten and P. Walter.

The following bodies promised their support: Kalisher Bruder Ferein, Isidore Pile, President; Kalisher Young Men's Arbeiter Ring, Branch 241, H. Klarman, Chairman; Kalisher Independent, Waxman, Chairman.

The Committee started its activities on January 18, 1953 by sending out letters and circulars to ex–Kalish folk in America. Meetings were held, both large and small, both public and in the private homes of members; and speeches were held explaining the cause. The members donated willingly. At the Memorial Meetings the fund raising went on and the results were satisfactory.

The ex–Kalish folk in America took part in the planting of the Forest as well as the Memorial Services held in Israel. Members of the delegations were: Joseph Arnold, Morris Walter, Kalman Aronovitch, Sam Bayrack, Israel Diamant, Paul Walter, Hershel Arkush and others.

One of the commemorative actions is the Kalish House in Tel–Aviv. Apart from its being the World Centre for Kalish Jewry, the house will contain books, pictures, documents and anything pertaining to the Kalish Kehilla.

An additional activity is the publication of the Kalish Book. Let us mention that the initiative came from Polish and French Kalish folk. Yehiel Grinspan of Paris and Itzhak Kletchewsky began to collect material, pictures and documents and wrote articles on the social institutions of the town. Grinspan contacted members in the United States and was assisted by the members Saltzman, Makowsky and others.

In 1957, joint steps were taken by the Kalish Societies in Israel and the United States. The Committee organized activities, held meetings and gatherings, maintained constant contact with Book Committees in Canada, France, Brazzaville, Uruguay, Australia and in particular with the Israel Committee.

[Page 242]

It also assisted in locating data, pictures and the publication rights of the works of Arthur Szyk. The Committee has helped in raising funds for the publishing of the book.

These three enterprises are an important contribution to the memory of Jewish Kalish.

In conclusion, we have summed up the varied activities of the Relief during the past thirty years. These have been like a message to all our dispersed brethren. The facts and figures show the sense of brotherhood in individuals and our public.

Before the deluge of blood, we found creative joy in our work through rehabilitating cultural and educational institutions. After the Holocaust, all our efforts were concentrated on assisting those who survived the gas–chambers and the camps. When war ended, we set out to help the few survivors and tried to do the best we could.

At the same time, we remained true to the principle of the revival of the people of Israel and helped the immigrants, the pioneers and the defenders of the State of Israel.

We proudly conclude that during days of sadness and joy, we stood together with our people. Our welfare activities may be noted as part of the total assistance activities that followed the Holocaust. We make our contribution in all urgency and loyalty.

———

Kalish Immigrant Societies in the U.S.A.

by Kalman Aronovitch

Like all immigrants from Easter Europe who began to arrive in the United States during the seventies and eighties of the 19th century, the Jews of Kalish came to know the meaning of loneliness in their new homeland. There were various reasons for their departure from their old home–town: economic crisis, Polish animosity, unwillingness to serve in the Tzar's army, etc. Once they were in the New World, they missed their families and homeland. Integration in the new country was not easy. Many hoped that their stay in the new land was only temporary and that once they had managed to save a few dollars they would return... But as the years went by, and the changes of return grew fewer, these 'greenhorns' began looking for townsmen who were better acclimatized in order to provide one another with mutual aid of all kinds.

In those days, life in New York was very difficult. A man had to work 14–16 hours a day in order to make a living. At times, he even had to carry his machine on his back in search of work which was not always plentiful. Even people who had been labourers and artisans in Easter Europe found it difficult to get used to the conditions of the sweat-shop, which were very different from the conditions they had been accustomed to in their former homes.

[Page 243]

It was this need to find a foothold and support which gave rise to the first Landsmanshaftn in the United States. To our great regret there are no documents dealing with the first Kalish Society. The majority of its members have already passed away and the remaining few do not recall the details. There is, however, more information about the later societies.

The Kalish Lodge

We have found out from former Kalish residents who have been living many decades in the United States that the first association of people from Kalish was founded in 1870. It was named: "American Kalisher" and later "Kalisher Lodge". This association was formed in the style of secret fraternal lodges and was conducted with all the ceremonies of the secret lodges.

When a meeting of the "American Kalisher" was opened, "Outer Guards" were placed in front of the entrance. They wore a strange uniform. "Inner Guards" were placed in the hall. When a stranger wanted to attend the meeting, the Outer Guard informed the Inner Guard by signalling through knocks at the door. A crack was then opened and the stranger's desire was brought to the attention of the president. If the president agreed to his entry, the Guards led the stranger around the table in the centre of the room before he was conducted to the officers of the Lodge. Admission of new members was accompanied by ceremonies and oaths.

This association did assist the Kalish Jews to a certain extent.

The Kalish Bruder Ferein (Fraternal Union)

This Society was formed in Harlem, New York in 1887 when most of the inhabitants of Harlem were Jews. In 1962 the Society celebrated its 75th anniversary. The society maintained contact with the Kehilla in Kalish and from time-to-time sent donations which were intended for welfare purposes. They had their own synagogue and to this day possess two private cemeteries.

The wives of the members formed a branch of the society by the name of "The Kalisher Sisterhood" and were active in the mobilization of help for people of Kalish in the United States and in the old homeland.

Of the founders and active members, we know of Zigmunt Galewsky, the President, Pile and others most of whom have passed away. The active members today are: Wittkover, Kauffman and others. Most of the present members are second and third generation Americans and to our regret they show little interest in other persons of Kalish origin, either in the United States or in Israel.

The Kalisher "Progressive Young Men"

The first meeting of the Society took place in 1904 at the home of Abraham Wolkowitch on Second Avenue, New York. In 1909, Wolkowitch and his family returned to Kalish. He was killed in the Warsaw Ghetto with his wife and his sons Sam and David. Abraham Wolkowitch was an active member of Poalei Zion and took part in the social life of the city and in community work.

[Page 244]

Most of the members of the Society were young people, many of whom had escaped military service. Some of them were political refugees who had fled from Siberia or the Tzar's prisons. They included members of the Bund, Social Democrats, and members of S.S., P.P.S., Zionists and Poalei Zion. These young men were unable to integrate in existing societies because of their opinions so they formed their own society.

The founders were: Sam Berke, Abraham Weiss, Moshe Walter, Kuyavski, Joe Kott, Jay Prashker, the late N. Kahn, the late Glatstein and others. Sam Segal was their secretary.

The purpose of the Society was: - supporting each new immigrant from Kalish; assistance in finding work and sending aid to Kalish. When the number of members of the Society grew, it was suggested that they join the Arbeiter Ring. On April 11, 1911, the Society joined the Arbeiter Ring as Branch 241. The secretary then was Sam Kauffman.

Arbeiter Ring, Branch 241

In its new image, the Society went its own way. Its members leaned towards Zionism whereas the Arbeiter Ring was then very much under the influence of the Bund. The leadership of the Branch did its best to include national and Zionist issued in its lecture programme in addition to issues concerning socialism. The Branch also supported various Kalish institutions and sent help to schools there.

During its first years the Society numbered over 200 members. Eventually, the membership grew smaller until there were only thirty old members in 1961. After the death of its secretary, Chaver Glatstein, the branch united with the Lodz Branch and today goes under the name of "Lodzer Kalisher Kreis Branch Numer 36".

The United Mutual Assistance Committee of Kalish Organizations

After World War I, the United Mutual Assistance Committee for Kalish Jews was founded in New York.

All the organizations which then existed in the United States joined this United Committee. The latter sent out a public appeal to all ex-Kalishers in America to support their townsmen. The answer was $3000 which was given to the emissary of Polish Jewry, Dr. Rosenblatt of Lodz.

An Inter-Party Committee was formed in Kalish for the distribution of the Relief funds and was active until 1930?

Kalisher Independent Society

After a few years, a number of members headed by Sam Berke, Joseph Kott, Max Meiner and other members of the Progressive Young Men left the Arbeiter Ring because of ideological differences of opinion. They formed their own organization which they named: "Kalisher Independent Society". Their secretary was Philip Weiss. In 1940 they took over the cemetery at Mount Moriah in New Jersey. They organized cultural activities, lectures and trips. When the Relief was established in New York, they joined its Committee.

[Page 245]

The Society is active to this day. It takes part in Jewish social activities and supports them. It also supports HIAS, the Histadrut, the U.J.A., the Jewish National Fund, etc. The second and third generations still participate in this work. The following members still continue to be active: Sam Berke, Max Meiner, Joseph Brilliant, Roth and others. They are headed by the persons who founded the Society some thirty-odd years ago. The active public worker, Sam Berke, acts as President.

Kalisher Social Ferein

In winter 1928, a group of ex-Kalish people founded the Kalisher Social Ferein. Most of the members had immigrated after World War I.

The initiators and founders were: Peretz Walter, Yehuda Aharon Brotman, Wolf Ziewush, Joseph Aronovitch (Arnold), Yaakov Yohanan Heber and others. These, together with their wives, met at the home of Joseph Arnold for prior discussions and in 1929 the Society was officially founded. At first they numbered 15 persons but in due course they grew to 100 members.

The aim of the Society was the support of secular Jewish schools in Kalish, the Borochow School and others. They also set up a Mutual Loan Fund for assisting needy members. It should be remembered that a year or two later, a major economic crisis began in the United States. Many members were in dire need. The Fund sold shares of $25 each and every shareholder was entitled to receive a loan.

The Society also held a theatrical performance in the cellar of Joseph Arnold's home, entitled: "The Man beneath the Table". The benefits from this show were sent to Kalish. Wolf Ziewush and his wife, Noskievitch of Zdunska-Wola and others took part in this show.

In 1935 the Society terminated its independence and became Branch 265 of the Internationaler Arbeiter Orden 'I.W.O.' Apart from relief work, there were also cultural activities: lectures and meetings with authors and cultural workers.

After World War II, a number of members demanded that they should withdraw from the Order. In 1955 the Government closed down the Order and the Social Ferein became independent once again. It has retained its character and functions to this very day.

The Social Ferein is represented in the Relief and supports it and its members have been active in it since it was first founded. The Society has its own cemetery at Mount Lebanon in New Jersey as well as its private Sick Fund.

Kalisher and Area Landsmanschaft Newcomers

After the destruction of Europe, new immigrants from Kalish and the vicinity began to arrive in the United States. They were people who had escaped from the camps and the gas-chambers and also partisans and exiles from Russia. All these newcomers needed the assistance of the Relief. Their common fate: - they had lost families and relatives in most cases – made them seek one another out in order to pour forth their hearts and help themselves in integrating into the new life. Aronowitch gathered these members to a meeting on January 14, 1951 at the Borochow Centre, 216 East 14 Street where a founding committee was elected. Its members were: Kalman Aronowitch, Joseph Lubelsky, Sam Krakowsky, Avraham Krotowsky, G. Meisner and others. The committee decided to found a society which was named "Kalisher un Umgegent Landsmanschaft fon Nei-Gekumene" (Newcomers from Kalish and the Vicinity).

[Page 246]

The aim of the Society was: Maintaining social contact, upkeep of the tradition of the older Societies of Kalish; active participation in the work of the Relief and assisting national and cultural Jewish life in the United States. Monthly meetings were held for discussing various subjects; a tradition of Hanukkah parties was established and the Banquet of the Society was set for Purim. On this occasion, funds were collected for the U.J.A. and Israel and were forwarded through the Relief. The Society also took an active part in the connection with the Martyrs' Forest and the Kalish Book. Sam Rakowsky, the Chairman; G. Meisner, Secretary and the committee members: L. Mintz, M. Weintraub, R. Wolnikov, A. Yachimowitch and others, were particularly active in these respects.

At one time, there were differences of opinion among the members. Some held that the Society should restrict itself to being a fraternal organization without taking part in national activities. In 1960, a group of members suggested that they join the Arbeiter Ring. This suggestion was taken up and the society became: "Arbeiter Ring Branch 361". Upon the union with the Arbeiter Ring, a number of members left the Society. The Branch now has a few dozen members. They meet regularly and hold their annual banquet on Purim. The Chairman of the Branch is J. Lubelsky and the Secretary is G. Meisner.

[Page 247]

Kalisher Non-Partisan Relief Committee in U.S.A.
Standing: r.to l: **Max Smolin, Mary Smolin, Yadzia Rother, Ludwig Walker, Peretz Walter – Secretary, Nahum Medine, Abraham Bandel – Chairman, Fela Bandel, Sadie Diamant, Samuel Rother and Frania Perle**
Seated: l. to r: **Sam Berke, Israel Diamant – Treasurer, Paulin Arnold – Secretary, Joseph Arnold – President, Samuel Okladek – Financial Secretary, Jeanette Okladek and Jacob Levy**
Not in the photograph: **Hershel and Regina Arkush, Rebecca Walter, Sarah Heber, Ida Berke and Helen Levy**

Organization of Kalish District Landsleit in Australia
Standing. R. to l: **Shalom Margolis, Yidel Shmerling – Chairman, Gedalia Kwiatkovsky – Secretary, W. Stollman, Sala Kwiatkovsky, Issac Jacobovitch and S. Moskovitch**
Seated. L. to r: **Paula Brooks, Leah Levy, Max Levy, Max Brooks, Aryeh Kwiatkovsky, Ruth Linch, Nahum Linch and Sala Shmerling**
Not in the photograph: **Ezekiel Joseph Margolis**

————

[Page 248]

Kalish Townsfolk in Australia

There is no information about Kalish townsfolk in Australia at the beginning of the 20th century. It is true that the first immigrants arrived between 1900-1912 but their influence was not felt at all in local Jewish life.

It was in 1927 that a number of people from Kalish arrived chiefly by way of Eretz Israel. During those years the economic, cultural and spiritual conditions were very difficult. Each man sought for his townsfolk in his loneliness. Between 1927 and 1939, about ten families arrived direct from Kalish. Closer contact between the Kalish townsfolk was immediately established.

A small group of landsleit headed by Feivel Yedwab, the oldest of the settlers, established the Kalish Landsmanshaftn in 1944 with the purpose of assisting those townsfolk who were still alive. When news was received through the Jewish Agency and other sources that there were still living Jews in the city, we took steps to obtain entry permits for them and received 150 in the course of three months. At the same time, we sent large quantities of food packets, clothes and blankets to Poland through the HIAS.

Not all the Jews of Kalish made use of the permits. Some of them settled in Sweden, America, Israel and elsewhere. For those who came to join us, we provided as much help as we could. If we take into account the difficult material situation of the first Kalish people in this country, we can recognize how much effort was involved in their help.

When the Jewish Committee ceased activities in Kalish, our help also stopped. We had some money on hand so we sent it to the Red Magen David in Tel-Aviv.

The Kalish townsfolk displayed no particular activity after that until 1949 when a new wave of immigration began bringing with it fresh needs and functions. Activities were then renewed. Newcomers were helped to find work, homes and loans. With our aid almost all of them succeeded in settling down. We still continue to receive requests for entry permits and the Committee complies as best it can.

There are now many Kalish townsfolk in Australia, chiefly in Melbourne. The Kalish Centre in Melbourne is known for its communal and cultural activities. Towards the end of November every year more than a hundred townsfolk meet for a Commemoration evening. Every year a large party is held which serves as a social meeting and increases the resources of the Committee. The Centre also participates in the activities of the United Appeal to which it devotes a special evening party. Over the years, family parties and joint rambles and hikes have been held. The General Meeting elects the Executive and the Committees for Immigration, Relief, and Help in finding apartments and work.

The Melbourne Centre has also helped to set up a Landsmanshaftn in Sidney which, it may be added, is the only one of its kind in that city. Within a brief period of time, it has already infused a spirit of life into the second largest Jewish Community in Australia where communal and cultural activities were almost non-existent.

We are very interested in all Jews from Kalish, particularly those now in Israel. We maintain contact with the survivors remaining in Kalish and with those wandering all over the world.

[Page 249]

THE
HOLOCAUST

[Page 250] Blank

[Page 251]

The End of the Community

by Dr. Moshe Gross (Henryk Zeligowski)

In memory of my parents Rachel and Bernard,
My sisters Devorah and Madzia,
And my nephew Jakob

KALISH
10-1939 – 8-9-7-1942

Hospital – Jew Camp – Labour Camp

After the Germans occupied Poland in October 1939, they began to implement their plans for the extermination of Polish Jewry by pillaging us of all our property and exploiting our strength to the very last. But they proceeded to do so step-by-step. Pending complete extermination, they set out to make maximum use of us for their war effort. They began by ascertaining the amount of Jewish property and restricting Jewish liberty.

The Judenrat

Their first step was to establish a Judenrat (Jewish Council) whose seat was at the Community Offices. Its members included: Luzer Mitz, Frankel, Katzinel, Advocate Perkal, Dr. Seid, Dr. Lubelski, Magister Rotzeig, the cantor of the 'German' Synagogue, Gustav Hahn, etc. A large staff of officials was promptly recruited to secure maximum promptitude and accuracy. A detailed register of the Jewish population of Kalish was prepared with precise data about property and numbers of old people, sick, children, craftsmen, intellectuals, physicians and lawyers.

New orders, censuses, lists, demands for war compensation to be paid in paper money, gold and jewellery quickly followed one another. From time-to-time, the representatives of the Judenrat were summoned to the Gestapo offices in Jasna Street and always returned with new proscriptions and orders.

Jewish shops and factories were repeatedly robbed and looted in broad daylight. However, the collection centres at the Municipality, Police and elsewhere were never full because trains loaded with Jewish property departed for Germany every day. Work, crafts and trade quickly came to a complete standstill. Wealthy people buried their valuables as best they could in the earth or in walls; or else, they sold them and fled from the city hoping to find better things elsewhere. But most of the population were poverty-stricken and simply resolved to put up with the oppression and persecution and wait for the end of the war.

Every day, a number of young men were requisitioned for labour. There were few volunteers and so the gendarmes would complete the quota by frequent manhunts. The Jews were required to empty Jewish shops, clear away ruins, clean the streets, restore destroyed buildings, clean barracks, police stations, Gestapo offices, etc. Sometimes they were required to bury those sentenced to death and shot in the Jewish cemetery. Treatment of these Jewish workers in Kalish was precisely the same as elsewhere. Once, for instance, the Gestapo ordered us to jump about on all fours and bark at the tops of our voices. On another occasion, we had to punch one another as hard as we could and anybody who was found cheating was generously assisted with rifle-butts. The Germans treated the members of the Judenrat in a similar fashion, and their numbers rapidly diminished. The only ones left were those who had no opportunity of running away and others who found the activities desirable in various respects. Many of the younger generation made up their minds to cross the frontier.

[Page 252]

We gradually grew accustomed to such daily sights as shearing off the beards of old Jews, street-chases for forced labour and kidnapping for the 'Shelter'. The latter was in the Municipality and was generally dreaded. Those taken there were beaten until they fainted. Young Jewesses were often taken there and ordered to undress, to the delight of drunken gendarmes and soldiers under the guidance of the notorious Mayor Grabowski, a bestial sadist. He played a major part in the destruction of the Jews of Kalish and the vicinity. For several years he was the chief instrument of the Gestapo and the equally satanic Gesundheitsamt (Health Office) and faithfully and efficient carried out all orders received. In this, he was assisted by a large band of officials of various origins.

In general, there was a state of sheer confusion and alarm which the Germans were interested in maintaining and they may have started many rumours for that purpose. Thus, early in November, a rumour spread from mouth-to-mouth that a ghetto was to be established in a very small area. This led to a prompt movement of the population to the indicated quarter away from the centre of the city and the major streets. On 15th November, tenants in certain streets were given a few moments to pack up and were led under guard to the monastery. Within a few days, the tenants of scores of houses in various parts of the town were uprooted in this way. The confusion increased when the order to wear the yellow badge was published.

The Market Hall

On 20th November, entire streets were cleared with the aid of several hundred gendarmes from the vicinity. A few moments were allowed for packing belongings and then everybody had to get out into the street. Within a very short while we were marching in threes under the guard of armed gendarmes. Then we found ourselves within the crowded 'Market Hall' where there were already many thousands. In another few moments, the mass of people were being kicked and forced back with rubber truncheons so as to make room for newcomers.

Money and jewels that had not been very well hidden had already been pillaged in the course of 'searches for weapons'. Packed as tight as herrings in a barrel, we could not even sit down. We trod on one another and kicked one another amid oaths and cursing. The little children wept; the bigger ones shrieked, the grown-ups shouted and people began fighting about a scrap of pavement or a lost bundle. Sick people moaned and the dying groaned while above all rose the roaring of the drunken gendarmerie. During that endless night it was rumoured that we were to be sent to work in Germany or to the General Government. But actually, this was only the first large-scale action and nobody could foresee what was to follow.

[Page 253]

Sure enough, the first groups were taken out the next day and led under guard to the station where they were packed like herrings in trains setting out for Warsaw, Rzeszow (Reisha) and elsewhere in the East. But others were brought to take their place. Many people decided that it was impossible to remain in Kalish and requested and received permission to go direct from their homes to the railway station.

I. The Jewish Hospital

The authorities permitted patients, those suffering from contagious diseases, the aged and the crippled to be housed in the Jewish Hospital for the time being. This hospital was set up early in November in its former building by order of the German Chief of Police and the Gesundheitsamt. Dr. Seid took charge. Both the building and the equipment were in ruins. Jewish joiners, plumbers, mechanics and painters engaged in the restoration work which progressed well. The public contributed money, linen, bedding and kitchenware. The Jewish doctors contributed the medical equipment. Beds were brought from all over town and the first ward was opened. Yet, each family preferred to keep its sick at home. But after the first transports, people realised that hospitalisation enabled the patients to remain in Kalish for the time being and they desperately clung to this last hope. So the wards and even the corridors filled up.

The patients were treated by Dr. Seid, Dr. Plotski, Dr. Lubelski and Dr. Devora Gross-Shinagel. The remaining Jewish physicians showed less interest either because they were preparing for flight or else were afraid of accepting any responsibility whatever.

After Dr. Seid left on 20th November, my older sister, Dr. Gross-Shinagel took charge. Drs. Beatus and Gath and Mrs. Walachowicz offered their help, but disappeared a few days later. Dr. Gross continued in charge with the devoted and self-sacrificing cooperation of the former hospital nurses Lola Margulis (little Lola); Hala Eliasiewicz; Helena Storch; my younger sister Madzia Gross who had just returned from a German war prison after serving as a Red Cross volunteer in the Polish army; I myself and the medical student Alex Bloch.

Workers in the Contagious Diseases Dept. were: Mrs. A. Zhulti, Yetka Koppel and each one of us as far as possible. Several members of the service co-operated without a break and with complete devotion. They were Feivel Chapnik and his mother who worked in the kitchen; Opochinska and her daughter; Wroblewski and his wife; Zucker the tailor, Wolkowitch and Kalmanowitch.

It must be said that under the conditions prevailing, the hospital was a model institution which enabled it to carry out the important tasks laid upon it during the coming years. The statistics I kept as long as it functioned showed that about a thousand patients passed through, most of them very ill or suffering from contagious diseases. Many grave operations were carried out and thousands of injuries and wounds were dressed. Thousands of patients were given medical treatment and many children were born. Later, patients from the ghettos and camps in the vicinity came here for longer hospitalization. The well-equipped operating theatre, the clinic and pharmacy made things much easier. With the approval of the authorities, we engaged an Aryan woman pharmacist as our own pharmacist M. Green was transferred elsewhere. A few months later, the student Stella Lieberman took charge of the pharmacy besides helping in the Dispensary and the wards. The hospital laboratory was set up and conducted by Chemical Engineer Artur Shinagel and proved to be very valuable.

[Page 254]

Administration was handled by Shmuel Arkush who afterwards became a member of the Altestenrat (Council of Elders). Subsequently he was assisted by Sender Zeidel who also made the purchases in town. The kitchen and laundry were managed by Mrs. Arkush who was assisted by Opochinska and her daughter, Mrs. Feivel and Mrs. Zeidel. Burials were performed by Berker, Prussak and Kowalsky. They had plenty to do as mortality was considerable at first. The gravely ill who were absolutely unable to travel were brought here from the Market Hall. There were also many old persons who had no resistance at all under these conditions. There were no burial ceremonies and few people were present.

This hospital became a strong unit with considerable independence and immunity. It also became a centre of the fading or vanishing Jewish life, being the last citadel which kept several hundred Jews in Kalish. The little synagogue of the hospital, and every room that could be used for dwelling purposes, were also filled very quickly. More than 150 patients were admitted. About 350 invalids, chronically diseased and old people were housed in the Talmud Torah. This institution was managed by Dr. Feigin-Danziger and she remained in charge until it was liquidated. Her faithful assistants were the Orderly Neuman, Male Nurse Green and his sister, Hella Nomberg, Irka Rosenfeld, Mrs. Somatitzka, Freedman the upholsterer, etc.

The more active of the old folk also helped as best they could. Administration was handled by Somatitsky, Skobron and Rosenfeld. This was actually a kind of Old Age

Home though some wards and a dispensary were provided. But those really ill or suffering from contagious disease, or requiring operations, were sent to the hospital. The other old folk were housed in the former Old Age Home which was managed by the industrialist, Isidor Wiszniewskl, Landau (of the Guttstat family and Hahn. We also took over the Jewish Orphanage which had been emptied. It housed several dozen families, largely workers of the hospital and the Talmud Torah, their wives and children.

The Orphanage remained in its own place from the start of the War until 18th November, 1941 and was managed by Mrs. Ella. It housed about twenty orphans who were kept in exemplary cleanliness in spite of the difficulties. The older ones studied. Later they were employed in sewing and in the tailor's workshop.

Meanwhile, the last transport had left on 3rd November 1939. By a heart-breaking chance, I saw them leave – that last grief-stricken caravan of wandering Jews exiled to an unknown land. It included many folk who were classified as "fit for transport" and were taken from the Talmud Torah. These, together with the people of the Old Age Home, some 120 in all, were sent to Lochow near Warsaw. We received letters from them for some time but do not know their final fate.

[Page 255]

The *Judenrat* had virtually ceased to function during this period although a few individuals maintained contact with the Germans. The only *Judenrat* member left was Hahn, the "Jewish Elder" who was trusted by the Germans after all the honoured representatives of Jewish society had fled. He was coarse, lively and sharp-witted and won the approval of the Germans in whom he, in turn, largely believed on account of his ignorance.

Landau appeared and was very active from the beginning of the transportation. He knew many of the gendarmes because he had been arrested early in September and taken to the Reich as a "civilian prisoner-of-war". During the transportation he was allowed to move around freely and arrange many official matters. He too skilfully won the confidence of the Germans. After the liquidation of the Old Age Home, these two, together with Isidor Wiszniewski (of the Ben-Zion Wartski family) were recognized as a Council of Elders. Wiszniwski took over supplies – Landau ran the Police and Hahn as Jewish Elder handled the Gestapo affairs. Shmuel Arkush, manager of the hospital, was appointed secretary.

To our great surprise, we were not transferred like the others to the General Government, possibly because the Jewish quarters of Warsaw, etc. had become congested and disorganized. Instead, Jewish camps were established in December 1939 and early 1940 at various places in our region (Warta, Turek, and Zdunska-Wola) each containing several thousand persons from the small towns. A larger camp of 2,500 was set up at Kozminek-Bornhagen which contained the Jews of Staviszin, Dobra, etc. This was headed by Haftka, Dudek, Knopf (chairman), Wilczinski and Roth. Health was handled by the orderly Grzemilas and later by Dr. Shalit who had escaped from Germany in 1938. Although it had a certain amount of independence, it was still under our authority in all respects for we retained the status of administrative and economic centre to the very end and became the most important health centre in the entire Kalish district. The authorities and District Physician Karsch took interest in our hospital and paid it many visits. We received considerable allocations of food and medical supplies for the patients and were also permitted to send them to the Municipal Hospital for special treatment, x-rays, pneumothorax, etc.

A typhoid epidemic began in Kosminek early in spring and Dr. Gross-Shinagel engaged in an energetic inoculation campaign extending to several thousand persons in the neighbouring camps. We had to isolate all actual and suspected patients and accordingly enlarged the Contagious Diseases Department considerably.

Immediately after Passover 1940, all Jews aged 10 or more were required to put on a yellow Shield of David 10cm in diameter with the word "Jude" in the centre. These had to be sewn on firmly on the upper garment, one on the right-hand side of the chest in front and the other on the right-hand shoulder behind.

In spring 1940 many Jewish soldiers returned from the war prisons. Among them were: Julek Wolkowitch, Shmulek Rakowski, Preger, Dzialoszynski, Moshe Moshkowitch, Heniek Breuer, Heniek Bleshkowski, Adolf Bloch, Leib Bejrach, Josef Diamant the shoemaker, Abraham Hirshbajn, Epstein and Smuliek Eliashewitch, the very experienced male-nurse of the former Jewish Hospital who immediately started working in our hospital.

[Page 256]

The total number of persons in the camp rose to 150. From Kosminek camp about 100 men were sent to set up a labour camp at Opatowek and a few weeks later, a smaller labour camp of 30 men was set up at Stary.

In June, 1940, the Talmud Torah had to move to a building in P.O.W. Street N°13 (former Nowa Street) which had once served as a lace factory. Most of the apartments were ruinous and many of the larger halls were still full of machinery. However, the transfer was completed within three days by dint of great effort and the offices of the *Wirtschaftsamt*(Economic Department) were housed in the Talmud Torah. A few days later the Hospital and Orphanage were also ordered to move to Szopena Street N°4. The whole building was dismantled while the patients were still lying in the wards. Several weeks later the large "German" synagogue and the old cemetery were broken up. The tombstones were taken as building material for shelters and for street paving. The bathhouse and community buildings were also destroyed.

The hospital was reopened on a smaller scale and without an operating theatre. However, the demand for hospitalization also decreased and it now served chiefly as a Health Centre. Patients from the surrounding camps came for prolonged treatment, chiefly surgical cases and contagious diseases, i.e. typhoid and scabies. Luckily, we checked the typhoid by the inoculations which were renewed every six months.

II. Judenlager

Every day, a few score workers now proceeded to the work required by the Labour Office, breaking up old houses, paving roads in town, blocking the course of the Prosna from the theatre to Wodna Street, etc. The police and Gestapo found work for a number of drivers and locksmiths: Moniek Lipinski, Shmulik Rakowski, Henek Brenner, Boobi Hahn, Leo Feigin and Aaron Winter. Every day our tailors and shoemakers, Berel Gross, Zelig Gross, Opas, Zucker and Schiller went off to the police workshops. Fuyara worked for an Ukranian who received permission to employ him. The housepainters Bloch Sr., Mendel Bloch and Adolf Bloch worked in the barracks ad at the police.

During the summer, our hospital and Old Age Home gradually turned into a Judenlarger where the Council of Elders exercised increasing authority. The nameplate of the hospital disappeared and was replaced by that of 'Arbeiter Kollone'. In order to increase the number of workers, the Council of Elders reduced the hospital staff to a minimum, disregarding requirements. The hospital management helped as best they could with this but in spring and autumn the percentage of patients increased and the staff could no longer do everything necessary. In spite of this, it was the practice to leave only one nurse for all the patients and the dispensary, arguing that the doctor could also go out to load up coal or dig. And indeed, a year later, when our situation was far worse, Dr. Gross-Shinagel also went out to work in the tailor's workshop, visiting patients only in the evening.

[Page 257]

There was constant friction between the Council of Elders and the hospital from the very beginning. First the Council seized all power and authority. Then it fought openly against the hospital doctor and staff giving them reduced rations and claiming that they were idling. It also stopped paying their 'wages' which had originally been set at 50 Reichspfennig per day. Things were no better in the Old Age Home for the manageress, Dr. Feingin-Danziger and the rest of the staff who worked beyond their strength. It is possible that they were treated even worse. However, the *Feldsher* (Barber-surgeon) Neiman, in spite of his age, continued to attend patients and most skilfully extracted teeth besides running the only barber shop left. By this time, our Judenlager had taken on a regular pattern with 2 houses for the workers at POW St. 16 and 18; the hospital at Szopena 4 and the Old Age Home at POW St. 13 (the former Nowa St). A canteen was set up for odds and ends in addition to rations and for rations too. We were not permitted to go out into the town without a special permit. All official affairs were handled by members of the Council of Elders, the messenger Seidel and the Springer brothers. Still, many would steal out after removing the yellow badges in order to earn a trifle. Poles often visited us to do business thought this was also prohibited. We had no cultural life or entertainment and lived not for the next day but for the next moment, for we never had an instant free for leisure.

In June 1940, we were visited by Grabowski, former Mayor and now head of the Health Department, accompanied by Gestapo men in uniforms. They inspected all the patients and made a note on the card of each one. They then announced that some of the patients would have to be sent to other towns where special hospitals and convalescent homes were being set up. To begin with, only the aged and chronic patients would be sent. Then they went their way leaving behind the usual depression that followed a visit by the Gestapo.

During the summer, the number of workers increased to about 120 in all. Work was compulsory for every Jew aged 13-15 or upwards. Most of them went on sewing. The tailors, shoemakers, mechanics and drivers worked for the police or wherever there was work. As we had many excellent craftsmen, they were often sent to work in the homes of officials, gendarmes and Gestapo men. This gave the Council of Elders excellent opportunities to establish contact with the various leading officials. More than once, some of the Jews succeeded in obtaining information, particularly about our camp. As a result, we often knew in advance about searches, orders and other oppressive acts which were being planned. Here much was done by Council member Vishnievski who found an entry to the home of the Mayor Fetzel and was well treated by Major Krauser, head of the Police and head of the Economic Department. Hahn also took his share in this. He won the confidence of Schönrogen, head of the Gestapo.

All this cost an untold amount in money and gifts.

That summer, we set up a dental clinic in the hospital which proved invaluable for teeth began to decay terribly on account of the lack of vitamins and other important elements in the food. An Aryan dentist came to the clinic twice a week by permission of the authorities. For a long time, her assistant was Zosia Freund.

[Page 258]

At the same time the chemical laboratory of the hospital was developed and expanded by chemical engineer Arthur Shinagel. Our medical supplies were cut down from time to time, but demand grew constantly with the arrival of patients from the vicinity and the surrounding camps. The laboratory began to manufacture its own preparations, particularly injections which were difficult to obtain. In autumn 1940 a big workshop was opened for the manufacture of wooden soles which carried out many orders for shops in Kalish and elsewhere. The workshop was founded by the brothers Abraham, Benek and Nathan Hirschbein.

We did our best to celebrate the festivals as well as we could. Prayers were held on the New Year and the Day of Atonement.

Arbeitslager

That autumn, the Germans decided to exterminate the sick and aged who could not work. It should be noted that they carried out their mass transportations and slaughter either in the autumn or in winter, apparently to reduce the danger of epidemics to a minimum. On 26th October, 1940, Grabowski arrived in our camp again and held a number of serious conversations with our representatives. He and his two Gestapo companions informed the Council that at 10 a.m. the following day, the patients selected by them for transfer to convalescent homes would be taken away. The patients had to be washed and dressed in fresh underwear. We did not need to worry about anything else and even bedding was unnecessary as everything had now been prepared. That day, our mechanics related when they returned from their work at Gestapo headquarters that a large number of strange Gestapo men had arrived with a mysterious large black lorry that was closed on every side and had no ventilation holes at all. It was easy to link these facts with the morning visit. We spent the day in feverish preparations, talks, discussions and leave-takings. There were still many optimists, hoping for the best but the majority were ill at ease and apprehensive. Yet, even the most pessimistic never foresaw that the entire 290 Jews who had been listed would be dead within a few hours.

The next day at precisely 10 a.m. on 27th October, a huge black lorry came to a standstill in front of the Old Age Home at No. 13 POW St. Its roof was as high as the first storey. It looked like a great black coffin. Two shiny black cars brought Grabowski at the head of a gang of uniformed and unfamiliar Gestapo men. We had to fetch those who were called by name for they were mostly chronic patients and cripples. The Germans ordered us to carry them, seat the patients or stretch them on the benches within the lorry.

"When you come down the steps, be careful nothing happens to the patient!" "Take it easy, we're not in a hurry". "Please put the man down here in the corner until he feels better!" Meanwhile, they saw to it that we should fill up the cold lorry. But they would not permit the younger folk to join their departing relatives.

[Page 259]

The metal doors were banged shut – the heavy bars were dropped in place and the large lorry set off silently but swiftly followed by the gleaming cars. The next day, 28th October, two more trips were made and about 110 persons were removed. Everything was done swiftly in order not to spoil the weekend. They must have grown tired of putting on a show and stopped being polite, calming the weepers with their whips and shooting at anybody who looked out of the windows. The only ones who did not feel the general apprehension and bitterness were the lucky insane.

The last two groups left on Monday, 30th October and included a few hospital patients. The chair of one of the old women was brought back on one of the trips. The Gestapo man who brought it explained, "She doesn't need it any longer because she's received a new one". That day the Council of Elders was required to pay the cost of transport at the rate of four Reichsmarks a person and to arrange all matters connected with the departure of 290 persons at the Economic Office.

The Germans gave evasive replies to the repeated questions of the Elders as to where the people had been taken. "At the moment they are in transit camps and from there the will be sent to the permanent convalescent homes. As we don't know in advance who is being sent, you will have to be patient for a few days until everything is in order." For many weeks we applied to the Krankenverlegung Institution which was supposed to deal with such matters but could not find out what had happened. Finally, we were told that news had just been received that a few of the old people had died of heart failure, brain fever or pneumonia. The rest were in Padernice and were in good health. But no map showed the spot because it did not exist.

Little by little we understood that we would never see the dead again unless we followed in their footsteps. After that we lived in a state of constant dread for we could see the sword hanging over our own heads and knew that we would go the same way sooner or later. The Germans were exploiting our working power but would clearly exterminate us too. The hermetically sealed gas-wagons which were first tried out on our old folk were about to commence the great action of "purifying" Europe of the Jews which was later perfected in the large extermination camps.

The old people, who had been choked by poison gas in the lorry while still on their way, were taken to the neighbouring forest and buried or burnt. It was rumoured that they had been buried near Winiary. Nobody knew precisely because the roads had been strictly blocked on that day, but it was clear that the action had taken place near Kalish for the lorries returned within three hours. However, as far as mass extermination was concerned, the experiment does not seem to have been too successful. It took too long and called for trouble and deception. It was not a way for finishing off eight million Jews "who were eating the bread of charity". It was then that they began to build the huge concentration camps at Auschwitz, Treblinka and elsewhere with their modern death-chambers and furnaces. At the same time the Jews began to be concentrated into gigantic ghettos from which they could not escape. However, the gas lorries were kept for auxiliary purposes in the small towns from which it was not worthwhile transporting the Jews and we no longer had any illusions about our fate.

[Page 260]

III. Workshops

In order to remain alive we had to convince the Germans that they needed us for the time being and that we were good workers. So the Council of Elders was given permission to operate large tailoring and shoemaking workshops, the entire income of which went to the Wirtschaftsamt (Economic Office). There was ample room. One of the empty buildings at POW St. No. 13 was refurbished. Machines were brought from all parts of the town for tailors, seamstresses and furriers together with other tools.

1. *The Tailor Workshops.* The tailors included: Zucker, Berl Gross, Selig Gross, Schiller, Ofas, the Neimann family, Berek Pilz and a few dozen more who were their assistants. The first sewing machines were soon whirring 'for the victory'. Several score were employed. The managers were my father, Berl Gross and Schiller. Later, the shop was expanded to sew women's clothes and underwear. This department was managed by Mrs. Arkush. We all understood the gravity of the situation and started working with all our strength. Even the old people helped for fear of new transportations. There were fewer people engaged in digging for they were all brought into the shops. Orders from German businesses in Kalish and elsewhere were plentiful and it was impossible to satisfy them all. In addition, many private orders were carried out. The best tailors sewed for the high officials who were swamped with gifts of clothing and other private

'mementos'. They were very important for they gained us help of one kind or another. We were visited by various supervisory delegations which came to ascertain the quality of the Jewish work and always left with hands full. The Volksdeutsch Woiciechowski, who was the manager of the Wirtschaftsamt, was a frequent visitor who was very pleased at our work because it increased both his private income and that of his department as well.

2. *The Shoemaker's Workshop* began operations early in 1941 and employed more than ten shoemakers and their assistants, including Katz and his son, Ruhr, Abeczadlo, Wygodski and Diamant. The workshop was managed by Mr. Freund of the Frenkel family. New shoes were made there; old shoes were repaired and all kinds of slippers, children's shoes, belts, bags, etc. were made from the waste which was brought from the local tannery. These products were excellently made and showed an exceptional inventive capacity which astonished the Germans. Later in the year they began the mass production of shoes with wooden soles which were also made from waste material. These soles were manufactured on the spot by the brothers Hirschbein. There was a big income from this branch as many large orders were received from Poznan and Ostrow.

3. In addition, a *Hat Factory* was founded and managed by the master craftsman, Bulka and young Schiller.

[Page 261]

4. The *Furriers' Workshop*. The furriers showed even greater energy and inventive capacity. The leading ones were: Yossi Baum, Yulek Wolkowitch and S. Kolsky. Apart from the various orders and 'presents' for the officials and their mistresses, furs were created here out of nothing. A few centimetres of fur trimmings, chiefly Caracul which the Germans had previously burnt, were used to make valuable articles. The trimmings and waste were brought from Berlin, cleaned and sewn together with much toil. There were plenty of machines and a great will to work. Everybody wanted to go on living.

By the following spring, production had doubled in every department. We were being urged on from every side though it was quite unnecessary. We were called on to do our best for the victory! And indeed, we were working for victory but for our own and not for theirs. Our camp was transformed into one huge factory, feverishly labouring and toiling in order to secure us all the right to live.

The Jewish Camp in Bornhagen-Kosminek

In those days, large workshops like our own were also established at Kozminek. However, they lacked expert workers and so did not develop so far nor did they give the local ghetto the aspect of a typical labour camp. In addition, there were 'too many' old people, women and children there and so Kozminek remained only a Juden-lager to the end.

Sanitary conditions in all these camps were very poor indeed. Doctor Shalit, the only physician, and Grzenilas, the *Feldscher*, could not handle all the work and so they sent many patients to us. Dr. Gross-Shinagel often had to go to the camps to help in difficult cases, receiving special permission from the authorities. We also went there twice a year to give inoculations against typhoid.

Contact between the camps was very close. They were all dependent on us in spite of the measure of autonomy found in each but we were linked by ties of mutual interests. They had horses and wagons with which they visited us twice a week to take the rations allocated to them by the Wirtschaftsamt; various goods, medicines from our dispensary which also served them and post. It should be noted that all this time we were permitted to send letters and parcels by post to other towns. We maintained contact with the other ghettos and in general knew what was happening there as far as the German censorship did not erase what was written.

Theoretically, only physicians and members of the Council of Elders were allowed to travel by special permit as well as patients. However, healthy people also travelled because the police could usually be bribed and illicit trade went ahead on a considerable scale. Hawkers would go out and would bring back butter, eggs and meat which could be bought more easily and cheaply if the authorities were not in the neighbourhood. Nobody paid attention to the penalties involved.

In general, the Kozminek Jews felt more at ease in their ghetto. There were more of them and they were not as shaken as we were by large-scale transportation, the removal of the old people and the endless oppression and extortion. Besides, the only Germans they saw were three local gendarmes. To begin with, they were not even interfered with when they celebrated Sabbath and Festivals. During Passover 1941, they had dry potatoes and coarse matzos for the Seder but the sanctity of the Festival was preserved. And surely, they thought, it would be the last Seder in wartime and next year in Jerusalem! Their only fear was the camp commandant, Buechler, a Volksdeutsch. He often burst into the ghetto when he was drunk and beat anyone he met with his stick. If anyone was found with an egg or a piece of butter, he was beaten and fined. If word came that the 'Greener' was on the way, they all hid like mice in their holes. The person in direct contact with him was our Council Elder Landau who was also controller of the Kozminek Judenrat.

[Page 262]

Our own camp was directly under the Municipal Authorities and District Authorities in Poznan. The Kozminek Judenrat (with Knopf as Chairman and Roth, Dudek and Wilcymski) was generally hated by the Jews, like our own and all the others, and for identical reasons. In the Kozminek ghetto there were several Jewish policemen without caps and sticks, it is true, but in charge of the detention cell and enjoying the assistance of the German gendarmes.

In Kalish we had no Jewish police until the end. It was true that our Chairman Hahn called for volunteers and tried to recruit a number but there were none. Maybe because we were too few – maybe because the handful of survivors stood firm together.

That year, 1941, we had a peaceful but gloomy Passover. Each family had lost at least one of its older members. It was hard to obtain matzos. We did not receive a baking permit, and the Kozminek matzos which were baked by hand, were very expensive, while our potato supply was also scanty. Nevertheless, the truly observant Jews observed the festival in meticulous detail after a hard day's work; for nobody could even dream of release from work.

The only pleasure left to us after work was to walk about the large courtyard in front of No. 16 POW St. or one of our buildings. Part of it had been cleared and planted with vegetables for the kitchen and the canteen. The fences were removed and the plot was expanded as far as the burnt flour mill of Kupfer so that the courtyard of the neighbouring house, n°18, was also added to it. This allowed the children to pass from house-to-house without going out into the street and infuriating the Germans. In addition, we could also pass from house-to-house at night without fear. There was another such courtyard at N°13 POW St. where grass actually grew though it was as thin as the faces of our children. However, there was no stench of sewage water there and it was farther away from the street and closer to the fields. Three times a day we were permitted to visit those houses and in any case, people did not pay particular attention to the regulations. Nor could the Germans really restrict our movements as the hospital was on one street, the canteen on another and the only kitchen and workshops stood separate. At first the brothers Asher and Simha Shepinger acted as doorkeepers but later they were transferred to the workshops.

[Page 263]

In spite of the prohibitions people would steal out into the town to sell something and buy a little food while some would visit Christian acquaintances to ask for something to eat. Naturally only those who had the right kind of appearance could venture this.

The Beginning of the End

The heat of June arrived. Endless military convoys, artillery, ammunition and aeroplanes had been moving eastward for several months. Though this looked as if it meant a conflict with Russia, there was no indication of it in the press. This went on until Sunday 22nd June, 1941 when I overheard a whispered conversation in one of the flats and someone saying: "So they attacked first and are advancing rapidly..." My friends and I embraced with tears in our eyes and we ran down to obtain details which had been brought from town and had spread through the camp like lightning. But our enthusiasm swiftly vanished. What would happen to us next? Would they let us live till the end of the war? Now they would either send us deep into Germany or else murder us here for fear of vengeance.

From this date our situation took a turn for the worse. The Fuehrer had declared that we were the arch–foes of the Germans and our treatment changed accordingly. The only weapon left to us was work. We had no alternative except to increase production and prove to the Germans that now, more than ever, we could help them at the front as a source of labour and supply. And we did. They recognized the value of our work, recognized us as a productive element and for the time being, deferred their plans to liquidate our ghetto. For as we afterwards learnt, they had intended to get rid of us together with the Kozminek people at that time.

After the first assault and the German victories, our situation seemed to improve slightly but not for long. In September, the Arbeitsamt demanded 200 young men to be sent from Kozminek for agricultural work in the Posen District. They were selected without any medical examination.

The Arbeitsamt announced that they would all be back in four weeks provided that they picked the potatoes as required. Those who left were allowed to take small bundles with them and the next day most of them were marched on foot and a few in carts to Kalish. On the way the Germans collected some more workers from the Opatuvek and Stavy camps. All of them were housed for the time being in the former Kalish vinegar factory which had belonged to Lustig and which was notorious among the Poles because it had been a concentration camp for those exiled to Germany. Several of the men ran away. The next day they were all sent by goods train to Gildenhof and Brunsdorf in the vicinity of Posen where there were large estates.

Several days later we were ordered to send a hundred men. Here as well the first to be sent were those who avoided work, the shouters and the dissatisfied. After picking the potatoes they were all due to come back. They were permitted to take some belongings and were led like sheep to the vinegar factory. Once again, a few of the bravest ran away and the next day, the rest followed their predecessors. Among them was my girl–cousin, Madza Borislowska who had been brought to us half a year earlier from the Warsaw ghetto by our Polish friend, Mr. Antoni Pawelski. About 337 persons were left and we now feared the worst for those who had gone. A week later we received the first letters. They had all arrived in Gildenhof and Brunsdorf in the Posen District and had been dispersed among the farms. Lodging and food were not too bad. They were engaged in picking potatoes and other agricultural work. We breathed easily. This time the Germans had not deceived us and they might be trusted up to a certain point. We began to go back to work. But this interval did not last very long.

[Page 264]

On Saturday 15th November, 1941 Kalish was again visited suddenly by the black gas lorries so our driver reported from the Gestapo. We took this as clear evidence that they intended to destroy us all and had first sent the strong young men away to agricultural work while the remaining 370 of us would meet the fate of the old people who had been killed the year before. We remembered that the Gauleiter Greizer had promised in a speech not long before to purify his region from all 'harmful elements' while the Fuehrer had said only a week earlier that the time had come to exterminate Jewry adding: "The Jews should not imagine that they will ever take vengeance on the Germans. Even if such a time should ever come, the memory of European Jewry will already have been blotted out."

The members of the Council of Elders proceeded to the Municipality to find out what was planned and take steps if possible while the workshops came to a standstill. Everybody went home. By evening the camp was like a big beehive and many people ran away to Kozminek and Varta. Late at night, the Elders returned declaring that the Germans were going to send us to Kozminek or Lodz because Kalish was a district town and would therefore be 'Judenrein'.

The endless night passed with the Council of Elders trying to persuade the Germans to leave the community shut away where they could work for the victory. But it was only when darkness fell that we heard motor engines and found ourselves under a strong guard of armed gendarmes. We knew that we were trapped with no way of escape. People dashed crazily from place to place. The younger men began to discuss feverishly whether they ought not to resist the Germans by force since, in any case, it was the end for us all? But what could we defend ourselves with? Sticks, axes, our hands and teeth or whatever came to hand, as long as we did not permit them to lead us away like sheep to the slaughter but to prove that Jews also knew how to fight and die.

More sober people went hunting for some weakly guarded point. There were no hiding places in the houses. Some of the more daring men managed to reach neighbouring houses over the roof and fled by night to Kozminek. The Gestapo men laughed aloud and did not even bother chasing them.

The God-fearing Hassidim tranquilly prepared for death. After carefully bathing themselves they put on shrouds, swathed themselves in prayer-shawls and began fervent prayer. They no longer sought for deliverance but for the forgiving of transgressions. They were happy men that handful. They were happy and proud because they knew that they had been privileged to die hallowing the Holy Name of God like our forefathers in Spain and elsewhere in Europe for so many generations. The women wept silently as they pressed their children to their hearts.

[Page 265]

With the coming of day, everybody felt slightly easier. It was the darkness that terrified. And yet, Jewish optimism proved to be more astounding than anything else. Though we could not delude ourselves as to our fate, our hearts refused to believe that we were all about to be destroyed. We felt it was impossible for so many innocent people to be killed together. But in any case, all those who had some property left hid it away and waited for what would happen next. To be sure, what difference would it make whether our neighbours pillaged our property or our murderers took it all? Yet still people worried as to what was going to happen to it.

On the afternoon of Monday 17th November, the two black lorries stopped again at the gateway. Now Hahn, the Chairman who had formerly been so noisy and impudent, was as bowed and bent, pale and submissive as we were. He called us all to line up in the courtyard. The Gestapo men then came and summoned each person by name from a list which they had. Each one called had to take three paces forward, turn around on his heels and return to his place while the chief executioner made some mysterious mark next to his name. When I was called, I sprang out of the row and fixed my eyes on the man who called me and whose face was familiar. After the parade and census, Hahn told us that they had intended to send them all but at the last moment the 'monster with the scar' had decided only to take the old people and the rest of the sick. Afterwards we learnt that the change had been brought about by a cable from Berlin.

Now came a most egotistic and ugly relief of tension. We found that Hahn was telling the truth this time. The Gestapo men came back in the evening and called a number of persons, chiefly old people and patients. Once again they noted something down beside each name as they observed the terrified faces. And we knew clearly who would be taken. When my parents were summoned I burst out weeping for the first time in many years. I do not know what happened in bygone times but in our case, we did not leave our parents alone for one moment – my sisters, my brother–in–law and I. We could not bear the thought that they would soon be lost to us forever – that they would soon die – stop breathing, thinking or feeling. And they kissed us goodbye while our tears mingled. Suddenly, I dashed to the attic as though possessed. It was still possible to climb over the roofs and escape. That was the last chance. But our parents preferred to die rather than endanger our safety. I wanted to force them to go but my father threatened that he would shout or jump from the roof... I never saw any man exercise such self–control. It was he who consoled us. My mother fainted but recovered after an injection and was angry with my friend who gave it. How much she wanted to die among her kinsfolk, in our arms.

At 9.a.m. on 18th November we had the terrible experience of parting from them when the men of the Council of Elders came with a list of those sentenced to death. The death lorry was due to come in another hour. I could hear weak voices raised in lamentation. They were particularly terrifying as they did not seem to come from this world. A last thought occurred of snatching an axe and bringing it down on the fat German necks and shaven skulls, splitting them so that their brains burst out even if I fell and drowned in their blood. I turned and was giddy but somebody supported me. I heard the sound of a motor and there the lorry was. We kissed for the last time, said a last word and looked at one another. Then they went. Now I was an orphan.

[Page 266]

I do not know how long I stood looking after the departing lorries and their convoy. I simply could not move but felt as though I was turned to stone. My sister led me home. We passed the empty room of the Hassid Neuhaus. He had left a soul light burning there before he went out and had covered the mirror with a white sheet. I fell weeping into my sister's arms. I think those were the last tears I ever shed.

There was a young girl called Malka Yakubovitch whose legs had been paralysed for years. Now suddenly she rose from her bed on her own. Some people escaped over the roofs – Kalmanovitch and his wife hid in the well in the courtyard. The Gestapo men fired warning shots and struck all who came their way with their whips. That 18th November, 1941 cost us 127 victims including 15 children from the orphanage. Five of the oldest girls and their director managed to escape at the last moment.

That same day we were ordered to leave the house at No. 4, Szopena St. The keys were received by the criminal German policeman Puppe who I believe was remembers from World War I. We were housed in the dwellings at Nos. 13, 16 and 18 POW St. which now stood empty under guard day and night without knowing what was going to happen next. The Elders knew no more than we did. But on Saturday we began to arrange our work at the shops in order to go back and work the next day.

But early in the morning of December 1ˢᵗ we were called to attention by the gendarmes and found ourselves surrounded once again. Before we knew what happened, the murderers had burst into the dwellings and took the families that had children up to the age of twelve, in accordance with a list. They were accompanied by members of the Council of Elders. Within half an hour, about a hundred people were loaded on to two lorries and taken off in the direction of Kozminek. The gendarmes went back to their own place having now done their job with perfect Prussian precision. Nobody escaped. But we all felt at ease when we saw that these were ordinary lorries.

Afterwards we found that the Council had known of this action several days in advance, but did not warn anybody for fear of their own fate and that of their relatives. Yet this was also a death transport and all the young people were destroyed.

By now, each one of us was the solitary survivor of a big family – the only person saved from a sunken ship. I was left with my younger sister Madzia. The economical Gestapo decided that it was not worth their while to bring the black lorry for a mere hundred persons and, therefore, ordered that they should be transferred to Kozminek where a major action was to be carried out. Our people were forced into the firemen's shed together with the Kozminek victims and taken out several days later in groups of seventy by the black lorry. Here the Germans showed their full brutality. They smashed the weeping babies, whom the mothers had left behind, against the sides of the lorry in order to enjoy the sight of the spurting blood and brains!

[Page 267]

But there it was possible to escape by giving large bribes. The members of the local Council of Elders bribed the gendarmes and saved themselves at least. Still, several hundred Jews were killed including a large number of women, old people and babies. By a virtual miracle, my sister, Dr. Devora Gross–Shinagel, with her husband and their child Jacob, were saved out of the Kalish people. When she told the guard that she was a doctor, he allowed her to leave, in sheer astonishment to find her among all these.

There were only about a hundred and fifty of us left now and we were crowded into two buildings – 13 and 16 POW St. Next day we went back to work as usual as though nothing had happened. The machines whirred and the hammers banged in our struggle for life. So far, we had chiefly carried out the orders of private firms for clothes and shoes and the Economic Department made a lot of profit on us. In the year 1941 alone, we provided them with several million Reichmarks. But to make our work even more important, the Council now made desperate efforts to obtain military orders. These might secure our residence in Kalish. And they did succeed in obtaining a large order for sheets, gloves, leggings of synthetic ram skin and high felt boots for the army. But these orders were irregular, to our regret.

Still, the Elders finally established contact with a big German industrialist from Berlin named Sannwald who had had to cut down the production of uniforms for the army because of a shortage of workers. He was happy when we offered him our services with the approval of the Economic Department and other Municipal Authorities. After our first trial order of several score of uniforms proved satisfactory, Sannwald asked the District Gestapo for a permit to exploit our working capacity. We were anxious that he should make our shops part of his factory, take over the administration and thus give them the status of a military supply factory. We, therefore, did our very best to make him feel satisfied with our work and finally learnt that his contract had been approved. We rejoiced believing that we now stood firmer.

Weeks had passed and the young people who had been sent to Poznan were long overdue. More than two months went by and they did not come back. In addition, the information in their letters described a worsening situation. From January 1942, they had been sent to camps where they were suffering from starvation and filth. They were working hard at land betterment and road repairing and their food was being steadily diminished so that they did not have the strength to work. We gave up all hope of seeing them. Then one day we were alarmed to hear that the "man with the scar" had been seen again. The news was enough to empty the camp of half of its inhabitants. Many went to stay with Polish acquaintances. By day we set up many observation patrols. After three days we learnt that he had left town and the tension died down. Still, many families left the camp in order to find refuge in 'safer' camps such as Zdunska–Wola and Lask. (These were the Bloch, Bulka and Lipshitz families, Mrs. Arkush, Mrs. Vishnievska and her children, etc.)

[Page 268]

Meanwhile, work in the shops was expanding rapidly. Worn out uniforms were brought in heaps and piles. We had to disentangle them very cautiously, clean them, patch them and put them together again so that they looked like new. Every seam, every stitch and the place of every button were carefully measured. Everything had to be done with absolute precision.

The newly-emptied halls were used for a special department for sorting and cleaning which employed all the women without exception, the children above twelve and all the men who did not know how to sew. The shoemaking shop was shut down as being less important and everybody was put to work tailoring to increase production to a maximum. The one purpose was to please the capricious Berliner who held our fate in his hands. He knew this and drove us without mercy. Now our task was to toil for the German Army day and night and sometimes on Sundays. We gave all the strength we had and even more: "all for the Wehrmacht!" That slogan gave us and the people in Kozminek several more months of life. But bad tidings reached us from the camps.

During spring, many of the young men died under dreadful conditions in the Labour camps near Posen while some went out of their minds. A few succeeded in escaping and reached our own camp. They would walk at night and hide in the forests by day. They were shadows dressed in rags and the tales they told were horrifying. Since they were tailors, we managed to have them registered as coming from another ghetto. They were most obedient and did not behave like the rebellious Krize, Hela Moscowitch and Lola Yedvah, the former two of whom lost their lives because of their rebelliousness. My younger sister Madzia Gross was handed over to the Gestapo on March 26th, 1942 on a charge of collaboration with the Polish Underground. Two gendarmes came to arrest her even though she was ill. They said she was being taken for a brief interrogation but we knew that we would never see her again. Polish acquaintances related that she marched like a soldier, as though she had arrested the others. After liberation many people related that they had found her signature on one of the walls in the Lodz Ghetto prison for she had been transferred there and was sent on by the judges and policemen of Romkowsky, the ruler of the Lodz Ghetto who sent hundreds of "saboteurs" like her to the Chelmno Death Camp near Kolo almost every day.

We knew that sooner or later we would be sent to camps or killed for we could feel that the attitude of the Germans had been changing for the worse. This became plain after their first defeats along the south-east front. We were going to have to pay for the victory of the Russians at Stalingrad. If we heard German being spoken or the roaring of a lorry engine, our hearts would cease to beat and the blood would freeze in our veins. We felt that the sooner they came to finish us off, the better. In spite of this, we were happy every day to know that we had lived one day, one hour and one minute longer. All we hoped was to be allowed to sleep on until the morning.

Toward the end of May, 1942, our camp was again surrounded by the gendarmes who took away several dozen men who were fit for work. The camps in Poznan were emptying too fast on account of the high mortality and the losses had to be made good.

[Page 269]

At this point I decided it was time for me to escape at all costs. I managed to get to one of the vacated houses, climbed a high fence and hid under the stairs of a ruinous cellar in a neighbouring house. There I found our shoemaker, Bendet Rohr. We put branches in front of the entry but heard the leaves rusting and twigs being crushed. We made a dash for the next fence. I believe that shots were fired after us but we reached the third garden belonging to Dobrowolski. We were separated from the street by a little wicket-gate and parted from one another. Strolling sedately so as not to attract attention, I walked along the streets to the house at 15 Ciasna St. where I had been born and lived for seventeen years. My former neighbour, Mrs. Zofia Lewandowska, hid me in the cellar where I spent several hours. In the evening I went back to the camp after the selection had been made.

The next day the only sign of a change was that a few dozen machines were not working and a few hearts mourned at fresh bereavements. But the machines that were working speeded up in order to make good the withdrawal of forty workers. We were now 120 in all.

During the hot days of June 1942, we learnt from bribed German officials that we were to be sent first to Kozminek and then to the Warsaw ghetto. We went on working but the work was no longer any good. Sannwald vented his fury on the terrified foremen. We had to repair every defect after our working hours and on Sundays. Yet, in spite of his fury, Sannwald did his best to ensure that we should be left in Kalish – in his own interest as well as our own.

The End

On the hot morning of July 8th 1942 I took the uniform which I was to pick apart by noon and set out to work on the roof of the low wooden hut in order to avoid breathing the dust which rose from the clothes as they were being picked apart. Suddenly, an unusual movement in the courtyard attracted my attention. I looked towards the field. The gendarmes had not arrived there yet. A single leap and I would be free but I remembered my last remaining sister above in the workshop. I slipped down in to the courtyard, not seeing what was going on or paying any attention, arrived upstairs within a few seconds and dashed into our room thrusting aside all who came my way. But my sister was no longer there. A neighbour told me that at the very last moment she, her husband Artur and two-year old child Jacob (the last child in the camp whom we had succeeded in hiding until now from the gendarmes) had managed to get away and find a refuge with a Christian family opposite at No. 18 POW St. I looked out of the window, saw the curtain move in the room opposite me and saw my sister's tearful face.

I was down in the street within a few moments and because I had no belongings with me and was not even properly dressed, the gendarme assumed that I lived in a different house and let me pass to No. 16. I dashed into the corridor dashed up to the attic and shifted a cupboard to reach a well-camouflaged entry in the wall which led into the attic in the next house, No. 18. The entry had been made in the previous November. Now I forced my way through it with difficulty and found myself in the now Aryan house. But I had to cross a big courtyard to reach the apartment where my sister had taken refuge. Luckily it was empty.

[Page 270]

I ran across, but in the corridor I found the way blocked by Schultz the shoemaker, a Volksdeutsch whom I knew well. My entreaties did not help. A gendarme appeared promptly. Still, I managed to scurry away and escape. I believe he shot after me but I was very quickly back in the camp. I then realized that there was no way out. I could not reach my sister. If I took a single careless step, the gendarmes would find her. Even if I should reach her, it was very doubtful if there would be any room for me as well with my distinctly Jewish appearance. So I had to stay where I was and hide until the fury had passed. I had to change tactics.

At this point, I heard the yells of the gendarmes: "Alle austreten!" (All out!) I dashed into the corridor where my companions were standing arguing furiously. "Don't waste a second. Follow me!" A few of them did so and within a few moments, we were back in the attic. After a brief consultation, we decided to get out onto the roof, cross three more roofs in succession and hide in the attic of the third house. After that, we would see. There were five of us: Haniek Blashkovsky and his wife Esther, Schwarzbard, Yulek Volkovitch and his wife Marisha Zeidel and I. First we got the women onto the roof, wiped out all the traces and then followed. We crawled over the glowing surface so as not to be seen. Finally, we reached the entry into the last attic of the Aryan house and forced the cover off. Slowly and furtively, we slipped down and crowded against the darkest corner where the roof met the wall. The walls and roof–beams were all dry and the slightest careless movement could start them creaking. So we lay pressed against one another listening to our hearts beating. The only thing that disturbed the silence was the buzzing of flies and the yelling of the gendarmes which reached us from the distance.

The clock in the Municipality Tower rang 11. A motor suddenly started roaring. I cautiously crept to the low attic window. Startled swallows flew away from their nests. I scattered dust on the panes and then approached. These were not the death lorries but ordinary ones. The people of the last group were being pushed onto them. I could recognize acquaintances. They were not alarmed because they had been promised that they were being taken to Lodz. When the lorry left, my heart pounded in grief knowing that I would never see them again.

Back with the others, the women were weeping. What would happen to us? Where would we find a hiding place? We could not stay here where nobody would lend us a hand. Nobody was going to risk his own safety for us. The women began to regret having come. They wanted to go back to their kinsfolk. And we were particularly worried about Esther who was ill and was expecting to give birth to a child any time. Still, she displayed astounding courage and calmness. It grew hotter and hotter. It became hard to breathe. We did not feel hungry though we had eaten nothing since the night before but we were very thirsty and had not the slightest idea how much longer we might have to crouch where we were.

[Page 271]

Suddenly, the rusty lock creaked and the wooden door of the attic opened. A young woman came in carrying a basket. The others looked at me. I was the closest and knew what they meant. If she should notice us, we would have to hold her, cover her mouth and tie her up until we got away. But the young Volksdeutsch woman quietly put the basket in place, undid the rope covering it and went off. And the hours continued to crawl by until at last darkness fell and it became a little cooler. That was what saved us for we were on the verge of collapse. Yulek and I proposed to go over to the empty house and fetch water, food and some clothes. But we had to give up the idea for fear of waking up the housefolk while crawling. Apart from that, the guards of the Voluntary Fire Brigade might observe us since they used to go around abandoned dwellings stealing whatever they could.

At six o'clock in the morning when the workers in the neighbouring factory went home after the night shift, we decided we would leave our hiding–place. Each of us would go separately for safety reasons. Maybe some of would be lucky. When the clock struck, we looked at one another for the last time and broke down the door with a joint effort. A moment later, I was standing at the gate of the house and slowly took a few dozen steps. When a group of workers passed me, I made a dash for the fields and for freedom.

Afterwards I learnt that the Germans had told the truth for the first time and had not deceived us. All the camp folk had been rounded for the time being in the empty mill which had formerly belonged to Reich and Chmielnicki. The next day they were all placed on the train and taken to the Lodz ghetto either 136 or 146 Jews in all. And that was the last transport in the history of Kalish Jewry. It took place on the 9th of July 1942. Just before the train started, the two sisters Klein, pupils at the orphanage, appeared at the station. They had run away from the Poznan camps and returned to Kalish at that moment and willingly joined the deportees for lack of any alternative. Henyek Blaszkowski and his wife did the same. They too had no alternative for Esther was about to have a child and already found it hard to walk.

The other couple, Yulek Wolkowitch and Marisha Seidel arrived at Warta on foot and after resting there for a few days proceeded to the Zdunska–Wola ghetto. But the whole of that ghetto was transferred to Lodz soon after. "All of them" means the handful that were left after the terrible slaughter which took place there first when almost all the Jews in the camp were cut down by machine gun.

During the transportation of Kalish, Isidor Wiszniewski also ran away but was unlucky. A few days later he was handed over to the Gestapo but his numerous gendarme acquaintances saved his life and he was sent to Lodz. I was, I believe, the last Jew left in Kalish. I spent a fortnight in the home of Polish acquaintances, first with Mr. Josef Jaworowicz and then with Antoni Pawelski who risked their lives and unhesitatingly lent me a fraternal hand in my distress.

[Page 272]

Two days after the last transportation, Mr. Pawelski told me that my sister was no longer in the apartment where she had taken refuge and that all the Jews were still in the Kalish area. I set out to Kozminek on foot to find out what was going on. No one recognized me on the way and here I found that the ghetto had already been removed. For a moment I entered the home of a Polish acquaintance hoping that my sister would be sitting there. While I was eating the food she brought me, a Volksdeutsch postman entered the house. It seems that somebody had recognized me in the street and had sent him there after me. I did not have the strength to run away and was taken to the Gendarme station.

Here I pretended to be a fool and told Wachman that I had come from Kalish to look for my family. Our ghetto had been transferred only yesterday so I had come here to join my kinsfolk. The fat Prussian shook his head not knowing what to do with me. He could have killed me but why bother for a single Jew? He looked at me dreamily but suddenly woke up. He angrily ordered me to go to the Warta ghetto. But I preferred to return to Kalish hoping to find my sister. There I learnt that she had been handed over in her hiding place and had apparently been sent on to Lodz with the others. What was I to do next? Reporting to the Gestapo meant death for they were not going to send a single Jew to Lodz under guard when one bullet could do the business.

Besides, I did not believe that they had really been sent to Lodz. My friend Antoni Pawelski advised me to proceed to the General Government area and try to cross one of the fronts there or wait in one of the ghettos for the time being until the front approached. But this seemed impossible to me too since I had no money. All I had was thirty Reichsmark, a torn shirt and trousers and an old pair of shoes. My Polish friend Josef Jaworowicz gave me an overcoat and hat.

To me it seemed preferable to go to Germany and work as a Pole. As I had no documents, Mr. Pawelski found a temporary refuge with acquaintances in Piwonice. For two days I remained hidden in the barn until I could no longer bear it and went back to Kalish to find out what had happened. It turned out that Poles were not being sent to work in Germany at the time. Now I began wandering from Piewnice to Kalish and back every day rather than lie hidden and tense. The Pawelskis encouraged me as best they could and tried their hardest to get me Aryan papers. I doubt whether I could have held out had it not been for them. Besides, in the barn at Piwonice there was a danger at any moment that one of the farm workers might come and take hay for the animals and discover me. I walked by day when people were going to work and carried a bottle of coffee and some sandwiches in my hand as though I were going to the works as well.

One day a gendarme came walking around the street corner so suddenly that I was caught unprepared. I slowly strolled past him without looking in his direction and went on without changing direction. At the road–block, I stopped, glanced in boredom at my watch and turned into the neighbouring street. Mrs. Pawelska saw this from her window and told me afterwards that the German had turned his head to watch me and stood there doubtfully for quite a while.

[Page 273]

At night it was safer in the village for searches were being conducted unceasingly in town. But one night the farm–woman told me in alarm that I could not stay because she was afraid that the gendarmes would be coming in connection with the arrest of her husband. I remembered that five kilometres away there was a peasant that I knew in Liss village. But he refused to give me any help and I spent the night in the fields.

The woman who allowed me to stay in her place did not know I was a Jew otherwise she would not have let me remain for a single moment. So, I made up all kinds of stories for her with the aid of Mr. Pawelski. As far as she knew, I was the son of one of the rebels who had met his death in Auschwitz together with her husband.

By this time I was on the verge of collapse but I still wanted to go on living. Now I spent weeks hidden in the high pile of hay. Searches were being conducted everywhere. I counted on a last chance. It was rumoured that the arrests and searches in Kalish had stopped on the Friday. I was hoping for Mr. Pawelski's visit since the convoy would be leaving the following day. And this time I was right. At about noon on 18th July 1942, he arrived. The Polish transportees to Germany were leaving that day and we must not lose a moment. I had to leave at once. And on the way we discussed the plan of action. I had no documents so I had to try to steal into the convoy. We went back to Kalish through the fields and reached the railway station through side streets.

The station was swarming with secret police. I stopped in front of the time–table as though I was studying it. Meanwhile, Mr. Pawelski brought me a platform ticket and shook my hand for the last time. I tried to thank him for his generosity and the brotherhood he had shown me but he would not let me do so. Be careful! A plain-clothed man approached. Once again I bent down to tie up my shoelace and when he passed, I went through to the platform.

It really was the last moment. A group of displaced Poles, men, women and children were approaching bringing any amount of luggage with them. I sized up the situation in the twinkling of an eye and ran over to one woman in order to offer her my help. I swung up a heavy sack of her belongings on my shoulder and marched along with all the rest towards the carriage.

The Ghetto – 4 Chopin St.

A fleshy German belonging to the Arbeitsamt (Labour Office) counted people off: "Thirty–five, thirty–six". All my bones were quivering…"Thirty–seven" and I was inside the carriage.

The engine whistled and the train started out. The peasant women wept. The peasants dropped their shaven heads in nervous worry. It was hard to depart from the beloved homeland, the village where they were born, the cabins and their own land, their own soil where they had grown up and struck root. I could share their grief – who better than I?

I approached the window. Mr. Pawelski was standing in the doorway of the waiting-room. His face showed how happy he was. We had succeeded. He waved his hand but surely could not have believed that he would ever see me again. He vanished from my eyes but remains firmly engraved in my ever–grateful memory.

[Page 274]

Darkness began to descend. The wheels spun faster and faster. The train began speeding up forging ahead into the grey distance. I was going to Germany for a fresh contest with my fate to go on struggling bitterly for life.

Lodz, 26th March 1947

[Page 275]

Kalish, Kosminek and the Camps

by Wolf Lassman

As soon as the war broke out on 1st September 1939, about three–quarters of the Jewish population left Kalish, dispersing in all directions. My two brothers and I also fled to Leszno but had to return because the Germans advanced so fast that they cut us off. Others came back after the surrender of Warsaw but a small proportion proceeded to Russia.

The Germans were rumoured to have entered Kalish on September 6th. When I came back on the 21st, Kalish was empty and like a city of the dead. Everything was closed and locked but most of the shops had been looted. Many Jews had already been shot. I heard that when the Germans entered the town they surrounded several Jewish streets, drove the Jews out of their beds in their night clothes, ordered them to run in circles and then practised shooting at them for several hours. After that, those who survived were sent home. But many bodies were left in the streets.

Jews were allowed in the streets until 6p.m. If a Jew with a beard appeared, it was promptly cut off often with pieces of skin as well. At this time the Germans were sending the Jews to the filthiest kinds of work, beating them murderously on the way.

In due course, Jews began to open their grocery shops. There was no hunger as yet but they lived in dreadful fear, feeling that they were captives in the hands of savage beasts. Early in November, 1939, the Germans suddenly cut off Gornoslonska Street, broke into the Jewish houses, ordered them to take some household linen, pillows, food, etc. and leave their homes at once. They were first taken to the Market Square and were afterwards driven into the large Market Square and were afterwards driven into the large market building there. More than 2,000 Jews were driven there on the first day. A hundred were separated and taken to the Town Hall shelter. They included lawyers, industrialists, merchants and physicians. They were cross–examined about the hiding places of gold, silver and jewellery. The Germans also demanded that they hand over all valuables that they possessed. Then, each one was taken to a dark room; a blanket flung over him and was then beaten until he was senseless. No food or water was given to them. Two days later they were brought back to the market building.

A total of about 10,000 people were finally crowded in there. In due course some food was provided. The building was surrounded with barbed wire and placed under S.S. guard.

One day, the Germans took the writer Flinker into the market place and simply cut him into pieces! His household help had told the Germans that she had heard him cursing Hitler. After he had been tortured to death, she took possession of his home and belongings.

A few Jews managed to escape from the building. The only question was – where could they go? They were being kidnapped and expelled everywhere. But most decided that there was no point in trying to run away. A dreadful epidemic of typhoid began in the Market Building and killed off hundreds of people. Only after this did the Germans remove people from the building, sending one transport to Lechow and another to Rembertow near Warsaw. After the first set of Market Building inmates had been removed, other Jews were caught and sent there.

[Page 276]

Kozminek

The remainder made the mistake of hoping that now they would be left alone. But the Germans promptly began transporting the second 10,000. Then they began kidnapping more Jews and concentrating them there once again. By the end of 1939 almost all the Jews of the city had been expelled. It was announced that any person with more than 10

Reichsmark in his possession would be executed. The Jews got rid of all their possessions, their gold, their jewelry and their valuables. Very few risked keeping anything for themselves. The only Jews remaining in the city were the hospital patients and staff and a handful of unskilled workers. Somewhat later, tailors were selected in order to establish a tailor's workshop.

A few weeks later the Germans sent all the hospital patients in the direction of Grochow. On the way they were gassed to death and flung into common graves. After this expulsion the Germans collected parcels for the patients among the Jews of Kalish. Later, one of the tailors recognized his father's fur coat which an S.S. man brought him to be made over.

The Germans gathered all the belongings of the 30,000 expelled Jews in large warehouses. They sold the less valuable goods to the Polish population for next to nothing, took the best for themselves and sent the rest to Germany.

[Page 277]

While the Jews were concentrated in the Market Square before the transportation, the Poles stood around and watched. Some of them asked S.S men to take bundles away from the Jews for them. Polish girls asked the Germans to take rings from the fingers of Jewish women for their sakes and the Germans obliged them. A few families succeeded in running away. Together with my father and two brothers, I got away to Brzezyny near Kalish where we met the Greenbaum family with 6 members. We all worked a fortnight for Marr the Volksdeutsch. But one day all the Jews in the neighbourhood were collected and sent to Kosminek, about 20 kilometres from Kalish. At the time, Kozminek was still an 'open ghetto' where people were packed together like sardines. But we did not starve because we could buy food from the villages. The ghetto was conducted by a Judenrat and there was a Jewish Ordnungsdienst (Police). Haftke was placed in charge of the Jewish Labour Office and later became notorious for his cruelty to his fellow Jews.

Meanwhile, the Jews of the Kalish District had almost all been liquidated or transported elsewhere. My family and I registered for work at the Opatowek Civilian Labour Camp, 11 kilometres away. There we were employed in work such as unloading coal, cleaning drains and ditches, making roads, etc., being sent out in groups when called for by various German factories.

We were housed at the former Elementary School. Our daily ration included 330 grs of bread and two plates of soup a day. From time to time we were given a piece of horse meat. As a rule, we had to work twelve hours a day but we were often compelled to continue until late at night and had to begin work at 7a.m. as usual the next morning.

The situation rapidly grew far worse. The overseers began beating us and we began to feel hunger. Then we stole coal and sent it to the Kosminek ghetto and they sent us bread in return. We also stole potatoes. In many cases those who were carrying the stolen goods were caught and murderously thrashed. But nothing could prevent us from stealing because that was the only way to obtain food. Otherwise, we would all have perished of starvation.

Early in 1940, the Germans began transporting Jews from Kozminek to other camps. When the unspeakable German Gett was appointed supervisor of the entire district, our situation became absolutely intolerable and we could feel that our days were numbered. Things went on like this, rumour after rumour, persecution growing steadily worse until March 1941. Suddenly, we saw one day that the ghetto had been surrounded. There was nowhere to hide. Gestapo and S.S. units burst into the ghetto and drove Jews into the synagogue courtyard. They drove the weak, the ill, the old people and the children and anyone else to whom they took a dislike into the synagogue. But anyone could be released for money! Haftke released people as he liked. He went through the Jewish homes, brought out those in hiding and took them to the synagogue.

Black lorries then came and the sick, weak and children were loaded on them – a total of about 150 in each so that many were choked while they were being loaded. Mothers climbed into the lorries themselves refusing to be separated from their children. By the time those lorries passed Opotowek nothing could be heard from them but occasional moans for all the people had already been choked. Poison gas was used on them to kill off the people and the bodies were emptied out and burnt. When Jews in Opatowek saw the lorries passing, they ran after them wailing bitterly. The S.S. men shot at their legs while the overseers beat them mercilessly. This action lasted three days while the lorries removed about 1500 as I saw with my own eyes in Kozminek.

[Page 278]

After this many Jews ran away to Warsaw and Lodz believing there was a better chance of surviving in the large Jewish concentration camps. Meanwhile, Gett, the District Commissioner came to the ghetto every day with a gang of drunken Gestapo men. At night, they drove the Jews naked from their dwellings, forced them to run through the streets and beat them murderously. Occasionally, they brought pretty Jewish girls to the gendarmerie station, violated them all night long, beat them early in the morning and drove them into the streets naked.

Jews were dying off like flies, starving to death. They were replaced by others. After the terrible action of Kozminek, there was no food available any longer for the others at Opatowek and it was clear that the days of both camps were numbered.

In May 1941, orders were given that all residents of Opatowek should prepare to leave. Jews from another labour camp were also brought and we were about 300 in all. On that day 30 peasant carts reached the camp and we were carried off to Kalish where we were forced into six railway carriages and brought to Poznan. There we were received by representatives of private factories. We were divided into two groups and the second group of about 150 Jews was sent to Schwanningen which belonged to the German Labour Front. There we were taken to a camp containing two large barracks. It was surrounded by a barbed wire fence and had a special guard. We had to fetch straw before we were given food, and had to move at the double When we returned, each two of us had to carry back a load of straw weighing 150 kilogrammes in our hands under a hail of merciless blows. We were then summoned for the first parade and informed: "You have come here to work and obey orders. Anyone who does not obey will be hung. So will every saboteur. You will be beaten for every breach of discipline." Our group was then divided into 10 units.

Though we were forbidden to speak to Polish workers who were employed with us, they soon told us that Jews had already been here and had been starved by the Germans and then sent to Konin where they were destroyed and their bodies given to the "Reiff" soap factory.

We had to work hard labour 10 to 12 hours a day on 300grs of bread and 2 mouthfuls of water. Within a fortnight, one Jew ran away and was followed by 5 more several days later. The regime then became even more severe and close guard was kept over us at work. We were not allowed to rest at all but had to work bowed down and could not raise our heads. We were kept separate from the Polish workers.

After much searching, the Germans caught the six Jews who had run away. The first one was placed in a hot disinfection oven "in order to fry".

[Page 279]

There was only a scorched black skeleton to be removed. The Germans allowed the other five to die easily – all of them being hung. One of them said in the eyes of all present: "We are innocent and the German murderers will pay for this!" A Gestapo man shot him and his corpse was hung as well.

Now the overseers thought up a new game at work. They would place a Jew in a little cart, cover him with sand, wheel him to some abyss and empty him out. The poor fellow tumbled down the slope breaking all his limbs and perishing in agony. Those who died while falling were the lucky ones. We were compelled to watch. Often a Jew would be covered up to the neck in sand and left to perish. Koerner, the German overseer, was particularly murderous and was the one who organized these "Jewish" games as he called them.

After three months at the camp we were absolutely exhausted. The Germans selected 60 Jewish "Mussalmen" – people who were too weak to do any work – and sent them to the Soap Factory at Konin. Only a handful were left and we were sure that we were going the same way. Instead, 200 other Jews were brought to the camp. One Jew succeeded in escaping from Konin. He was caught, brought to our camp for execution but was kept in detention for several days. The Jewish camp attendants who brought him his food learnt from him that after Jews had been gassed to death in the entire region, their bodies were brought to the soap factory. He himself was hung.

One winter night, all the camp heads made a party to celebrate the German victories at the Front. At midnight, the Camp Heads and the Gestapo burst into our huts and drove the Jews out naked, making us run across the snow and beating us murderously. Then the Germans lined up on either side of the entry to the tents. We were ordered to return and they made us run the gauntlet, killing eight Jews. One was first flung into a pit and afterwards dragged out and tied to a telephone pole at a temperature of minus 30 degrees centigrade. He froze to death. Czekala, chief of the guard who was a savage sadist, took the lead in all of this.

The searches conducted when entering the Camp were a chapter in themselves. If a Jew was found bringing anything in, his number was noted down and he was tried on parade, the usual sentence being 50 strokes on the naked body. The Germans used damp rubber whips which cut up the victim's flesh. The victim was then placed in an unheated but hermetically sealed disinfection oven where he choked to death.

One evening in July 1942, we were ordered to leave with our bundles. We were called out on parade at 11p.m. and left standing until dawn when we saw that the camp was surrounded by S.S. men and gestapo. There were then about 500 of us in the camp.

About 60 armed Germans led us to the railway station where almost 60 goods wagons were on the line. We heard groans and moans and human shadows peeped out from time to time through the tiny barred windows. Four additional wagons were coupled on and we were loaded into them. But the train did not take us in the direction of Konin as we had expected.

[Page 280]

The Synagogue in Kozminek

We journeyed for six days and six nights without food or water. Of the 2,000 Jews in the train, many perished.

In due course the train stopped and we were ordered to get out within ten minutes leaving our belongings behind. The survivors were arranged in groups of five. Three S.S. officers made a selection – the healthy to this side and the others to that. About 600 men were selected, loaded on to lorries and carried off to a camp. At first we did not know where we were but later we found out that we were in Auschwitz. The others were taken off to Birkenau.

We found people dressed in what looked like pyjamas. This we did not understand. We knew that there was mass extermination of Jews going on so how could they suddenly be walking around like that?

Now we were conducted into a transit hut were we stripped and went out naked through another door. There we were left standing all night until 8 a.m. It was cold and raining. The Kapos of the neighbouring hut mocked us, threw stones at us, poured water over us, etc. In the morning, our heads were clipped and we were taken for delousing. We were then conducted to Quarantine Block No. 30 which already contained about 3,000 people.

We went up to the attic where each man was given his piece of bread. Thereafter, a new life in a real concentration camp began. We were not sent to work but were tortured with parades and had to stand with knees bent for three hours before the parade. Anybody who fell was beaten unconscious. Bread was brought in huge baskets. Each man had to approach and take a piece of bread without looking in. The moment the man's hand closed on the bread, he would be hit over the head. Often enough he would receive the blows but not the bread and was left to starve all day long They kept us busy doing drill accompanied by beatings. Dozens of people died every day.

[Page 281]

One day the authorities began to select men for work outside. Everybody tried to think up a suitable occupation and look as young and healthy as possible. About 300 men were selected including my father, my two brothers and me. There could be no greater good fortune than to have the whole family leave together.

Kalish in August 1939 and After

From the Ringelblum Archives

In August 1939, the public became clearly aware that war was inevitable. This led to greater excitement and all kinds of preparations. The Poles were imbued with a spirit of patriotism and displayed their readiness to defend their fatherland. General mobilization was proclaimed and preparations began. In Kalish, the local Jews were convinced of the justice of the cause of those who were defending themselves. As war grew closer, the relations between Poles and Jews improved for they knew they had a common enemy and a united popular front had to be set up against it. The anti–Semitic propaganda of the Polish Endeks almost ceased. While the Poles knew how powerful the Germany enemy was, they felt they could rely on the spirit of their own soldiers.

The fate of the Jews was also bound up with the war for the attitude of the Germans toward Jewry was familiar. They also knew that the Germans were encouraging the

Endeks and their anti–Semitic activities. The conscious sections of the Jewish population had condemned the Fascist Regime of the Third Reich. A defeated Germany would certainly improve the position of Polish Jews.

They all believed in victory and this led to the consolidation of the patriotic Front in Poland. But events moved fast. There were provocations on the frontiers, incidents in Danzig and mobilization. A whole series of year–groups were called back to the army and the Kalish groups began to grow. The barracks were too small to hold all the mobilized men so they were placed in schools, cinemas, government buildings etc. The City began to look like a military camp.

Tension increased steadily when the German–Soviet Agreement became known and general mobilization was proclaimed. The military authorities resolved to dig trenches and erect barbed wire barricades. Civilians were mobilized for these tasks and responded with devotion. Groups of civilians marched out of town with flags accompanied by bands. The Jewish population took a very active part in all of this. Various organizations like the Bund, Betar and Maccabi mobilized their members and marched under slogans such as: "Jewish workers are digging a grave for Hitlerism". Jews also dug shelters in town against air attacks. There could be no doubt that as soon as military action began, the city would be bombed. The Air–Raid Precautions Committee recommended that women and children should be sent to neighbouring small towns and villages and a special office was opened by the Town Council for evacuating the population.

[Page 282]

These instructions caused much excitement in the town. Everybody understood that it was necessary to leave quickly. The rumour that the Government archives had been taken out of the town increased the commotion. Long files of people began to stand at the offices of the P.K.O. (Polish Saving Bank) made up of people who wished to withdraw their savings and keep them in spot cash. People on holiday came back in alarm from holiday and rest resorts. The prices of travelling bags, baskets and cases began to rise. The railway station was thronged. Only really well–to–do people could hire lorries and taxes. People were packing their belongings everywhere and setting out on their wanderings to find a safe place.

Towards the end of August, the stream of refugees from the city began to increase as long caravans of peasant wagons full of evacuees from the frontier villages began to reach the town. The peasants loaded whatever they could on wagons, put their cattle out and began moving eastwards. Now even the poorest left the town moving with their knapsacks on their backs towards Lodz, Warsaw and other towns lying to the east. Nobody considered whether he was doing the right thing. There was a general panic and flight.

Three–quarters of the population left the city during those days before the war.

12.7.1941.

From Kalish to Warsaw

The events of September led to a general flight, absolutely confused, without any consideration or preparation. People went off without belongings, in their morning suits and without overcoats. Everybody could feel that another hour in Kalish was as good as destruction.

The following fact indicates how nervous and terrified the townsfolk were. My mother, my younger brother and I went to acquaintances in the morning to take advice. The streets were quiet. Most of the shops were closed and a large part of the Jews were already detained in the Market building. Our acquaintances had already finished packing and were about to go to the railway where the train was due to leave in twenty minutes time. Without further consideration, we decided to join them although we had nothing with us. We entrusted our apartment with everything in it to a Christian neighbour, a blacksmith's wife with whom we were on good neighbourly relations. She promised us that if we had to go away she would send our belongings on to wherever was necessary. In due course, she took everything herself and claimed that the Germans had expropriated the lot.

[Page 283]

The railway station was packed full. The trains could not contain all the passengers. Jews waited, grew nervous and were apprehensive about new excesses that might occur at any moment. They climbed onto the steps and fenders of the carriages. The carriages themselves were packed and choking. Everybody was standing. Yet they began to feel more at ease. As soon as the train began to move, they breathed easily. They were outside the city at last.

The train stopped at Sieradz and Zdunska Wola. Jews were standing in groups and also wanted to travel. Their faces were stamped with fear, anxiety and grief because they could not join us. In Lodz we had to wait several hours for the train that left for Warsaw. Here as well there were masses of Jews from Lodz and other cities and small towns. They could feel what a long time it was for they wished to escape after all that had happened to them. The yellow badges which they wore gave the Germans reason to mock and torment them. They expelled all the Jews from the waiting room at night and ordered them to crowd together on the platform. They arranged them all in a long column and ordered them to open their bundles and bags for inspection. When the Jews obeyed, the Germans moved from bundle to bundle taking whatever they liked the look of. Anybody who dared to object was immediately beaten, including women.

When the train arrived at last, the Germans put all the Jews in one place and kept them there until the Poles were all on board. One minute before departure, they made the Jews run to two goods wagons that were hitched onto the train. The crowding and confusion was indescribable People trod on one another. There were terrifying shrieks. Families were split up, children were left without parents and many lost all their belongings. When the train started out at last, half the Jews were left at the station not knowing what to do and cursing the day they were born. The Germans enjoyed themselves, mocking the barbarous Jews who did not know how to behave quietly like civilized people.

Thoroughly dejected, the passengers arrived at Koluszki where we had to get off and wait for the train to Warsaw. This was the frontier station between the areas that had been annexed by the Reich and the General Government of Poland Thousands of Jews were walking nervously up and down the platform, looking out for the train. Between Lodz and Koluszki, the Jews had removed the yellow bade hoping that they would not have to wear it any longer. But they were wrong! The Germans at once saw how many Jews there were at the station and went on tormenting as before. The German railway workers took them all to one spot, beating and cursing them for removing the badge. The Jews swiftly put it on again but it did not help. The Germans had decided to torture them. There was one young German who walked up and down in front of the terrified Jews as they trembled and pushed them about saying: "These cursed Jews." Suddenly he stopped and ordered them all to repeat together at the top of their voices: "We wanted war." The Jews obeyed.

The Polish passengers gathered around, laughed and did their best to show the Germans how much they appreciated these tricks. One of the Poles offered to translate the German's order into Polish. The young German felt encouraged and went on inventing torments. He ordered all the Jews who had served in the Polish Army to take one pace forward. About fifteen men or so advanced. The German arranged them in two rows and rebuked them for having shot at German soldiers. He then began to drill them ordering them to fall and stand and helped them to obey by kicking them. He then commanded them to pick up their bundles, cases and knapsacks and made them run a hundred metres along the railway tracks. Many of them stumbled and fell. Before the train left, the Germans again 'inspected' the baggage and took whatever they wanted.

[Page 284]

When the Jews finally forced their way into the Warsaw train, they moaned with relief. People climbed through the windows and onto the roofs. Weary and exhausted they reached the Warsaw terminus late at night. Apart from the many Jews, the station was full of peasants and food hawkers who had brought supplies from near and far. Everybody waited for the morning. They then went into town to search for a refuge and some way of earning a living.

23.8.1941

The Jews in Kalish from September to November 1939

Early in October, anti-Jewish measures began to increase. Until then the situation had not been too bad. When the Jews returned to their former occupations, operating the workshops, opening their shops and things were almost as they had been. As masses of German soldiers passed through Kalish there was a great increase in business, particularly in cafes and restaurants. The Jewish pastry cooks and cake shops worked hard and made plenty of profit

The German character of the town became steadily clearer. All Polish signs were removed and replaced by others in German. The streets were given German names. Photographs of Hitler began to appear in shop windows and swastikas fluttered everywhere. The Polish population swiftly adapted itself to the new conditions and many Poles set out to prove to the Germans that they were even prepared to run ahead of them in some respects. Many shop windows began to display not only swastikas and portraits of Hitler and Goering but also notices: "Aryan business", or "Jews not admitted", whereas formerly they had merely written: "Christian business."

By the 10th of September, in some mysterious fashion, an old Endek pre–election propaganda sheet was strung across a cross–road. It read: "Kalish without Jews."

As soon as the Germans entered Kalish, they arrested many of the Jews and Poles who had remained in the town. Five or six weeks later, these Jews returned and described how they had been taken to various towns in Germany and exhibited to the population with the explanation: "These are Jewish swine that shot at German soldiers."

When the town was occupied, German soldiers confiscated all kinds of goods from Jewish and Polish shops alike, particularly cotton goods. Gradually, orders began to appear which affected Jews alone. An order was published that Hitler flags were to be removed from all Jewish houses. German officers had already confiscated all the goods from the Jewish shops. Furniture was taken from the dwellings. Many shopkeepers and apartment owners were ordered to vacate their premises within a few hours or even a few minutes and German or Polish families took over. The whole appearance of the town changed within a few days.

[Page 285]

So did the external appearance of Kalish Jews. Before the war many had continued to wear the traditional Jewish garb, beards and ear locks, kapota and Jewish caps. Now these disappeared. Everybody wore either ordinary caps or hats. After the many cases in which beards and ear-locks had been ripped from the faces of the Jews by German soldiers, there were scarcely any beards to be seen.

One day the Germans ordered that all Jewish shops had to display a placard of a standard size containing the word: "JUDE". On 10th October the Germans ordered the establishment of a "Council of Elders of the Jewish Community." However, none of the former leaders were left in the town so the governor of Kalish summoned Hahn the cantor of the new synagogue and placed him in charge as Senior of the Elders and ordered him to set up a Council of 25 members to represent the Jews of the city before the authorities and ensure that they obeyed all orders and regulations. The Council members were to be responsible for obedience with their lives and property.

Within two days the Council had been set up. Its offices were placed in the former Kehilla building and its first task was to conduct an accurate census of the Jewish population, property, money exceeding 2,000 zloty and all jewellery. Between 15 and 20 persons worked on this task for ten days and nights and 20,000 Jews were recorded.

The Germans began making all kinds of demands of the Council. On one occasion they demanded 50 sets of mattresses within four hours. All goods of this kind in the Jewish shops had been confiscated weeks before so the mattresses were collected by Jews from Jewish homes. If the Jews refused to hand over the bedding, the collectors took them by force. When the Germans demanded money, as they often did, the Council imposed a tax on the rich Jews. But the Council's chief range of activities was the supply of workers for daily labour.

The Labour Department supplied the Germans with 150–200 workers daily on average and as many as 400 on special occasions. The Jews were summoned for two or three days' work a week. Those who wished for exemption paid two or three zloty instead of a day's work or 36 zloty a month. In addition, half a zloty was charged for deferring work for one day on medical exemption authorized by the Council's physicians for which one zloty a day was charged. Many Jews redeemed themselves with money and 60–70% of those sent to work every day were hired substitutes to whom the Council paid 2 zloty for each day's work. This money came from the receipts for exemption and deferment which left the Council with a daily surplus of 50–100 zloty.

The Germans imposed various kinds of work on the Jews who buried Poles that had been shot in the new Jewish cemetery, the barracks, the Hospital of the Holy Trinity, the District Government Building, the Public Insurance Building, the Auxiliary Police and the Gestapo. Four Jews were regularly employed removing Polish sign–boards or erasing whatever was written on them, or other Polish texts. A reserve of 10 workers was regularly on duty at the Council offices to deal with sudden demands by the Germans. As a rule, the orders for workers arrived on day before the date they were required. The Germans did not pay any wages but gave bread and lunch in a few places.

[Page 286]

The Jews were treated differently in different places. Here and there relations that were almost friendly were established between the German soldiers and the Jews. In such places, the German would give the Jews cigarettes and beer and talk to them freely. Elsewhere, the Jews were beaten, pushed about and hurried up. One day a German stamped the word "Swine" on the foreheads of all the Jews working under him. He ordered them to leave it there for the whole week and inspected them daily to make sure it could still be read. For three weeks, 25 Jews worked on a farm near Kalish. The German soldiers stationed there treated the Jews better than the owner who was a Volksdeutsch woman.

The attitude of the German authorities towards the Council varied from time to time. They made all kinds of demands which were fully satisfied. But there were also cases showing a very different attitude. Once two members were summoned to the Gestapo, arrived at 11a.m. and were locked in a room until dark but no harm was done to them. On another occasion, the Germans took 10 Council members away including the 80 year old Dr. Beatus who was there by chance. They were all savagely beaten, compelled to drill and then given pavements to scrape. Meanwhile, a few Germans were busy photographing the activities. Another time, they went to the Kehilla building and smashed furniture, screens and chairs. They turned the Jewish Gymnasium quarters and the Jewish Elementary School building into a hospital for Polish Prisoners of War.

The New Synagogue was locked up and had not yet been damaged. The Germans temporarily housed Polish prisoners of war in the Great Synagogue and the Talmud Torah Building. There were many cases of desecration by them. Thus, they removed the Torah Scrolls from the synagogues at 21 and 29 Ciasna Street and burnt them in the courtyards; and Jewish girls were ordered to dance around the fire. They destroyed another synagogue and flung the Torah Scrolls and religious literature into the river, with blows and shooting. German soldiers entered the home of a poor family on the excuse of sanitary inspection and ordered the mother to strip her seventeen year-old daughter and give her a bath.

Flinker, a flour mill owner who had once edited the local Jewish paper, was murdered following denunciation by his Polish household help who claimed that he had weapons hidden in his home. He was arrested, had a heart attack on the way to prison and was shot by German soldiers. Using the same excuse, the Germans, early in November, also murdered a Polish priest. The Jews were ordered to bury his corpse at the entrance to the Jewish Cemetery.

[Page 287]

When Germans from the Baltic countries were settled in the Reich most of the good flats of Jews and Poles alike were expropriated early in November. Those expelled from their homes were allowed to take next to nothing of their property and were all housed in a monastery. The Baltic Germans who came to Kalish were promptly housed in these apartments. The Poles were gradually released from the monastery and a few were permitted to leave town. All the others were taken to the Market building which had previously housed prisoners of war and army horses.

About the 10th of November, the method of expropriating apartments changed and only those of Jews were taken. The Jews were driven to the Market building. The German gendarmes would close off a street on all sides, order all the Jewish tenants to clear out within a few moments and then conducted them in groups to the Market building. Every few moments fresh Jewish families could be seen crossing the city under guard and carrying little bundles, knapsacks or pillows. They had had so little time and were so confused that each one had snatched what first came to hand.

———

Some Figures
(from the Ringelblum archives and elsewhere)

by S. Glicksman

The following meagre data to be found in the Ringelblum Archives and the documents of the Joint can help to give a picture of the destruction.

There were 24,000–28,000 Jews in Kalish before September 1939 when hundreds of families left the city. Some of them returned as soon as military operations were over. In December 1940 refugees from Kalish were to be found in the following places: 6830 in Warsaw; 75 in Cracow and Glogow; 30 in Tyczyn; 84 in Lancut; 50 in Lezaisk; 1224 in Rzeszow (Reisha) and 150 in Rembertow.

Four large transports left the city, the last departing on Monday 12th December 1939. One train went to Lublin, the second to Sandomierz, the third to Kaluszyn and the fourth to Lukow. Additional four or five trains also left. Patients from the Old Age Home were sent to Baczki near Lochow on 15th December. It is reported that in January 248 Kalish Jews were to be found there including 100 old people and 53 children.

After the great expulsion, 400 gravely ill patients remained in the Jewish Hospital including 280 chronic bed cases that could not be moved. A physician and two grave diggers were left to look after them and they were permitted to remain until spring. Those looking after them might requisition food for them from locked Jewish apartments. A special permit was necessary to open such dwellings.

There were 1912 Jews in the Market building between the 1st and 22nd of February 1940 who received extra food from the Hospital. On 23rd February 1940, they were transferred to Kozminek where a camp was set up for them. The Jewish Council distributed the following rations in1940: Half a loaf of bread; 50 grammes of butter and 100 grammes of jam a week. The whole population of the Jewish camp ate in the Kehilla kitchen. There were also children aged less than 14 for whom an elementary school of two classes was set up. They were taught German, Polish, arithmetic and Torah. A kindergarten was set up for 25 children aged less than seven.

[Page 288]

The first Kalish Action was conducted between 27th and 30th October 1940. Its victims were about 250 persons incapable of work, half of them chronic patients from the hospital. They were taken off to an unknown destination, apparently for extermination. The Germans pretended that they had been sent for convalescence. There were 437 persons left including hospital patients. On 1st January 1941, 439 persons were enumerated. After the Action with the black lorries, about 50 able–bodied young men were left in Kalish. One tailor's workshop was left. In July 1942, the survivors were transferred to the Lodz ghetto and the Jewish community of Kalish ceased to exist.

———

Kalish in May 1962

by Abraham Milgrom

I did not meet a single Jew at the railway station or on the way into town. In general, there is little traffic. I did not find a porter and did not catch a taxi. There were two at the station altogether.

The fate of the handful of Jews who had remained alive was symbolized by my talk with a woman aged about 45 who had a Polish appearance. She asked me whether I was a Jew and when I said I was, she confessed that she was also a Jewess and now married to a Pole. When she had succeeded in escaping from the ghetto, this Pole had helped her to survive the war period.

I saw that it was hard to find living Jews so I went to the dead. There was complete ruination at the cemetery. The gravestones were scattered in the field, smashed to pieces, with little bits lying here and there. The last grave was that of Sonik the dentist who had died in Danzig and had left a will asking to be buried beside his mother's grave. His gravestone recorded that he had been a colonel in the Polish army. I gave the keeper a few zloty and asked him to take a little care of the graves but doubt whether he will do anything. The cemetery calls for attention.

Naturally, industry and trade are all government enterprises. The members of the free professions work in cooperatives: cooperative of lawyers, of barbers, etc. I heard complaints about the absence of private trade and told them: "You always preached that Poles should not buy from Jews. There are no Jews no – go and buy from one another!"

The workers are not satisfied with their wages either. I found satisfaction only among the pensioners. They had never dreamed that they would receive a pension from the government. But actually, none of this was my affair. I did not find Jews.

———

[Page 289]

The Finish

by Dov Zielonka

It was April 1945. After many air attacks we were ordered to leave the camp. I worked on the day shift. Work stopped right away. The S.S. men drove us out. Meanwhile, people ran to the kitchen to find some food. I tried my luck as well. The kitchen was full and the men fought one another in order to grab something. The Nazi Commandant drew his pistol and ordered us to get out But he shot at the ceiling and the window and nobody moved though a couple had been already injured while fighting for food. A squad of S.S men burst in and began beating us At last we went out, marching I had not succeeded in grabbing anything in the kitchen.

The streets were empty and shots could be heard on every side. Aeroplanes were diving and shooting Our guards were moving close to the walls while we were in the middle of the street. Where were we going? Nobody knew.

That evening we reached some camp or other On the other side of the barbed wire fence boys aged ten to thirteen were dragging heavy beams of wood two by two while a German followed them carrying a rubber truncheon We did not know who the children were.

All of a sudden we saw a twelve-year old boy among us. Clearly he was not one of ours for our children had already been exterminated in Auschwitz. We spoke to him in many languages. He did not answer. A German aged about sixty went over to him but the boy did not answer him either The German took a slice of bread out of his wallet and the boy dashed to take it but the German signed to him to go behind him to the wall of the nearest house. He gave him the bread, turned him with his face to the wall and shot him.

We had been marching for a fortnight now, sometimes by day and sometimes by night. We had long lost every human likeness. Men who were wizened with starvation kept on dropping without interruption. We reached a town that was being bombed constantly. Here we hoped we would be saved. But the Germans led us by side roads to a branch of a narrow gauge railway. Here they crushed about 100 of us in a goods wagon and locked the doors. Our guards vanished We felt that we were choking and yelled. But nobody heard our voices. The time seemed to pass like an eternity.

They opened the wagons in the morning. A dense vapour burst out like steam from a boiler. The S.S men drove us on. It was the end of April, a fine day! We were marching through the mountains between Marienbad and Karlsbad. Laznowski was almost exhausted. Aeroplanes appeared very high up. Sender was still full of faith and confidence. All of a sudden, the German officer yelled: "They're diving!" All the S.S men dashed to shelter in a wood nearby but ordered us to lie down. The plane came diving down a moment later and began circling around us. I could see the muzzles of the machine guns only ten metres from me. Another plane arrived They did not shoot. After circling for about ten minutes, they cleared off.. They must have seen that we were prisoners. "Nothing is going to happen to you anymore" said the German officer jokingly.

[Page 290]

We went on. It was Friday evening. Rain was falling without a break. We were wet through and our souls were weeping Joseph Meir Seidel, our spiritual leader who always put heart into us, now began to lose his faith. There was some inhabited place five kilometres further on. Maybe we would rest there. They ordered us to stop. Rain was pelting down. Two S.S. men rode off to town to see whether we could pass through. An hour later came the order: Turn back! Where to? It was dark. We turned back for a distance of two kilometres. There was a stable with a broken roof. They marched us in. Wet animal droppings. Our feet sank in manure. We burst out weeping. Simeon Zucker wept and cried: "Lord of the Universe, end our troubles".

Now we decided not to march any further I fell down. I fell asleep and dreamt of Passover at home. The table was covered with the best of everything The family was seated around it. I was asking the Four Questions All of a sudden I felt a sharp pain and opened my eyes. A German had hit me over the head with a stick. Everybody went out except eight who were not awakened even by the German sticks. I gazed with envy at these men who had already been delivered.

It was the 6th of May. Men were collapsing on the road. Anybody who could not run was shot by the German who had murdered the hungry boy. I no longer had the strength to move. My sandals were worn out and their soles were tied around my feet with rope. My strength was giving out. Two companions supported me and brought me into the font line so that the professional murderer should not shoot me It was already dark and we were still running. It was after midnight At last they put us in a stable. This time it was dry. I tumbled down. I think it was our fifth day without any food. If only I could lie and not stand up again.

It was still dark and they were already beating and yelling. On the march again. The S.S. were no longer counting us. The officer was carrying a knapsack. We already had marched 15 kilometres. Now we heard that the village through which we had passed that morning had already been liberated. Was it possible?

Passing through another village, two men tried to hide. The S.S. men beat them murderously. All of a sudden, a roll of bread fell beside me. I could not believe my eyes Somebody had thrown it from a window. I shared it with my five companions. There was no desire to go on. We were only 15 kilometres away from freedom!

Once again we decided we would go no further. Without a word, we all sat in the field. The commander was nervous. In his knapsack he had a civilian suit. He left us sitting while he himself dashed this way and that, looking at his watch every few moments. After ten minutes had passed, he ordered: "Get up, get on!" We remained sitting. He yelled again. We did not budge. He summoned the S.S. men – drew his pistol and shot in the air.

[Page 291]

Our companion Moshe stood up bared his body which was covered with bruises and sores and said: "Leave us alone. I've left a wife and child and I want to see them again. The war is over. Why should we die at the last minutes?"

His words made their impression. The German lowered his pistol. At that moment, we rose and dispersed in all directions. I ran through a sown field with a strength which suddenly appeared although my companions had had to support me only a few minutes earlier. I heard shots but I went on running.

*

I was too impatient to stay at this hospital in Saatz in the Sudetenland. The war had ended a month earlier and something was driving me back to Kalish. I had seen my two younger sisters leave for Auschwitz in 1944. They must surely be back in Kalish desperately awaiting my arrival. After all I was responsible for them. I tried to walk but my legs would not carry me. The doctor refused to allow me to leave. In spite of this, I decided to go.

I learnt to walk again and a few days later I was out in the streets asking how I could get back to Poland. I met a group of Poles who had been doing forced labour here. They would be leaving for Poland by a special train in a few days. I promptly joined them.

Now at last I was on the way. The train crawled. I felt really ill. We reached Kattowitz after a fortnight. There I left the others to make my way to Kalish. At six o'clock in the morning I got out at the railway station amid a huge crowd. My eyes were searching for a Jew. What had happened to all the Jews of Kalish? The municipal bus took me to town. I got off at the Town Hall.

It was a fine summer's day and I was back in the city where I had been born and grew up. Yet, how alien the whole place was! I searched for a Jew in the Old Market. There were none! With a beating heart, I dashed to No. 5 Babina Street where we had lived. I went in a spoke to the janitor. At first he did not recognize me: "Jusef, don't you know me?" He recognized me, crossed himself and asked whether anybody else of the family had come. I told him that my sisters ought to be here. He shrugged his shoulders. He had not seen them.

I asked for water. The fellow could not understand what was going on inside me. He said that he would give me coffee in a little while and that we would have some breakfast. I sat in his dwelling for an hour. I then rose and departed. I went out and came back at once to ask: "Maybe you know where a Jew lives here?" He answered that one had been living in Babina Street but had already moved away.

The moments that followed were maybe the worst in my life. What was I to do? I had reached my destination. Here I was in Kalish. I had managed to reach the end of the war. Was this the life that would follow? Why, I was an unnecessary person in the world, without a penny in my pocket, ill, in rags and tatters and without a roof over my head!

[Page 292]

The Town Hall clock struck the hour of ten. I had been walking through the streets for four hours and had gone around the park five times already. Where could I go? Tears fell from my eyes and once again I found myself by the Town Hall. My legs were failing. I sat down on a stone opposite the bus station. I dropped my head and fell asleep. A woman woke me up and asked if I was a Jew. Yes, I answered, I am a Jew. She pointed to the house of Apt and said: "You'll find Jews there".

I went up and met with the Jewish Committee of Kalish.

Barbed Wire Fence

[Page 293]

My Dream

by Halina Liebeskind

I dream of a journey afar
That is quiet and storm less and good.
I dream of a distant corner
Far away in the peace of a wood.

And I dream of a lonely island
Under the shade of a tree
Where I shall not long for people.
Yes, that is the dream I see.

The beauty of Nature I'll cherish.
All along I shall swallow the air
Oh, how sweet my life will become
When I'm done with all bitterness there.

The grasses will serve me for food.
I shall live on the fruit of the trees.
I shall pick corals for berries
While the birds will sing me of peace

And when I shall have to depart
From that loveliest world of them all,
The forest will sing me a death-song
And I shall give up my soul.

And no one will shed tears for me,
My memory will vanish away,
And none will lament for my passing
Save the winds as they wander and stray.

Halina Liebeskind was thirteen years old when she arrived in the Warsaw ghetto with her parents. During the Revolt in the ghetto she sheltered in a bunker which the Germans discovered. She was sent from Warsaw to Lublin, but by a miracle, she was not sent to Maidanek. Instead, she reached the Birkenau camp with her aunt and was sent from there to Ravensburg where she remained until the liberation.

The original poem was written in Polish.

[Page 294]

Those Who Fought Back

[Page 295] Blank

[Page 296]

Joseph Kaplan

Joseph Kaplan was born in 1913, passed through Heder and Yeshiva and spent a little time at the Hebrew Gymnasium but had to stop studying because of the material situation of his family. He attended evening classes instead. While very young, he joined the Hashomer Hatzair with which he identified himself. He studied Hebrew and made a living as a carpenter.

In Hashomer Hatzair, he was first a guide then unit head and then head of the group. From there, he became the leader of the Lodz-Kalish District and later proceeded to Wolhynia. H. Geller reports on his activities there. The entire region had been left without guides and instructors who had all proceeded to Eretz Israel or else had been summoned to the headquarters in Warsaw. It was 1937 and they were awaiting the new representative urgently. One rainy morning a young fellow in a tattered overcoat arrived at the Rovno Ken (club centre). He had a head of thick black hair, a sunburnt face and a rather mischievous smile and his name was Joseph Kaplan. A few moments later, he opened his bag, produced a few hectographed sheets and said: "I put out these circulars in Kalish. I prepared them myself." The next day our own First Circular appeared. The leadership in Wolhynia had gone into action. The leadership of course consisted of a typewriter, a hectograph and Joseph Kaplan.

The next day, he vanished for two months while he went to all the little Clubs in the small towns. There was no railway – no highroads. All journeys were made by wagon or on foot. But warm Jewish hearts were to be found in those little towns. He had to advise, instruct, scold and encourage and hold back those who wished to go to Eretz Israel before they had completed their full instruction period. On his own, he came to know the thousands of Hashomer Hatzair members in Wolhynia.

[Page 297]

Two months later he returned, weary, more tattered than before but full of life and declared that he had cracked the nut. For now he knew the entire district and had found faithful assistants everywhere. A few days later he published a detailed report covering each place separately. Then he vanished again, returning to Rowno only from time to time. On one occasion he told the story of his own hard life, the childhood without happiness and the frequent intervals of hunger

In due course he wished to proceed to Eretz Israel but was summoned to the Warsaw headquarters from which he maintained his contact with Wolhynia.

In 1938, he was still planning to proceed to Eretz Israel. By the beginning of 1939 his passport was ready. The war broke out. The Halutzim poured eastwards. He spent a long interval in Lida and used the time in sending Halutzim on to Wilna from which there were prospects of aliya. The Movement was left in the hands of boys in Poland He himself reached Wilna in January 1940.

However, he only spent a month there for the Movement in Poland had been abandoned. In February 1940, he returned as a member of the Delegation of Warsaw to handle activities under the Nazi occupation The other members were Mordechai Anilewitz, Tosia Altman and Shmuel Bratzlaw. Joseph coordinated activities and was justly regarded as the head of the Movement. The Delegation did a great deal. The Movement was restored and began to expand. Two Kibbutzim were set up and Hachshara was organized as an underground activity, the members engaging in urban work. Two underground National Councils and two Seminar Courses were held.. The Warsaw Ken numbered more than a thousand members who issued ten different journals in hundreds of copies and maintained contact with every other Ken in the small towns

Joseph's special function was contact with the various institutions. He kept in personal touch with Dr Ringelblum, the heads of the Joint, the underground and representatives of communal institutions. He was the established 'contacts' man with the various centres. Though he had an exceedingly Jewish appearance, he went everywhere in spite of the danger involved. In the ghetto it was he who delivered the educational lectures. It was Joseph who organized Hachshara in order to make sure that the older members did not break off their ties with the Movement even if they could see no way of continuing their activities.

During his first Warsaw year, he set up Hachshara at an estate which was found to belong to an anti-Semite whose only purpose was to exploit his cheap workers to the utmost. The lads worked from morning to night and were fed only on left-overs. This Hachshara was closed down and he sought Hachshara elsewhere.

The famous Hachshara farm at Czenstochow had been taken over by the Wehrmacht – the German army. He resolved to get the farm from them and succeeded. He also obtained the abandoned estate of a Jewish landowner near Zarki with the assistance of the local Judenrat. There he established a Halutz training farm. He and Zvi Brandels had travel permits as sick persons and within a few weeks, had transferred the older Hashomer Hatzair members to the Hachshara centres, two or three at a time.

[Page 298]

He devoted all his efforts to the issue of newspapers, first for the Movement and later as an underground press. Only in these papers was it possible to find military reports with expositions of war and political developments. It was exceeding difficult to get the paper out of Warsaw and he, therefore, decided to publish special issued for other towns. These took the form of three books each of 160-180 pages. They were given a special cover bearing in Polish the name: "Agricultural Calendar for 1942". They contained a selection of the Warsaw press, news from Eretz Israel and the smaller branches and were distributed by special underground methods.

Early in 1942, a left-wing anti-Fascist Resistance Organization was set up on the initiative of the Jewish communists. The other participating groups were the left Poalei Zion, Hashomer Hatzair, Dror and the Z.S. Joseph was a member of the command. Its significance was that it brought the various groups together, but it achieved nothing and did not last long.

That spring, the Germans entered the ghetto one night, took 50 Jews from their beds and shot them in the street. Joseph escaped and concealed himself at Zarki. The mass transportations began on 22nd July 1942 and more than 300,000 Jews were removed from the ghetto within 55 days. Joseph returned to Warsaw and began to make further plans He found work in a wood manufacturing factory and became expert at forging stamps and documents.

When leading survivors met to discuss what should be done, Joseph was one of those who demanded that they should defend themselves; but there were no arms. Hashomer Hatzair, Dror, Akiva and Gordonia together established the Jewish Fighting Organization but there were neither arms nor money. Meanwhile, the debate continued. The younger ghetto residents wished to fight and die while the others wished to hold out as long as possible. But the younger people saw no prospects of rescue. They knew what was going on in Wilna and precisely what was taking place in Treblinka. Arieh Wilner managed to smuggle ten pistols and five hand grenades into the ghetto and some benzene was obtained for preparing Molotov cocktails. Joseph continued to insist that proper preparations must be made for resistance.

On 3rd September, 1942 the German Commissar Hansel came to the factory where Joseph worked and asked for him. Some of the workers went to find him As soon as he returned he was handcuffed and taken out to a closed car. When another member of the Command went out to look for ways and means of liberating Joseph, he was stopped by the Gestapo men in the street. They began to search him and he drew a knife but they killed him on the spot. Thereupon instructions were given for all underground members to move to new addresses. The only one caught was a girl who was carrying arms.

When Joseph and another Jew were being taken from the Pawiak Prison to the Transportation Centre, they were conducted into one of the gateways as they marched and were shot. It is possible but not certain that the second Jew shot was an informer.

[Page 299]

In his last letter Joseph had written: "Don't believe the Germans any more. All their promises are just satanic tricks to split the community. If we are fated to die, let us die honourably. Resist the Germans by force everywhere. Organize the youth. Protect yourselves. Don't go to the railway wagons!"

Details of Joseph's personality were described by Irena Adamowicz, a pious Catholic who helped the members of Hashomer Hatzair and visited Israel in June, 1958. The personal details shed additional light on Joseph's interesting personality and bring him even closer to us.

"....Joseph went from Wilna to Warsaw at his own demand. He felt he was the father of the Movement and thought that there was no one else to do the work. I last saw him in Wilna on January 14th, 1940. He went southwards and reached Warsaw by way of Brisk (Brest Litowsk). He travelled as a returning Jewish refugee because he had a typical Jewish appearance and that caused him much trouble He used to travel a great deal to the small towns with a Judenrat Permit which did not give the right of travel by train. But the main difficulty was to get him through the streets to the railway station and he was always very worried about whoever accompanied him.

....His outstanding quality was his organizing capacity and success in all negotiations In Radom, the Judenrat caused trouble to the Movement. Joseph arrived there and straightened matters out. He dealt with every issue energetically and obstinately. He dedicated himself so much to each detail that he was afraid that he would lose his mind. He used to say that he had a great deal to do before he went mad.

...Other qualities were his level-headedness, a gift of distinguishing between main issues and trifles and a power of swift decision He used to deal with details a great deal but never forgot the main purpose, the aim to which the details were subordinate. If he made a mistake, he was prepared to confess it but usually he displayed ample self-assurance. Agriculture was his aspiration When he met Polish agriculturists; he always impressed them as a very great expert.

...Sometimes he would behave like a child. One day I met him in the Nalewki. He began to pull me by the sleeve and dance. Passers-by began to stare at us. It turned out that he had just heard that his Kibbutz "Maanit" had settled on the land. He also had a weakness for bright little objects, for fine notebooks and fountain pens When he received something of the kind he was as happy as a child. But he really loved working with his hands and was always pleased when he could use them.

...He was of middle height and thin with a mop of black hair. He had large black smiling eyes and his smile was a little bit lopsided. He was not a good looking man but had an attractive exterior. His clothes were usually dark grey.

...Until the truth was known about the slaughter at Ponar in the spring of 1942, he believed that it would be possible to outlive the years of fury. But after that he ceased to believe and opened the eyes of others. He began to be active – to travel. On one of these journeys, he was caught. I believe it was at Skarzysko. He was placed against the wall and told that he had the right to write a letter. But, he told himself: if I do write they'll think they will have to kill me, so I shan't write. And sure enough, some Nazi appeared and allowed him to clear off. He managed to pick up his money that had fallen to the ground.

[Page 300]

...Together with his practical sense and level-headedness, he tended to engage in adventures. When there was talk of the possibility of getting out, he told me he was prepared to go out and come back. I looked at him as though he were crazy. On one occasion, he told me, that in his opinion the Jews ought to go on wearing the yellow badge after the war as well!

...He always spoke about the principle duty of every Halutz which was to go to Eretz Israel. He also believed in a World Soviet Republic that would bring redemption to all. But as long as there were frontiers it was necessary to rehabilitate Jewish life.

...In June 1942, I went to Wilna for the last time and went to meet Joseph before leaving. A few days earlier we had quarrelled as usual about different matters. Now I came to make it up and say good-bye. We knew that there were not many prospects of surviving.

...I saw him for the last time during the great transportation from Warsaw, a few weeks or maybe days before his death. We met at the Jewish Cemetery. I brought him letters from Wilna. He took bread and eggs out of his pocket and we ate. He spoke to me about weapons and about the need to arrange people on the Aryan side. He spoke in a business-like tone without generalizations.

...This was at the time when the whole ghetto was waiting for death."

Memorial Stone for Joseph Kaplan at Kibbutz Maanit

[Page 301]

Adek Boraks

Adek Boraks of the well-known Boraks family reached Wilna from Kalish soon after the beginning of the war and helped to transfer members of Hahalutz to Soviet-occupied territory. His free and colloquial Polish served him in spite of his distinctly Jewish appearance as a passport with non-Jews, peasants, smugglers, etc. He was appointed a member of the Reserve leadership of Hashomer Hatzair. Between 1939 and 1941 he and the others moved from place to place together with the Jewish masses but almost all of them returned to Wilna including Adek when news of the German occupation arrived. He used to leave the ghetto at night, remove the yellow badge and try to find allies who would supply him with arms. He began to be an expert at forging documents.

One evening when he left the ghetto and came to the house of a girl who lived outside, two gestapo agents rang at her door and demanded to see their papers. She explained that he was her fiancé and before showing his own forged documents, he requested to see their authorization. They merely glanced at his papers and apologized before leaving.

He left Wilna and found his way to the Warsaw ghetto where he met the representatives of the Joint, the Parties and whatever Jewish Community there was. He was the first person who brought them the whole truth in simple language. Naturally, the majority either did not believe him or felt for sure that it would not happen in Warsaw. After receiving money promised him by the Joint and a travel permit, he began to make his way back. In Grodno he and his companions were arrested by gendarmes but escaped through the ruins of the bombed-out street in the darkness. When they reached Warsaw by car they were caught again while they were trying to find a way into the ghetto. It is not clear how they got away but they arrived in the ghetto chained and handcuffed without overcoats or hats in the chilly night.

[Page 302]

On proceeding to the railway station to reach Bialystock and Wilna some extortionist tried to get money out of him. He did not answer them and they summoned a policeman. "Where did you get this transit paper from? From the Judenrat?" asked the policeman ironically. Adek did not lose his head but became very angry and answered in his good street Polish: "Mister, from what Rat – where is that Rat? Is there a town called Rat in Poland? I got it in Grodno and not in any of your Rats!" They cleared off. Afterwards people said of Adek that he could even escape from the hands of the devil himself.

Adek returned to Bialystock where he met his Kibbutz comrades. The closet of these was Zerah who had grown up with him in the Kalish Ken. After studying the situation he realized that he ought not to leave this place for it had no Military commander. He was the only one who had ever obtained any real military training. Discipline required him to proceed to Wilna while logic told him that the needs in Bialystok were more urgent. When asked to stay, he said: "Discipline and responsibility require me to go back to Wilna first and then appeal". The argument that he was risking his life did not help. Adek stood firm. It would not be a good example if a member of the leadership should engage in a breach of discipline for reasons of mere logic. He decided that he would not go back empty-handed but would smuggle gold coins in order to buy arms. The coins were then sewn into the pads in the shoulders of his jacket. A week later, he sent a cable: "I have a job and would like to ask your advice Edward". Which meant that he had arrived safely and that there was money for weapons.

Now it was decided that he should return to Bialystok and take charge of the military command. He prepared a code in order that they should be able to use postcards. Weapons would be called furniture, rifles would be cupboards, and dollars would be Stefan and so on. The key to the code was in the hands of Adek, Joseph Kaplan and Rozka. In a single postcard he could supply ample information which often made a dangerous journey unnecessary.

He needed plenty of patience. The partners were not in a hurry to supply the arms freely. Promises were broken. Disappointments followed one another. Adek, Zerah and Yoshka (from Wylkowiski) planned the organization of the 'cells', each of five. Cell members were admitted one by one after two or three talks face-to-face; sometimes even more. Each member knew only the other four. The activities of the Cell were not discussed among the larger Hashomer groups as though they did not exist.

In a debate on Forest and Partisans as against war in the ghetto, Adek said: "Haverim, I want to clarify our attitude to the ghetto once again.

[Page 303]

Maybe there are better prospects for effective war in the Forest. But are we going to be satisfied with that and abandon the masses to be led like sheep to the slaughter here too as they were in Wilna while seeking martial effects in the Forest? I do not belittle sabotage activities. We would blow up so many bridges; we would explode so many ammunition trains; we would cut so many telegraph wires, etc. All these are of the greatest importance. But they do not offer any answer to the main question: How are we to organize a mass response? How do we find a way of giving expression to the resistance of the people? How do we lead to the revolt of Jewish masses that are closed away in the ghetto awaiting the fate of sheep led to the slaughter? Suppose we fight in the Forest? Do we then wash our hands clean because we have done our duty? That is a solution for individuals who wish to lend a hand to the war against fascism.

But where is the communal and national solution? Are we to abandon the unorganized ghetto with its old folk, women and children and say "we have saved ourselves?" Where is the responsibility to the history of the People? Where is the vanguard character of our Movement? I see our Movement as the head of the masses in their revolt, not as an elect group who satisfy their own consciences but as the pioneers of a nation; for surely we have educated our comrades to that end! The War of the Masses will have to be fought in the ghetto and we have to head it together with others who think as we do. First and foremost the ghetto! And first and foremost, the National War. The War of the Jews. They are killing us as Jews and as Jews we shall fight back. And we shall not give answers as individuals but as an organized community. That is the kind of thing which will have its value in history."

At about this time one of the fellows brought the first rifle to the ghetto and it was used in training. The butt was removed and Adek used to move it from place to place. He was selected for this underground activity and also organized the Cells.

He directed attention to the establishment of a Fighting Front of all the movements which supported the principle of combat. The easiest way led to the communists. First meetings were held between him and their representatives. Later there was also a meeting with Shlomo Poporetz who represented the most nationalist and revolutionary section of the Bund. In this way, a High Command was established between the Shomer Hatzair, the communists and the Bund consisting of Adek, Yoshke Kawe and Poporetz. This was the basis for the broader Front which was established in the course of time. Adek was sent to the Military Centre of the Command. With the establishment of the second Block, consisting of the Hashomer Hatzair, Dror, the Zionist Youth, the Revisionists and part of the Bund, Adek's slogan became: Unification of the two Blocks into a single fighting Front.

In February 1943, Adek began to betray his nervousness at meetings. He feared an Action in the ghetto. One day he announced with certainty that the Action would be carried out and did not permit those who were on the Aryan side to enter the ghetto. A day later, Zerah sent a slip of paper to the workers outside the ghetto wall: "Haika, the Action is over Our comrades tried to fight. Here is the list of our losses: Frank, Yoshke, Isruelik, Zivia, Rozka, Yankel and Sender. Nineteen in all and the last on the list – Adek".

[Page 304]

This is how he met his end: Adek's post was discovered. He shot with his pistol and the fellows attacked the S.S. with their fingernails! Traitors had played a part here. And since Adek had lost the essential basis of defence and surprise from ambush, he also had no power of manoeuvring. Gedalia managed to catch Adek's words: "We will pay them back yet! Continue!" Their hands were raised. The Germans searched their pockets. Adek stood at the head of the squad, his face flaming and his eyes shooting fire. After that we no longer saw Adek. The transport left the ghetto and from the distance we saw how they were being hit over the head and how the fighters were behaving "impudently" towards the Germans.

-Echoes came from afar. Jews who were in the same goods wagon and who had escaped the furnaces told about the remarkable commander and rare companion who decided together with his comrades not to jump out of the wagon but only helped others to jump.

On the very threshold of the Furnaces, Adek and his companions organized a revolt so that the Jews should not enter of their own free-will. They were killed just outside the furnaces and fell proudly and bravely.

Adek (Elijah) Boraks was born in Kalish in September 1918. His father was a progressive Zionist and the owner of a Tricotage Factory. He studied at the Jewish gymnasium and joined the Hashomer Hatzair Movement. In 1933 he proceeded to Wolhynia on Hachshara. In the army he was a corporal.

During the fighting in Bialystock on 5th November 1943, he headed a group in Smolna Street.

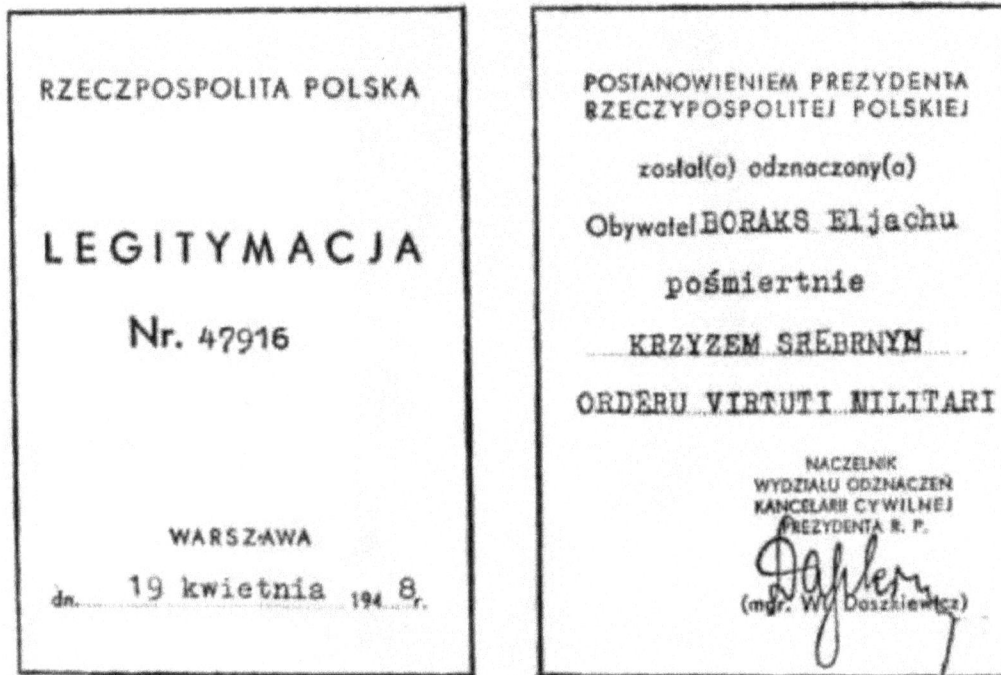

Certificate of Polish Order of "Virtuti Militar!"

[Page 305]

Jacob David Sitner

He was born in Kalish in 1897 to a well-to-do orthodox family. His father was one of the wardens of the Kehilla and a well-known communal worker. So was his mother, whose heart was always open to general distress. Educated in the traditional spirit, he helped to establish the Tseirei Zion Movement in the city and headed it during and after World War I. Later, he established one of the first Leagues for Labour Eretz Israel which had hundreds of members. He visited the small towns in the region, delivered speeches, organized and acted on behalf of the Central Office. In 1925, he moved to Warsaw where he headed a large firm of transport agents but there as well, he devoted much of his time and energy to the Poalei Zion (ZS) Party and was a member of its Warsaw Committee for many years. At one time he was a member of the Party Council and later member of the Central Committee which often used to meet in his home where various discussions were held during the most difficult period of the Movement.

He and his wife Havera Leah – one of the oldest and most devoted in the party – saw to it that every haver should feel at home and he encouraged many members at times of distress and crisis. They were both kind-hearted, delicate and liked by all. The theoretical monthly of the party, "Die Neie Gesellschaft" was founded on his initiative and with his help. He took part in establishing most of his party's enterprises and institutions and was a delegate to the Congress for a Labour Eretz Israel in Berlin in 1930. He visited Eretz Israel in 1935 and submitted a plan for establishing a Histadrut enterprise for goods transport between Poland and Eretz Israel. His plan was approved but the implementation was delayed.

[Page 306]

He was one of the devoted and active members of the underground and represented it in enterprises for social aid in the Warsaw ghetto. He served as Chairman of the Local Committee of Poalei Zion (SZ) in Warsaw during the days of the underground. During the first ghetto period, he managed a brush-making factory which employed members of the Kibbutz of Dzielna Street. For some time he manufactured jam at home. Afterwards, he went over to brush-making shop. In October, 1942, he was murdered. His wife Leah who was also active in the underground gave her life in April, 1943 with their son Joel (Yulek who wrote poems which were published in the Polish underground press). In a letter by the Party in Poland to the Ihud Olami and dated 15th November, 1943, his name is listed among the active party leaders who died at their posts.

Abraham Diamant

We know little about Abraham Diamant. What is known as: He was an active member of the Poalei Zion in Kalish; was a corporal in the Polish army and fell on 1st or 2nd May, 1943, when he was forty-two years old. In the List sent from Warsaw in May 1944, Hersh Wasser writes about him as "the Corporal":

"He was one of the few soldiers of the ghetto who as a mark of distinction was entrusted with a rifle – a very rare treasure among the fighters. Abraham Diamant was a worked aged 42, tall and broad-shouldered whose face expressed gentleness and strength at the same time. A serious, concentrated man and an ideal comrade, he was prepared to share his last slice of bread or spoonful of food with others. He had an absolutely firm character, was daring and despised death – qualities which are not very common.

From his childhood, he was connected with the Jewish Labour Movement and was an active Poalei Zion member in Kalish. On his way from communal and political activity to sharing in the battles of the Jewish Fighting Organization, he went through all the Nazi hells. The Germans exiled him from Kalish to Warsaw in October 1939 together with his wife and child. He had 20 zloty in his pocket and a little bundle in his hands and lived in one of the deathly refugee camps. He felt the German whip, the pangs of starvation, distress and typhoid. During the first expulsion to Treblinka on 22nd July 1942, his wife and daughter were taken from him and sent to the death camp. In spite of all these harsh blows of fate, which broke thousands of other people, Abraham's spirit did not fail. He became even more silent. The furrows on his forehead grew far deeper, his gaze became angrier and his hands clenched into fists".

[Page 307]

The idea of resistance and active battle against the raging Fascist beast found a fervent supporter in him. He identified himself with the new Movement from the moment it was organized. The Polish Corporal, the brave soldier, gripped the rifle in his hands once again.

He did not wish for praise and honour. He used to tell his friends that the war of the Jewish fighters, and even their deaths, would not be a useless sacrifice. The struggle of the ghetto fighters would be part of the War of the Forces of Freedom against Fascism and the basis for a better future for Jewish masses everywhere in the world. The Ghetto Fighters would be the builders of the future.

When the day of action came, the fighter Diamant occupied the position assigned to him at an attic in 32 Swiento-Jerska Street. That was on the 20th April 1943. On that day he picked off seven Germans with his rifle and silenced a German machine-gun nest. He stood on guard by day and night and would not be parted from his rifle even for a moment. He repulsed German attacks with a savage fury. When the S.S. men surrounded the house and burst into the upper floors, Diamant would not leave his post but returned fire. Only after the Germans had already reached the roof did he make his way to another area together with other fighters. After that he was always on the move, on patrol, on guard, on sorties, alone or with the other fighters. He had no pity for himself, never hesitated even for a moment and resolutely stared death in the eyes.

On May 1, he fought amid ruins in the burning remains of the house at 30, Franciszkanska Street, in which there was a large shelter for the civilian population. A unit of the Fighting Organization defended the entrance. All of a sudden, news arrived that the Germans had discovered another entry to the shelter and were coming in. The fighters opened fire. The Germans answered with hand grenades. Three fighters headed by Diamant went out through a different side of the shelter and attacked the Germans from the rear. Two Germans were killed and the rest dispersed. Our objective had been achieved for the moment. The fighters took up positions in the ruins of the neighbouring house. A second unit of S.S. men approached and a struggle for life and death began. Abraham's shots did not miss their mark. The Germans did not dare approach their positions but shot with machine guns from the distance. All of a sudden, Diamant began to reel. A bullet had gone to his heart. He wanted to hand his rifle over to Hersh Berlinski who headed his group but did not manage. From the ruins, he fell into a burning cellar. His body was not found. It was entirely burnt.

––––––

[Page 308]

Zerah Silberberg

Comrades relate that Zerah was taciturn, close-mouthed, firm, deep-thinking and used to give good reasons for his words. He was heavy but gentle and had a sense of proportion. Nobody imagined that he could lie or do anything that was not noble or abandon anybody. Haika Grossman writes:

"Adek and Zerah were very close friends and neither of them ever hid anything from the other. I never saw them in an intimate conversation and used to wonder how they could be such good friends. To which Adek would tell me: "With a mere glance." The ripe masculine friendship was both considerate and reserved. – "Zerah, what will happen if I should die a natural death?" Adek would ask. "You'll die twice" Zerah would answer. "Once from the illness and a second time out of grief at such an ordinary way of dying." It was only rarely that their source of humour would dry up.

One evening Adek asked whether the day would ever come when they would reach Eretz Israel. And Zerah answered: "Why don't you ask whether you'll remain alive?" And that led to a discussion about survival after death Zerah said that he did not care whether they would cut his body up into pieces. "The important thing is to be here and fight here as long as you have life let in you."

[Page 309]

When the lungs of a haver were affected and he did not wish to go to the doctor, Zerah tricked him. He fixed an appointment and sent the haver there, claiming that it was an important meeting. The fellow was insulted but began to accept treatment and recovered.

Zerah also took part in the debate on Forest Resistance or War in the Ghetto. This is how Haika Grossman describes the discussion.

"The deliberateness of Zerah always led to silence in the room. I do not know how Zerah came to be so respected by all the haverim that they used to listen to him so attentively. But they used to say: "Silence, Zerah has asked for the word". He spoke as though he was thinking aloud, stressing his peculiar pronunciation of the letter L, he would talk very slowly without any apparent emotion. Yet, everybody knew that Zerah was boiling. Zerah was tensely living through the problem. He began by saying: "Frank is right.. If we have to weigh the problem we are entitled to weigh it in terms of the war against fascism. Any other approach, no matter how dressed up in the ideology of helping Jewry or helping yourself as best you can, means treachery. Anybody who says that the masses can be saved through the forest is either misleading himself or is purposely misleading others. How can we save the masses if we are in the forest? Is that the way you are going to save the ghetto; the old people, the women and children? And will you leave the war against the fascists to the gentiles? What? I see that there are some here who wish to take us back to a discussion we finished with long ago. Doesn't this lead us back instead of forward? First of all, it is impossible to save masses. That is a utopia – a dangerous illusion which leads to an acceptance of fate. It is possible to save only individuals and even if somebody talks of saving masses, he only seems to mean saving individuals, consciously or unconsciously. And maybe he is counting himself among them? It doesn't matter if somebody is hurt by my words. Maybe I am being unjust. But this is not a private or a personal matter, neither are mine nor yours. If we were only among ourselves we might be able to fix it up. But we have to decide how to educate masses – a Movement – and how and what can demand of others. So first we must make sure that everything is in order among us: and as for the ghetto and the partisans, I identify myself with the opinion of our haverim in Wilna - with the opinions of Adek and Haika."

After that Zerah was sent to Grodno to help the young haverim to carry out the armed revolt.

"I still remember how the resolution was adopted. The room was very sad. The only bright thing was Zerah's face. It burnt and glowed. He urged that the resolution should be acted upon at once. We wanted him to stay with us another day, to discuss matters and to prepare a plan. It was the first time that we saw the well-balanced Zerah so tense. At once, he demanded – at once! The earth is burning under their feet already. Many Jews have already been uprooted. The transports are already on the move, the crowded railway wagons are passing the stations without stopping and it is only through the tiny barbed windows that they are making their last despairing call to the world, telling passers-by and railway workers that they are Jews from Grodno. Those transports disappear in the West and we know that this means Treblinka. Can we still do anything?

[Page 310]

"The next day Zerah hurriedly packed his bag, took the only 'Aryan hat' which was a sort of property of the Movement and which Adek had used on former 'Aryan' journeys. (We used to say: The hat makes the man.) Yendza forged him a permit at short notice and as before, we accompanied Zerah to the exit. We entreated him to wait until tomorrow for at this time of day, Jews had to work and nobody went out or came in. "I am going over the fence" he insisted. We accompanied Zerah to the fence. Adek, Zerah and I went through the ghetto streets in order to be with one another as long as possible. Zerah and Adek entered the courtyard. Before Zerah had climbed on top of the out-house in the courtyard, one of the Jews who lived there dashed out, caught him by the leg and dragged him down. 'I shan't let you pass! They'll punish us all because of you! Clear away from here' And he added good wagoner curses. This was a huge, broad-shouldered fellow. He grabbed the bag in his powerful arms and began to hit out from right to left. Adek nimbly caught hold of him. The battle lasted several minutes. Zerah mounted the roof and Adek caught the bag, tripped the giant up, flung the bag up on to the roof and Zerah jumped over the low fence and vanished."

Zerah spent a fortnight in the closed ghetto, trained the leaders of the 'Fives', planned attack points, organized the bringing in of materials and arms. The weapons were neither good nor plentiful. Once again electric bulbs filled with vitriol, iron knuckledusters, sticks and various other primitive weapons. Zerah and Yocheved looked for a way to establish a united front with other movements. He looked for contact with the communists, the few remaining Bundists and the Revisionists but he found all of them helpless. He looked for a way to the 'decent Jews' of the Judenrat in order to get money from them. They warned him that they would not take part in any hotheaded or mischievous tricks.

Zerah could see the end of the ghetto and wished to establish the organizational contact between the Grodno and the Bialystok undergrounds. The majority had decided to remain where they were and organize a defence as far as possible. Once again Zerah devoted himself to fixing defence points and allocating duties. He inspected the weapons and shared them out, gave instructions for their use and prepared a general plan.

When the effectives demanded that he should return to Bialystok he did not accept orders. And he returned only when the chapter of bloodshed was over. When people were heard in the Bialystok ghetto demanding a revision of the policy of resistance, it was Zerah who stood in the breach.

"I still remember his face, his compressed lips, his quivering voice and his powerful but somewhat restrained appearance. He did not make any charges; he made no personal attacks, he only explained, convinced, showed why there was no other way, that there were more failures in stores for us besides our failures until now; that there was no other way except the way of complete devotion and self-sacrifice. That Adek was right when he had not abandoned the positions, otherwise we would have emerged from the Action with a mark of shame burning on our brows. We would have caused demoralisation in the ranks of the fighters and would have shaken their confidence in us as a leadership and a Fighting Movement. He asked to speak a number of times and grew neither weary nor despairing. - - Gather your strength don't abandon the proper way; don't waste time on a debate that has neither social nor moral significance! That was what the piercing eyes of Zerah told me."

[Page 311]

Following the liquidation of the Bialystok ghetto, the Underground made a final attempt to accompany the masses and rouse them to revolt at the Concentration Point. Zerah and Yoshka undertook this task. Zerah was in command of one sector and fell in the battle.

Zerah Silberberg was born in 1916 and was a member of Hashomer Hatzair from his childhood. He went to Slonim for Hachshara and was there when the war began.

Temkin

I telephoned. Mr. Tanski was waiting for me at the other end. He was very happy that we were still holding out but had no news for us. He had already had all the necessary permits but had gone off to have them approved by the gestapo. The officer had inspected them with care, tore them to little pieces and then scolded Tanski for still making efforts on behalf of the Jews. According to him, we had to do something for ourselves. He wished us success and that was the end of our conversation. The last hopes of deliverance had burst like a soap-bubble.

In due course, the secret of Tanski was revealed. He was the manager for Koznikowski and thanks to him Jewish workers were assigned to this place. It can almost be said that my family and I remained alive thanks to him. During the first expulsion, he housed all the workers and their families in his cellars. He obtained dwellings in the ghetto for us, took us through the barriers in his motor-cars and equipped us with all kinds of permits which meant work. He had considerable influence and extensive connections. During the January Action he came to us with a car in order to carry us from our hiding place to work. He helped anybody who wished to find a refuge on the Aryan side.

He was a mysterious figure. Opinions differed as to whether he was a German or a Pole or a Volksdeutsche. But it was also suggested that he was a Jew though we did not think that was likely.

[Page 312]

He fell in August 1943 after being arrested in his workshops on a charge of false papers. The denunciations of the Kapos were what put him into the hands of the Germans. When he was arrested he seized the weapons of two detectives belonging to the Criminal Police and escaped in his car. But the next day he was caught on the denunciation of one of his good German friends and was executed.

Only then was everything known. Tanski was none other than Temkin of Kalish. His sisters, Mrs. Katz, her husband and daughter worked for him. His father, an old man of seventy-five, was reciting Psalms in our cellar. The son had wanted to take him to the Aryan side but the old man wanted to be buried in a Jewish grave.

From: "Three Hundred Hours in the Burning ghetto" by M Berland, Yad Vashem, Jerusalem 5719

Israel Shari

He fell on 13th April, 1943. But before that, the Kalish tailor Israel Shari had taken part in many battles and had made his mark as a fighter and patrolman. He was the commander of a patrol unit and carried out very responsible tasks. He used to ascertain the objectives of the German columns, the number of soldiers in a village, their arms and similar information.

On 23rd January 1943, we were fighting a savage battle with the occupants who had suddenly attacked us. We retreated without losses. The Germans avenged their defeat on the village of Svatnitza which used to help the partisans. After seven days of wreaking havoc, the Germans pretended to be leaving the village in order to entice us back.

Our commander sent Shari and another two Jews to scout the region. Near a cow-shed, Shari saw a German but the other saw him too. The whole neighbourhood was lit up and Shari buried his head in the snow. The Germans emptied a whole belt of machine gun bullets but Shari killed him with a single shot. The whole German orchestra then began shooting. Shari exploited the confusion and crawled back. A bullet hit him in the hand and he spent two months in bed.

At last, the Gestapo learnt where our camp was and they prepared a punitive expedition against us. They did not catch us by surprise – Israel Shari whose wounded hand had not yet healed, took his rifle in both hands.

[Page 313]

"Retreat!" he shouted. "I'll hold them up here."

It was clear to us that Shari had made up his mind to sacrifice himself and save the unit. After we withdrew, he remained alone. He hilled the commander of the German unit with two bullets and brought confusion into the German ranks for a moment. That moment saved us but then the Germans came down on him. He fell like a hero. All honour to his memory.

Einikeit, Moscow No. 150.

Misha Adelstein

He was born in Kalish in 1923. In 1939 he settled in the village of Bursk where he organized a group of Jews to acquire arms and go to the forests. On 16th August 1942 he went to Luberk Forests and joined a company of Russian partisans. He was appointed commander of a section at Otriad Kartokhin.

After the liberation, he was killed by the Bandera Men.

Yossele Goldshmidt

In 1942, he escaped from the ghetto in Nowogrodek to the Poshtshe of Lipitsisonska. To begin with, he was in family camps and later joined the "Orlianskaya Borba" Lenin Brigade. In September 1943, he was wounded in the head and fell into the hands of the Germans, unconscious. They shot him at Zhetel. He was 24 years old when he fell.

[Page 314]

Yehiel Tenzer

His parents were poor and he worked hard from his youth. While still young, he joined the Youth Movement of the Left Poalei Zion. For some time he worked as a weaver and lost his place more than once because of his excessive activity in the Movement. For many years he was chairman of the Textile Workers' Trade Union in Kalish, which was one of the few unions in Poland to which both Jews and Poles belonged. He represented his Union in the Institutions of the General Trade Union Movement and as the vital spirit of the Left Poalei Zion and its youth in Kalish. Tall, strong and healthy with a friendly expression, he was considerate to all who came to him. He worked a great deal among the youth, guiding and teaching. He finally opened a coal shop but struggled hard to make a living for his family for all his time was dedicated to his public activities. Often enough he did not demand payment when poor people came to his shop.

He was a warden of the Kehilla and a member of the Municipality for his party. Party men were not the only ones who came to him for advice and help. He devoted his time and heart to all who were in need. He was the chairman of the Curatorial of the Borochow School and took part in various other Kalish Institutions.

When war broke out and the District was annexed by the Reich, the Jews were expelled. Tenzer moved to the town of Rzeszow (Reisha) in Western Galicia and from there to Warsaw where he was active in the underground of his Movement. For some time he worked at Tebens Metal Factory. When he was imprisoned at the Poniatowo Concentration Camp, he continued his communal activity and took part in the Fighting Jewish Organization at the camp where he was murdered. His name is included in the List of 320 Jewish communal workers, scholars, scientists and artists that were murdered.

———

[Page 315]

Kalish Women in the Resistance – Vitka Kempner

Hava Shurek

Vitka Kempner of Kalish has an honourable place among the women who fought in Vilna. She studied in Kalish, was an active member in the Hashomer Hatzair Movement and when studying at the Warsaw University, was an active member of the Avuka Students Society. In 1939, she crossed the frontier and reached the Halutz Concentration in Wilna. In the ghetto she was a member of the Hashomer Hatzair Secretariat and helped to organize the Fighting Jewish Organization. Later, she was in the Nekama Partisan Group where she commanded a unit and headed a patrol unit. She received the 'Red Flag' Order of Distinction. Later she helped to organise the Haapala (Immigration without Certificates) to Eretz Israel from Eastern Europe.

In June 1942, the Command of the P.P.A. Fighting Organization decided on the first act of sabotage against a train. The Haverim stole dynamite from German bunkers. In a dark cellar at N°3 Carmelite Street, people worked by candle light to prepare a mine in a piece of metal pipe. The elementary information they had acquired came from Soviet pamphlets which were stolen from the Archives of the YIVO (Yiddishe Wissenschaftliche Institut). Vitka went out to find a suitable place to place the mine along the railway line.

Her dark hair became blond and Aryan. In the morning she went off to work among a group of Jews. She slipped away from them in the street, removed the Jewish badge from her chest and back and mounted the pavement. Now she was an Aryan and went out of town to the railway leading to Vilioka. Germans were on guard there and civilians were not allowed to approach. They stopped Vitka.

She played the innocent, told them that she was going to the neighbouring village and did not know that she was not allowed to cross there. They warned her that if she was caught again, she would be arrested. Vitka went away and appeared not long after at some other place that was not being guarded at the time. But she then found that there were Jewish workers nearby. Apart from this, a steep slope was necessary if the operation were to succeed.

So Vitka went out each morning from the ghetto for three days, spending the whole day near the railway line and searching for the right place for the operation. All the 'joie de vivre' went from her face. She became silent and her eyes seemed to look inward. She was thinking about the operation and the responsibility.

[Page 316]

When dawn rose on July 8ᵗʰ, Vitka, Isa Matzkevitz and Moshe Brause left the ghetto carrying the mine. Their objective was to blow up a German train seven kilometres south-east of Vilna. The operation had to take place at night and they would have to be back in the ghetto by dawn the next day so that they could go out to work as usual.

At dawn, Vitka reached the ghetto, her legs torn and bleeding but her face radiant. The mine had been planted and nobody had noticed them. There was strength in her eyes which gave them an unusual brightness while her face had a different expression. When she was asked what she had thought during the long night, she answered: "How to do the job without falling into their hands? I was sorry that I had no cyanide of potassium with me."

News of the explosion arrived at 3p.m. The train was destroyed, both engines and ammunition wagons. The Germans were at a loss for this was the first operation of its kind near Wilna where there were many garrison troops. They did not suspect the Jews for they were sure that the Jews were already defeated and would not raise their heads. Such a deed could only be done by free men.

It was a happy day for the Fighters of the Ghetto. They laughed in the streets. Passers-by shrugged their shoulders thinking that the others had gone crazy.

Many coaches containing German soldiers and ammunition in the train, which was on its way to Polotsk, were smashed. In the morning, the peasants counted 200 bodies of soldiers, apart from those who were completely blown apart and could not be counted. After their census, the peasants collected pistols, rifles and many bullets.

Vitka Kempner displayed her full capacity in the Forests. One night in October, 1943, she went 40 kilometres on foot carrying a suitcase full of mines and entered Vilna. There she blew up an electric transformer. Next day, she entered the Keilis Concentration Camp and took 60 people out to the Partisan bases. In the Nekama Camp she organized the survey patrol and headed it. She took part in blowing up a train near Oran where 200 Germans were killed. With the aid of five other Partisans, she set the Turpentine Factory at Olkiniki on fire. She distinguished herself at the battles of Deinimova in January, 1944 and captured two Gestapo agents. She took part in blowing up 2 railway engines and 2 bridges.

In November 1943 she had to fetch important documents in Vilna. On the way she was caught by a German patrol that took her to the Gestapo. She escaped from their hands and vanished. The next day she brought an important Kovno member of the Underground to the base.

A Society of Jewish women in Brazil has been named after her.

———

[Page 317]

Hannah Aronovitch-Rackman

In 1940, the Nazis began to exterminate Jewish children. They expelled the Jewish mothers from their homes collecting them in a certain Square which they surrounded with S.S. soldiers. A Nazi Officer delivered a speech to the mothers and called on them to hand over their children who would be sent to special Children's Institutions where they would be provided with better care.

Unfortunately, not all the mothers understood that this was all lies and deception. Many of them handed their children over to the Germans. When the polished German Officer tried to take Hannah Rackman's child from her arms by force, she slapped the office twice across the face. He put his hand on his pistol while she, according to a witness, stuck her nails in his face and tried to scratch his eyes out. She fell while defending herself in this way.

———

Rivka and Vera Shurek

Rivka and Vera Shurek were the wife and young daughter of Abraham Shurek of Kalish. According to the accounts of A. Sutzkever and B. Mark, they were both active in Bialystok ghetto. They became famous in the struggle against the Germans who made special efforts to capture them alive. Both of them fell in a clash with a German patrol.

[Page 318]

Yizkor

May God remember the souls of our Brethren of
Israel who resided in the city of Kalish and
became martyrs and heroes during the Holocaust;
thirty thousand Jews who were slain, murdered,
strangled and buried alive; the entire holy
congregation of Kalish who were destroyed and
hallowed the name.

May God remember how they were offered up
with the other martyrs and heroes of Israel since
time untold; and may their souls be bound up in
the bundle of life. they were lovely and pleasant in
their lives, and in death they were not divided.
may they rest in peace where they lie. and let us
say Amen.

[Page 319]

[Blank]

[Page 320]

The Roll of Honour

[page 321]

THE ROLL OF HONOUR

IN MEMORY OF THOSE WHO FELL
IN THE WARS OF ISRAEL

Let the People of Israel remember their faithful and courageous sons who gave their lives in the Wars of Israel. Let Israel remember their offspring and find blessing in them. and mourn the radiance of their youth and their splendid bravery, the hallowed readiness for all deeds, dedicated souls of those who were slain in bitter battle, May the heroes of our Wars of Liberation and of Victory be set as a seal upon the heart of Israel for age on age.

AVRUNIN, JOSEPH son of SAMUEL and ESTHER

Born 1925 in Tel-Aviv. Educated at the Ben Yehuda Secondary School and active in the "Sea Scouts", where he was an Instructor. He was sent on an advanced course in Maritime Services on board the Neptune and was killed in action at sea. He was brought to burial on 4th Tishri 5704 (1943).

BET-HALEVI, ABRAHAM BEZALEL son of ISRAEL DAVID and HAYA PEARL

Born in Kalish on Lag Be-Omer 5673 (1913). In 1939 joined a Football Team which went to Australia, and remained there to study at a High School for Science and Commerce. Upon the outbreak of the Second World War he volunteered to join the Australian Army with the aim of returning to Eretz Israel in its ranks. He fell in the line of duty on 25th Tevet 5704 (1944).

FEIERMANN, BARUCH son of YEHIEL MEIR and .JUDITH

Born in Blaszki, arrived in Israel 1948 as a member of MaHaL (Overseas Volunteers) and joined the Givati Brigade. Fell in battle on 14th, Tishri 5709 (1948) and was buried at the Military Cemetery in Kfar Warburg.

[page 322]

FENICHEL, HAYYIM son of MENAHEM and NEHAMA nee ENGEL of Kalish

Born in Kfar Saba in 1947, graduated from his Secondary School, was an Instructor of the Noar Oved and a Sergeant in the Israel Defense Army. He fell in the Battle of Rafiah during the Six Day War, and on 29th June 1967 was buried in Kfar Saba.

FROMMER, ABRAHAM HAYYIM son of NAHMAN and JUDITH

Born in Tel-Aviv 1938. Secondary School education. Entered in the Israel Defense Army. He fell in the Battle of Rafiah suitability for Officers' rank. On 22nd Iyyar 5718 (1958) he was mortally wounded during training, when a grenade he carried in his belt exploded, and was buried in the Military Cemetery of Kiryat Shaul.

GLOWINSKI, ARIEH son of ISAAC and HINDA

Born in Kalish in 1920, came to Eretz Israel with his parents in 1935, completed his studies at an evening Secondary School. He was active in Gadna and the Hagana, volunteered in December 1947, took part in the defense of the Sharon villages, the opening of the road to Jerusalem, the battles for Lydda and Ramleh and the attempt to breach the Faluja Pocket. He fell at Irak al Manshiah and was buried at Faluja on 20.10.1948. His remains were afterwards transferred to the Military Section of the Nahlat Yitzhak Cemetery.

GOTCHAL, ZVI son of JOSEPH and HANNAH nee ANZER

Born in Tel-Aviv on 2nd Tammuz 5688 (1928) and studied at the Balfour Secondary School. After serving as Supernumerary Constable at Beit Shean, he commenced his studies at the Hebrew University on 29th September, 1947. When the Call to Arms came he abandoned his studies and together with dozens of his companions volunteered and was sent to the Etzion Block. He participated in battles in and around Jerusalem for the liberation of the Jewish Quarters. On 1st May, 1948 he fell on the Katamon Front. He was buried in Sanhedria, and on 9th Marheshvan 5712 (1951) his remains were transferred to the Military Cemetery on Mount Herzl.

INBAR (MELTZER), ALEXANDER son of ARIEH and ADA

Born in Haifa 28th December 1939, completed the Technical School of the Haifa Technical Institute. Captain in the Air Force, Navigator-Pilot. Died 7.6.1967 during the Six Day War in an attack on the H3 Airfield in Iraq. Buried in Haifa on 2.8.1967, after his remains were returned from Iraq.

[page 323]

ISRAELOVITCH, ISAAC son of ABRAHAM

Born in Kalish, 1923, received an elementary education and found employment as a metal worker at an early age, A member of Hashomer Hatzair, he came to Eretz Israel in 1947 and joined the Palmah. Fell in the attack on the Nebi Yusha Police Station in Upper Galilee on 20.4.1948 and was buried in the Nebi Yusha Military Cemetery.

KAPLAN, AVNER, son of ISRAEL and RACHEL (daughter of the late Jerusalem Chief Rabbi Zvi Pessah Frank)

Born 25th Sivan 5797 (1937) in Jerusalem, the first-born child of his parents, showed his devotion to his studies and rare spiritual qualities from his early childhood. Graduated with distinction from the Ohel Shem Secondary School in Ramat Gan, was active in the Halutz Youth Movement where he was an Instructor, and later joined Nahal.
During the Sinai Campaign in 1956 he was injured in the spine on the way to Sharm es Sheikh (Mifratz Shlomo). After his recovery he became a member of Tel Katzir Kibbutz. He was killed in an accident at Tel Katzir soon after Passover 1959.

KOCHMAN, SIMEON son of YEHIEL and ESTHER RIVKA

Born on 6th Marheshvan 5685 (1924). On finishing Secondary School he enlisted as a Supernumerary Policeman at Kiriat Hayyim and was an active member of the Hagana. Upon the outbreak of the War of Liberation he left his work and engaged in defense activities. He fell in the Battle for Bet Afa on 11th Tammuz 5708 (1948).

LEWKOVITCH, JOSEPH son of ZVI

Born in Kalish, 1927. When the War broke out he was cut off from his family, moved from camp to camp and suffered starvation and other distresses under the Nazis. In 1945 he was liberated by the Allied Forces and joined a group of Halutzim. With the aid of the members of the Jewish Brigade he proceeded to Hachshara in Italy, reached Eretz Israel as a Maapil at the end of 1945 and became a member of Kibbutz Hulata. There he found his place in work and social life, and fulfilled his duties on guard and in defense. While on his way to aid Mishmar Hayarden on 5.6.1948 he was injured by a shell. He was buried in Kibbutz Hulata.

[page 324]

LITTMAN (AVTALION), PINHAS son of RABBI JACOB ZEEV and GITTEL

Born in Kalish on 21st Marheshvan 5686 (1926) and came to Eretz Israel in 1936. Went through Secondary School. At the age of 17 he responded to the wartime summons "to Arms or Farms" and proceeded to serve at Sdeh Eliahu Kibbutz, where he joined the Jewish Settlement Police. In a fray with Arabs he was severely wounded but recovered. After two and a half years of service in the Special Police he became a student at the Agricultural Faculty of the Hebrew University. In December 1947 he enlisted and fought in the vicinity of Jerusalem. During the fighting at Ramat Rachel he was severely wounded and died.

LUBELSKY (ALON), DAVID son of MOSHE and DEBORAH

Born in Tel-Aviv 1925, received an elementary education. Served in the Palmah for five years. Upon completion of service joined an independent Kibbutz which settled at Nirim, where he was in charge of security. In the attack of 15th May, 1948 the Nirim settlers under his command repulsed the enemy but he himself was mortally wounded by shrapnel. He was buried the same day in Kibbutz Nirim.

NAPARSTEK, SAMUEL son of DAVID and HANNAH

Born in Kalish 1920, ran away to the Russian Zone at the outbreak of the Second World War. Served in the Red Army from the age of nineteen and was sent to a Training School for Officers. After the War he came to Eretz Israel and immediately volunteered for military service. He fought in the Hills of Jerusalem and was wounded near Kibbutz Harel. Next day he went into action at Bet Jemal. On the way back his car was blown up by a mine. He died of his wounds on 19.10.1948 and was buried in Kiryat Anavim.

PULVERMACHER, ABRAHAM son of ISAAC and MINA ABRAHAM

Born in Kalish 1924, came to Eretz Israel in 1935, received a secondary education. Joined the Hagana in which he served for seven years. At the outbreak of the War of Liberation he enlisted in the Givati Brigade, participated in opening the road to Jerusalem and the Battles of the South and the Negev. Fatally injured in the Battle for Bet Afa on 18.7.1948, and was buried in the Military Section of the Nahlat Yitzhak Cemetery. He was awarded the rank of Lieutenant posthumously on 23.1.1951.

[page 325]

SILBERMAN, ISAAC son of ELIEZER and ESTHER

Born in Eretz Israel 1929, member of the Hagana from the age of fourteen. He studied at the Montefiore Technical School and worked at the Tel-Aviv Electricity Plant. In December 1947, after the United Nations vote approving the establishment of the Jewish State, he volunteered and took part in the Battles for the Sharon settlements and Tel Aviv. He was sent to Military Hospital by order of the Medical Officer, but left it of his own accord and returned to his unit. On 26.5.48 he fell in the Battle for Latrun and was buried there. His remains were transferred to the Military Cemetery at Mount Herzl on 17.11.1949.

SHELAK, MOSHE YAAKOV (MELNIK) son of ZVI and SARAH

Born in Kalish 1924, attended Secondary School. During the Second World War was imprisoned in a Camp but shortly before the liberation escaped by jumping from a train. He came to Eretz Israel and volunteered for Aliya B work, particularly frontier crossing. Disguised as a Greek he led immigrants across the frontiers of Austria and Italy, and was wounded several times by frontier guards. He reached Eretz Israel again in 1946. At the commencement of the War of Liberation he joined the Palmah and served in the Portzim (Break-through) Unit of the Harel Brigade. On 10.6.1948 he was wounded at Kiryat Anavim and died two days later. He was buried at Sanhedria and on 16th Marheshvan 5712 (1951) his body was transferred to the Military Cemetery on Mount Herzl.

SHILOH, JACOB son of MOSHE and YONINA (SHELAH)

Born in Kalish 1935 and came to Eretz Israel from Belgium in 1949 as a member of the Youth Aliya. Educated in Gan Shmuel Kibbutz . Volunteered at 17, remained in the Standing Army reaching the rank of Rav Seren (Major), and was sent to a course of Paratroop Training in France. Upon completion of the Course he received an International Prize for Free Parachuting. Took part in all paratroop activities of the Israel Defence Army and trained beginners. In the Battle of Shechem during the Six Day War he was fatally wounded by a sniper and was buried in Afula on 7.6.67.

[page 326]

SHKLANOWSKI, SAMUEL ISAAC son of YEHIEL YEHUDA and SHOSHANA

Born in Tel-Aviv 1925 and studied at Secondary School, member of the Hagana from 14. At the age of 17 he joined the Supernumerary Police and served at Shaar Hagolan until 1945. Upon the commencement of the pre-State fighting he took part in the defense of the Tel-Aviv suburbs. He was sent to the Negev in December 1947, helped to guard the Water Pipe Line and the Supply Convoys to the Negev and Jerusalem, in the vicinity of which he also fought. On 13th Iyyar 5708 (1948) while training he felt that the safety catch of the grenade in his hand had opened. There were more than 20 members of his Unit in the Training Hall with him. He dashed out and the grenade burst in his hands. He was buried in the Military Section of the Nahlat Yitzhak Cemetery.

WACHS, ZEEV son of ISAAC DAVID and NEHA

Born in Kalish in 1922, came to Eretz Israel and afterwards went to France. During the Second World War he returned and worked at the Government Printing Works in Jerusalem. In 1944 he volunteered for the Jewish Brigade and took part in its Campaigns. After demobilization he went back to his former work in Jerusalem and lived in the Old City. Upon the outbreak of the fighting at the end of 1947, and while still working at the Government Printers, he and his comrades organized the defense of the Jewish workers at the Press. He was then called to the Jewish Defense Services and participated in the guarding of the convoys which brought supplies to the settlements round Jerusalem. On 6.4.1948 he fell in the Battle of Mount Castel and was buried in the Maaleh Hahamisha Kevutza. On 12th Kislev 5714 (1953) his remains were transferred to the Military Cemetery at Mount Herzl, Jerusalem.

YITZHAKI, ARIEH son of ELIJAH ITZIK and DEBORAH

Born in Kalish, 1914, came to Eretz Israel with his parents in 1924, studied at the Tahkemoni Religious School. From his childhood he was an active member of the Betar Youth Movement, afterwards joined the Irgun Zevai Leumi and was active in the Underground. He fell while preparing explosives in the vicinity of Tel Aviv during 1939, and on 21st Av 5699 (1939) was buried in the Nahlat Itzhak Cemetery.

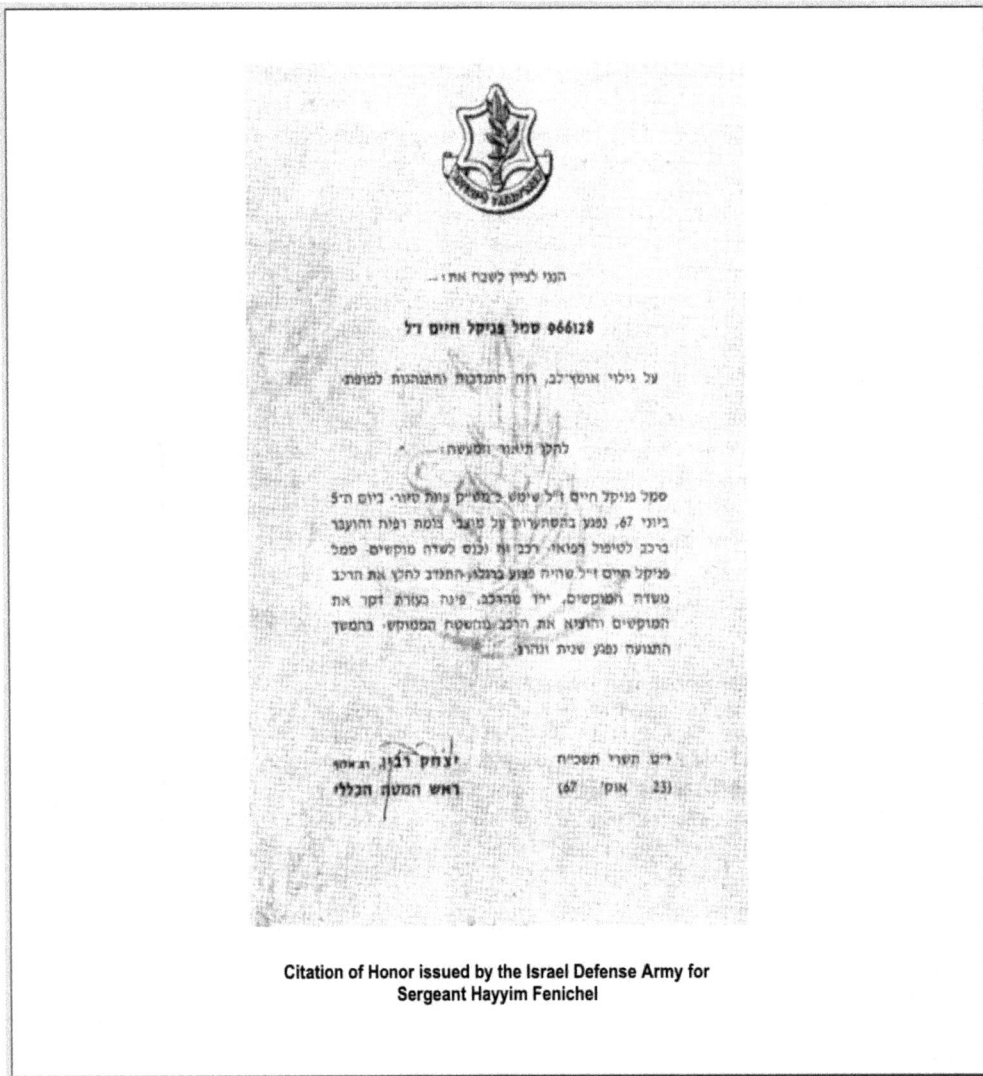

Citation of Honor issued by the Israel Defense Army for Sergeant Hayyim Fenichel

The Kalish Book Committee in U.S.A.
Standing, r. to l.: **Hershel Arkush, Jacob Levy, Samuel Okladek, Samuel Roth, Nahum Medien, Max Smolin**
Seated, r. to l.: **Israel Diamant, Abraham Bandel, Joseph Arnold, Sam Berke, Peretz Walter**

Editorial Committee in Israel
Standing , r . to l . : **Gershon Wrotslavsky, Eliezer Birnbaum, Menahem Shklanovsky, Zvl Arad**
Seated, r. to l.: **Mendel Sieradzki, Dr. Saul Zalud, Baruch Tall, Abraham Zahar**

[Page 329]

The Tale of Kalish Jewry Ends Here

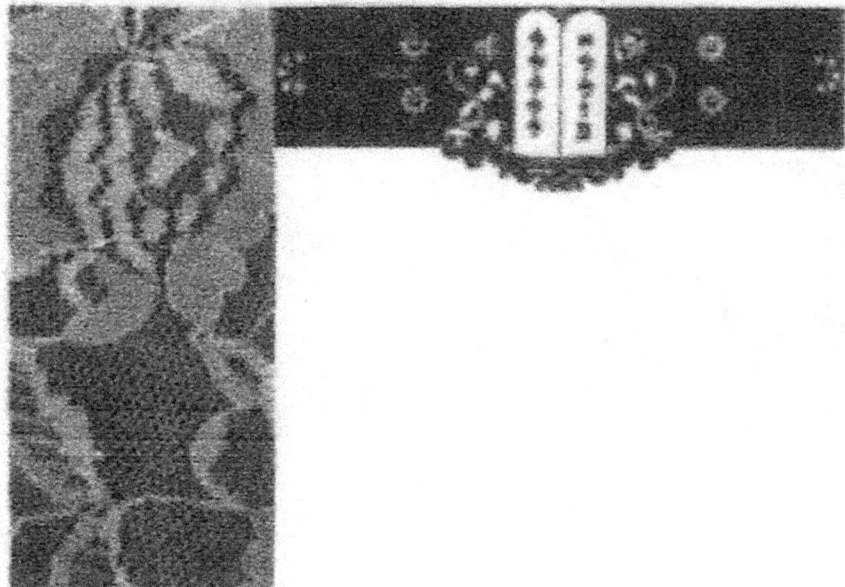

KALISH JEWRY
DAY BY DAY

On the march

Daughters of Israel

Daughters of Israel

Public Activities

School Children

School Children

School Children

The Younger Generation

The Younger Generation

Youths

Youths

Craftsmen and the Technical School

A Dramatic Circle

Blind Gabriel

Societies and Organizations

Societies and Organizations

Wide Branching Families

Wide Branching Families

Children

Children

Children

Family Festivities and Social Gatherings

Children

Family Festivities and Social Gatherings

Family festivities and social gatherings

Great Synagogue Choir

Band of the Athletics Association

The Older Generation

The Older Generation

The Older Generation

A family

A Young Couple

Jews in and out of Procession

Sportsmen and Athletics

Sportsmen and Athletics

Passover Seder at the Jewish Hospital

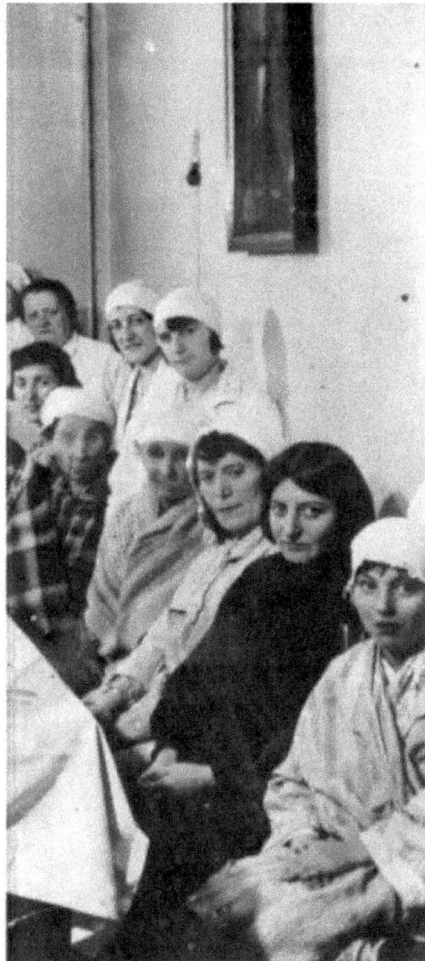

Passover Seder at the Jewish Hospital

Going to the Sukkah

Going to the Sukkah

Going to the Sukkah

Buying willow twigs for the Hoshana Prayers on the Last Day of Sukkoth

Distributing Bread at the Kehilla Offices

In the Fish Market

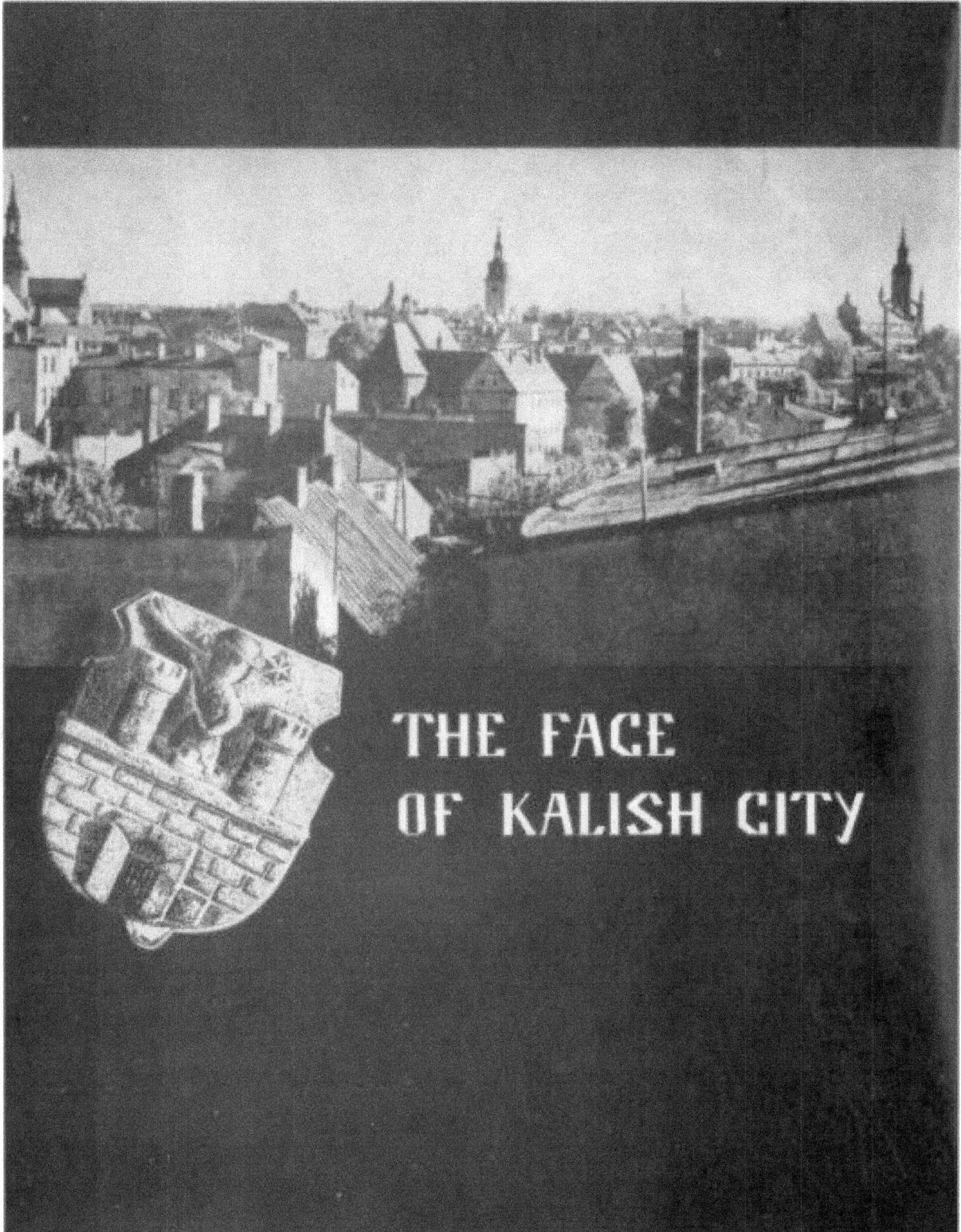

THE FACE
OF KALISH CITY

The Town Hall

In the Park

The River Prosna

Corner of the Park

On the Banks of the Prosna

The Island in the Park

The Rowing Club

Wodna Street

The River Prosna

Avenue in the Park

The Old Market

Kilinski Square

Municipal Theatre

Municipal Theatre

A Cross-Roads

Chopin Street

District Government Building

The Market Building

The last Trees of the Synagogue Garden

The New Market

Babina Street

Josephine Allee

The Old Market

Zlota and Nowa Streets

The District Law Courts

Ciasna Street

Chopin Street

Corner of Zlota and Warszawska Sts. And the Old Market

Piskozewska Street

Zlota Street

Nowa Street, corner of Babina Street

Ciasna Street

The Great Synagogue and Talmud Torah

The Heart of Kalish

Kalish from Above

Name Index

www.ingramcontent.com/pod-product-compliance
Lightning Source LLC
Chambersburg PA
CBHW082006150426

42814CB00005BA/238